D0021535

# THE TRIUMPH
# OF IMPROVISATION

# THE TRIUMPH
# OF IMPROVISATION

### GORBACHEV'S ADAPTABILITY,
### REAGAN'S ENGAGEMENT, AND
### THE END OF THE COLD WAR

## JAMES GRAHAM WILSON

CORNELL UNIVERSITY PRESS
*Ithaca and London*

First published 2014 by Cornell University Press

Printed in the United States of America

Library of Congress Cataloging-in-Publication Data

Wilson, James Graham, 1980– author.
    The triumph of improvisation : Gorbachev's adaptability, Reagan's engagement, and the end of the Cold War / James Graham Wilson.
        pages cm
    Includes bibliographical references and index.
    ISBN 978-0-8014-5229-1 (cloth : alk. paper)
    1. United States—Foreign relations—Soviet Union.
    2. Soviet Union—Foreign relations—United States.
    3. United States—Foreign relations—1981–1989.
    4. Cold War—Diplomatic history.  5. Gorbachev, Mikhail Sergeevich, 1931–  6. Reagan, Ronald.  I. Title.
        E183.8.S65W56    2014
        327.73047—dc23        2013027121

Cornell University Press strives to use environmentally responsible suppliers and materials to the fullest extent possible in the publishing of its books. Such materials include vegetable-based, low-VOC inks and acid-free papers that are recycled, totally chlorine-free, or partly composed of nonwood fibers. For further information, visit our website at www.cornellpress.cornell.edu.

Cloth printing    10 9 8 7 6 5 4 3 2

*For My Dad*

# CONTENTS

# ACKNOWLEDGMENTS

I am deeply indebted to a number of individuals and institutions. Research was made possible by travel grants from the University of Virginia's Corcoran Department of History, Society of Fellows, and Graduate School of Arts and Sciences as well as the Society of Historians of American Foreign Relations and the George H. W. Bush Presidential Library. I thank Daniel Linke of the Seeley J. Mudd Manuscript Library at Princeton University, Robert Holzweiss of the George H. W. Bush Presidential Library, and Sherrie Fletcher and Cate Sewell of the Ronald Reagan Presidential Library.

I extend my gratitude to the academic community of Vassar College—in particular, Rebecca Edwards, Michael McCarthy, and James Merrell. I thank Robert Brigham for his mentorship and tireless support.

I am especially grateful to the faculty of the University of Virginia's Department of History: to Michael Holt, Sophie Rosenfeld, and John Stagg for early and sustained encouragement; to Peter Onuf, Jeffrey Rossman, and Philip Zelikow for their mentorship in teaching and scholarship; and to Jason Eldred, Kate Geoghegan, Lawrence Hatter, Barın Kayaoğlu, Christopher Loomis, Stephen Macekura, Kathryn Shively Meier, Harold Mock, Victor Nemchenok, Martin Öhman, Robert Rakove, Hilde Restad, Rachel Sheldon, Scott Spencer, Dana Stefanelli, Lauren Turek, and Kelly Winck. I would like to thank Artemy Kalinovsky, Svetlana Savranskaya, Josh Itzkowitz Shifrinson, Ambassador Anatoly Adamishin, and Ambassador Jack Matlock for sharing research and recollections and Holger Nehring and Tom Nichols for wisdom and encouragement.

I spent the 2009–10 academic year in Geneva at the Graduate Institute of International and Development Studies, as an Albert Gallatin Fellow in International Affairs. I thank Jussi Hanhimäki and Davide Rodogno for the opportunity to participate in a year-long seminar there; I also thank Thomas Fischer, Kars Aznavour, John Goodman, and Merdan Gochkarov. During that year, Ruud van Dijk, Jessica Gienow-Hecht, and Leopold Nuti allowed me to present portions of what became this book in Amsterdam, Cologne, and Rome.

I spent the 2010–11 academic year at the Miller Center of Public Affairs in Charlottesville, Virginia. I thank Sheila Blackford, Juliana Bush, Michael Greco, Kyle Lascurettes, Anne Carter Mulligan, Amber Lautigar Reichert, Herman Schwartz, and Marc Selverstone. Jeremi Suri served as my "dream mentor." Will Hitchcock and Allen Lynch offered invaluable insight during this period. Brian Balogh has been a role model and true friend.

I thank my colleagues at the Department of State's Office of the Historian—especially Elizabeth Charles, David Nickles, Paul Pitman, Stephen Randolph, Avshalom Rubin, and Daniel Rubin. Joshua Botts, Seth Center, and Laura Kolar have been far more than colleagues over the past quarter of my life; I could not have completed this book without them.

I thank Michael McGandy and Sarah Grossman of Cornell University Press as well as the two anonymous readers for their sustained attention and constructive criticism. Yvette Chin prepared the index; Martin Schneider and Erin Cozens edited the manuscript. All mistakes are my own.

I lack the words to thank Mel and Phyllis Leffler, Robert Pounder, Blanca Uribe, Richard and Adene Wilson, and Katherine, Anthony, and Rhys William Edgar.

# A Brief Note on Sources

In August of 2011, I started work at the Office of the Historian of the U.S. Department of State to compile volumes of primary sources documenting U.S.-Soviet relations during the 1980s as part of the *Foreign Relations of the United States* (*FRUS*) series. While this position provided access to documents on the U.S. side beyond those available to the average researcher, this book relies entirely upon the evidentiary source base that is available to any researcher. Every document cited, in other words, is declassified and available to researchers at the following repositories: the Ronald Reagan Presidential Library; the George H. W. Bush Presidential Library; and the James A. Baker III Papers and Don Oberdorfer Papers, both at the Department of Rare Books and Special Collections, Mudd Library, Princeton University.

I interviewed Jack Matlock at his home, discussed the end of the Cold War with Anatoly Adamishin and Pavel Palazchenko in private settings, queried Philip Zelikow on a number of occasions, and have interviewed Elliott Abrams, Andrew Marshall, Bud McFarlane, John Poindexter, Rozanne Ridgway, and Tom Simons for the *FRUS* series. These interactions led me to reflect upon the proper approach to documents and conclusions; I have not quoted them in this book. The views expressed in this book are those of the author and do not necessarily reflect those of the U.S. Department of State or the U.S. government.

For foreign sources, I have attempted to quote from repositories of the most easily accessible sources. When possible, I cite English translations available on the websites of the National Security Archive, the Cold War International History Project, and the Parallel History Project or in volumes published by these organizations. When it is not, I cite from the Gorbachev Foundation Archive in Moscow and the volumes of Gorbachev's papers that that organization has published over the past few years.

# Abbreviations

| | |
|---|---|
| ABM | Anti–Ballistic Missile |
| AFL–CIO | American Federation of Labor and Congress of Industrial Organizations |
| APEC | Asia–Pacific Economic Cooperation |
| BBC | British Broadcasting Corporation |
| BNOC | British National Oil Company |
| CDU | Christian Democratic Union of the Federal Republic of Germany |
| CFE | Conventional Forces in Europe |
| CIA | Central Intelligence Agency |
| CNN | Cable News Network |
| CPD | Committee on the Present Danger |
| CPSU | Communist Party of the Soviet Union |
| CSCE | Commission on Security and Cooperation in Europe |
| DARPA | Defense Advanced Research Projects Agency |
| EC | European Community |
| EU | European Union |
| INF | Intermediate-Range Nuclear Forces |
| FDP | Free Democratic Party of the Federal Republic of Germany |
| FRG | The Federal Republic of Germany (West Germany) |
| GATT | The General Agreement on Tariffs and Trade |
| GDP | Gross Domestic Product |
| GDR | The German Democratic Republic (East Germany) |
| GE | General Electric |
| ICBM | Intercontinental Ballistic Missile |
| IDF | Israeli Defense Forces |
| IMF | International Monetary Fund |
| KAL 007 | Korean Airlines Flight 007 |
| KGB | Komitet Gosudarstvennoy Bezopasnosti (Committee for State Security) |

| | |
|---|---|
| MAD | Mutually Assured Destruction |
| MIRV | Multiple Independently Targetable Re-entry Vehicle |
| MX | LGM-118A Peacekeeper missile (Missile-eXperimental) |
| NAFTA | North American Free Trade Agreement |
| NATO | North Atlantic Treaty Organization |
| NORAD | North American Aerospace Defense Command |
| NSC | National Security Council |
| NSD | National Security Directive |
| NSDD | National Security Decision Directive |
| NSPG | National Security Planning Group |
| OMB | Office of Management and Budget |
| OPEC | Organization of Petroleum Exporting Countries |
| PATCO | Professional Air Traffic Controllers Organization |
| PRC | People's Republic of China |
| Project RYAN | Raketno Yadernoye Napadenie (Nuclear Missiles Attack) |
| SALT and SALT II | Strategic Arms Limitation Talks (also Strategic Arms Limitations Treaty) |
| SDI | Strategic Defense Initiative |
| SPD | Social Democratic Party of the Federal Republic of Germany |
| START | Strategic Arms Reduction Talks (also Strategic Arms Reduction Treaty) |
| UN | United Nations |
| USSR | Union of Soviet Socialist Republics |

# THE TRIUMPH
# OF IMPROVISATION

# Introduction
## Individuals and Power

At three hours past midnight on November 9, 1979, U.S. National Security Advisor Zbigniew Brzezinski woke up, answered his phone, and learned that World War III had begun. Two hundred and twenty Soviet intercontinental ballistic missiles were hurtling toward the United States, his military assistant informed him. Call back to confirm, Brzezinski responded. The phone rang again, and the news had gotten worse: twenty-two hundred inbound missiles. Just before dialing the White House to alert the president, he received a third call. NORAD was no longer detecting any missiles; it was a false alarm. On that night—and throughout the Cold War—the prospect of global thermonuclear war between the Soviet Union and the United States was very real indeed.[1]

Ten years later to the day, on November 9, 1989, word spread in East Berlin that the East German government intended to lift travel restrictions to the West. A crowd of ordinary people—couples, students, a grandmother in her nightgown—gathered outside the Bornholmer Strasse border crossing. Anxious guards awaited orders. Thirty minutes before midnight, they lifted the gates at Bornholmer Strasse and at checkpoints around the city. Throngs of East Germans walked into West Berlin.[2] Friends embraced; families reunited. Germans danced in the streets and on top of the Berlin Wall.

Between these two November nights the world changed. Nuclear weapons, the division of Germany and Europe, and the ideological contest between capitalism and communism defined the Cold War between the United States and the Soviet Union. Brzezinski's 3 a.m. phone call came as détente between the two superpowers was collapsing. The end of the 1970s was a very tense time between the two superpowers. Then, in the middle of the 1980s, relations improved. Hope dawned, and the global balance of power shifted. In time, the Berlin Wall came down, and a new world order emerged.

This book comprehends these diplomatic and political developments and seeks to explain how the Cold War ended. Here I take a long view, from the Soviet invasion of Afghanistan in December 1979 to Operation Desert Storm in January 1991. Hundreds of books and articles have looked at particular episodes from this critical period. Efforts to tell the broader story tend to focus on one of four explanations: (1) Mikhail Gorbachev was wholly responsible; (2) changes in the distribution of power in the international system determined leaders' preferences; (3) U.S. policymakers crafted and executed a grand strategy to defeat communism; (4) nongovernmental actors pressured leaders to halt the nuclear arms race and liberate Eastern Europe. The debate over how the Cold War ended commenced the moment it ended, and it is an argument without end. Perhaps the most significant change in thinking over the past two decades has been over the role that Ronald Reagan played. Whether he was in fact hawk or dove, hedgehog or fox, Reagan as statesman now commands a presumption of greatness. Those who subscribe to the third explanation regard him as a grand strategist.

Fresh evidence has guided me in a new direction. Much of the material in the next seven chapters—whether from the United States, Russia, China, Germany, France, Poland, Hungary, or Czechoslovakia—was either declassified or became available over the course of writing this book, which I began in 2005. These documents speak clearly and consistently: observers misunderstood the end of the Cold War, and historians have mischaracterized it. The passage of time and the proliferation of sources allow for a clearer view of what happened. This book employs both of them to tell the story of a revolution in human affairs.

The basic argument here is that adaptation, improvisation, and engagement by individuals in positions of power ended almost a half century of cold war and the specter of a nuclear holocaust. Four of these leaders stand out: Mikhail Gorbachev, Ronald Reagan, George Shultz, and George H. W. Bush. Amidst ambivalence and uncertainty, Gorbachev, Reagan, Shultz, and Bush—along with a host of other actors—engaged with adversaries and adapted to a rapidly changing international environment that saw the recovery of international capitalism and the paralysis within command economies.

Decisions shaped how history unfolded in the 1980s. Economic recovery after the stagnation of the 1970s resulted from difficult and often unpopular choices. Leaders faced daunting challenges and succeeded when they improvised in response to dramatic and surprising events. The most instructive example of success was the astonishingly quick and almost entirely peaceful response to the protests and demonstrations in East Germany and Eastern Europe—which led to the collapse of communism. Individuals in Moscow and Washington did not catalyze these demonstrations but instead reacted prudently, imaginatively, and courageously to events they did not foresee. No master plan explains either the developments in Eastern Europe and East Germany or the response to those developments in the West.

The Cold War did not end on equal terms. The United States and its allies prevailed. The Soviet Union collapsed in December 1991, but it had lost the Cold War well before that. Defeat notwithstanding, Mikhail Gorbachev was the most important individual in the story of the end of the Cold War. He believed that his country possessed sufficient military strength to focus primarily on domestic priorities, and he ultimately sacrificed an empire to advance his reforms.[3]

Selected general secretary of the Communist Party of the Soviet Union in March 1985, Gorbachev pursued new political thinking and new policies to adapt to an evolving world. Changes in the international system in the 1980s altered the dynamics of the Cold War. The boom and bust of oil, global movement away from state control of markets and industry, capital flows into Eastern Europe and the undertow of debt it created, and the information revolution, with its transformative effects on basic human interactions, created fresh challenges. New technologies prompted leaders to adapt to a freer exchange of ideas and to connect markets on a global scale, and Marxist-Leninist theories did not readily provide the tools to meet these challenges. Gorbachev attempted to reconfigure his ideology accordingly. His devotion to reforming communism inspired him to make concessions that reversed the course of the U.S.-Soviet confrontation and then allowed East Germany, Poland, Czechoslovakia, Hungary, Romania, and Bulgaria to bring the Soviet Bloc to an end.

Gorbachev struggled to align means with ends. His slogans "acceleration," "perestroika," "glasnost," "common European home," and "new world order" often amounted to just that. His mission to revitalize communism and the Soviet Union failed, however. His new thinking did not provide a tangible alternative for structuring the international economy and preserving order in unstable regions. Much of the world regarded him as a savior, yet he lost the Soviet Union. His limitations reveal that he was human; like all leaders, he faced choices, and those choices came with costs.

Growing up during World War II, Gorbachev's view of humanity was shaped by that conflict. He had no use for martial valor, could not abide the prevailing tenets of Mutual Assured Destruction (MAD), and took little pride in the size or the quantity of Soviet missiles. He discarded Moscow's commitment to international class struggle and embraced strategic sufficiency. In January 1986, he gave a speech calling for the abolition of nuclear weapons by the year 2000. Three months later, the catastrophic nuclear meltdown at Chernobyl led him to redouble his efforts. At Reykjavik, in October 1986, Gorbachev engaged with an American president who shared this vision.

That man, Ronald Reagan, the fortieth president of the United States, was not the cowboy his critics alleged. He long dreamed of a world without nuclear weapons, and he had a strategy to meet this evolving vision. By building up arms, Reagan was convinced, the United States would compel the Soviets to agree to build down. Beginning in March 1983, the Strategic Defense Initiative (SDI, also known as "Star Wars") gradually became the essential component in this plan. It was neither an invulnerable shield against missiles, nor a negotiating chip, nor a plot to bankrupt communism. After getting to know Gorbachev and deeming him to be trustworthy, Reagan envisioned SDI as a massive insurance policy; he would share the system with the Kremlin to make sure that both sides stuck to their arms reduction agreements.

Reagan's SDI program was enigmatic. It accelerated arms control at some moments, decelerated it at others, and probably influenced Reagan's strategic thinking more than it did Gorbachev's. No one at the start of the decade would have expected that a man who had called for a massive nuclear buildup would offer to share with his Soviet counterpart the technology to shoot down missiles. In the president's mind, SDI was not a deception, and sharing was not a ploy.

Reagan, by means of SDI and other initiatives, did not win the Cold War. Rather, he established the terms for the big debates between Washington and Moscow in the 1980s. He championed drastic reductions of strategic arms, the elimination of medium-range nuclear missiles, and the acceptance of strategic defenses. He spoke of an economic turnaround and a technological revolution in the West that did indeed come to pass. In 1983, to a gathering of evangelicals in Florida, he called the Soviet Union an "evil empire"; in 1988, standing in the middle of Red Square, he declared that it was not. By the end of his presidency, he had substantially reduced the Soviet perception of American threat.

When it came to foreign policy, Reagan's thoughts and emotions were conflicted. He wanted both to abolish nuclear weapons and to eradicate communism. At times, he recognized that the first goal required engagement with Soviet leaders and recognition of their legitimacy; at others, he did not. Given his abundant optimism and conservative political philosophy, tradeoffs did not interest him.

A key assertion of this book is that Reagan was fundamentally of two minds about whether to undermine the Soviet Union or to engage with its leaders. No doubt all political leaders experience periods of uncertainty, and these do not necessarily preclude their successes. Throughout his political career, however, Reagan was ambivalent and contradictory about how to deal with the Soviets. As president, these qualities were compounded by his passive style of management. He did not give clear guidance to subordinates, and he depended on others to reconcile conflicting aspirations. He surprised supporters and critics alike and, more to the point, his own top advisers. From the very start of his presidency, Reagan wanted to negotiate with Soviet leaders, his tough talk about the impending collapse of communism notwithstanding. He wrote letters to three successive general secretaries—Leonid Brezhnev, Yuri Andropov, and Konstantin Chernenko—asking them to sit down, man to man, to find a way out of the Cold War. This was not the Ronald Reagan the American public thought they knew.

Reagan's oldest political associates discouraged these overtures. Secretary of Defense Caspar Weinberger and other hardliners distrusted the Soviets and feared the unintended consequences of the president's optimism and goodwill. They disapproved of arms treaties and encouraged a crusade against communism. Alexander Haig, who was secretary of state from January 1981 to July 1982, expected to dominate foreign policy and was inclined to negotiate with the Soviets, but he failed to establish a solid working relationship with the president and alienated nearly everyone around him. As a result of the president's conflicting aspirations and reluctance to intervene in the personality conflicts among his national security team, ambivalence and sometimes outright confusion reigned during the first year and a half of the Reagan administration.

In July 1982, George Shultz replaced Haig as secretary of state. Over the remainder of the first administration and throughout the second, Shultz was the critical agent of U.S. foreign policy. Shultz garnered the trust of his president and deflected the blows of hardliners in the executive branch and in the U.S. Congress. He concentrated on the Soviet Union and labored to steer relations with it from confrontation to cooperation even before Gorbachev's ascent in March 1985. His bond with Gorbachev turned out to be as important as the Soviet leader's relationship with the president.

Shultz wanted to engage the Cold War adversary, establish trust, share ideas, and promote human rights everywhere. He found optimism in the coming information age and the promise it held for capitalism, and he did not regard the relationship between East and West as a zero-sum game. With Gorbachev as well as with Soviet Foreign Minister Eduard Shevardnadze, he established trust. At the superpower summits in Geneva, Reykjavik, Washington, Moscow, and New York and in the delegations he led to Moscow in 1987 and 1988, Shultz often took on the role of outside adviser to perestroika. At home, he blunted the efforts of hardliners who did not want arms control agreements and considered the Soviet Union an implacable foe incapable of change.

Shultz empowered Reagan's impulse to bargain with the Soviets. He supported the redoubling of efforts to achieve an Intermediate-Range Nuclear Forces treaty in the wake of a stalemate at the Reykjavik Summit in October 1986 and after the Iran-Contra scandal weakened Reagan's presidency. In April 1987, following the KGB's penetration of the U.S. Embassy in Moscow, he brushed aside critics and the U.S. Congress to travel to Moscow. That summer, he prevented Secretary of Defense Caspar Weinberger from cutting off arms negotiations. Ultimately, Shultz outlasted Weinberger and all of his other rivals.

When Reagan and Shultz left office in early 1989, they believed that the Cold War was basically over. George H. W. Bush, forty-first president of the United States, understood the ways in which that was not fully the case. Gorbachev, Reagan, and Shultz arrested the nuclear arms race. The economic recovery that started in the West in 1983, amidst continued stagnation in the East, demonstrated the endurance of market-based economics and democratic institutions. Yet the division of Germany and Europe remained. Reagan famously challenged Gorbachev to "tear down this wall" in 1987, but these words did not translate into policies that achieved that objective.

Bush's manner was cautious, and he lacked Reagan's ebullience, but he had a better sense of how to steer the changes occurring in Eastern Europe and the Soviet Union toward a resolution of longstanding challenges. He prudently led the nation through the unpredictability of 1989 and skillfully managed his national security team. He did so in the face of domestic political constraints that included a hostile Congress, public clamor over the federal deficit, and support for rapid Baltic independence on the part of Americans who shared this ethnic heritage. Bush managed competing domestic aims while maintaining the priority of dealing with Gorbachev and minimizing violence as the Soviet empire withered.

A closing argument of this book is that Bush oversaw the construction of a new configuration of power after the fall of the Berlin Wall, one that resolved the fundamental components of the Cold War on Washington's terms. The Conventional Forces in Europe Treaty undercut the rationale for nuclear weapons to defend European security. Shrewd diplomacy allowed for the swift reunification of Germany and European integration. Reform of existing international institutions and promotion of new ones revived the capitalist globalization of markets, trade, and investment that had existed before World War I.

Confirmation of the Cold War victory occurred when Bush put together a grand coalition to expel Saddam Hussein from Kuwait. The Soviet Union did not act when its client was thwarted by a coalition of Western and Arab states that aided the U.S.-led military action. The 1991 Persian Gulf War demonstrated that the Cold War, finally, was over and that U.S. power and American values reigned supreme—with all the consequences that supremacy implied.

Gorbachev, Reagan, Shultz, and Bush relied on astute and imaginative advisers. Alexander Yakovlev and Anatoly Chernyaev were essential to new thinking at home and abroad, and Eduard Shevardnadze reshaped the conduct of Soviet diplomacy after his stolid predecessor, Andrei Gromyko. Jack Matlock advised Reagan on Soviet matters at key moments and worked in concert with Shultz after replacing Richard Pipes, who, in stark contrast to Matlock, regarded the Soviet people as capable of withstanding a nuclear war. National Security Advisor Brent Scowcroft and Secretary of State James Baker presented President Bush with a national security team that worked in harmony toward common purposes.

Other leaders played key roles as well. Margaret Thatcher's economic policies paved the way for Reaganomics. François Mitterrand's reverse course in 1982 underscored a growing neoliberal consensus. Both leaders engaged Gorbachev constructively in the mid-1980s. Helmut Kohl took the lead on German reunification during 1989 and 1990, and before that, he was Reagan's closest ally on the deployment of INF systems. Pope John Paul II, throughout the 1979–1991 period, was the world's foremost anticommunist. He buoyed the spirits of Polish Catholics and sustained the hopes of the Solidarity movement in Poland. These individuals in positions of power and influence were important, though ultimately not as critical in ending the Cold War as Gorbachev, Reagan, Shultz, and Bush.

This is a book, then, about structure and agency as well as planning and improvisation. It is a book about the burdens of responsibility, the obstacles of domestic politics, and the human qualities that constitute leadership. It is about the surprises of history—and the possibilities of the future.

# CHAPTER 1

# Reagan Reaches

*January 1981–June 1982*

"I know of no Soviet leader since the revolution, and including the present leadership, that has not more than once repeated in the various Communist congresses they hold their determination that their goal must be the promotion of world revolution and a one-world Socialist or Communist state," Ronald Reagan declared at his first press conference as the fortieth president of the United States. Soviet leaders, he went on to say, "have openly and publicly declared that the only morality they recognize is what will further their cause, meaning they reserve unto themselves the right to commit any crime, to lie, to cheat, in order to attain that, and that is moral, not immoral, and we operate on a different set of standards."[1]

Ronald Wilson Reagan took office hoping to reduce the size of government, reinvigorate the economy, reaffirm the American way of life, and reach for something grander. "Why are you doing this, Ron? Why do you want to be President?" a top political adviser asked him during the 1980 campaign. "To end the Cold War," was his answer. How did he plan to do that? "I'm not sure, but there has got to be a way," the former governor insisted.[2] Three months after that conversation, Reagan bested Jimmy Carter in the most resounding defeat of a sitting president since Franklin Delano Roosevelt's victory over Herbert Hoover in 1932.

Reagan had voted for FDR four times—he, too, believed that America had a "rendezvous with destiny." That destiny, as Reagan saw it, was to oppose the Marxist "philosophy of world revolution and a single, one-world Communist state."[3] On February 27, 1981, he welcomed British Prime Minister Margaret Thatcher to Washington and delivered a speech reaffirming the Atlantic Charter. "We've all heard the slogans, the end of the class struggle, the vanguard of the proletariat, the wave of the future, the inevitable triumph of socialism," the president concluded his remarks, "clichés that rapidly are being recognized for what they are, a gaggle of bogus prophecies and petty superstitions." The future lay elsewhere. "Prime Minister, everywhere one looks these days the cult of the state is dying, and I wonder if you and I and other leaders of the West should not now be looking toward bright sunlit uplands and begin planning for a world where our adversaries are remembered only for their role in a sad and rather bizarre chapter in human history."[4]

Over the next year and a half, Reagan repeated the charge that communism constituted a bizarre chapter in human history. His rhetorical offensive climaxed in a speech to the British Parliament on June 8, 1982, in which he spoke of "the march of freedom and democracy which will leave Marxism-Leninism on the ash heap of history as it has left other tyrannies which stifle the freedom and muzzle the self-expression of the people."[5] These were bold words. Indeed, the central theme of this chapter is that Reagan's reach exceeded his grasp. Cold War victory, to him, meant eradicating communism and abolishing nuclear weapons. Yet reducing nuclear weapons required that he deal directly with the Soviet Union and respect its legitimacy. During this period and throughout his eight years in office, Reagan's approach toward the Soviet Union was contradictory. The existence of those contradictions, along with the president's lack of guidance and assertiveness, meant that dynamics between individuals and among groups within the Reagan administration determined U.S. policies toward the Soviet Union and the Cold War.

## President Reagan

His talk of the Atlantic Charter notwithstanding, Reagan signaled elsewhere that he might not intend to take an active foreign policy role. He did not mention the Cold War in his inaugural address, and he devoted his first two months in office to persuading a handful of Democrats in the House of Representatives to vote for a massive tax cut that he insisted would fire up the American economy. "Our one hundred day plan says we have three priorities," the president's chief of staff, James Baker, advised him, "and those three priorities are economic recovery, economic recovery, and economic recovery."[6]

Secretary of State Alexander M. Haig Jr. thought he had a pretty clear idea what this meant: he would be the "vicar" of foreign policy.[7] The retired four-star general exuded physical confidence.[8] Haig also took the Cold War personally. As Supreme Allied Commander of NATO in the 1970s, he narrowly escaped an assassination attempt by the Baader-Meinhof gang. Since the terrorists had planned the attack from a KGB safehouse, Haig concluded that the Soviet Union had ordered the attempt on his life and that they were orchestrating a network of international terrorism.[9] Haig possessed supreme confidence in his ability to draw such conclusions. Upon returning home from Vietnam, he obtained a master's degree in international relations from Georgetown. Later, as military attaché to Henry Kissinger, he learned statecraft from the man he considered the master.[10]

As with Kissinger, Haig considered himself a realist uninterested in what the governments his interlocutors represented did back home. He also espoused "linkage," which cast the United States and the Soviet Union as players seated at a global chessboard. Each side had knights, bishops, and pawns, but there were just two kings. "Our primary adversary in Vietnam was the Soviet Union," Haig asserted at his confirmation hearings.[11] If the Soviets wanted the United States to lift its grain embargo in 1981, they should force their Vietnamese clients to withdraw from Cambodia. If they wanted a nuclear arms treaty, terrorist groups needed to stop wreaking havoc throughout the Middle East. In Poland, a revolt against communism was simmering, Haig stated at a meeting of the National Security Council in February 1981. If the Soviets were about to invade, the United States "must get them somewhere else first, and that means Cuba."[12]

Reagan probably did say something to the effect that Haig would be "the vicar." His aides, however, did not trust the general. On Inauguration Day, Haig handed Reagan's top domestic adviser, Edwin Meese, a document that laid out his prerogatives as secretary of state. Meese never passed it on to the president.[13] Haig, for his part, treated Meese with contempt. In fact, he treated nearly everyone in the administration with contempt. In NSC meetings, he pounced on the young White House budget director, David Stockman. He did not forgive Meese for burying his memo. Yet he later recalled the palace intrigue with a sense of bravado: "Do you think I gave a shit about guerilla warfare with a bunch of second-rate hambones in the White House?"[14]

Haig's feuds spilled over into the headlines. The evening news on March 25, 1981, broadcast an angry Haig speaking out against an announcement that Vice President George H. W. Bush would head the administration's crisis management team.[15] Rumors circulated that the White House might soon expect Haig's resignation.[16]

And then crisis struck. At around 2:30 in the afternoon of March 30, 1981, upon leaving a gathering of AFL-CIO representatives at the Washington Hilton Hotel, President Reagan was shot in the chest by a mentally unstable man named John Hinckley Jr. Sixty-nine years old, Reagan very nearly died from his wounds. The president's survival spoke to his strong constitution, unflagging spirit, and tremendous luck. "Perhaps having come so close to death made me feel I should do whatever I could in the years God had given me to reduce the threat of nuclear war," Reagan later recalled.[17] While he was recovering from the assassination attempt, he wrote a letter to his Soviet counterpart, Leonid Brezhnev, imploring him to help find a way out of the Cold War.

Ever since taking office, Reagan had grappled with whether to lift the grain embargo Carter imposed on Moscow after the Soviet invasion of Afghanistan. "I've always felt it hurts our farmers worse than it hurt Soviets," he confided in his diary in February of 1981. "Many of our allies?? filled the gap & supplied Soviet[s]. But now—how do we lift it without sending wrong message to Soviets?" Reagan pondered: "Wouldn't we be doing more for their people if we let their system fail instead of constantly bailing it out?"[18] The brush with death clarified the president's thinking: he would lift the embargo. He made the decision on his own. Around the time Reagan was putting pen to paper, Vice President Bush was hosting the Dutch prime minister and praising him for holding the American line on the grain embargo.[19] Bush had no clue what Reagan was up to. Haig did—and he was furious. The president was sending a gift to the Soviets for which the United States would receive nothing in return—an affront to Haig's realism. At the very least, the message needed to be tougher. No problem, Reagan told Haig: you send your letter, I'll send mine.[20]

In his letter, Reagan called on the Soviet leader to take steps to ratchet down the Cold War. He reminded Brezhnev of their introduction in California a decade earlier: "When we met I asked if you were aware that the hopes and aspirations of millions and millions of people throughout the world were dependent on the decisions that would be reached in your meetings [with Richard Nixon]," after which "you took my hand in both of yours and assured me that you were aware of that and that you were dedicated with all your heart and mind to fulfilling those hopes and dreams." Now was the time to act upon this pledge to help foster peace. "It is in this spirit, in the spirit of helping the people of both our nations," Reagan wrote, "that I have lifted the grain embargo. Perhaps this decision will contribute to creating the circumstances which will lead to the meaningful and constructive dialogue which will assist us in fulfilling our joint obligation to find lasting peace."[21]

## Reagan's Thinking

Reagan's emotional appeal reflected more than just his convalescence. He had always sought a lasting peace but had been deeply conflicted about whether the United States could bargain with the Soviet Union or whether communism needed first to be eradicated. Throughout his political career, he regarded the stakes as paramount. "You and I have a rendezvous with destiny," Reagan proclaimed in his 1964 advertisement for Barry Goldwater's presidential campaign. "We will preserve for our children this, the last best hope of man on Earth, or we will sentence them to take the first step into a thousand years of darkness."[22]

Reagan hoped that his countrymen would choose wisely. At the Republican National Convention in August 1976, he spoke of an America as "beautiful a hundred years from now as it was on that summer day" when he drove down the coast of southern California between the vast Pacific Ocean and the majestic Santa Ynez mountains, an America that had overcome the two fundamental challenges of the day: "the erosion of freedom that has taken place under Democratic rule in this country" and the danger that "the great powers have poised and aimed at each other horrible missiles of destruction, nuclear weapons that can in a matter of minutes arrive at each other's country and destroy, virtually, the civilized world we live in. ... Will they look back with appreciation and say, 'Thank God for those people in 1976 who headed off that loss of freedom, who kept us now 100 years later free, who kept our world from nuclear destruction'"?[23]

Reagan hoped so. Yet however eloquently stated in 1964 and 1976, his vision for the future left unanswered the fate of the people living in the rest of the world. What about the inhabitants of the Soviet Union, of leftist regimes in Eastern Europe, Latin America, Asia, and Africa? Did Reagan believe that America's preservation of peace and freedom required liberating the communist bloc? Or could America achieve its goals while coexisting alongside the communist world? The answers did not come easily. Human dignity, individual freedom, free markets, and equality of opportunity were all universal values Reagan believed America should foster and project everywhere. A missionary impulse was ingrained in him at an early age. Raised to live a spiritual life by his mother, Nelle, an active member of the Disciples of Christ, young "Dutch" Reagan learned Christian values and even, at age eleven, requested to be baptized after reading a modern-day parable called *That Printer of Udell's: A Story of the Middle West.*[24] Becoming an active member of the church, he forged a strong bond with his family's pastor, Ben Cleaver, whose daughter, Margaret, became his first girlfriend. The elder Cleaver served as a surrogate father figure to Reagan, whose own father had been an alcoholic. Cleaver taught him about the "atheistic doctrines" on which communism rested and instilled in the boy the founding principle of the Disciples of Christ: the world "must look [to America] for its emancipation from the most heartless spiritual despotism ever. .... This is our special mission in the world as a nation and a people, and for this purpose the Ruler of nations has raised us up and made us the wonder and the admiration of the world."[25]

Reagan did not base his vision of the future solely on a mission to spread American and Christian ideals. As much as he believed in that cause, Reagan also valued peace and strength; he considered them intertwined. "America has never gotten into a war because it was too strong," he used to tell his supporters. Those closest to him understood what he meant. An important and sometimes overlooked influence on Reagan was his second wife, Nancy. "For years it had troubled me that my husband was always being portrayed by his opponents as a warmonger," she later recalled, "simply because he

**FIGURE 1.1.** Reagan and Weinberger, 1983. Secretary of Defense Caspar Weinberger encouraged the president to take a hard line on negotiations with the Soviet Union. Courtesy of the Ronald Reagan Library.

believed, quite properly, in strengthening our defenses."[26] Nancy wanted Ronald Reagan to be remembered as a man of peace. So too did the former lifeguard from Tampico. "I have seen four wars in my lifetime," he declared during the 1980 campaign. "I'm a father of sons; I have a grandson. I don't ever want to see another generation of young Americans bleed their lives into sandy beachheads in the Pacific, or rice paddies and jungles in Asia or the muddy, bloody battlefields of Europe."[27]

These two sets of values shaped Reagan's character and help explain why he spoke alternately of two very different long-term goals. The first was the eradication of communism. Reagan contended that communism was a "disease" for which Americans required "frequent vaccination to guard against being infected until the day when this health threat will be eliminated as we eliminated the black plague."[28] Reagan thus saw the Cold War as an epic struggle, not merely between capitalism and communism. A divided world could not survive "half-slave, half-free," he wrote a supporter. "We must also keep alive the idea that the conquered nations—the captive nations—of the Soviet Union must regain their freedom."[29]

Reagan's second long-term goal was not destroying communism but reducing arms to foster peaceful coexistence. He opposed SALT II because he believed that it would lock into place a strategic balance that favored the Soviet Union. "We are negotiating the SALT II treaty from a position of weakness," he asserted.[30] The way to tackle this problem was to let "the Soviets know we are going about the business of building up our defense capability pending an agreement by both sides to limit various kinds of weapons." Yet in building strength, Reagan cautioned, the United States should not abandon trying reach to an agreement: "I have repeatedly stated that I would be willing to negotiate an honest, verifiable reduction in nuclear weapons by both our countries to the point that neither of us represented a threat to the other."[31]

Reagan was torn between a "crusade for freedom" and "peace through strength." A "crusade for freedom" aimed to cast the Cold War struggle in terms of moral clarity. From the Founding Fathers to the present day, American leaders stood for "social justice, decency, and adherence to the highest standards [to which] man has evolved in his climb from the swamp to the stars." Soviets, for their part, had always called for "treachery, deceit, destruction, and bloodshed."[32] Reagan yearned to broadcast this message to the world and to support voices of freedom within the Soviet Union. "A troubled and afflicted mankind looks to us," he proclaimed, "pleading for us to keep our rendezvous with destiny."[33]

"Peace through strength," for its part, meant restoring America's strength, irrespective of changes to the Soviet system: "When John F. Kennedy demanded the withdrawal of Soviet missiles from Cuba and the tension mounted, it was Nikita Khrushchev who backed down, and there was no war. Our nuclear superiority over the Soviets [then] was about 8 to 1." In the aftermath of the Cuban missile crisis, "no attention was paid to the declaration by the Soviet foreign minister that they would make sure they never had to back down again." Reagan grasped the meaning of this statement: "He was announcing the intention of the Soviet U. to begin a military buildup."[34] Reagan assured his supporters that the Soviets had made good on that pledge. Détente had provided them the opportunity. While the United States reduced its strength, the Soviet Union surged ahead. As a member of the Committee on the Present Danger, Reagan subscribed to the "Team B" alternative National Intelligence Estimate that the Soviets possessed strength far beyond what the CIA was claiming. Yes, Soviet leaders spoke of peaceful coexistence and parity, but their benevolent language obscured their desire for nuclear superiority. A shift in the strategic balance had emboldened the Soviet Union, Reagan was convinced. It had made the Kremlin more willing to stand up to the United States and its allies, even at the risk of threatening the peace.

The USSR was alternately on the brink of collapse, according to Reagan, or strong enough to present the United States with the ultimatum: "surrender or die." Liberating the communist bloc entailed undermining Soviet leaders and allowing their decrepit regime to collapse. It meant treating them not just as bogus emperors but as illegitimate representatives of the Russian people. Pursuing arms reductions required establishing long-term trust between the two superpowers and their leaders and, in certain important ways, bolstering the authority of Soviet leaders. When he promoted "a crusade for freedom," Reagan characterized the Soviet system as weak. Communism had ruined Russia's economy and failed to provide for its people, he averred. In one of his radio broadcasts after losing the 1976 Republican primary, Reagan told the story of a shipyard worker who wanted to bring his family to the West and whose living conditions the former governor deemed emblematic. Reagan surmised that America "could have an unexpected ally if citizen Ivan is becoming discontented enough to start talking back. Maybe we should drop a few million typical mail order catalogs on Minsk and Pinsk and Moscow to whet their appetites."[35]

"Peace through strength," however, portrayed the Soviets as ferociously strong. "When it comes to the Soviet Union," he declared, "no one denies they have assembled an offensive force of tanks [and] mobile artillery, support aircraft and armored personnel carriers on the Western front in Europe that are superior to our forces and those of our NATO allies."[36] The Soviets had also, he claimed, deployed a "hunter-killer" satellite "which could 'home in' and destroy a target in space during a single orbit." They possessed a "laser beam capable of blasting our missiles from the sky if we should ever try to use them" and had launched a crash program to build "orbital bombardment vehicles and laser weapons."[37] In the most extreme case, the Soviet leadership, Reagan warned, was preparing the Russian people to withstand a nuclear war. He described a vast system of Soviet military and civil defense: 30,000 hardened military installations; 10,000 hardened surface-to-air missile sites; industrial shelters prepared to sustain 60 million evacuees.[38] "Do the Russians subscribe to our belief in 'mutual assured destruction' as a deterrent to war?" he asked. "Apparently we think so but just as apparently the Russians do not. We say, 'thermo-nuclear war is unthinkable by either side.' The Russians have told their own people that while it would be a calamity it is not unthinkable; that it very well might happen & if it does the Soviet U. will survive & be victorious."[39]

What was America to do about it? Reagan railed against the so-called Vietnam syndrome yet balked at the suggestion that he wanted to project American power to ward off communist gains in the periphery or to roll them back in Eastern Europe. He wrote a supporter: "Apparently, my message ... isn't getting circulation. I've never advocated armed intervention in any of the troubled areas of the world."[40] Reagan purported to want mutual arms reductions in the long term, yet he questioned whether arms control agreements with the Soviet Union could ever be enforced. "I don't really trust the Soviets," he wrote a friend in 1980, "and I don't really believe that they will really join us in a legitimate limitation of arms agreement."[41]

Reagan was also ambivalent over whether to jettison the doctrine of Mutual Assured Destruction. On one hand, he passionately opposed it, ridiculing its architect, Robert McNamara, as "that efficient disaster." He likened MAD to "two westerners standing in a saloon aiming their guns to each other's head—permanently" and described it to intimates as "the most ridiculous thing" he had ever seen.[42] Reagan's strategy of "peace through strength," however, rested on the notion that deterrence worked—and by deterrent he really meant preponderance. "Until recently our deterrent was nuclear superiority," he stated. "If the Soviets attacked Western Europe we could threaten Russia with nuclear destruction. That of course is no longer true."[43] Americans had "reason to question" whether MAD was "an adequate defense."[44]

Reagan wanted America always to win. Sometimes, this meant disavowing diplomacy to pursue an ideological crusade against communism. Other times, it meant negotiating with communists to get a better deal. Reagan never saw a contradiction between his grand ambitions of eradicating communism and abolishing nuclear weapons, something he could do only by bargaining with communists and implicitly recognizing their right to exist. Real arms reduction was possible only if the Soviet leaders trusted Reagan. And they could not trust him if it appeared he was out to destroy them.

Reagan did not see a fundamental contradiction because he believed in the unlimited potential of American strength as defined by the vibrancy of the nation's institutions, the dignity that individual freedom and equality of opportunity bestowed on its citizens, and the men and women of the U.S. armed forces. He believed that in every facet of life this strength had been allowed to erode over the two decades preceding his presidency.

## Hardliners

In the spring of 1981, as the president recovered from the attempt on his life, his administration embarked on defense expenditures that totaled $1.5 trillion over five years and included a host of new weapons systems: 100 MX missiles (later scaled back to 50), each equipped with ten multiple independently targetable reentry vehicles (MIRVs) to deliver 300-kiloton warheads (equivalent of twenty times the destructive force of the atomic bomb dropped on Hiroshima); the B-1 bomber; the Trident Submarine; the neutron bomb; the F-14 fighter jet; and outlays for two new aircraft carrier groups priced around $18 billion each. There were also new research projects to develop particle beam technology, high-energy lasers, and space weapons.[45]

His physical strength restored and his entreaty to Brezhnev rebuffed, Reagan embarked on a rhetorical offensive. "The years ahead are great ones for this country," he told Notre Dame's class of 1981, and "for the cause of freedom and the spread of civilization. The West won't contain communism, it will transcend communism. It won't bother to dismiss or denounce it, it will dismiss [sic] it as some bizarre chapter in human history whose last pages are even now being written." The stakes had never been higher, Reagan told cadets at West Point a month later. "You are that chain holding back an evil force that would extinguish the light we've been tending for 6,000 years."[46] In an NSC meeting about whether to try to block a natural gas pipeline linking Siberia to Western Europe, Reagan vented his frustration in close quarters. "I for one don't think we are being harsh or rigid" in attempting to disrupt the gas pipeline, he told his team. "The Soviets have spoken as plainly as Hitler did in 'Mein Kampf.' They have spoken world domination—at what point do we dig in our heels?"[47]

Advisers close to Reagan welcomed this talk. Haig considered himself to be tough on communism, but the California crowd and their allies believed that the secretary was actually holding the president back. Foremost were Edwin Meese and William Clark, two lawyers who had served successively as chief of staff to Governor Reagan and who professed to have no foreign policy experience other than an innate understanding of communism's evil. Meese became counselor to the president with a cabinet rank and a seat on the NSC. His official purview was domestic affairs, but he paid little heed to the distinction between domestic and foreign policy. In the early days of the administration, Meese met with the NSC's counterterrorism adviser, Colonel William Odom. "He wanted to launch covert operations all over the world," Odom later recalled.[48] Meese took a commanding role at NSC meetings, moving the agenda along and summarizing major conclusions at the close. In an incident in August 1981 that drew ridicule as well as concern about the integrity of the chain of command, Meese waited until the next morning to inform the president that American F-14 fighters had shot down two Libyan MiGs.[49] "I know nothing about foreign policy or foreign affairs," William Clark told Reagan when he learned he was to be deputy secretary of state.[50] The former California Supreme Court justice struggled to answer basic questions about international affairs during his confirmation hearing and failed to charm Senator Joseph Biden with talk of having once spent "seventy-two hours in Santiago."[51] With the Republicans newly in charge of the Senate, Clark squeaked through. He purported to "represent the United States" at the State Department. Neither he nor Meese had any foreign policy credentials. Yet both men exerted tremendous influence over U.S. foreign policy in 1981 and 1982.

More formidable was Caspar Weinberger. A Harvard graduate, Weinberger often seemed out of place amidst a conservative movement that extolled midwestern values and scorned East Coast intellectualism. He had carved out a niche by outpacing potential rivals in his zeal for cutting government waste. "Cap the Knife," as he was known during his tenure as the director of finance in California and director of the Office of the Management and Budget during the Nixon era, proved to be anything but that in his first year as secretary of defense. When Reagan's own OMB director David Stockman realized that his budget estimates had not taken into consideration huge military outlays at the end of the Carter administration, Weinberger shrugged. He welcomed the bank error in his favor.[52] Weinberger took responsibility for crafting America's arms buildup. He was often out in front of the president. "I think there is bound to be a continuing interest in ballistic missile defense," Weinberger told the Senate Armed Services Committee in one of his first testimonies. "We have a situation in which there is a very strong first strike Soviet capability and ... basically my feeling is that if we are able to develop a much more credible and much more reliable kind of defense against an incoming attack, it will be to all of our interests." At a May 22, 1981, meeting of the NSC, Weinberger attempted to spur the president on missile defense, but it does not appear that Reagan ever noticed.[53]

Weinberger professed horror at the defense budget he had inherited. After the Soviet invasion of Afghanistan, the Carter administration had called for a defense budget of $142 billion, a 5 percent increase. It was not enough for Weinberger. "I was already aware of the general deterioration of our military during the Carter years," he later wrote, "but as I began receiving the classified data on our capabilities, I found that it was even worse than I had thought. It was truly appalling."[54] The briefings Weinberger received "revealed that we were losing the respect and support of our allies . . . , and the Soviets suspected we lacked the conventional military strength—and perhaps the will—to prevent a Soviet advance into Western Europe."[55]

Weinberger was convinced that the United States was facing a window of vulnerability. He proposed a six-month moratorium on negotiations while America rebuilt its strength.[56] The word went out to service chiefs to tell the defense department what they needed. "This was Christmas in February," Weinberger's military attaché, Colin Powell, later recalled. "This was tennis without a net. ... The requests initially totaled approximately a nine percent real increase in defense spending. ... That was not enough.

**FIGURE 1.2.** Ronald and Nancy Reagan, 1984. The First Lady wanted her husband to be remembered as a "man of peace." Courtesy of the Ronald Reagan Library.

Weinberger ordered the chiefs back to the drawing boards. They went from their wish lists to their dream lists. ... The latest figures went to the Office of Management and Budget, and the word came back, not enough."[57] Weinberger's proposal garnered broad support outside the Pentagon—especially among neoconservative Democrats. Reagan prided himself on his ability to draw support from old-school Democrats like Eugene Rostow, Senator Henry "Scoop" Jackson, and the latter's ambitious aide, Richard Perle, whom he had grown to respect in the 1970s. He cherished the connection with Paul Nitze, who, with his mentor, Dean Acheson, had been "present at the creation" of U.S. Cold War strategy. One of Reagan's fondest memories from the campaign season in 1980 was the endorsement of former senator Eugene McCarthy, who told Reagan that he could be the next Truman.[58]

In Jeane Kirkpatrick, Reagan found a registered Democrat with an intellectual framework that rationalized his own geopolitical instincts. Reagan chose her to be his ambassador to the United Nations sight unseen after reading an article in which she laid out the differences between authoritarian right-wing and totalitarian left-wing regimes. Authoritarian right-wing regimes that favored private property rights and sanctity of contracts, such as that of General Augusto Pinochet in Chile, sometimes evolved into pluralistic democracies. In contrast, totalitarian regimes of the left had no history of evolution. Support for authoritarian regimes could thus be justified, the human rights abuses they engendered notwithstanding.[59]

In Richard Pipes, Reagan found a registered Democrat who professed to understand what made the Soviets tick. That fact made him essential to Reagan as he assembled his administration. Pipes had escaped Poland and immigrated to the United States in 1940. Through intellect and determination, Pipes earned a doctorate in history and began teaching at Harvard University ten years later. He established his academic reputation by disaggregating modern Russia from the development of the West. While feudal structures had largely eroded by the seventeenth century in England, France, and the remnants of the Holy Roman Empire, Pipes contended, the concepts of private property and individual liberty remained alien to tsarist Russia until its collapse. The Soviets, in his account, resembled their predecessors far more than they cared to admit.

Liberal in outlook, Jewish in faith, a Harvard man after the war, Pipes gravitated to the Democratic Party. He voted for Henry Wallace in 1948 but by the 1970s fell in with neoconservative Democrats who had been, in the words of Irving Kristol, "mugged by reality." Pipes joined Rostow, Nitze, Fitzpatrick, and other disaffected Democrats to rally around Senator Henry "Scoop" Jackson. He authored the Team B Report that rejected the CIA's intelligence estimates and warned of a growing Soviet military threat. As the Soviet specialist on Reagan's NSC, Pipes stood out when his lack of political experience led him to make statements exemplifying what others around him probably thought but refrained from stating because they were politically toxic. Behind all the studies, the data, and the analysis, there was something elemental—something that Pipes, owing to his study of history as well as his own personal history as a Polish Jew, understood: Russian people did not think in the same terms as Americans. They were tougher, they were more accustomed to sacrifice, and more of them were conditioned to do horrible things. He believed that they were capable of fighting and winning a nuclear war.[60]

Pipes did not believe the USSR would change, because "totalitarian regimes are by definition incapable of evolution."[61] Necessity lay in rebuilding America's strength—not negotiations. The Soviet expert saw neither the softer side of Reagan nor the sense of the entreaties he wrote Brezhnev. "In fact, as I can testify from personal experience," Pipes later recalled, "during this period Reagan was determined not to negotiate with the Soviet leadership."[62]

Pipes and the rest of the new administration sought to arrest the narrative that democracy and capitalism were in decline. It wanted to harness soft power. Reagan himself had spent his formative political years doing just that, pitching consumer products for General Electric—literally selling the American Dream. He appointed his old friend Charles Z. Wick to head the United States Information Agency. Wick took the assignment seriously. "In view of the extreme urgency of coping with the effectiveness of Soviet Disinformation," he wrote in an early report, "I propose that the administration immediately mobilize with Wartime Urgency all the resources for information available to it."[63] Of particular concern to Wick were alleged KGB efforts to spread disinformation among America's European allies. A growing antinuclear movement in Western Europe challenged U.S. strategic flexibility. New technologies emerging in the mid-1970s raised questions about America's commitment to West Germany and France. Would the neutron bomb turn Germany into a battlefield for a war fought by countries that could escape unscathed? After the Soviets installed SS-20 missiles, which targeted the capitals of Western Europe, suspicions reemerged over whether the United States would actually risk retaliation against its homeland to defend its European allies. These questions rallied broad coalitions that seldom fell into categories of left versus right, but Wick had no taste for such niceties. To him, it was information versus disinformation. Any demonstration against further nuclear armaments in Western Europe was perceived to be either the result of direct KGB involvement or lies propagated by Soviet intelligence services.[64]

When soft power proved insufficient, the role of spreading America's message fell to the Central Intelligence Agency. During the campaign Reagan had promised to "unleash the CIA," and once in office he chose his campaign manager, William Casey, to spearhead this effort. A veteran of the original Office of Strategic Services during World War II, Casey idolized William J. "Wild Bill" Donovan, who had gone on to be one of the people who founded the agency. Casey had made a small fortune in Wall Street while preserving connections to the intelligence community. By all accounts, he wanted to be secretary of state, but his poor speaking style precluded his being the spokesman for America to the world. Settling for the CIA, Casey aimed to take the fight to the communists. "Just as there is a classic formula for communist subversion and take-over," he explained toward the end of his service, "there is also a proven method of overthrowing repressive government that can be applied successfully in Nicaragua"—and by extension all of the Third World.[65] In this, Casey was mistaken. Yet he and Reagan were intent on distinguishing themselves from the previous administration, and talk of counterinsurgency was one way to mark that difference.

On January 20, 1981, Reagan was briefed by the outgoing CIA director, Stansfield Turner, on the nature of the Soviet threat. After Reagan had based his political campaign on the premise that the Soviets possessed superior nuclear capability, Turner explained "that the question was not the numbers of bombs and missiles but the operational capacity to use them, and that according to CIA estimates, the USSR had no advantage over the United States." CIA data indicated that "even after a Soviet first strike, the U.S. would have enough strategic nuclear weapons to destroy all Soviet cities with populations over 100,000." Reagan responded with silence, and Turner understood that his "days as a passenger in an official CIA armored limousine were over."[66] Team B effectively became Team A once Reagan was elected. Its members welcomed the exaggeration of threat posed by the Soviet Union. "Democracies will not sacrifice to protect their security in the absence of a sense of danger," Richard Perle explained to a reporter midway through the first term. "And every time we create the impression that we and the Soviets are cooperating and moderating the competition, we diminish that sense of apprehension."[67]

Each of Reagan's advisers sought to prove that he or she truly represented what Reagan wanted. No one could say definitively just who was doing Reagan's bidding. In 1981 and 1982, the most hawkish position tended to win out. As Reagan vacillated in tone, his advisers clashed over petty matters; the president chose not to intercede.

Haltingly, Reagan struggled to set priorities. Doing so meant tradeoffs, and the president loathed sacrificing anything. When David Stockman tried to explain to Reagan that he simply could not have guns and butter, the president "noted that his silence on this matter was not from lack of interest but rather because he was afflicted with two allergies: the allergy of wanting to control government spending and the allergy of wanting to increase our national security posture." Reluctant to choose, Reagan decided that "Mr. Stockman should see what could be done from the current budget."[68] This was about as clear as the president would get.

The challenges of the job were daunting; by the end of spring the president appeared exasperated. "Sometimes I wonder if we are destined to witness Armageddon," he wrote after an NSC meeting on Lebanon in May. "Got word of Israeli bombing of Iraq—nuclear reactor," he wrote a month later. "I swear I believe Armageddon is near."[69] The president labored to convince his supporters that the ship of state was headed forward. "I know I'm being criticized for not having a made a great speech outlining what would be the Reagan foreign policy," he wrote a longtime friend. "I have a foreign policy; I'm working on it. I don't happen to think that it's wise to always stand up and put in quotation marks in front of the world what your foreign policy is."[70] If his policy remained undefined, Reagan never wavered in his confidence in the righteousness of the American system in contrast to the moral and spiritual poverty of communism. The world was beginning to see "not in only in Poland but the reports that are beginning to come out of Russia itself about the younger generation and its resistance to longtime government controls, is an indication that communism is an aberration," the president declared at a news conference on June 16, 1981. "It's not a normal way of living for human beings, and I think we are seeing the first, beginning cracks, the beginning of the end."[71]

Reagan certainly sensed an opportunity, a historic moment in the Cold War. In the summer of 1981, however, the United States was still mired in a deep recession. "Their economy is going bust," he wrote in his diary after an NSC meeting on Poland. "Here is the 1st major break in the Red dike—Poland's disenchantment with Soviet Communism. Can we afford to let Poland collapse? But in the state of our present economy can we afford to help it in a meaningful way? We can't alone but if our NATO allies could really unite we could handle it."[72]

That summer, Reagan traveled to his ranch in California. The respite was brief. On August 3, 1981, the nation's largest air traffic controller union,

PATCO, went on strike. Reagan acted swiftly. Citing national security, he fired all of the air traffic controllers. The decision appeared to reverberate beyond America's borders. "The way the PATCO strike was handled impressed the Russians . . . and gave them respect for Reagan. It showed them a man who, when aroused, will go to the limit to back up his principles," wrote Pipes.[73] It mattered not whether the Soviet leadership actually paid attention—but whether Reagan and his advisers believed that they did.

The next week, Reagan signed off on his chief domestic priority, a tax cut of over $750 billion over the next five years. Reinvigorated, he returned to Washington to address foreign policy. The six-month moratorium prescribed by Weinberger had expired; Reagan addressed himself toward proposing a new arms deal. The United States would adhere to the unratified SALT II Treaty that limited nuclear weapons, but it would also pursue a new agreement that reduced them.

At an October 13, 1981, meeting of the NSC, the administration grappled with how to achieve arms buildup and arms reductions. They were in a tight spot, Weinberger acknowledged. "If we are perceived as not engaging in serious negotiations, our modernization program will not go through," he stated. "If we succeed in reaching only a cosmetic agreement, our modernization program will also come to a halt, being perceived as no longer necessary. Or if we are viewed as not making progress in negotiations, the Soviets will make it seem to be our fault, and our modernization program will be endangered." Weinberger urged Reagan to "consider a bold plan, sweeping in nature, to capture world opinion." He proposed a "zero option," whereby the Soviets eliminated their SS-20s on the condition that the United States would not deploy the Pershing II missiles and the ground-launched cruise missiles.[74] That is to say, the long-term goal would be the elimination of an entire class of nuclear weapons. The president was intrigued but initially skeptical. "Do we really want a 'zero option' for the battlefield?" he asked. "Don't we need these nuclear systems? Wouldn't it be bad for us to give them up since we need them to handle Soviet conventional superiority?" Weinberger's response evinced a cynicism he always denied. "The Soviets will certainly reject an American 'zero option' proposal," he acknowledged. "But whether they reject it or they accept it, they would be set back on their heels. We would be left in good shape and would be shown as the White Hats."[75]

On November 18, 1981, Reagan delivered the bold speech Weinberger had advocated. He called for strategic arms reductions and announced guidance for the next round of theater-range nuclear arms negotiations due to begin later that month. "I have informed President Brezhnev that when our delegation travels to the negotiations on intermediate range, land-based nuclear missiles in Geneva on the 30th of this month," the president announced, "my representatives will present the following proposal: The United States is prepared to cancel its deployment of Pershing II and ground-launch cruise missiles if the Soviets will dismantle their SS-20, SS-4, and SS-5 missiles."[76] The proposal led critics to conclude that Reagan had been duped by his own advisers, who did not actually want a deal. It strained credulity that the Soviets would dismantle their own weapons on the condition that the United States would not deploy.[77]

The motives of Weinberger and other skeptics of arms control bred cynicism, but Reagan's were genuine. After his initial skepticism, he grew to like the zero option. He saw nothing pernicious about a plan to eliminate nuclear missiles. It comported with his grand narrative of American history as a story of innocence and noble intentions. The United States had no wish to threaten Soviet security, Reagan vowed in his November speech, because "territorial ambitions" were anathema to the American character. "When World War II ended," Reagan told his audience, "the United States had the only undamaged industrial power in the world. Our military might was at its peak, and we alone had the ultimate weapon, the nuclear weapon, with the unquestioned ability to deliver it anywhere in the world. If we had sought world domination then, who could have opposed us?"[78] Arms reductions alone were not enough to achieve a lasting peace, Reagan went on to say in his November speech, for "the American concept of peace goes well beyond the absence of war." A lasting peace meant the "flowering of economic growth and individual liberty." For "terms like 'peace' and 'security' ... have little meaning for the oppressed and the destitute ... to the individual whose state has stripped him of human freedom and dignity," the president explained. "We must recognize that progress and the pursuit of liberty is a necessary complement to military security."[79]

On the day that he spoke these words, Reagan also wrote to Brezhnev. "We should strive to find a common ground for agreement on matters of vital interest to our two countries and the rest of the world," wrote Reagan. "The cause of peace, and particularly the threat of nuclear destruction hanging over mankind, require that our two countries make an effort, together with our partners, to resolve our differences peacefully. I assure you the United States is committed to such a process."[80]

Reagan's aides hoped that this letter would be tougher. Excised by the president's hand were significant portions of the draft text, including demands that the Soviets call on Vietnam to withdraw its troops from Cambodia and that they apply pressure on Cuba to halt its meddling in Angola. In another section, Reagan moderated the language, striking "The Soviet military buildup of the past two decades has resulted in Soviet military capabilities well beyond any reasonable need for self-defense" and scribbling "what do you think about dropping this?" next to a passage expressing concern for Soviet dissidents Andrei Sakharov and Anatoly Shcharansky.[81] In these edits and in other ways, Reagan showed that he wanted to engage Brezhnev, but he could not contain his administration. Allen and Haig, for instance, were given to shouting at each other in NSC meetings.[82] The press focused on tension within the White House at the expense of publicizing the administration's initiatives.[83] Frustrated, Reagan called up a respected Washington journalist to deny that personnel changes were to be expected. Alexander Haig was "the best Sec. of State we've had in a long time," the president recorded in his diary after the call.[84] He recognized that there was tension, but he wanted to move forward. He summoned his secretary of state and national security advisor and ordered "a halt to the sniping."[85]

## Crisis in Poland

It appeared increasingly likely in the winter of 1981 that the Soviet Union would invade Poland to quell Solidarity, whose strikes were grinding the country's economy to a halt. An invasion would not alter the configurations of Cold War power, but the specter of Soviet tanks moving into Poland would evoke memories of Hungary in 1956 and Czechoslovakia in 1968. And such an event would humiliate the new American president. "Information available to me indicates a growing possibility that the Soviet Union is preparing to intervene militarily in Poland," Reagan wrote Brezhnev earlier that year. "I wish to make clear to you the seriousness with which the United States would view such an action, to which we would be compelled to respond. I take this step not to threaten the Soviet Union, but to ensure that there is no possibility of your misunderstanding our position or our intentions."[86]

After General Wojciech Jaruzelski declared martial law in Poland on December 13, 1981, Reagan gathered his national security team for the first of a series of contentious meetings. Haig expressed outrage at the suppression of freedom but urged his colleagues to remain calm. "The real question," the secretary of state queried, is whether "some degree of repression [is] tolerable from our standpoint, or do we stand only for total victory and are we prepared to pay the price necessary to achieve total victory?" He effectively answered his own question. In crisis mode, Haig walked away from his earlier bluster. He broached the prospect of applying pressure to Cuba—only to oppose it. The worst thing the administration could do, he stated, "would be to divert world attention from Poland by U.S. muscle flexing elsewhere."[87]

Reagan disagreed. For "the first time in 60 years" the United States had a chance to call the Soviets on their crimes. "I'm talking about a total quarantine on the Soviet Union. No détente!" Solidarity and its leader, Lech Wałęsa, resembled America's Founding Fathers. Their plight called to mind "the opening lines in our own Declaration of Independence. 'When in the course of human events. ... ' This is exactly what [the Poles] are doing now."[88] Weinberger seconded the president's outrage. It was hardly the first time in sixty years that the Soviets had squelched the forces of liberty in Eastern Europe, he pointed out. It did not matter that they now did so indirectly. "Let's not be mistaken," said Weinberger. "What Poland has now in Jaruzelski is a Russian general in Polish uniform. The Soviets are getting what they want." The president had an opportunity to seize the initiative. "It is the time to do it."[89]

"Let me tell you what I have in mind," Reagan stated. "I am talking about action that addresses the Allies and solicits—not begs—them to join in a complete quarantine of the Soviet Union. Cancel all licenses. Tell the Allies that if they don't go along with us, we let them know ... that we may have to review our Alliances." Reagan then invoked a precedent: "I am thinking back to 1938 when ... FDR asked the free world to join in a quarantine of Germany."[90] Yet Haig reiterated the need for prudence. Closing American embassies or breaking off diplomatic contact with the Soviets would be the wrong move, he insisted: "We don't want to get into a World War III scenario." A precipitous move would be sure to kill INF talks and perhaps lead to riots in Europe. "Let us make no mistake," he warned: the potential breakup of its empire was "a matter of life and death for the Soviet Union. They would go to war over this."[91]

No agreement was reached around the table, and the NSC meeting the next day was equally animated. "I think to consider [the] Helsinki [accords] null and void would hit them hard," the president stated. "Europe will go bonkers if we do that," Haig responded. If America's allies did not go along with the "revolution started against this 'damned force,'" Reagan countered, "they, too, will pay a price." He did not back down when Haig warned that a tough speech "will bring the specter of the terror of World War III on Christmas Eve."[92]

Later that day, Reagan met with the Polish ambassador, who along with his wife had decided to defect to the United States. Amidst a tepid response from Western Europe, this meeting and a letter of encouragement from Margaret Thatcher stiffened the president's resolve. "We can't let this revolution against Communism fail without our offering hand," Reagan wrote in his diary. "We may never have an opportunity like this one in our lifetime."[93]

In the days that followed, however, the president softened his rhetoric. Despite his talk of a "once-in-a-lifetime opportunity," the nature of that opportunity never became entirely clear. When his anger subsided, Reagan realized that his options were limited. On December 23, 1981, he ordered a host of sanctions ranging from suspending Aeroflot flights to closing negotiations on new long-term grain sales.[94] What else could the president do? Soviet tanks had not actually rolled into the streets of Poland. America's European allies did not seem terribly perturbed—at least not enough to imperil the construction of the Siberian pipeline. Washington and Moscow had their differences, Reagan told a reporter that day, but ultimately both needed to find a way out of the Cold War. "I have met Brezhnev. I met him 10 years ago. And lying in the hospital last April, after March 30, I wrote a handwritten letter recalling that meeting to Mr. Brezhnev, and sent it to him, because ... we must find a solution."[95]

"It sounds as if Jaruzelski is not a puppet, but is under the gun," Reagan speculated at an NSC meeting on January 5, 1982. Fresh intelligence suggested that Jaruzelski had ordered martial law to forestall a Soviet invasion. Weinberger could not agree. "Poland has been invaded, albeit indirectly." The secretary of defense wanted to strike back. The Polish crisis came as the NSC had planned to deliberate whether to allow a struggling American company to sell International Harvester farming equipment to the Soviet Union. Weinberger sought to cancel the export licenses. It mattered not that experts discounted any prospect that they could be weaponized. "It helps them to harvest more efficiently—it improves their economic conditions," Weinberger told the NSC. "This at a time when a few more pushes would contribute substantially to their economic problem."[96] The president expressed ambivalence. "Cap, I still say if we had not continued to bail out the Soviets over all these years, if we had all stuck together, we wouldn't have the problems we have now," he stated. "But, on International Harvester, I find myself thinking, selfishly, does this hurt us more than it hurts the Soviets? Could International Harvester go belly up and throw people out of work?" There was also no guarantee against the Soviets' buying equipment from European firms. "The moral thing is not of much use if the Allies go their own way."[97]

Haig still considered Weinberger's plans alarming. Calling in Poland's outstanding loans, as the defense secretary proposed, might start a chain reaction. "We must be careful," Haig warned. The United States had no interest in seeing a country like Romania go bust. "You are pursuing policies that will lead us in that direction," he asserted. "The Soviets can't take over all the tottering economies of Eastern Europe," Weinberger shot back. "If they had to support them all, it would speed the day when their system would collapse."[98]

The president straddled the line between his two outspoken advisers: he did not take decisive action. He was furious when the Soviets induced the Polish government to declare martial law, but his emotions subsided in the weeks that followed. He yearned to demonstrate America's newfound will and strength, but he was loath to pay the price of harming a U.S. corporation as the country remained mired in economic doldrums. He invoked FDR and the moral clarity of World War II because he abhorred communism and equated it to fascism. Yet as much as Reagan craved victory in the Cold War, he did not articulate a realistic vision of what victory entailed. So he continued to talk tough about the Soviets—and to build strength—even as he tried to negotiate with them.

## NSDD-32

On January 1, 1982, Reagan appointed Deputy Secretary of State William Clark to be his new national security advisor.[99] Few within the administration spoke ill of "the Judge" at the time of his promotion. Clark had convinced Haig not to resign after having been denied the role of crisis manager the past March and then assured Reagan that Haig remained viable, but Haig could not abide seeing his former deputy in a position of equal authority and with better access to the president.

The resulting disputes went beyond personalities. The priorities Clark laid out resembled those of Weinberger. He supported efforts to derail the Siberian pipeline. "[The] goal was to stress out the Soviet economy, particularly its hard currency cash flow, and fully exploit its rigidities, to engage Moscow on every front—through our military buildup, the war of ideas and the battleground of the Third World," one of Clark's aides later recalled. "It was a systematic assault on the Soviet Union in virtually every category of activity."[100] A devout Catholic, Clark intuited a shared destiny between Reagan and Pope John Paul II. "Both men took shots in the chest by would-be assassins only four weeks apart," he later recalled. "With a smile they decided that that was God's wake-up call that they had to work even faster in bringing down the Soviet empire."[101]

Clark's promotion also created new patterns of influence. One of the beneficiaries of this change was Richard Pipes, who now briefed the president directly on Soviet affairs. "He was not especially knowledgeable on the subject of foreign policy," Pipes later said of Clark, "but I found that, like Reagan, he had very good judgment."[102] Clark called on Pipes to help

Thomas Reed, a former U.S. secretary of the air force, construct a national strategy statement in the early months of 1982. The result was NSDD-32, a document that integrated hardline elements into a plan aimed "to foster, if possible in concert with our allies, restraint in Soviet military spending, discourage Soviet adventurism, and weaken the Soviet alliance system by forcing the USSR to bear the brunt of its economic shortcomings, and to encourage long-term liberalizing and nationalist tendencies within the Soviet Union and allied countries." The authors advocated a shift in Cold War strategy: the United States should seek not only to contain the Soviet Union but also to "reverse the expansion of Soviet control and military presence throughout the world, and to increase the costs of Soviet support and use of proxy, terrorist, and subversive forces."[103]

"The threats we face and the nature of our objectives are such that we are at a time of greatest danger to our national security since World War II," Reed told the NSC when presenting the report. At the same time, "it is unlikely the Soviets will challenge us directly in the near future." They would, however, continue to challenge the United States indirectly. To meet this challenge, the United States needed to prioritize "North America, NATO, Southwest Asia, the Pacific, Latin America, and Africa, in that order." Using economic pressure, assistance to friendly governments, and covert action if needed, the United States could reverse the tide. "The bottom line," Reed asserted, "is we are helping to encourage the dissolution of the Soviet Empire."[104] Neither Reed nor Pipes articulated just how the means were to produce the ends.

The result of Pipes's and Reed's efforts marked a triumph for the administration's hardliners. NSDD-32 technically remained classified, but its framers did not intend for their work to go unnoticed. Reed urged Clark to "go public," because "the President should get credit for having a plan."[105]

The Reagan administration intended to force the Soviet Union to "bear the brunt of its economic shortcomings," Clark declared in a speech at Georgetown University in May 1982. The hope was that it "might one day convince the leadership of the Soviet Union to turn their attention inward, to seek the legitimacy that only comes from the consent of the governed, and thus to address the hopes and dreams of their own people."[106] To the delight of Pipes, Clark's language caused a stir in the pages of official communist organs—the speech provided further evidence to them that the new administration sought to destroy the Soviet system. Aware of their own vulnerability, Pipes wrote Clark after the speech, Kremlin leaders had begun to realize "that it is our purpose to have the Soviet Union bear the consequences of its economic mismanagement and that we want to turn Soviet energies from expansion to internal reform." Indeed, the Soviet leadership appeared "extremely sensitive" to this plan, and "it ought to be hammered home time and again until the message gets through to the Soviet people."[107] Reed agreed. The Reagan administration was no longer content to manage the Cold War: "We believe the free world can prevail."[108]

Clark's speech came at a time when conservatives outside the Reagan administration were expressing concern. Writing about foreign affairs in the *New York Times,* neoconservative intellectual Norman Podhoretz lamented what he saw as the administration's lack of direction. Only if means comported with ends could the United States have an effective foreign policy, he wrote. "Yet judging by the discrepancy between the stated objectives of the Reagan Administration in foreign policy and the actions it has so far taken," he went on to say, "I am driven to one of two conclusions. Either this Administration does not in fact know what it wishes to do, or what it really wishes to do does not correspond to what the President himself has said." The president had "said that he welcomes the signs of an impending breakup of the Soviet empire from within and he has looked forward to a time when Communism itself will disappear. Yet presented with an enormous opportunity to further that process, what has President Reagan done? Astonishingly, he has turned the opportunity down."[109]

Faced with this pressure from the right, Reagan followed the lead of his national security advisor and got the message of NSDD-32 out. He gave a series of high-profile speeches that spring. The key objective of each one was to herald talks on strategic arms reductions. Each contained eloquent passages that promoted strength, peace, freedom, and the visceral—not necessarily logical—bonds that drew these ideas together. For example, in a commencement address at his alma mater, Eureka College, Reagan drew on the substance of NSDD-32 to promote peace through strength. The challenge America faced, Reagan declared, required an effort "to establish a framework in which sound East-West relations will endure ... [and in which] we can build a more constructive relationship with the Soviet Union." Confronting this challenge successfully depended on achieving five goals: (1) restoring a military balance; (2) stopping the transfer of high-end technology to the Soviet Union; (3) promoting regional stability in the Third World; (4) pursuing arms reduction; and (5) fostering dialogue with Brezhnev.[110]

Reagan used the Eureka speech to elaborate the vision he had shared with a television audience in 1964 and with delegates at the Republican National Conventions in 1976 and 1980. "Peace is not the absence of conflict," he stated in May 1982, "but the ability to cope with conflict by peaceful means. I believe we can cope. I believe that the West can fashion a realistic, durable policy that will protect our interests and keep the peace, not just for this generation but for your children and your grandchildren."[111] Coping with conflict meant reform of Soviet policies, Reagan explained. Yet reform did not necessarily constitute a revolution. "Both the current and the new Soviet leadership should realize aggressive policies will meet a firm Western response," he declared. "On the other hand," Reagan went on to say, "a Soviet leadership devoted to improving its people's lives, rather than expanding its armed conquests, will find a sympathetic partner in the West."[112] Reagan, after all, was not unreasonable. Throughout his political career, he had castigated liberals for perpetuating the myths of socialism but then worked effectively with Democrats to reform the tax code and strengthen social security. Provide him a demonstration of good faith, Reagan seemed to be saying, and he would negotiate with any Soviet leader.

The day after the Eureka speech, Reagan read a letter from Brezhnev responding to his announcement of strategic arms reductions. The letter contained little more than the standard Soviet line; Brezhnev cast blame on Reagan for the breakdown in arms control, and he singled out Reagan's Eureka speech. "I deem it necessary to say it with all clarity," Brezhnev wrote, "since the position with which the U.S., judging by your speech of May 9, is approaching the negotiations cannot but cause apprehension and even doubts as to the seriousness of the intentions of the U.S. side." The letter displeased Reagan. "He has to be kidding," the president wrote in the margin. "He's a barrel of laughs."[113]

Rebuffed in his latest call for arms reductions, Reagan complained about the Soviets four days later in a meeting of the NSC. The administration found itself in a quandary over the Siberian pipeline, which both the American business community and Western Europe wanted to see built. Even the most hawkish advisers conceded that the best the United States could do would be to delay the pipeline, not stop it. "I will not decide on this matter today," Reagan concluded at the end of the meeting, "but I will tell you how I feel in a manner that perhaps will indicate that I lean one way rather than the other."[114] The notion that the United States would ease up on the Soviets while Poland remained in a state of martial law elicited from the president nothing but scorn. "I am feeling ... like that mule who is ready to kick," he told his national security team. Earlier that year, he had told the Soviets "there would be more punishments coming and here Wałęsa is still in jail and we are already talking about relaxing the sanctions." The Europeans needed to "have a bit of guts," and the administration needed to "provide the leadership and tell the Europeans who is the enemy." The time had arrived for the United States to take off its gloves. "The Soviet Union is economically on the ropes—they are selling rat meat on the market," Reagan declared. "This is the time to punish them."[115]

Reagan was proud of his performance. "There was a lot of talk about not having a set to with our allies," he wrote in his diary afterward. "I finally said to h—l with it. It's time we tell them this is our chance to bring the Soviets into the real world and for them to take a stand with us."[116]

On June 8, 1982, Reagan ratcheted up his rhetoric in a speech to the British House of Parliament at the Palace of Westminster. Tracing the cause of freedom back to the "exodus from Egypt" as well as "the stand at Thermopylae, the revolt of Spartacus, the storming of the Bastille, the Warsaw uprising in World War II," Reagan cast anticommunist "freedom fighters" in Nicaragua and elsewhere as inheritors of a proud and noble lineage of mankind's struggle against slavery and tyranny. He spoke of the "grim reminders of how brutally the police state attempts to snuff out [the] quest for self-rule—1953 in East Germany, 1956 in Hungary, 1968 in Czechoslovakia, 1981 in Poland" and of helping "those who strive and suffer for freedom within the confines of the Soviet Union itself." Communism was on the wrong side of history, and "we must take actions to assist the campaign for democracy."[117]

"Let us now begin a major effort to secure the best," the president declared, "a crusade for freedom that will engage the faith and fortitude of the next generation." Inverting Trotsky's famous line, Reagan called for a "march of freedom and democracy which will leave Marxism-Leninism on the ash heap of history as it has left other tyrannies which stifle the freedom and muzzle the self-expression of the people." Reagan continued to turn communist rhetoric on its head: "In an ironic sense Karl Marx was right. We are witnessing today a great revolutionary crisis, a crisis where the demands of the economic order are conflicting directly with those of the political order. But the crisis is happening not in the free, non-Marxist West, but in the home of Marxist-Leninism, the Soviet Union."[118]

Reagan's speechwriters devoted tremendous energy into crafting the Westminster speech. Its principal author was Tony Dolan, a former protégé of William F. Buckley who had won the Pulitzer Prize for reporting on mafia activities in Connecticut. "The human conscience is such that evil acts bother people," Dolan later recalled, "and I've found that if you let the bad guys talk, they'll get preoccupied with trying to rebut, and in the end they concede it. ... That's why they have coined phrases like Wars of National Liberation and the People's Republics."[119] The Soviet Union was not a normal state, according to Dolan's early drafts for the speech; it was "the focus of evil" in the modern world, a "militaristic empire whose ideology justifies any wrongdoing or use of violence if done in the name of the state," and a "sad, bizarre, dreadfully evil episode in history, but an episode that is dying." After consulting with an enthusiastic Pipes, Dolan included in the final version a paragraph emphasizing the "great revolutionary crisis" that communism now faced.[120]

The ideological crusade Reagan enunciated at Westminster pleased Clark, Pipes, and Weinberger, but it hardly resembled the Eureka speech, in which the president had called for a verifiable treaty on arms reductions. As his emotions grabbed hold of him in meetings of the National Security Council, his cold warrior instincts ruled the day. When these emotions subsided, Reagan resumed overtures to Brezhnev to seek accommodation. As Reagan vacillated between pursuing "peace through strength" and a "crusade for freedom," his foreign policy team squabbled. Nitze, for whom Reagan had tremendous respect, fell out of favor with the hardliners in early 1982 after his "Walk in the Woods" proposal to limit NATO deployment and allow some Soviet SS-20s to remain undercut Reagan's "zero option." Whenever the chance arose, subordinates justified their actions as simply doing what Reagan intended. "Because Reagan knew what he wanted but could not articulate his feelings in terms that made sense to foreign policy professionals at home and abroad," Pipes later recalled, "I took it upon myself to do so on his behalf."[121]

The president did make one unequivocal decision. By the start of summer of 1982, Haig had alienated everyone around him. He blamed Weinberger for plotting against him, accused Jeane Kirkpatrick of siding with Argentina rather than with the United Kingdom during the Falklands crisis, and cursed out James Baker for booking him an airplane without windows. Haig then crossed the line by insulting Nancy Reagan on the trip to an economic summit in France. On June 24, 1982, Reagan relieved him of his duties as secretary of state. The president loathed personal confrontation, but after Haig threatened to quit for (at least) the third time, he accepted the letter of resignation. "I must say that it was O.K. He gave only one reason and did say there was a disagreement on foreign policy," Reagan recorded in his diary. "Actually the only disagreement was over whether I made policy or the secretary of state did."[122]

As Haig departed, Reagan was indeed determined to set foreign policy objectives. He understood that the stakes were high. "Right now in a nuclear war we'd lose 150 mil. people," he wrote in his diary after approving a civil defense buildup in December 1981. "The Soviets could hold their loss down to less than were killed in W.W. II."[123] "Had a briefing on Soviet Arms," he wrote on February 18, 1982. "It was a sobering experience. There can be no argument against our rearming when one sees the production complex they have established for the mfg. of every kind of weapon & war machine. Their sophistication is frightening."[124] The Soviet Union was dangerous, in other words, and driven by a Marxist ideology that aimed to take over the world. Reagan reached for a way out of the Cold War, but the Soviets demonstrated through their actions, before and after he took office, their reluctance to reciprocate.

# CHAPTER 2

# Stagnation and Choices

*January 1979–November 1983*

The Soviet invasion of Afghanistan in December 1979 evoked international outrage and frustration. It conjured up memories of World War II and followed a decade of psychological blows to the West—humiliation in Vietnam, the rise of OPEC, the proliferation of domestic and international terrorist networks, Islamic revolution in Iran, and the hostage crisis that ensued. Hardliners in Reagan's cabinet, who considered Nixon and Ford to have been amoral and Carter a wimp, presumed these events to be interconnected. They were not.

The men within the Kremlin subscribed faithfully to the ideals of communism. They lent support to thugs and made decisions that led to atrocities in Afghanistan and elsewhere, but few of them, we know now, expressed confidence that communism was on the march in the late 1970s and early 1980s. Put simply: leaders on both sides believed they were losing the Cold War. For the first few years of the 1980s, both sides faced economic, political, and moral stagnation; both sides contemplated how best to proceed from the positions of weakness inherited from the early 1970s, when the ability of great powers to impose order declined precipitously. Leaders made decisions to adapt to perceived weakness between 1979 and 1983 in ways that shaped the rest of the 1980s. Stagnation in the West inspired certain leaders to undertake actions that proved to be wise, while stagnation in the East led the Kremlin to make ones that were foolish. Global communism, a movement once brimming with vibrancy and excitement, had crested. One of the most fateful decisions of the whole Cold War occurred not in Moscow but in Beijing.

## Global Capitalism and the Western Alliance

The global economy grew very little between 1971 and 1982. Capitalism appeared the worst hit. After a miraculous recovery from 1945 onward, the economies of most West European countries were sputtering at the end of the 1960s. The need to stabilize and retool the economies of the World War II aggressors tested the victors' commitment to free trade and open competition.

In the United States, goods produced in Japan and West Germany crowded out those produced at home. In large swaths of the South and the Rust Belt stretching from New York to Ohio and Michigan, manufacturing jobs disappeared. The centerpiece of postwar capitalist finance, Bretton Woods, collapsed when Richard Nixon took the United States off the gold standard in 1971 and imposed wage and price controls. OPEC's embargo during the October 1973 Arab-Israeli conflict closed the spigot on the flow of cheap oil that had fueled the recovery of international capitalism after the Great Depression had imperiled it and World War II had nearly destroyed it. The rise of OPEC called into question the notion of a coalition of great powers that could impose political and economic order on their terms. It caused tremendous angst. "Can Capitalism Survive?" read a cover of *Time* in 1975. "Is Capitalism Working?" read a slightly less ominous one in 1980.[1]

Weakened abroad by the catastrophe of Vietnam and at home by the social turbulence of the 1960s, the United States saw its position decline further. Its preponderant power had shaped the immediate postwar era, but that was no longer so.[2] The quadrupling of oil prices in 1973 led to widespread inflation, which plagued everyday Americans and bedeviled elected officials. The rise of oil prices did not prevent economic contraction, however. Economists were accustomed to seeing periods of extended inflation and recession as mutually exclusive. The advent of "stagflation" dispelled this illusion.

When Jimmy Carter appointed Paul Volcker to head the Federal Reserve in 1979, the six-foot-seven economist, "Gibraltar-like in appearance and policies," in the words of historian Charles Maier, set about tackling inflation even at the expense of growth.[3] The ensuing recession did Carter no political favors; nor was Reagan helped when Volcker hiked interest rates to 20 percent in 1981. The short-term results were painful: real wages of American workers dropped over 10 percent from 1978 to 1982.[4] During the recession of

1981–1982, U.S. unemployment figures approached 11 percent. Exasperated at the sluggish pace of the recovery, the American people rolled back GOP gains in the House of Representatives in the 1982 midterm elections.

Reagan's former company, General Electric, exemplified capitalism's stagnation. A legacy of the iconic inventor, Thomas Edison, GE sold the American dream. It produced power turbines, jet engines, locomotives, televisions, microwaves, and light bulbs. The performance of the company reflected the health of sectors of the American economy ranging from construction and utilities to healthcare, financial services, and entertainment. "GE: We bring good things to live in. We bring good things to life," pledged its commercials. Yet despite pioneering innovations such as the CT scan in the 1970s, GE ambled through a decade in which the Dow Jones Industrial Average closed at 785.57 on January 2, 1970, and 785.75 on January 2, 1980. GE's plans for the new decade reinforced many of the negative stereotypes of capitalism as a whole and American conservatism in particular. Shortly after Reagan declared in his inaugural address that "government is not the solution; government is the problem," Jack Welch took the helm of the president's former employer. His unstated message: the problem was too many jobs. "Neutron Jack," as he was quickly dubbed, left the machines intact and operational while dispatching with the humans—just like the "enhanced radiation weapon," or neutron bomb, Reagan ordered the U.S. military to stockpile. Welch sold off large parts of the company and laid off workers by the thousands. It was not at all clear, even after these severe employment measures, whether the company could restore long-term fiscal growth and profitability.[5]

Declining economic fortunes reverberated abroad, and they cut into the strength of the NATO alliance. Economic malaise hastened a sense of moral crisis. Parties on the political left blamed the collapse of détente not on Moscow's repression of human rights and invasion of Afghanistan but on the policies of Western Europe and the United States. They pointed to the Helsinki Conference of 1975, which was to have settled the remaining unresolved questions of World War II. Why continue to wage cold war? At least, why do so when the West was facing its own bruising economic problems? Embedded in these questions posed by the left were judgments of moral equivalence, disillusionment, resentment over real and perceived injustices resulting from the application of American power, and the insinuation that capitalism could function only while waging cold war.

After the punishing winter of 1978–1979, when strikes almost ground the United Kingdom to a halt, Margaret Thatcher seized on the unrest to win a smashing victory at the polls. Driving home the message "Labour Isn't

Working" (complete with an image of dozens of workers queuing up for the dole), Thatcher attacked the basic tenets of the welfare state and confronted the fundamental question of authority. Just who ruled Britain? On paper, as historian Niall Ferguson has written, the situation looked perhaps not so dire.[6] Yet there was chaos in the streets, and trade unions were choking the entrepreneurial spirit. Economic uncertainties were exacerbated by the campaign of terror waged by the Irish Republican Army. Many Britons perceived that regulation stifled innovation, but they were less inclined to sacrifice the social welfare benefits accorded them under postwar governments. Fed up with the status quo, however, they responded positively to the defiant aphorisms of Thatcherism, a politics-ready version of Friedrich Hayek and Milton Friedman. As historian Tony Judt put it, "In many places this rhetorical strategy was quite seductive to younger voters with no firsthand experience of the baneful consequences of such views the last time they had gained intellectual ascendancy—half a century before."[7]

Thatcher's initial prescriptions reduced government spending, cut taxes on the wealthy, and restricted the money supply. Setting a precedent to be upheld by Volcker's Federal Reserve the following year, Chancellor of the Exchequer Geoffrey Howe raised interest rates in the United Kingdom from 2 percent to 14 percent. Change did not occur overnight. In the short term, Thatcher's austerity package and privatization schemes appeared to be disastrous. Unemployment rose from 5.5 percent in 1979 to 13.3 percent in 1983, making it the highest rate in Europe. GDP shrank while riots broke out in the streets of England's biggest cities in 1981, but Thatcher doubled down on her policies. "You turn if you want to; the lady's not for turning," she proclaimed. The country was turning, and by the fall of 1981, her popularity level was on par with that of Neville Chamberlain at his lowest. Yet she did not relent.

Across the English Channel that year, François Mitterrand became the first prime minister of the Fifth Republic affiliated with the Socialist Party. Few knew what to expect from the mercurial Frenchman, a conservative in his youth who had switched from Vichy collaborator to resistance member in time to remain politically viable after World War II. Notwithstanding the appointment of several communists to his cabinet, Mitterrand moved swiftly to distance himself from them. On June 12, 1982, he signed off on an economic "U turn" that froze prices and wages and cut public spending. Mitterrand's retreat from the "failed experiment" of conventional Keynesianism, writes historian John W. Young, "sounded the death knell of old-style state intervention as a cure-all for the woes of free-market economies and confirmed that the future lay with rolling back state expenditures, limiting taxation, and encouraging private enterprise, as in Reagan's United States and Thatcher's Britain, even if the short-term cost was high unemployment."[8] Left-wing governments in Italy and Spain followed Mitterrand's lead. His case for French leadership in European integration confounded his critics and insured his political survival.

Less fortunate was his German counterpart, Helmut Schmidt. The chancellor, representing the left-leaning Social Democratic Party of Germany (SPD), bucked the trend of most social democrats in the 1970s by enunciating perceptions of Soviet threat. Schmidt regarded the deployment of SS-20 missiles, which targeted all of the European capitals, as having altered the strategic landscape. In a speech to the International Institute for Strategic Studies in London, he praised strategic arms limitation between the United States and Soviet Union before cautioning that "strategic arms limitations confined to the United States and the Soviet Union will inevitably impair the security of the West European members of the Alliance" unless NATO removed "the disparities of military power in Europe parallel to the SALT negotiations."[9] Schmidt presumed that American deployment of the neutron bomb would redress the imbalance of nuclear terror on the continent. Yet domestic political considerations led the Carter administration to cancel what antinuclear activists branded a "killer weapon."[10] Schmidt, who had expended considerable political capital to retain support for the neutron bomb within his own party, was not consulted on the decision.[11]

Following the recommendations of a NATO High Level Panel, the alliance committed in December 1979 to deploy Pershing II intermediate-range ballistic missiles as well as cruise missiles. Germans could not be the sole recipient of these advanced nuclear missiles—nor did any other country desire that distinction. Prime Minister Bettino Craxi of Italy proposed a plan by which no single country would be the only member of the alliance to accept the missiles. From NATO's declaration in December 1979 onward, the so-called Euromissiles crisis became a dominant topic in electoral politics throughout Western Europe.

Schmidt might have led this process to a successful conclusion, but he was curiously easy to dislike. He annoyed members of the Reagan administration who might otherwise have extolled his conviction. "It was not possible ... to wish away realities" in Eastern Europe, he scolded Haig, who probably did not appreciate the rebuke, having told hardliners the same thing during the Polish crisis.[12] With Schmidt's support eroding both at home and abroad, in September 1982 Hans-Dietrich Genscher's Free Democratic Party threw its support behind the right-leaning Christian Democratic Union (CDU), allowing Helmut Kohl to become chancellor following an October 1 "constructive vote of no confidence."[13] Even then, deployment of Pershing IIs was not assured. Hundreds of thousands of Germans protested in the streets. The Green Party called members of the CDU and the Free Democratic Party (FDP) Nazis on the floor of the Bundestag. A series of contentious votes tested the resolve deployment's proponents, culminating in a key vote in the spring of 1983 and a final vote that fall. The Federal Republic of Germany (FRG) and the core of the NATO alliance weathered the storm. The resolution of the debate transcended historic rivalries and painful memories. Alarmed by the prospect of West Germany adrift from NATO's shore, Mitterrand became one of the most vocal supporters of missile deployment.[14]

These decisions proved to be investments over the long term. Kohl's economic policies reflected the conservatism that Thatcher and Reagan had put into place. The ability of the FRG to shore up government finances, and that of German banks and corporations to return to profitability, were propitious. Few at the time were thinking beyond the Cold War, however. Nuclear weapons posed the greatest concern to the most people. The Cold War was reality; its fundamental components seemed immutable. The best that most people could hope for was that confrontation would recede, détente would be restored, and some measure of prosperity would return.

## Soviet Stagnation

The men inside the Kremlin did not agonize over strikes, student movements, and public opinion polls. They did, however, make fateful choices during the 1978–1983 period as well. Soviet leaders initially welcomed Ronald Reagan simply because he replaced a man they had grown to despise. "The desperate flailing about of this petty politician, who has tried in all things to be like the other atomic maniac, Harry Truman," read *Pravda*'s account of Jimmy Carter's farewell address, "can only give one the impression that he has, from all indications, forgotten that Washington is not ancient Rome and that all attempts to remake the world in America's own image are simply chimerical." The American people must have "sighed with relief when they learned that he will be returning to his native Plains to grow peanuts once again."[15]

Soviet commentators who followed American politics had rooted for Reagan during the campaign, even despite the nasty things he said about the USSR. "We believed we had a pretty good picture of Reagan," one of them later recalled. "He was a conservative, a man who had already put his views forward many decades ago in a very straightforward way." He was tough on communism, but "the mood in Moscow was 'anyone but Carter.'"[16] The day after Reagan defeated Carter, Soviet Prime Minister Nikolai Tikhonov expressed "hope that the new administration in the White House will demonstrate a constructive approach toward relations between our two countries."[17] The election over, Tikhonov and his colleagues expected Reagan to moderate his stances and soften his tone. "The Kremlin found it impossible to believe that Americans would want to turn their backs on détente and return to the suspicions, the warlike behavior, and the huge military spending of the cold war," longtime ambassador to the United States Anatoly Dobrynin later recalled.[18] Its inhabitants remembered how Richard Nixon spent his political career bashing communists before becoming president—only to launch détente once in office.

But no one in the Kremlin was speaking in these terms after Reagan held his first press conference. "During my long career as ambassador the collective mood of the Soviet leadership had never been so suddenly and deeply set against an American president," Dobrynin put it. "It was a catastrophe in personal relations at the highest level."[19]

The man in charge, Leonid Brezhnev, did not resemble the man Reagan had met in California in 1973. He once cut a dashing figure, but a decade and a half in power had reduced the Soviet leader to a shell of his former self. Battered by years of palace intrigue, addicted to sleeping pills, and diminished by a series of strokes, Brezhnev lumbered his way through public events, sometimes reading the wrong speech or greeting foreign leaders by the wrong name.[20] This lethargy in leadership was mirrored in the economy and society. Relative strategic gains purchased by Soviet missiles had hardly engendered a vibrant consumer society. As it became clear that the Soviets had no hope of catching up with the West by the end of the 1970s, Brezhnev contributed another phrase to the communist lexicon: *developed socialism*. "In the USSR a developed socialist society has been built," read the 1977 version of the Soviet constitution. "Developed socialist society is a natural, logical stage on the road to communism," it went on to elaborate. Soviet academicians gave convoluted explanations for what they presumed this to mean. "Developed Socialist society is not considered by us as something midway between socialism and communism," according to one of them. "It is a socialist society attaining a developed condition, characterized by the all-round disclosure of the advantages of socialism."[21]

What were these advantages of developed socialism? No World War II and no Cuban Missile Crisis. To the average Soviet citizen living in the Brezhnev era, "developed socialism" sacrificed the fantasy of utopia for the reality of peace. Vowing never to repeat Khrushchev's mistake of negotiating from a position of weakness, Brezhnev ordered a sustained buildup of Soviet missiles beginning in 1965. He built unconventional weapons in a conventional way: determine the cheapest model that works, and build as many as possible. "Khrushchev only bragged," the former Soviet diplomat Oleg Grinevskii wrote, "but in the Brezhnev era the Soviet military-industrial complex squared its shoulders and began a massive build-up."[22] Brezhnev felt he was responsible for gains in Soviet security. In 1972 he and Nixon vowed to prevent nuclear war and signed agreements restricting the growth of strategic arsenals and limiting antiballistic missile defenses to one per side. A year later, he became the first Soviet leader to travel to West Germany, where he received a lavish welcome. And in 1975, Brezhnev presided over the Helsinki Conference, which seemed to legitimize the postwar division of Germany as well as the borders in Central and Eastern Europe that the Soviets had carved out at the end of the World War II. The event marked "a crucial victory for our foreign policy," a prominent Russian historian wrote over a decade after the collapse of the Soviet Union, one "comparable with Yalta and Potsdam."[23]

Not since Stalin's brief stint as "Uncle Joe" during World War II did a Soviet leader garner such acclaim abroad. In the early 1970s, some foreign observers viewed Brezhnev as a different type of communist—perhaps a different type of Russian. Throughout its history, Russia's most revered leaders had established their reputation in some grand and violent struggle. Its citizens lionized those who repelled foreign invaders, imposed order where there had been chaos, or sacrificed hundreds of thousands of lives for the stated purpose of saving millions. Brezhnev aspired to break the mold. "The main life project of Brezhnev is the idea of peace," Anatoly Chernyaev, later a top aide to Gorbachev, wrote in his diary in 1975. "With this he wants to stay in people's memory."[24]

Brezhnev was also enamored of the prestige the new fleet of missiles lent his country. In 1976, he appointed the head of the Soviet military industrial complex, Dmitry Ustinov, to lead the Ministry of Defense. Ustinov immediately called for deployment of a new missile, the SS-20 "Pioneer." With three independently guided warheads atop a solid fuel booster, an SS-20 could destroy Paris, Hamburg, or Rome in a matter of minutes after launch from a site in the Soviet Union. These missiles were ferociously powerful; they were not intended to be used. Their deterrence capacity was needed because even before the deployment of NATO's next generation of nuclear weapons—Pershing II ballistic missiles and highly accurate cruise missiles—the Soviet general staff feared encroachment.[25] "Write down all the launchers of nuclear weapons deployed in Western Europe directed against us," Marshal Ogarkov told Grinevsky, who had asked him to explain the rationale behind the SS-20 deployment. "Not only were there American tactical nuclear weapons, but also the nuclear weapons of Britain and France, the American F-111 bombers in England, and all that flies in the air and floats in the seas around Europe."[26] For the Soviet survivors of World War II, no amount of military hardware could assure security. Some 28 million Soviets had died as a result of the Nazi invasion in June 1941. Many of the top brass had served in the siege at Leningrad. Marshal Sergei Akhromeyev, chief of the General Staff of the Soviet Armed Forces in the 1980s, had endured two Russian winters without sleeping inside a building, and was one of two survivors from his high school class of thirty-two.[27] Never again, these veterans insisted, could an adversary be allowed to gain an advantage that might tempt it to attack Soviet Union. "For the Soviet military, and for millions of Russians," recalled Oleg Kalugin, a KGB general during the 1970s, "the tragedy of World War II, the so-called unexpected attack was something they would never forget. That was a painful, tragic experience. It was a national disgrace for the armed forces."[28]

Brezhnev certainly would never allow it to happen again. By the start of the 1980s, he relied increasingly on a troika to make foreign policy. Ustinov, Yuri Andropov, and Andrei Gromyko became Politburo members in 1973 and worked reasonably well together. Aware of his own physical limitations, Brezhnev tasked them with solving what he considered the most pressing challenges the country faced.[29] Together, they made three choices that kept the Soviet Union mired in stagnation.

## Afghanistan

The tragic and unnecessary decision to invade Afghanistan was one for which Ustinov, Andropov, and Gromyko bore great responsibility. In April 1978, the People's Democratic Party of Afghanistan (PDPA) overthrew the moderate leader Mohammed Daoud Khan and set about building socialism. Less than a year later, an Islamic insurgency ground this process to a halt. In March 1979, the PDPA sent an army division to Herat to quell the rebellion, only to witness most of its troops turn against the government. The Kremlin grew concerned that, like Iran two months earlier, Afghanistan would fall victim to Islamic fundamentalism. The Afghan communist leader, Nur Muhammad Taraki, begged the Soviets to send troops.[30]

Brezhnev refused. "The involvement of our forces in Afghanistan would harm not only us, but first all of them," he told the Politburo on March 19, 1979. Gromyko feared the international reprisals. "We would be largely throwing away everything we achieved with such difficulty, particularly détente; the SALT-II negotiations would fly by the wayside." Western leaders would cancel planned summits with Brezhnev. They would not take seriously the notion that the Red Army had been "invited."[31]

Taraki made life miserable for his Soviet "friends." They offered him one hundred thousand tons of wheat; he asked that they give three hundred thousand, defer all loans and interest payments, build him a thousand-kilowatt radio station, and provide pilots for advanced helicopters.[32] The notes from Politburo meetings in March point to grave doubts on the part of Ustinov, Andropov, and Gromyko as to whether the communist government in Afghanistan could survive. They resisted involvement because they doubted whether it was possible to build socialism in a country where Islam was so potent a force.[33]

The Soviet leadership failed to steer clear of Afghanistan. After the pacification of Herat, Taraki found himself undermined by his ruthless second-in-command, Hafizullah Amin. The Kremlin conspired with Taraki to get rid of Amin that August, but the effort failed. In September, after a series of plots and double crosses, Amin's men executed Taraki.[34]

From the Kremlin's perspective, Amin proved to be even more of a nuisance. He had studied for four years at Columbia University Teachers' College in New York City and was alleged to have taken money from CIA operatives upon his return to Kabul, using it to train communists and build up his own power base.[35] The Soviets had little choice but to support him immediately after the coup in the fall of 1979. Yet they resisted his exorbitant demands for economic and military aid to put down an insurgency. They simply did not trust him after Amin hinted that he might seek help from Iran or Pakistan—or, worst of all, from the United States.

Amin was secretly an agent of the West, Andropov's KGB sources told their boss. In an atmosphere already fraught with suspicion, NATO's December 12, 1979, announcement to deploy Pershing II and cruise missiles in Western Europe elicited fears within the Kremlin that Afghanistan might be the next recipient. Missiles in Afghanistan meant that the West could strike nuclear facilities far inside the Soviet homeland. Ustinov concurred with this assessment of threat. The United States stationed naval vessels in the Persian Gulf in the fall of 1979, he presumed, because it intended to invade Iran. According to Georgii Kornienko, Gromyko's longtime deputy, the attitude in the Kremlin at the time was that if the United States could meddle ten thousand kilometers away in the Persian Gulf, then surely the Soviet Union could be allowed to tend to its own backyard.[36]

Andropov and Ustinov convinced Gromyko of the need to intervene militarily; together they approached Brezhnev. It would take only a small force to repel the forces of imperialism and restore communism, they assured him. According to Valentin Varennikov, deputy head of the Soviet General Staff, Ustinov paid no heed to the reservations expressed by his top generals on December 7, 1979.[37] Marshal Ogarkov, Varennikov's boss, tried to dissent in front of the full Soviet leadership on December 10, 1979. "What are you saying, are you going to teach the Politburo?" defense minister Ustinov retorted. "Your job is to follow orders."[38] On December 24, Ustinov gathered the leadership of the Defense Ministry to announce that the Soviet Army was going in "for the purposes of rendering internationalist assistance to the friendly Afghan people, and also to create favorable conditions to prevent possible anti-Afghan actions on the part of the bordering states."[39]

Nothing about the invasion went as planned. After KGB agents poisoned Amin but failed to kill him, the Red Army launched Operation Storm-333, a brutal assault on the state palace that did kill him and some two hundred of his guards. As they attempted to restore a new government under Babrak Karmal, the Soviets saw the scale of their intervention expand and their losses mount. "We believed that the troops would be located in garrisons in the key parts of Afghanistan and their presence would support the viability of the regime of Babrak Karmal, who would gradually find advocates and gain force to control the situation in Afghanistan independently; then, we would withdraw our troops," recalled Major General Aleksandr Liakhovskii. "Plans remained just plans, and, in reality, everything turned upside down."[40] In fact, by the spring of 1980, the Afghan army that Soviet troops were attempting to shore up had shrunk to a quarter of its original size of 145,000.[41] The Red Army found itself committing more than 80,000 troops in the first six months just to hold major cities and defend the withering Afghan army from the mujahedeen. "As feared," writes historian Matthew Ouimet, "Soviet forces found themselves at war with the vast majority of the Afghan people in support of an unpopular government."[42] Their Cold War adversary found common cause with the Afghan resistance. Starting soon after Soviets boots hit the ground, American covert aid flowed to Afghanistan. Already begun by Carter before the start of his administration, aid would be ramped up during Reagan's watch. Between the fiscal years 1981 and 1984, the CIA budget for Afghanistan swelled from $30 million to $200 million.[43]

The brutality of the fighting exceeded anything the Kremlin had expected. In their quest for victory in Afghanistan, the Red Army committed horrible atrocities. One Soviet soldier later described blowing up a building in a village in the Kunar Valley after his platoon heard shots coming from that direction. "Among those running out the door was an old man who tried to escape," the soldier recalled. "My friend shot at his feet. The old man jumped in fear and sat behind a bush to hide. My friend aimed directly at the bush and fired a round, after which just the legs slid into view under the bush. He was supposed to be hiding, my friend told me, laughing." On another occasion, the same soldier recounted tracking down a small boy and taking him to the company commander. "He split the boy's skull with his rifle butt, killed the boy with one blow, without even getting up from his place."[44]

The Soviet invasion of Afghanistan led the Carter administration to reconfigure its Cold War policies and acknowledge that détente was dead. "The implications of the Soviet invasion of Afghanistan could pose the most serious threat to the peace since the Second World War," Carter said in his State of the Union address on January 23, 1980.[45] He called back the SALT II Treaty from Senate consideration, imposed a grain embargo on the Soviets, and declared that the United States would not participate in the Summer Olympics held in Moscow. On the campaign trail during this period, Reagan assailed what he perceived to be Carter's timidity. He ascribed the invasion of Afghanistan to American weakness. "This bespeaks an arrogance to me that is born of knowledge of their strength and feeling that they don't have too much to worry about with us," the former governor declared in an interview on January 10, 1980.[46] The next week, he speculated that Iran might be the next target on the Soviet agenda.[47]

In the heat of the Republican primary, Reagan certainly had political incentive to talk tough. Yet the men and women advising him on foreign policy, as described in the previous chapter, believed the gist of what he was saying. "Well, I think that they were first of all . . . still in pursuit of traditional warm water ports down in the Gulf that's been their goal for hundreds of years," Caspar Weinberger later recalled.[48] "We are dealing with an adversary who is driven not by fear but by aggressive impulses," Richard Pipes wrote in April 1980, one "who is generally more innovative in the field of political strategy than we are, and who selects his victims carefully, with long-term objectives in mind."[49]

Weinberger and Pipes were wrong: there was no ambition to pursue warm water ports. The Soviets had acted out of fear in Afghanistan. From a position of weakness, Kremlin leaders made a disastrous decision. Their planning was negligent; their political strategy for reconstituting Afghanistan was nonexistent. They did not select Amin as their "victim." The invasion was brutal and murderous, and it did not forward long-term objectives.

The Soviet invasion of Afghanistan killed détente, but that was also not a Soviet aim. It certainly ushered in the atmosphere of confrontation that Reagan inherited. The perception among Brezhnev and his foreign policy troika, however, was that the United States had already abandoned détente. The Soviets had not believed that in March 1979. By December, with the

SALT II Treaty stalled in the U.S. Senate, NATO's announcement of its missile deployment, and hints that Carter might intervene in Iran to rescue U.S. hostages, the view from the Kremlin was that détente was already dead—done in by American actions.[50]

## Poland

With the Red Army bogged down in Afghanistan, Moscow's foreign policy troika detected a new crisis brewing in Poland. In August 1980, Brezhnev appointed Andropov, Ustinov, and Gromyko to a committee tasked with figuring out how to stop the labor movement Solidarity. One of its first decisions was to mobilize three Soviet tank divisions and one mechanized rifle division to signal to Poland's communist leadership: fix the problem.

But the Polish leadership could not fix the problem, no matter the incentives from the USSR. Communism faced a genuine revolt led not by intellectuals but by salt-of-the-earth workers like Lech Wałęsa, who organized Gdańsk dockworkers to join with coal miners to demand more input on the shop floor, better wages, and more dignity. No credible person could pigeonhole this opposition—many who supported Solidarity were devout Catholics; others even read aloud passages from Marx and Engels during work stoppages. The Soviets attempted to define them anyway. News that the labor union wanted to shorten the work week to five days "confirms our evaluation ... that the activity of 'Solidarity' is more and more focused on vigorously attacking the very foundations of socialism" in the Polish People's Republic.[51] It was enough that the union had flouted the authority of the socialist establishment. "It's impossible to overstate the danger posed by Solidarity," Gromyko warned at a January 22, 1981, meeting of the Politburo. "Solidarity is a political party with an antisocialist bent."[52]

"Despite our recommendations," the "Polish friends" refused to take emergency measures, Gromyko lamented; "they've essentially abandoned this idea altogether."[53] Meanwhile, the Polish government predicted that economic output would decline fully 20 percent by the end of 1981. Structural problems well beyond labor unrest and Gdańsk were even worse. A decade-long "Polish Disease," whereby the Polish United Workers' Party (PUWP) borrowed billions of dollars from capital markets to stimulate consumption-based economic growth, had left a mountain of debt. According to Soviet estimates, Poland owed roughly $23 billion and needed $9.5 billion more in credits to import vital goods, while its exports totaled $8.5 billion. It needed to pay off $1.5 billion over the coming year—most of which was merely the interest on debt owned by Western banks. Diminished resource extraction caused by striking coal miners reduced Poland's supply of hard currency.[54] And efforts to raise prices on consumer staples had proven disastrous. The government had no effective solution. As the historian Stephen Kotkin writes, "Imagine a state with monopoly control over everything—economy, education, the media, cultural institutions, unions, police, the military, entertainment—which could not raise the price of sausage without risking mass social protests."[55] Exactly that was the case. "Of course we can't possibly come up with such a sum," stated Ivan Arkhipov, the Soviet deputy prime minister, after Poland requested an immediate loan of $700 million in the spring of 1981. The Soviet Union was already selling 13 million tons of oil annually to Poland at roughly half the world price, amounting to a real subsidy of 10.4 billion rubles (some $7.5 billion). Now Poland was asking for more. The only other option seemed to be that Poland prostrate itself before the International Monetary Fund.[56]

Discussions within the Kremlin established the choices as either sending in Soviet troops or convincing the Polish regime to declare martial law, but the Soviets could not get through to the Polish leadership. At an April 2, 1981, meeting of the Soviet central committee, Brezhnev boasted of a telephone call in which he had scolded Stanisław Kania. "They shouldn't have just criticized you [at a recent meeting of the Polish central committee]; they should have raised a truncheon against you," Brezhnev allegedly told the Polish prime minister. "Then, perhaps, you would understand."[57] Notwithstanding this bluster, Brezhnev doubted whether his message had truly been heard. "What's worst of all is that the friends listen and agree with our recommendations, but in practice do nothing," Brezhnev complained. "In the meantime the counterrevolution is on the march all over." Andropov called for one last meeting with the Polish communists "so that we can urge them to adopt severe measures and not to be afraid of what might result, possible even bloodshed."[58]

Andropov and Ustinov traveled hastily to Brest, Belarus, to find two demoralized and dejected Polish leaders. Kania pleaded with Andropov to be relieved of his position as prime minister. "With regard to the introduction of troops," Andropov reported back to the Politburo, "they flatly said that this is absolutely impossible, just as it is also impossible to introduce martial law." The Soviet leadership failed to comprehend Polish reluctance. "Take Yugoslavia: when demonstrations were held in Kosovo, they introduced martial law and no one said a word about it," Ustinov unhelpfully pointed out.[59]

Soviet "friends" in the Warsaw Pact grew anxious. The most strident calls for tougher action against Solidarity came from Erich Honecker of the German Democratic Republic. After overseeing the construction of the Berlin Wall, Honecker had risen to become first secretary of the Central Committee of the Socialist Unity Party in 1971 and then head of state in 1976. The Polish crisis had instilled in him a sense of foreboding—particularly since East Germany's economy depended on access to Polish coal. Honecker feared that the ruling Polish United Workers' Party might become "a social-democratic party that works closely together with the Church and the leadership of Solidarity with the sole goal of leading a renewal process, in the spirit of the goals of the counterrevolution, to its victory." He warned Brezhnev and Gromyko in August 1981: "We must not underestimate the possibility that the Polish disease will spread."[60]

The Soviets took action. On September 17, 1981, Brezhnev dismissed Kania and promoted Jaruzelski. Still, the situation did not improve, and the alliance frayed. Honecker balked when the Soviet emissary broached the subject of reducing his oil quota. Brezhnev seemed to have run out of ideas. "I still think that although we gave 30 thousand tons of meat to Poland," he told the Politburo on October 29, "our meat will scarcely be of help to the Poles. ... Jaruzelski is not showing any sign of initiative. ... Honecker is especially dissatisfied." Nor did Arkhipov, the economic specialist, have any answers. "The coal miners will fall short by 30 million tons of coal," he told the Politburo. "How can we make up for it? The oil industry is not going to exceed its plan, which means we'll have to make up for these 30 million tons in some other way."[61]

At a December 10 meeting of the Politburo, Nikolai Baibakov, the head of the Soviet State Committee for Planning, estimated that the total assistance to be given the Poles in 1982 would amount to 4.4 billion rubles (some $3 billion). The only ways to finance this, he explained to Brezhnev, were either to draw on state reserves or to forgo deliveries to the internal Soviet market. "The Polish leadership must decide the question," Gromyko replied. "Either it relinquishes its positions by failing to adopt decisive measures, or it adopts decisive measures by introducing martial law, detaining the extremists of Solidarity, and restoring public order. There is no other alternative." At the same time, the Soviets could not themselves participate in the crackdown. Even Gromyko, who possessed a rare talent for justifying dubious Soviet behavior to the outside world, had to admit that one Afghanistan was more than enough. "There cannot be any introduction of troops into Poland."[62]

On December 12, 1981, the Polish government met late into the night and came to the decision to introduce martial law. The next morning, Lech Wałęsa and other Solidarity leaders were taken from their homes and put in jail. Ustinov's instructions were unequivocal: "It is essential to emphasize that 'The Poles themselves must resolve the Polish question.' ... We are not preparing to send troops onto the territory of Poland."[63]

From Moscow's perspective, martial law amounted to a temporary stop-gap, not a resolution of the crisis. It did little to ameliorate the economic woes the country continued to face. "We already are stretched to the limit in our capacity to help the Poles, and they are making still more requests," Brezhnev told the Politburo on January 14, 1982. "Perhaps we can do a bit more, but we certainly can't give a lot more."[64]

## Project RYAN

The third fateful decision made by the Soviet leadership was Project RYAN—an acronym for *raketno yadernoye napadenie,* or "nuclear missile attack." While most Soviet leaders attributed Reagan's tough talk to political bluster, Yuri Andropov suspected pernicious intent. He interpreted Reagan's talk of a crusade against communism and his arms buildup as the prelude to a preemptive nuclear attack against the Soviet Union. Acquiring the plans for this attack should be the KGB's chief priority, he told Brezhnev shortly after Reagan's inauguration.[65]

In March 1981, Andropov instructed senior KGB officers to look for any signs that would confirm his suspicions. Word went out to chiefs of intelligence stations throughout the West to count the lights left on in military installations. Andropov warned KGB officers of an impending "nuclear apocalypse."[66] "Operation RYAN had one aim: to give advance warning in good time," recalled Andropov's deputy, Vladimir Kryuchkov. "Fail to give advance warning that the missiles had flown, and it would already be too late."[67]

The premises of Project RYAN were false, of course, but since military alliances on both sides routinely drew up and revised contingency plans they prayed they would never have to use, facts could be massaged, capabilities exaggerated, and intentions distorted. So every potential shred of evidence made its way to Moscow, and there were plenty of hypothetical plans to play into the Kremlin's hands. In December 1982, East German spies passed an operational plan of the U.S. Fifth Army Corp to the KGB. The United States seemed to be planning a preemptive strike with tactical nuclear weapons, after which it would employ nuclear mines to stave off a Soviet counterattack.[68]

In interviews years later, Marshal Akhromeyev downplayed the depth of Andropov's fears, but at the time they were real enough. In September 1982, when the chiefs of the General Staffs of the armed forces of the Warsaw Pact met in Minsk, General Orgakov was particularly dour. The international system, he said, resembled the 1930s. "The beginning of the Reagan Presidency calls to mind the Fascist seizure of power." The USSR had not heeded warnings about Hitler, and it must not repeat that mistake. When Andropov addressed the heads of state of the Warsaw Pact the next year, he declared that America's "perfect rocket systems" were "destined for a future war." Marshal Viktor Kulikov, commander-in-chief of the Warsaw Pact, warned that NATO's preparations would "allow the leaders of the [NATO] bloc to initiate an attack against the member states of the Warsaw Treaty practically without carrying out major preparatory measures, under the cloak of large-scale exercises which are conducted annually."[69] Andropov's fears emanated not just from a mistaken assessment of NATO's capabilities and intentions but also from the disparity between the actual Soviet capabilities and the Reagan administration's allegations. According to the papers of Vitalii Leonidovich Kataev, the senior adviser to the Chairman of the Central Committee Defense Industry Department from 1967 to 1985, the Soviet ICBM force throughout the 1980s was far less numerous and accurate than the U.S. assertions, and the vast majority of its silos were not hardened to protect against a nuclear attack—as the neoconservative critics of détente alleged.[70]

In other words, at no time did the Soviets possess the capability to launch a bolt-from-the-blue attack against American missile bases. They could not deliver the ultimatum: surrender or die. Indeed, Soviet strategic planners bore the same apprehensions as their American counterparts. "We assumed that the U.S. would launch first and, given your focus on accuracy and relatively smaller yields per warhead," Kataev later recalled, "that you intended to strike our weapons and control systems in an attempt to disarm us."[71] As head of the KGB, Andropov in 1982 knew that the Soviets possessed no strategic advantage—why did Reagan keep saying that they did? His only explanation was that Reagan was seeking superiority. And his only explanation for seeking superiority in the nuclear age was that the Americans intended to use it.

Project RYAN created an atmosphere where blocking Intermediate-Range Nuclear Forces (INF) deployment was a precursor to progress on arms negotiations. It was not that deployment would restore parity, in the eyes of the Kremlin, but that it would bestow on NATO a strategic advantage. Brezhnev's frailty, Gromyko's intransigence, and fears of conveying weakness meant that Reagan's private overtures regarding arms control went nowhere.

When Reagan wrote Brezhnev after the attempt on his life, the Soviet premier responded in earnest, pleading with the president to restart negotiations. "The main idea," he wrote in May, "that I would like to convey through my letter is that we do not seek confrontations with the USA or infringement upon American legitimate interests. What we seek is different—we wish peace, cooperation, a sense of mutual trust, and benevolence between the Soviet Union and the United States of America."[72] "Try, Mr. President," Brezhnev implored, "to see what is going on through our eyes. Attempts are being made to revitalize the USA-made military and political alliances, new ones are being added to those which already exist thousands of kilometers away from the USA and aimed against our country, the American military presence abroad in general is being increased and expanded, large areas of the world are being declared spheres of 'vital interests' of the USA."[73]

From the Soviets' perspective, Reagan's "zero option" in September 1981 ignored the broader strategic balance that favored the United States as well as America's allies, who already possessed medium-range nuclear systems. Brezhnev could not understand why he should take seriously a plan that did not consider the strategic arsenals of Great Britain and France. In a letter sent in December 1981, Brezhnev charged Reagan with engaging in double bookkeeping, "whereby in counting the Soviet arms in question their numbers are made to look many times higher, and—conversely—when it comes to the U.S., such numbers are drastically understated."[74] Reagan's arms proposals bred such cynicism. Georgy Arbatov, head of the Soviet Institute on American and Canadian studies, summed up the reaction. "Since the very first days of the Reagan administration," Arbatov wrote, "its leading spokesmen have missed no chance to make abusive charges against the USSR, like the charge that the Soviet Union supports international terrorism, uses chemical or bacteriological weapons, and so forth. The bully-boy rhetoric was supplemented by corresponding policies—primarily, by whipping up the arms race." How was the old guard within the Kremlin to interpret Reagan's intentions? "I think that an important motivation of such rhetoric and policy was an intention to provoke the Soviet Union into changing its policies, and thus justify a return to cold war."[75] Arbatov was a professional propagandist who did not wield the influence he claimed, but his words conveyed the Politburo's collective response to Reagan: if not détente, then what?

Brezhnev's physical decline precluded the one-on-one meeting that Reagan so keenly desired. In his stead, the role of Soviet emissary to the world was now Gromyko's alone. Known to his counterparts in the West as "Mr. No," or "Old Stone Face," Andrei Gromyko had been a fixture in the world of international diplomacy for some forty years. Fluent in English, Gromyko had dealt with every American secretary of state going back to Cordell Hull in World War II. His loyalty to the communist cause was unshakable. "Khrushchev once boasted to a foreign visitor that if Gromyko were asked to sit on a block of ice with his pants down he would do so unquestioningly until ordered to leave it," Henry Kissinger wrote in a 1979 memoir.[76] Gromkyo disliked this anecdote, and he also did not care for Kissinger's former military attaché, Alexander Haig, because the general seemed more interested in making statements than progress. Haig wrote Gromyko a personal letter shortly after his appointment but then released its contents to the press. Annoyed by this breach of diplomatic protocol, Gromyko reciprocated. The Soviet-U.S. relationship faced many problems, he wrote back to Haig: "One may only regret that these problems, judging by your message, have escaped the new Administration's attention."[77]

Gromyko's chief priority was to prevent NATO's planned deployment of the Pershing II and cruise missiles. He wanted to lock in the gains of the SS-20 deployment and seize the high ground on arms control. As a sign of "goodwill," he declared that the Soviets would slow down their deployment of SS-20 to allow for meaningful arms negotiations. He sought to counter Reagan's initiatives but did so in ways that were neither imaginative nor effective. Accordingly, he accused the Reagan administration of seeking military supremacy. It did so at its peril, for "those who worship the idol of the arms race forget that the same laws exist in politics as in a stadium where the runners are trying to outdistance each other," Gromyko said publicly in June.

**FIGURE 2.1.** Brezhnev and Gromyko, 1978. The general secretary and the foreign minister attempt to stand up. West German Chancellor Helmut Schmidt and Foreign Minister Hans-Dietrich Genscher look on. © Bettman/Corbis.

"If one person succeeds in moving ahead another person does everything in his power in order not to lag behind, or even to outdistance the other person."

In September, Gromyko traveled to New York City. He declared at the United Nations that the Soviets renounced the first use of nuclear weapons. It was a propaganda ploy. He knew that the United States relied on nuclear weapons to defend Western Europe from the overwhelming conventional military strength of the Soviet Union and that Washington would never renounce the first use of nuclear weapons should war erupt. This Soviet line might, however, embolden the antinuclear movement in Western Europe to pressure governments to reject NATO's deployment of new missiles. If the deployment could be thwarted, the Kremlin would be able to say it had decoupled the security of Europe from the United States and altered the correlation of forces in its favor.

The day after his UN announcement, Gromyko met with Haig. Differences between the United States and the Soviet Union, he said, resulted from historical forces that favored socialist development. "There were objective processes," he explained. "They had existed in the past, they existed at present and would exist in the future, and they governed occurrences in the world."[78] And Gromyko firmly believed that the Soviet Union was acting in concert with these "forces." The United States, by contrast, was opposing the march of history. In the nuclear era, each side needed to respect the opposing views and legitimate interests of the other. Gromyko could not ascertain Washington's intentions. The United States identified countries bordering on the Soviet Union as part of its own vital interests and was conspiring to keep the Red Army bogged down in Afghanistan. Were this meddling to cease, Gromyko told Haig, Soviet troops would leave.[79]

Haig appeared to speak the same diplomatic language, but he regarded history and "objective reality" differently. He associated Soviet behavior in areas of instability with how the United States should approach arms control. "Linkage was a fact of life," Haig told Gromyko. He would not repeat the mistakes of his predecessors. While embracing détente with the West, the Soviet Union had actively sought a strategic advantage over the United States beginning in the early 1970s and had violated principles of freedom and self-determination across the globe. "It was not during the Carter Administration, but during the Ford Administration," Haig stated, "that the American people began to witness a number of events which made a profound impression on the U.S. mood and attitude regarding U.S.-Soviet relations."[80]

Subsequent encounters were no more productive. Meeting with Haig in June 1982, Gromyko led off with the dubious assertion that "the Soviet

Union has never undertaken any action in the international arena to implant revolutions in other countries." Neither he nor Brezhnev nor "other Soviet officials when negotiating with the U.S. side" had ever brought "ideological views into the field of foreign policy." Gromyko "never mentioned ideology to Haig" and had not "tried to convert him to Marxism," read the notes of their conversation. The United States had an ideological foreign policy, but the Soviet Union "did not believe in mixing ideology with foreign policy."[81]

For all his bluster and bravado, Haig was more inclined to negotiate in good faith than the rest of Reagan's national security team. Yet Reagan loyalists never trusted him, and the "vicar" failed to establish a personal relationship with the president. On the other side of the Cold War, Gromyko did himself no favors. From the first encounter with Haig to the last, the Soviet foreign minister offered no opportunity to ratchet down tensions and make headway on nuclear arms control.

Gromyko's denials notwithstanding, ideology and foreign policy were linked throughout Soviet history. At nearly every point, historian Vladislav Zubok has written, its foreign policy operated within the framework of a "revolutionary-imperial paradigm" or a "symbiosis of imperial expansionism and ideological proselytism."[82] Starting out, Lenin had devoted himself to preserving the revolution. Once in power, Stalin sought to create a peculiar form of empire—even as the official Soviet line denounced imperialism and colonialism that was nationalism in form, socialism in content. In the drive to Berlin during World War II, Stalin had added an outer empire in central Europe as a defense in depth for an imperium consisting of lands traditionally controlled by the old tsarist regime.

After World War II, decolonization brought new opportunities. From 1945 to the mid-1960s, as nearly a billion people wrested themselves from the yoke of European colonialism, the Soviet Union used the ideology of anticolonialism to expand its influence. By the early 1980s, however, the well had dried up. As the military offensive in Afghanistan stalled, Soviet leaders were reluctant to intervene on behalf of socialist movements throughout the world. After the collapse of the Portuguese empire in 1975, opportunities for socialist revolution were elusive; every small victory became a cause for celebration. At the Twenty-Sixth Party Congress in 1981, Brezhnev boasted of the triumphant addition into the socialist camp of Ethiopia, Mozambique, and North Yemen.[83] The Carter administration had fixated on these Soviet incursions, but they were hardly of monumental consequence.

The great prize in the Soviet empire—the Cuban revolution located a mere ninety miles from the heart of capitalism—was also its greatest nuisance. Heavily subsidized by Moscow, Cuba's authoritarian prime minister Fidel Castro used Soviet aid to finance his own incursions into Central America and Africa. Castro was perpetually dissatisfied with his patrons in Moscow.[84] After Reagan's inauguration, he called on the Soviets to consider using nuclear weapons against the United States.[85] Moscow did not want to hear this. "We cannot fight in Cuba because it is 11,000 kilometers away," Brezhnev explained to Raúl Castro, brother and close adviser to Fidel, around that time. "If we go there, we'll get our heads smashed."[86]

Elsewhere, the Kremlin struggled to calibrate its ideology to the developing world. In the Middle East, the rise of Islamic fundamentalism in the 1970s provided a third way in the ideological struggle between capitalism and communism for which neither superpower was prepared. As hard as they tried, Soviet ideologists could not successfully fit the narrative of oppression against Muslims into a socialist account of history. Even if they could, there was no compelling reason for Islamic states to place Russia (whose history of Muslim conquest exceeded even that of Western Europe) at the helm of a vessel moving toward social equality. The United States may have been the chief practitioner of evil, according to Ayatollah Khomeini, but the Soviet Union was "the other Great Satan."[87] Under the leadership of Anwar El Sadat, Egypt's gravitation toward the West in the 1970s more than compensated for Soviet gains elsewhere.

When Brezhnev and Gromyko approached the Middle East after 1979, it brought them more harm than good. In Syria, Hafez al-Assad envisioned the establishment of a Soviet outpost not as a bastion against imperialism but merely as a way to defend Syria in a potential war with Israel. When the matter was taken up in the Politburo, Ustinov expressed support, as did Andropov, who envisioned the plan as part of the global struggle against imperialism. Amid Gromyko's opposition, however, Brezhnev, wary of adventurism after Afghanistan, let the matter drop. In 1982, following Israeli's invasion of Lebanon, Assad reached out to Moscow and asked for unconditional aid. By then, the prospect of full-throated support threatened confrontation with the United States to a degree that Brezhnev was not willing to tolerate.[88]

Prospects seemed better in Africa, where the Soviets could more vividly articulate the distinction between communism and European colonialism. In May 1981, Brezhnev welcomed the president of Congo, Denis Sassou Nguesso. Brezhnev gave a speech that directly linked the United States to the legacy of colonial oppression in that country. The people of Africa had achieved a role in international affairs that was "weighty and unquestionable," Brezhnev told the Congolese delegation. "The imperialists, the direct heirs of those who through iron, fire, and blood enslaved the free peoples, who for decades plundered and oppressed them, do not wish to reconcile themselves to this … [and] are attempting to impose upon the international communist their own conception of order … which would justify neocolonialist robbery and the methods of *diktat* and violence, and would give full scope for the suppression of the national liberation movements."[89] Sassou Nguesso may have taken this talk seriously at the start of the 1980s—he remained a committed Marxist until 1989—but not every leader in the communist world did.

## China Seeks a Way Out

In Washington, Democrats and Republicans overestimated the importance of Soviet gains in the 1970s. So did Americans writ large, because they regarded the status of their own country to be in decline, which led them to fixate on the USSR. Yet the grand total of Soviet gains in the 1970s did not, in importance, come anywhere near the decision of the People's Republic of China to reorient its economy to state capitalism. That was not precisely how China's leader, Deng Xiaoping, phrased it in 1978. Over time, however, his talk of new norms and cryptic aphorisms such as "it is good to be rich" led to free enterprise zones and a system of capitalism even while eschewing political liberties. "The core issue is to improve efficiency in production, construction, distribution, and other aspects of the economy in every possible way," wrote Zhao Ziyang, one of Deng's protégés, in a 1981 government report. GDP had quadrupled since the start of the People's Republic of China (PRC), and industrial output had increased eightfold. Yet average consumption had only doubled, Zhao noted. "Produce more products that society truly needs," he exhorted party members, "using the least amount of labor and material resources." How to do this? Zhao realized that "the system had to be transformed into a market economy," and to do that, "the problem of property rights had to be resolved."[90]

The path forward was tortuous, and the direction not always apparent. During the decade that followed, China's exports rose from under $10 billion to nearly $50 billion. Its output per person doubled. In contrast, the Soviet economy during the same period grew by a net total of 7 percent. China looked to the Asian Tigers; and developing countries, unhappy with communism yet unwilling to trust the old colonial powers, began to look to China.[91]

On January 1, 1979, the United States normalized relations with communist China. At the end of that month, Deng traveled to the United States, where the image of the compact leader of a billion people wearing a cowboy hat turned him into a media sensation. In private, however, Deng's trip presaged a surprising—and slightly alarming—change in attitudes within the communist world. "Now we have a strategic relationship, and in that regard, I want to use it to tell you what my plans are," Deng told Carter and Brzezinski behind closed doors. "We intend to invade North Vietnam to teach them a lesson." Carter inquired whether Deng might be concerned about how the Soviet Union, with its sixty divisions on the Chinese border, would react to an invasion of one of its patron states. "We thought about that," Deng responded. "And if they start using those forces we will use nuclear weapons on Moscow. We have decided through our calculations that while we don't have enough nuclear weapons to handle all of the Soviet Union we can at least hit the capital." What would Beijing do if that plan failed? "Well, if they start coming in with their new tank formations we will declare People's War. We will surround them with people and we will dissolve them."[92]

Beijing's outlook alarmed Moscow. "As for the possibility of war with China, we planned everything in this respect very seriously," a Soviet general later recalled. "We developed military strategies and tactics to combat China's huge masses of infantry. They could have brought an army of 25 million to the front line. ... We took the danger from China very seriously because it was a real danger." In a war game the Warsaw Pact ran in June of 1982, planners calculated that China would enter a hypothetical conflict on NATO's side.[93]

U.S. intelligence picked up what was happening in China. At the start of the Reagan administration, the State Department's Bureau of Intelligence and Research reported that China was moving in a new direction. "The Chinese see themselves for the foreseeable future as essentially a regional power contributing significantly to the U.S. and Western cohesion, but self-sufficiency in defense as well as in its economy remains a fundamental PRC policy." In the past, Chinese foreign policy had been guided by a model of "three worlds" in which the American and Soviet superpowers both contended and colluded with each other while China lay somewhere in a third category. The report continued: "Domestic as well as international developments over the past few years, however, have resulted in a major transformation of this world view, bringing it into close alignment with U.S. national interests."[94] In 1982, Reagan got a firsthand account from Richard Nixon after his return from Beijing. Nixon told Reagan that he was impressed by Party Chief Hu Yaobang, who professed to have read translations of Nixon's books, and Zhao, who drank beer during their morning conversation. The former president noted the visceral hatred of the Soviets that these men displayed. Foreign Minister Huang Hua told Nixon that "there was no doubt in his mind and in the minds of his colleagues in the government that the Soviet Union still seeks world hegemony." Moscow was thrusting southward in the tsarist tradition of conquest and expansion, Deng told Nixon: "It was ridiculous for anyone to pretend that the Soviet Union was not a ruthless, hegemonic power."[95]

In subsequent discussion of China with his national security team, however, Reagan did not demonstrate much interest in the changes under way or in how they might affect the Cold War as a whole. In a September 20, 1983, "Review of U.S.-China Relations," Reagan's only contribution to the NSC meeting was to interject: "You mean our position should be 'no ticky, no laundry'?" Nor did Reagan respond when the secretary of state told the NSC: "The Chinese have taken a number of steps in the economic area which we would like to encourage. They are experimenting with the rudiments of a market system. They have also introduced private incentives into the communes and into industry." Ultimately, attachment to Taiwan on the part of Reagan and the hardliners always restrained them from "playing the China card."[96]

For his part, Brezhnev could not deal with China. He detested Deng, whom he referred to as the "anti-Soviet dwarf."[97] Toward the end of his rule, Brezhnev did attempt to improve relations with China, but these overtures were stifled by the Vietnamese-Cambodian war in which Moscow and Beijing had backed different sides. His policies in the 1970s had left the Soviet Union with little leverage. While the Soviet Union benefited from the increase in the price of oil after 1973, it spent most of its profits supporting its huge military-industrial complex. Meanwhile, sovereign wealth from Saudi Arabia and other oil-rich states flowed into Western banks, which invested heavily in Eastern Europe and other regions, presuming that autocratic governments could guarantee loans by pulling the levers of their command economies. Yet the inefficiencies of a command economy drove these nations deeper into debt. From 1976 to 1979 alone, the sum of Poland's outstanding loans went from $10 billion to $17 billion.[98]

East and West operated in different worlds when it came to the scales of their economies. In the lead-up to martial law in Poland, the Soviet deputy prime minister had complained about the hard choices his country faced in order to come up with $700 million. One year later, when Mexico threatened to default on its foreign loans in 1982, the United States and the International Monetary Fund (IMF) constructed a package to give the country loans of $8.2 billion. Raising this amount of money in the West meant turning to international capital markets, which by the early 1980s had a total pool of some $1.5 trillion, of which about $300 billion was lent out each year.[99]

The 1970s left the United States and Western Europe in a weakened state. It left the Soviet Union far weaker. Perhaps the only bright spot for Soviet leaders was a pipeline that would connect Siberian gas fields to markets in Western Europe. The prospect of fueling the industrialized core of Western Europe promised a steady revenue stream and also the potential for Moscow to obtain economic leverage. It challenged the Western alliance on grounds similar to the Euromissiles crisis. The extent to which NATO should—or even could—stop the pipeline was an ongoing debate within the Reagan administration.[100] Seeking contracts for construction companies that needed business, most politicians in London and Paris did not oppose it.

Neither did Secretary of State Haig, who departed the administration in July 1982. Haig's reasoning reflected his realism: the United States risked alienating its allies in trying to stop something that was probably inevitable. His rivals within the Reagan administration, including Weinberger and Casey, considered that reasoning a capitulation. Acting on such thinking, they believed, was the reason the United States was losing the Cold War. Their counterparts in Moscow believed the mirror image when it came to INF deployment. Brezhnev, Gromyko, Andropov, and Ustinov also saw compromise as capitulation. Absent new individuals in positions of power, stagnation shaped the international environment in the early 1980s, and old thinking determined the relationship between the United States and Soviet Union.

# CHAPTER 3

# Shultz Engages

*July 1982–January 1985*

The new secretary of state, George Shultz, was an economist by training. He understood that the stagnation of the late 1970s and early 1980s had affected both sides of the Cold War, yet he retained tremendous confidence that the United States and its capitalist allies were about to recover. What was happening in Beijing, moreover, could happen in Moscow. Shultz wanted to talk to Soviet leaders about how market-based reforms could improve their economy, and he believed that an improved Soviet economy would curtail their aggressive foreign policies and strengthen the cause of peace. In other words, Shultz believed that the Soviets had the capacity to change. But the two superpowers had to keep talking. With the aid of the new Soviet specialist on the National Security Council, Jack Matlock, Shultz helped rationalize Reagan's conflicting impulses toward Moscow in order to engage the Cold War adversary.

Neither Shultz nor Matlock speculated much about whether or when the Cold War might end. Their ambitions were less grand, but no less important. They aimed to put U.S.-Soviet relations on a path toward a firmer détente that accentuated human rights, reduced stockpiles of nuclear weapons, and improved trust between the two superpowers. Unlike the hardliners William Casey, William Clark, Richard Pipes, Jeane Kirkpatrick, and Caspar Weinberger, Shultz and Matlock believed that the Soviet Union possessed the capacity to reform. Through toughness and persistence, they hoped, the

United States could affect changes in Soviet behavior. Shultz commanded the president's attention from the start. By the end of Reagan's first term, Shultz's four-part framework was guiding U.S.-Soviet relations.

## Secretary of State Shultz

The résumé of George Pratt Shultz was impressive. After serving in the Marines in World War II, he returned from the Pacific to complete a doctorate in industrial economics at the Massachusetts Institute of Technology and join the faculty of the University of Chicago. Active in Republican circles, he served as director of the Office of Management and Budget, secretary of labor, and secretary of treasury in the Nixon administration.

Shultz brought to the administration impressive credentials, tremendous self-confidence, patience, and a saturnine wit. Whereas Haig harbored a grudge against the Soviets for the attempt on his life in the 1970s, Shultz recalled positive memories of working with them. As secretary of the treasury, he had traveled to Moscow and Leningrad, where he was shown evidence of the nine-hundred-day siege by the Nazis during World War II. "I had learned something of the human dimension to the Soviet Union," Shultz later wrote. He "also learned that the Soviets were tough negotiators but that you could negotiate successfully with them." Their diplomats were typically smart, well-prepared, and unflappable. "I respected them not only as able negotiators but as people who could make a deal and stick to it."[1]

Shultz did not shy away from tough decisions. Along with Paul Volcker, he shared responsibility for persuading Richard Nixon to abandon Bretton Woods in the early 1970s. At the time of his nomination for secretary of state, Shultz lacked the traditional foreign policy experience of an Al Haig, a Cyrus Vance, or a Henry Kissinger; but as CEO of the construction giant Bechtel, he had established a network of contacts throughout the Middle East and Southeast Asia.[2] Shultz did not espouse a grand theory of international relations. Yet he believed in planning. "The way I like to go about things is to sort of think them out," he later explained, "to have a sense of direction, and not just be coping willy-nilly."[3]

Shultz loved telling the story of his first political crisis, a labor dispute left over from Lyndon Johnson's presidency. LBJ had invoked Taft-Hartley to stop the strike for eighty days, and the Supreme Court had upheld his decision. As the new secretary of labor, Shultz inherited the problem once the eighty days were up. "I have a strategy for how to handle this strike," Shultz recalled telling Nixon. "Let the pressures produced by the strike cause the union and management to settle it themselves through the collective bargaining process."[4] Patience worked; that was the lesson Shultz wanted to apply to the Cold War. "Coming into office as secretary of state at a time when we were confronted with tremendous problems," he later explained, "the economist in me asked, 'Where are we trying to go, and what kind of strategy should we employ to get there?' recognizing that results would often be a long time in coming."[5]

"I had a different way of thinking about the Soviet relationship than my predecessor, who was hooked to the Kissinger period," Shultz later recalled. Haig had focused on linkage, had downplayed human rights with the Soviets, and was open to back channels through private emissaries. "And I was uneasy with all that," Shultz recalled. "I didn't like the linkage, I felt that human rights [and] our values had to be prominent in our foreign policy, and that official contacts were not the same as public contacts."[6]

In their first meeting, Shultz flatly told Andrei Gromyko, "The deterioration of our relations is the result of Soviet conduct."[7] The Helsinki Final Act guaranteed freedom to worship as well as to move abroad, yet the Soviet Union refused to accord these rights to its citizens. Prominent Jewish dissidents like Anatoly Shcharansky had been denied permission to emigrate; Shultz insisted that their plight be discussed. "Is it so important that Mr. or Mrs. or Miss so-and-so can or cannot leave such and such a country?" replied

**FIGURE 3.1.**   Reagan and Shultz, 1982. Secretary of State Shultz garnered the trust of the president and encouraged him to negotiate with the Soviets. Courtesy of the Ronald Reagan Library.

Gromyko. "I would call it a tenth-rate question." Shultz was disappointed. "That is one of the difficulties facing our relationship. Human problems always enjoy the highest priority in the United States."[8]

Shultz took a dim view of Gromyko. Yet he retained optimism that with firmness and patience the United States could broker deals whereby the Soviets might improve their human rights record, reduce nuclear weapons, withdraw from Afghanistan, and refrain from meddling in Latin America, Africa, the Middle East, and Southeast Asia. Shultz did not know whether all of these goals were achievable. His penchant was to wait and see. Nothing was possible, he knew, without engaging the Cold War adversary. And that required recognizing the legitimacy of the Soviet regime.

NSC staffers such as Richard Pipes and Thomas Reed and their boss, William Clark, purported to know better than Shultz. The Soviet Union had violated every arms agreement it had ever signed, they believed, and the only thing the Soviets respected was strength. After Reagan had finished a speech and the crowd had dispersed, political expediency could not detract from the overriding priority: restoring American preponderance. Restoration of strength would then compel Soviet leaders to reconsider supporting regimes hostile to the United States and its allies and compel the Kremlin to real-locate resources in ways that weakened its control over the Soviet imperium. Hardliners professed to be following Reagan's lead. The president remained inclined to negotiate but was deeply conflicted over whether agreements born of these negotiations could ever hold. He often referred to Laurence Beileson's *The Treaty Trap*, which contended that no treaty in the history of the world had ever ushered in a lasting peace.

Reagan was unequivocal in one respect when Shultz joined the admin-istration: the United States was still playing catch-up in the Cold War. Not even the tremendous military buildup he had ordered assuaged the president's fear that the Soviets held a commanding advantage. "There's no question but that they have a superior military force than we do now," Reagan told an audience in May 1982.[9] Frustrated over how she had portrayed him in her weekly column, Reagan wrote to Ann Landers: the Soviets "have such an edge on us now we have no choice but to rearm. As their superiority grows so does the danger of confrontation."[10]

## NSDD-75

On November 10, 1982, Leonid Brezhnev succumbed to a fatal heart attack, an event that ushered in a fresh dilemma for the administration. Its speechwriters had prepared for the president to deliver a forceful speech chastising the Soviets for dragging their feet over strategic arms reduction negotiations. Should the tone be modified in light of the recent event? NSC staffers dismissed such thinking: Brezhnev's death merited no change in the administration's plans. As Pipes put it, the United States was dealing "with regimes, not individuals."[11] In the months following Brezhnev's death, Reagan sought ways to speak directly to the American people about the danger they faced. He did so amidst eroding political support; Democrats made significant gains in the midterm elections in November of 1982. As the new Congress was sworn in, the president's approval rating hovered under 40 percent. Reelection the next year appeared far from certain. With several polls showing the president behind his likely opponent, former vice president Walter Mondale, Reagan's political future was uncertain. Lou Cannon has best summed up this period: "The first two Novembers of his presidency were unkind months for President Reagan and the interval between them cruel and costly for the Americans who had accepted his invitation to dream 'heroic dreams.'"[12] Anxieties were not limited to domestic policies. Polls indicated that a growing number of Americans actively feared the prospect of a nuclear war.[13] Across the country, ordinary citizens voiced concern that Reagan's arms buildup spelled doom and organized a nuclear freeze movement that called on Congress to stop it.

The president shared their fear of nuclear war yet regarded the prospect of a nuclear freeze as more dangerous. He too dreamed of eliminating nuclear weapons, and that could never occur as long as the Soviets remained ahead. Only after the United States had built up its arsenal, Reagan believed, could both sides reduce weapons. Politics conspired against him, however. A December 1982 vote in the House of Representatives against his plan to build one hundred MX missiles left Reagan apprehensive about the future. "It's coming, Bud," the president told Deputy National Security Advisor Robert "Bud" McFarlane. "This inexorable building of nuclear weapons on our side and the Russians' side can only lead to Armageddon. We've got to get off that track."[14] But neither Reagan's anxieties nor his sagging popularity deterred hardliners from pressing forward with a rhetorical offensive. When Richard Pipes's sabbatical from Harvard expired at the end of 1982, his assistant, John Lenczowski, a thirty-two-year-old Ph.D. from Johns Hopkins, hoped to be promoted. He drafted a memo for Clark to send to the president. "The Truth and The Strength of America's Deterrent," as he titled it, replicated much of Pipes's view of the Soviets—and went further.

"The Soviets make all their strategic decisions—whether to advance or retreat—on the basis of their assessment of the strengths and weaknesses of their opponents," the memo began. "The key element in this assessment is the adversary's strength of moral-political conviction—i.e., his will to use force if necessary to defend his vital interests. In practice, as the Soviets see it, this means the willingness of their opponent to speak plainly about the nature and goals of communism." Cold War rhetoric and power were linked. "By simply telling the truth," Lenczowski addressed the president directly, "you incalculably strengthened the credibility of our military deterrent." There was no reason to let up. "So long as our leaders deliver this message, the Soviets will know that we are not spiritually weak, that we are not Finland-ized and that we have not permitted wishful thinking to obscure a clear understanding of Soviet intentions."[15]

Lenczowski's points aimed to bolster the strategic directive Pipes had submitted upon his departure. The product of two years of preparation, National Security Decision Directive 75 encapsulated the hard line that Pipes presumed to reflect the "real Reagan." Endorsed by Clark, NSDD-75 articulated three basic goals:

> To contain and over time reverse Soviet expansionism by competing effectively on a sustained basis with the Soviet Union in all inter-national arenas—particularly in the overall military balance and geo-graphical regions of priority concern to the United States. This will remain the primary focus of U.S. policy toward the USSR.
>
> To promote, within the narrow limits available to us, the process of change in the Soviet Union toward a more pluralistic political and eco-nomic system in which the power of the privileged ruling elite is grad-ually reduced. The U.S. recognizes that Soviet aggressiveness has deep roots in the internal system, and that relations with the USSR should therefore take into account whether or not they help to strengthen this system and its capacity to engage in aggression.
>
> To engage the Soviet Union in negotiations to attempt to reach agreements which protect and enhance U.S. interests and which are consistent with the principle of strict reciprocity and mutual interest. This is important when the Soviet Union is in the midst of a process of political succession.[16]

On January 17, 1983, Reagan signed off on the plan. Clark presented NSDD-75 as the logical extension of Reagan's words and deeds. Reagan did not see fit to argue, nor did he regard the new strategy statement as a repudiation of diplomacy. "With firmness and dedication, we'll continue to negotiate," Reagan declared in his State of the Union address the following week. "Deep down, the Soviets must know it's in their interest as well as ours to prevent a wasteful arms race. And once they recognize our unshakable resolve to maintain adequate deterrence, they will have every reason to join us in the search for greater security and major arms reductions."[17]

Notwithstanding the president's State of the Union remarks, Clark believed he had scored an important victory over the State Department. Weary after two years in Washington, Clark met with Reagan on January 7, 1983, to broach the prospect of quitting. The president dismissed the idea out of hand, ordering his beleaguered national security advisor instead to California for a month's vacation.[18]

With Clark temporarily sidelined, opportunity beckoned Shultz. On January 19, 1983, two days after had Reagan signed off on NSDD-75, Shultz sent the president his own vision of a way forward, a memorandum titled "U.S.-Soviet Relations in 1983." The substance of this memo differed considerably from that of NSDD-75. Instead of containing and reversing Soviet expansionism through military and economic pressure, it called for countering the "new Soviet activism by starting an intensified dialogue with Moscow" on the basis of realism and mutual interests.[19] Reports from Moscow confirmed the need for realism. Administration members hoped that the passing of Brezhnev might yield new thinking within the Kremlin. Yet "it is becoming increasingly clear that the Andropov approach is not marked by significant experimentation or initiative," Ambassador Hartman cabled Shultz. Andropov's foreign policy "has departed in no way from the Brezhnev policy." In fact, Hartman reported, Andropov appeared to be going out of his way to demonstrate his toughness—not only in Poland and Afghanistan but in a region like southern Africa, where Moscow held interests less vital. The only constructive development Hartman could detect was that Andropov might seek a rapprochement with the People's Republic of China—"a development which is not in our interest."[20]

Shultz pushed ahead. He devised a plan to get Reagan to do what the president had long sought: engage directly with a high-ranking Soviet official. Ambassador Anatoly Dobrynin seemed well suited for the role. A resident of Washington, D.C., for twenty years, Dobrynin possessed a cosmopolitan outlook and a gregarious demeanor. He had, over the years, established friendships with Bobby Kennedy and Henry Kissinger. He was not known to spout the rhetoric of international class conflict and the eventual triumph of communism. So Shultz orchestrated a plan to accompany Dobrynin to the White House on February 15, 1983. Having only recently returned from California, a furious William Clark called the secretary of state to express his disapproval (he had already shared his misgivings with their mutual boss). Clark's objections went nowhere. Shultz believed that Reagan's direct participation in the U.S.-Soviet dialogue accorded with the president's impulses to achieve arms reductions in spite of hardliners' objections. "The efforts of the staff at the NSC to keep [Reagan] out," Shultz recalled, "were beginning to break down."[21]

"We talked for 2 hours," Reagan wrote in his diary after the meeting. "Sometimes we got pretty nose to nose. I told him I wanted George [Shultz] to be a channel for direct contact with Andropov—no bureaucracy involved." Reagan also broached the subject of the Soviet Pentecostals seeking asylum, who were living in the basement of the U.S. embassy in Moscow. If the Soviets would allow them to leave unharmed, the president promised not to grandstand.[22] "George tells me that after they left the Ambassador said 'this could be an historic moment.'"[23]

Reagan's meeting with Dobrynin did not receive widespread attention. Newspaper editorials and network news broadcasts focused on the nuclear arms race. They pegged the U.S. administration—not that of the Soviet Union—as the greatest threat to peace. On February 25, 1983, Reagan convened a meeting of the National Security Council to discuss ways to counter the "latest propaganda threat" from antinuclear advocate Helen Caldicott—who had gone so far as to turn the president's own daughter against him. Criticism of his efforts to match Soviet strength was "ridiculous and harmful," the president declared. He was trying to save lives, not start a nuclear war, and his intentions were being distorted. He wondered whether "people appreciated how many men in our armed forces had died unnecessarily in conflict because of previous underfunding of training and equipment modernization."[24] Reagan feared that clergymen might succumb to the pressure of the nuclear freeze movement and abandon him in the following year's election. As he later wrote, Reagan "wanted to reach them, as well as other Americans who—like my daughter Patti—were being told the path to peace was via a freeze on the development of nuclear weapons that, if implemented, would leave the Soviets in a position of nuclear superiority over us and amount to an act of unilateral disarmament on the part of the United States and NATO."[25]

The president decided to take his case to the American people—"only this time we are declassifying some of our reports on the Soviets and can tell the people a few frightening facts." Fed up with the "d—n media," which had "propagandized our people against our defense plans more than the Russians have," Reagan was also worried about the future. "We are still dangerously behind the Soviets & getting farther behind."[26] The next day, Reagan addressed the Annual Convention of the National Association of Evangelicals in Orlando, Florida. The president called the Soviet Union an "evil empire" and urged his audience "to beware the temptation of pride—the temptation of blithely declaring yourselves above it all and simply call the arms race a giant misunderstanding and thereby remove yourself from the struggle between right and wrong and good and evil."[27] The next day, the phrase "evil empire" dominated all press coverage of the speech. "If the Russians are infinitely evil and we are infinitely good, then the logical first step is a nuclear first strike," read one assessment from a reporter. "Words like that frighten the American public and antagonize the Soviets. What good is that?"[28]

Once again, Reagan believed his critics had distorted his message. Yes, he had called the Soviet Union an evil empire, but one of the key themes of the speech was that the United States still needed to negotiate with it. Although Reagan made significant revisions to drafts of the speech, the phrase "evil empire" had not caught his eye.[29] His speechwriter, Tony Dolan, had inserted that phrase, convinced his superiors that it was to be only a minor speech, and then leaked the salient points of the speech to a *New York Times* reporter the night before Reagan delivered it.[30]

## Strategic Defense Initiative

Shultz regarded the "evil empire" speech as another victory for those who opposed engagement with the Soviets. He encouraged the president to take a more active role in foreign policy, speculating that this would discount the influence of hardliners. The president did so in a way neither Shultz nor anyone else anticipated.

Thwarted by the unwitting coalition of Soviets, liberal media, recalcitrant Democrats, and international nuclear freeze activists, Reagan vented his frustration. "I'm sure the bishops supporting the 'freeze' and unilateral disarmament are sincere and believe they are furthering the cause of peace," he wrote a supporter. "I'm equally sure they are tragically mistaken. What they urge would bring us closer to a choice of surrender or die. Surrender of course would mean slavery under a system that would banish God."[31] Not long after writing that letter, Reagan decided to level with the America public in one of the most surprising presidential announcements ever. "We can't afford to believe that we will never be threatened," Reagan stated in a nationally televised address on March 23, 1983. "There have been two world wars in my lifetime. We didn't start them and, indeed, did everything we could to avoid being drawn into them. But we were ill-prepared for both. Had we been better prepared, peace might have been preserved."[32] He then urged Americans to tell their representatives to support his arms buildup to redress Soviet superiority.

Reagan went further on the matter of deterrence. "What if free people could live secure in the knowledge that their security did not rest upon the threat of instant U.S. retaliation to deter a Soviet attack, that we could intercept and destroy strategic ballistic missiles before they reached our own soil or that of our allies?" the president asked. Recalling the spirit of the Manhattan Project, which had led to the creation of nuclear weapons, Reagan challenged the scientific community to come up with a device to defend American lives rather than simply avenge them.[33]

The Strategic Defense Initiative, as Reagan called it, did not come to him overnight. To start with, he had always opposed the ABM Treaty. In 1979, he traveled with his friend Martin Anderson to NORAD headquarters, where he was astounded to hear that Cheyenne Mountain could not withstand a direct hit by the new generation of Soviet ballistic missiles. Anderson and others convinced Reagan that the United States lacked not technical know-how but imaginative strategic thinking. "It isn't a question of technology; it isn't a question of money," according to Anderson. "The technology is already here, on the shelf, waiting to be used. And the cost is easily affordable."[34] This piqued Reagan's interest. A couple of years later, Edward Teller, the father of America's hydrogen bomb, would lead the charge to convince the Reagan administration of the feasibility of missile defense. On July 23, 1982, he wrote Reagan asking "for a mandate to vigorously explore and exploit the technological opportunities in defensive applications of nuclear weaponry." He warned of the troubling prospect that the Soviets might deploy their own system first. Even if the technology proved to be years away—something he did not think was actually the case—Teller hinted at an enticing political dividend for the president. "Commencing this effort may also constitute a uniquely effective reply to those advocating the dangerous inferiority implied by a 'nuclear freeze.'"[35]

Intrigued, Reagan invited Teller to the White House in September 1982, after which the president noted "an exciting idea that nuclear weapons can be used in connection with Lasers to be non-destructive except as used to intercept and destroy enemy missiles far above the earth."[36] The meeting between Teller and Reagan elicited a three-part *New York Times* series on a project to build "killer lasers" that would disable Soviet ICBM's midflight. Already, the concept was dubbed "Star Wars."[37]

A meeting with the Joint Chiefs of Staff on February 11, 1983, imbued Reagan with a sense of optimism. He apparently came away from it convinced that his top military brass wanted him to abandon dependence on mutually assured destruction and to move ahead quickly with research and development of a missile defense system.[38] Pledging support would allow

Reagan to seize the initiative in the stalled arms negotiations. And, as Teller suggested, it might also coopt the appeal of the antinuclear movement.

Notwithstanding this optimism, Reagan remained unsure at the time of SDI's ultimate purpose. "Frankly I have no idea what the nature of such a defense might be," he wrote a supporter. "I simply asked our scientists to explore the possibility of developing such a defense."[39] At a press conference on March 25, 1983, Reagan reiterated that he was merely instructing the scientific community to continue research into the project and not with any particular urgency. If, "maybe 20 years down the road," he said, "somebody does come up with an answer, I think that that would then bring to the fore the problem of, all right, why not now dispose of all these weapons since we've proven that they can be rendered obsolete?"[40] On another occasion, he suggested that SDI could replace the doctrine of Mutual Assured Destruction entirely. For "to look down to an endless future with both of us sitting here with these horrible missiles aimed at each other and the only thing preventing a holocaust is just so long as no one pulls the trigger—this is unthinkable."[41]

Convalescing after kidney dialysis, Soviet premier Yuri Andropov believed he had a good understanding of SDI's ultimate purpose. The only "impotent and obsolete" missiles under Reagan's plan would be Soviet ones. Feasible or not, he told Soviet arms negotiator Oleg Grinevski from his hospital bed, SDI had now become part of U.S. strategic culture. "All this confirms our worst fears—the U.S. ruling circles have embarked on a sudden application of a nuclear attack on the Soviet Union, and now they are trying to protect the U.S. from our retaliation, or at least minimize it."[42] The SDI announcement took not just the Kremlin but the rest of the Reagan administration by surprise. Neither the hardliners nor the moderates had anticipated such a tactic. Over time, it would become an essential component of Reagan's view of the world, and an article of faith for everyone in his administration.

Shultz learned of SDI shortly before the president's speech. Two weeks earlier, the national security advisor had stung him. In advance of a March 10, 1983, meeting in the Oval Office, Clark summoned Pipes back from Harvard to lend support to Lenczowski's hard line. The two Soviet experts proceeded to eviscerate Shultz's efforts to set up a meeting between Reagan and Gromyko in New York that October.[43] In their view, the Kremlin needed to modify its behavior before serious negotiations could get under way. Weinberger and Casey seconded the notion that Shultz was too soft.[44]

Shultz was aggravated, but he also sensed opportunity. On March 16, 1983, he sent the president a memo replete with phrases such as "in accordance with your instructions," "the criteria you have established," and "in accordance with your guidance." Shultz sketched out plans to meet with Dobrynin and to engage the Soviets "in discussion of human rights, regional issues, and our bilateral relations." "While continuing to stress the continuity of our policy of realism, strength, and dialogue," he wrote the president, "we can proceed with confidence to take limited steps in our bilateral relations with the Soviet Union where it is in our interest to do so."[45] What Shultz discovered only after the SDI announcement was that Reagan, too, had been dissatisfied by the March 10 meeting. A day after Reagan's SDI press conference, the president summoned Shultz and Clark again to the Oval Office, this time without the Soviet experts. Reluctant to confront Shultz in the Oval Office alone, Clark did not attend the meeting, explaining his absence in a handwritten note: "Mr. President, if our plans for the Soviets (or any other issue in my area of responsibility) are not coordinated with Cap and Bill [Casey] and Jeanne [sic], we will fail."[46]

Faced with a choice, Reagan began to gravitate toward Shultz. He authorized the secretary of state to use his upcoming testimony to the U.S. Senate to call for a reversal of the slide in U.S.-Soviet relations—without preconditions. "Some of the N.S.C. staff are too hard line & don't think any approach should be made to the Soviets," Reagan recorded in his diary on April 6, 1983. "I think I'm hard-line & will never appease but I do want to try & let them see there is a better world if they'll show by deed they want to get along with the free world."[47] At the same time, developments south of the U.S. border stoked his apprehensions. Jeane Kirkpatrick warned in a meeting of the National Security Planning Group "that a guerilla takeover of El Salvador would lead to stepped-up insurgent activity sweeping across all of Central America."[48] That summer, Clark and Casey paid a visit to the president to outline plans for fighting communism in Central America that would push the envelope of what Congress mandated. "We're losing if we don't do something drastic," Reagan recorded in his diary. His opponents in Congress were playing a treacherous game, he thought; they wanted "to give enough money to keep us in the game but El Salvador bleeds to death." Then they would call it Reagan's plan and blame him for losing. "If the Soviets win in Central America we lose in Geneva & every place else."[49]

Shultz was inclined to avoid such linkage. He did not oppose aid to the Contras and El Salvador, but Central America did not interest him as much as direct relations with Moscow. On June 15, 1983, he testified in front of the Senate Foreign Relations Committee. "In the past two years this nation ... has made a fundamental commitment to restoring its military and economic power and moral and spiritual strength," he declared. "And, having begun to rebuild our strength, we now seek to engage the Soviet leaders in a constructive dialogue through which we hope to find political solutions to outstanding issues."[50] There were clear and understandable sources of tension, Shultz went on to say. The Soviet Union lay in close proximity to America's closest allies. Its Marxist-Leninist ideology presented a prediction of the future opposed to that of the West. "But we are not so deterministic as to believe that geopolitics and ideological competition must ineluctably lead to permanent and dangerous confrontation." Cooperation could be achieved—but not by the same means as in the 1970s. So long as the president did not stake too much political capital on achieving a deal—as his predecessors had done—he could avoid the pitfalls of unforeseen events. Expectations needed to be kept in check. Strength and realism would guide America's dialogue with the Soviet Union. Human rights should be included. So should Soviet behavior in Afghanistan—but their withdrawal was not a precondition for an arms agreement. Point by point, Shultz articulated the four-part framework—bilateral relations, regional matters, arms control, and human rights—he had presented to Reagan that January.

Disapproving of this testimony, Clark attempted an end run around the secretary of state. On July 9, 1983, Clark recommended to the president that he and McFarlane be sent to Moscow as emissaries. Shultz, "a solid economist," should take charge of the Pacific Basin initiative and steer clear of the administration's Soviet policies.[51] Word of this memo quickly got back to Shultz. He marched into the Oval Office and threatened to resign. Reagan persuaded him to stay, promising greater authority and regular one-on-one meetings.[52] As it turned out, Shultz had cultivated the person who mattered most to Reagan. The next week, after a *Time* cover story playing up Clark's hard line toward the Soviets and labeling him the "second most powerful man in the White House," Nancy Reagan called up the secretary of state to say that Clark ought to be fired because he did not have her husband's best interests at heart.[53] Never again would Clark wield as much influence; by the end of the year, "the Judge" no longer worked in the White House.

Shortly before his Senate testimony, Shultz gained an ally on the NSC. On June 4, 1983, Reagan named Jack Matlock his senior specialist on Soviet affairs. A career foreign service officer, Matlock had served three tours in Moscow and was the U.S. ambassador to Czechoslovakia. Fluent in five foreign languages, Matlock appreciated nuance. In briefing books as well as drafts speeches and letters, Matlock flattered Reagan, advocated engagement, and led the president to believe his own thinking had been consistent all along. Of course, Pipes also spoke several languages; he, too, appreciated nuance. The difference was that Jack Matlock did not think that Soviet citizens believed they were capable of withstanding a nuclear war.

Matlock joined the administration in time for a tense period in the Cold War. All year tensions simmered in Lebanon. The previous summer, Israel had sent the Israeli Defense Forces (IDF) toward Beirut to attack PLO strongholds. After its withdrawal, the United States had deployed Marines as part of a multinational peacekeeping force, while neighboring Syria waged a number of proxy fights. On April 18, 1983, an explosion outside the U.S. embassy in Beirut killed sixty-three people. The attack came as Moscow was providing Damascus surface-to-air missiles manned by Soviet officers. The possibility of a direct U.S.-Soviet conflict in the heart of the Middle East aroused Reagan's fears. "Syria is poisoning the well & the possibility of an Israeli-Syrian (plus Soviet) confrontation cannot be ruled out," he recorded in his diary on May 4. "Armageddon in the prophecies begins with the gates of Damascus being assailed."[54]

As danger lurked in the Middle East in 1983, the U.S. Navy and Air Force probed the Soviet defense perimeter. Hardliners encouraged this saber-rattling in sight of Soviet armed forces. Reagan had apparently approved a plan of intimidation and probing in the early days of the administration and had never told anyone to stop. "It was very sensitive," according to undersecretary of defense Fred Iklé. "Nothing was written down about it, so there would be no paper trail." "Sometimes we would send bombers over the North Pole, and [Soviet] radars would click on," recalled the head of the Strategic Air Command, General Jack Chain. "Other times fighter-bombers would probe their Asian or European periphery." The exercises unnerved the Soviet air force. "It really got to them," recalled an undersecretary of state. "They didn't know what it all meant. A squadron would fly straight at Soviet airspace and their radars would light up and units would go on alert. Then at the last minute the squadron would peel off and return home."[55]

On the night of September 1, 1983, Korean Airlines Flight 007, a passenger jet on the way to Seoul, strayed into Soviet airspace west of Sakhalin Island. As the Boeing 747 approached the Kamchatka coast, three Soviet MiG fighters scrambled to intercept what they presumed to be an American reconnaissance craft. Over the next hour, KAL 007 crossed back into international airspace before again entering restricted Soviet territory. Failing to establish communication with the commercial airliner at the time of this second incursion, the commander at nearby Smirnykh Air Base classified KAL 007 as a military target. At approximately GMT 18:26, a Soviet Su-15 interceptor fired two air-to-air missiles, sending the plane into the Sea of Japan, killing 269 passengers and crew, including a U.S. congressman.

"What can we think of a regime that so broadly trumpets its vision of peace and global disarmament and yet so callously and quickly commits a terrorist act to sacrifice the lives of innocent human beings?" Reagan declared publicly the next morning. "What could be said about Soviet credibility when they so flagrantly lie about such a heinous act? What can be the scope of legitimate and mutual discourse with a state whose values permit such atrocities? And what are we to make of a regime which establishes one set of standards for itself and another for the rest of humankind?"[56] The KAL 007 incident provided an opportunity to embarrass the Soviet Union that the president could not resist. The Soviet response was indeed shameful, but the downing had been precipitated by an error on the part of an ill-trained Korean pilot and compounded by rashness on the part of a Soviet air commander. It had not been an act of terrorism, as Reagan quickly labeled it. He held a subsequent press conference in which the world heard the audio from the U.S. Signals Intelligence station in Japan (blowing the cover of one of America's most effective intelligence systems).[57] "And make no mistake about it," Reagan declared after playing the tape of the Soviet pilots for the press, "this attack was not just against ourselves or the Republic of Korea. This was the Soviet Union against the world and the moral precepts which guide human relations among people everywhere. It was an act of barbarism, born of a society which wantonly disregards individual rights and the value of human life and seeks constantly to expand and dominate other nations."[58]

Bud McFarlane, soon to replace Clark as national security advisor, saw tremendous political gains to be had. He wrote a memo to Shultz boasting that because of the "President's immediate and forceful expression of outrage" as well as his support for punitive actions directed against Soviet Aeroflot lines, "the cherished Soviet image of a peace loving and law-abiding great power has been tarnished beyond hope of immediate refurbishment."[59] NSDD-102, which the president signed on September 5, 1983, called on the international community to punish Soviet civil aviation. Voice of America producers received orders to intensify multi-language broadcasts to the Soviet Union and play up the incident in all language services. Following the administration's lead, Americans blamed Soviet leaders for wanton aggression. The message got across. A few weeks after the incident, a poll showed that by margin of 49 percent to 24 percent, Americans believed that Andropov was both cognizant and supportive of the decision to "kill innocent people"—even though 42 percent of those polled also believed that Andropov was "a very sick man, and may actually be dead."[60]

Reagan's team detected indications that the Soviets were frightened. On October 11, 1983, Jack Matlock met with Sergei Vishnevsky, a *Pravda* columnist widely believed to have close ties to the CPSU and the KGB.

Vishnevsky confided in him that the Soviets had handled the incident atrociously, telling Matlock that "President Reagan is mentally and physically ten years younger than his age; our leaders are ten years older." At the same time, his American counterpart needed to understand that Soviet officials possessed genuine fears that war was imminent. In this atmosphere, "the [Soviet] leadership is convinced that the Reagan Administration is out to bring their system down and will give no quarter; therefore they have no choice but to hunker down and fight back."[61] On October 28, 1983, Ambassador Arthur Hartman summarized a meeting with Gromyko: "The major problem the Soviets have with the Reagan administration is that they believe we are not prepared to accept their legitimacy."[62]

Several weeks after the KAL 007 incident, NATO launched a military exercise simulating a full-scale release of nuclear weapons against members of the Warsaw Pact. On the night of either November 8 or 9, the KGB sent a flash memo to its West European posts warning that U.S. and European forces had gone on nuclear alert and that the exercise was in fact a cover for a surprise nuclear attack. The exercise, called Able Archer 83, played into the suspicions that had led Andropov to launch Operation RYAN. Reagan's harsh reaction to the downing of KAL 007, it seemed, had convinced the Kremlin that some grander plot for retribution was afoot.[63] Later that month, the German Parliament gave final authorization for NATO to install American Pershing II missiles. Soviet negotiators responded to NATO's deployment by walking out of arms control talks in Geneva.

## The Four-Part Framework

The fall of 1983 was a dangerous season in which the president's political standing improved. The near-flawless invasion of Grenada in late October diverted attention from an attack in Beirut two days earlier in which 241 U.S. servicemen were killed. By the start of 1984, the president's approval ratings finally crossed 50 percent after fifteen months below that figure. Later that year, Ronald Reagan would be the oldest candidate ever to run for president; he was now favored to be reelected.[64]

Shultz benefited as well from the events of 1983. His adversary, William Clark, quietly submitted his resignation that October.[65] Clark's departure made the secretary of state's job only slightly easier. When Gromyko and Shultz met in Madrid on September 8, 1983, Shultz professed horror at Soviet callousness over KAL 007. Gromyko refused to discuss the incident before finally storming out. The meeting ended badly, but Shultz had no regrets. "You don't get anywhere by not meeting with people," Shultz later said of this period. "The question is what you tell them. And it's important to let them know how you feel."[66]

The position Shultz wished to convey to the Soviets was that the Reagan administration truly desired to eliminate intermediate-range nuclear weapons—even though NATO was about to deploy them in Western Europe. Around the time the Soviets walked out of arms control talks in Geneva, Shultz organized a series of Saturday breakfasts for senior officials on the eighth floor of the State Department. "With deployments under way, our position was one of strength," he later recalled.[67] He meant to harness this strength to outflank his rivals in Washington and engage the adversary in Moscow so that they would return to Geneva.

Jack Matlock chaired the first meeting on November 19, 1983. The format adhered to the four-part framework for negotiations with the Soviets: bilateral relations, regional matters, arms control, and human rights. The purpose of these meetings was to establish a credible American position from which to bargain. The agenda at that first meeting, according to Matlock's notes, included ways to reduce Cold War tensions and lower stockpiles of arms through fair and verifiable agreements. "While there were sharp differences regarding the specific steps that should be taken to reach the goals, nobody argued that the United States should try to bring the Soviet Union down," he later wrote. "All recognized that the Soviet leaders faced mounting problems, but understood that U.S. attempts to exploit them would strengthen Soviet resistance to change rather than diminish it."[68]

Throughout the spring of 1984, Shultz, Matlock, and McFarlane crafted a policy of engagement using this four-part framework. They aspired not to bankrupt the Soviet empire or to destroy its way of life but to negotiate based on firmness, strength, and realism. They hoped to isolate areas of disagreement between the two sides. A dialogue about Soviet dissidents fit into one set, chemical weapons fit into another, academic exchanges still another. Lack of progress in any one area was not to impede improvement of relations between Moscow and Washington. McFarlane and Matlock liked a recent article by James Billington, a Russia scholar heading the Woodrow Wilson Center, who called on the administration to begin a "generous and general" dialogue with the next generation of Soviet leaders. Attaching Billington's article, Matlock sent McFarlane a proposal for reinstating cultural and scientific exchanges shut down by his predecessor, Richard Pipes.[69]

As Reagan's first term neared completion, the attitudes of his top Soviet advisers did not resemble those at the start. In the midst of this rethinking of Soviet policy, word came from one of Senator Edward Kennedy's aides that

Andropov lay gravely ill. Whoever was to be appointed his successor needed to decide whether to "intensify centralization, repression, and militarization of Soviet society, or to improve incentives, decentralize decision making and rely more on market factors," Matlock wrote McFarlane. The United States had limited options for determining how that person might act, he acknowledged; it should nevertheless take proactive measures. "While we can have only a marginal effect on the outcome of this internal Soviet process," he wrote, "we should do what we can to strengthen the tendencies toward greater decentralization and openness, since this would produce a Soviet Union with less commitment to the use of force and less willing to engage in costly foreign adventures."[70]

U.S. policymakers should engage Soviet citizens on an individual level, Matlock believed. He had been in the room a month earlier when Gromyko told Shultz that "nowhere else were human rights violated so much as in some of the places in the Western hemisphere that were so dear to U.S. hearts, not to mention in the U.S. itself."[71] To move beyond these bromides, the administration needed to look beyond the old guard in Moscow and to show the next generation of leaders that it was no longer the segregated society of the 1940s, which Gromyko had seen firsthand (and selectively chosen never to forget). That was the purpose of rekindling exchange programs and reinvigorating cultural diplomacy. "Opportunities to meet with Americans and to come to the United States can undermine officially-sponsored negative stereotypes about the U.S. and stimulate private doubts about the veracity of propaganda caricatures," Matlock wrote the national security advisor.[72]

McFarlane was inclined to agree. In his previous position as Clark's assistant, he oversaw production of strategy statements like the hardline NSDD-75 but retained skepticism about the finished product. The NSDD evinced "no basis [for] believing that a framework for stability exists," he later recalled; it sought merely to "stress [the Soviet] system as best we can."[73] McFarlane hoped to move beyond this mindset by reengaging the Soviets on less contentious issues such as boundary treaties, cultural exchanges, and airline agreements. He hoped to draft new guidelines so that the hardliners could no longer invoke strategies that went nowhere. On February 18, 1984, McFarlane sent Reagan a memo, drafted by Matlock, titled "U.S.-Soviet Relations—A Framework for the Future," reiterating Shultz's four-part framework. Several of the processes described in the subheadings had been stalled, but setbacks, McFarlane wrote, need not derail the overall goal of diplomacy built upon strength.[74]

## Reagan Modulates His Tone

Reagan struggled to comprehend the Soviet reaction to Able Archer 83, the lousy state of affairs between the two superpowers, and the prospect of running for reelection when U.S.-Soviet relations were no better than in 1980. And although he still despised communism, he expressed more and more interest in learning about the Russian people. During this period he met for the first time with a scholar of Russia named Suzanne Massie, who told him of an era when entrepreneurship and orthodox Christianity defined Russian life.[75] Intrigued, the president wanted to learn more.

Although they had stormed out of negotiations after the INF deployment, Reagan beseeched the Soviets to return. "I continue to believe that despite the profound differences between our nations," Reagan wrote Andropov on December 23, 1983, "there are opportunities—indeed a necessity—for us to work together to prevent conflicts, to expand our dialogue, and to place our relationship on a more stable and constructive footing. Though we will be vigorous in protecting our interests and those of our friends and allies, we do not seek to challenge the security of the Soviet Union and its people."[76] Reagan promised to stress these themes in public statements over the next few weeks and to send a personal emissary to Moscow to explore new avenues of cooperation. Two weeks later, the president met with Shultz and McFarlane; afterwards, he expressed confidence in Andropov's reply. "The Soviets have indicated they would like a back door set up for private communications (as we proposed)," Reagan wrote in his diary. "Things may be looking up."[77]

On January 16, 1984, Reagan spoke in a televised address about a Soviet couple sitting down with an American one. "Just suppose with me for a moment that an Ivan and an Anya could find themselves, oh, say, in a waiting room," it began, "or sharing a shelter from the rain or a storm with a Jim and Sally, and there was no language barrier to keep them from getting acquainted. Would they then debate the differences between their respective governments? Or would they find themselves comparing notes about their children and what each other did for a living?"[78]

Ivan and Anya were not enemies—just ordinary people. Informed on February 1 by the visiting Yugoslavian president that the Soviets were "insecure and genuinely frightened of us" and that, were they to open up, "leading citizens would get braver about proposing change in their system," Reagan grew optimistic. "I'm going to pursue this," he wrote in his diary.[79] Jack Matlock welcomed this approach; he had drafted the majority of the "Ivan and Anya" speech and did not want the Kremlin to overlook its message.

On February 9, however, General Secretary Andropov died. The following week, Matlock met with Vadim Zagladin, a member of the International Department of the Central Committee of the CPSU, to allay the Soviet leadership's fears during another period of transition. Matlock shared his thoughts about a president he had not voted for but had grown to admire.[80] "Yes, he does not like communism and is profoundly disturbed by many Soviet policies and actions," Matlock told Zagladin. "At the same time, he is genuinely a man of peace and understands clearly the necessity of the U.S. and U.S.S.R. managing their inevitable ideological rivalry peacefully."[81]

The Soviets needed to bear something else in mind: "President Reagan can deliver on any agreements he signs." That had not always been the case with American presidents during the Cold War. Matlock could "understand the frustration of other countries when they must deal with an American president who may not be able to mobilize the support of 67 senators to ratify treaties." But Reagan was not Jimmy Carter. "History shows that American conservatives are better able to deliver than liberals," Matlock told Zagladin. And no one had more credibility among American conservatives than Ronald Reagan.[82]

The selection of the infirm Konstantin Chernenko as the new Soviet leader was not inspiring. Convinced of the need for a hardliner to combat the American cowboy, Politburo members scuttled Andropov's efforts to have a younger man named Mikhail Gorbachev appointed as his successor. However uninspiring, Chernenko was a man with whom Reagan prepared to do business. "I have a gut feeling I'd like to talk to him about our problems man to man & see if I could convince him there would be a material benefit to the Soviets if they'd join the family of nations," Reagan wrote of the new Soviet leader.[83] Then, in early March, West German Chancellor Helmut Kohl met with the president to encourage him to reach out to Chernenko. A summit might provide a way to get around Andrei Gromyko as well as insight into who might ultimately succeed Chernenko. The chancellor, believing that communism had lost much of its appeal, expressed optimism about the future. Every day, the forces of freedom were growing stronger. Religion might even be flowering in the Soviet Union: Kohl had seen Mrs. Andropov make the sign of the cross over the casket at the memorial service for her dead husband.[84]

On March 5, 1984, Reagan convened a meeting with his advisers. He wanted them to prepare for a summit with the new Soviet leader—perhaps to occur that August.[85] Subsequent reports from Moscow tested his determination to negotiate. On March 14, 1984, Shultz recounted to Reagan a meeting between Ambassador Arthur Hartman and Gromyko in which the Soviet foreign minister rejected any moderation of the Soviet line.[86] Furthermore, following through on the idea of a establishing a private emissary, former national security advisor Brent Scowcroft traveled to Moscow in March in the hopes of meeting Chernenko, only to be sent packing by Gromyko.[87]

On April 7, 1984, Reagan sent a letter to Chernenko calling for a new beginning. The president wanted to convey to the Russian people the message that he understood the tragedies of their past. "In thinking through this letter," read Reagan's handwritten postscript,

> I have reflected at some length on the tragedy and scale of Soviet losses in warfare through the ages. Surely those losses, which are beyond description, must affect your thinking today. I want you to know that neither I nor the American people hold any offensive intentions toward you or the Soviet people. The truth of that statement is underwritten by the history of our restraint at a time when our virtual monopoly on strategic power provided the means for expansion had we so chosen. We did not then nor shall we now. Our common and urgent purpose must be the translation of this reality into a lasting reduction of tensions between us. I pledge to you my profound commitment to that goal.[88]

The response from Chernenko was less than encouraging. It repeated many of the standard lines Gromyko employed in his meetings with Shultz. "Try to look at the realities of the international situation from our end," Chernenko wrote Reagan on June 6, 1984. "And at once one will see distinctly that the Soviet Union is encircled by a chain of American military bases. These bases are full of nuclear weapons. Their mission is well known—they are targeted on us." What was needed was not an agreement for the sake of an agreement, according to the Soviet leader, but for the United States to renounce any intention to press forward with SDI.[89]

Rather than dismiss the letter outright—as he might have done in the past—Reagan appeared to absorb the notion of Soviet fears. "Do you suppose they really believe that?" he had asked McFarlane, after reading a CIA report stating that Soviets feared an American nuclear attack the previous fall. "I don't see how they could believe that—but it's something to think about."[90] After reading this latest letter, the president met with McFarlane and Shultz and again broached the subject of a summit. "I have a gut feeling we should pursue this," he wrote in his diary. "His reply to my letter is in hand & it lends support to my idea that while we go on believing, & with some good reason, that the Soviets are plotting against us & mean us harm, maybe they are scared of us & think we are a threat. I'd like to go face to face & explore this with them."[91]

Later that summer, McFarlane sent Reagan an article by a Harvard professor named Nina Tumarkin entitled "Does the Soviet Union Fear the United States?" The president read the article and was impressed: "Bud, this is very revealing and confirms much of what I've been trying to say but didn't have the knowledge or the words."[92] Cognizance of Soviet fears further impelled Reagan to seek negotiations, but it never fully obscured his cold warrior instincts. As Reagan beseeched his Soviet counterparts to tone down the rhetoric of the Cold War, he continued to speak the language of the early Cold War era. He invoked the Truman Doctrine in a speech about Central America. Just as the United States had once staved off communism in Greece, it faced new dangers that must be confronted in the Western Hemisphere. The Sandinistas in Nicaragua and Marxist opposition in El Salvador constituted direct threats to U.S. national security—although the nature of that threat was never entirely clear. "Communist subversion is not an irreversible tide," Reagan declared. "We've seen it rolled back in Venezuela and, most recently, in Grenada. And where democracy flourishes, human rights and peace are more secure. The tide of the future can be a freedom tide."[93]

Notwithstanding the departure of William Clark, initiatives to engage with the Soviets evoked consternation among the administration's hardliners. John Lenczowski wrote a stern letter strenuously advising Reagan to forgo attending Andropov's funeral. According to Lenczowski, some were tempted to regard the installation of the INF as evidence that the United States could now negotiate from a position of strength; these people were mistaken. "The real source of our new national strength," he insisted, was "our national will—our will to use force if necessary to defend our interests." Reagan's presence at Andropov's funeral "would send the Soviets a major signal that this real strength was severely eroding." While many Americans refused to believe it, the Soviets held global ambitions that included the destruction of American democracy. They continued to operate an enormous gulag with millions of slave laborers, he alleged, and the academics and journalists they sent to the United States were likely engaged in methods of subversion.[94]

Hardliners did not lament that the Soviets had walked out of the Geneva talks. At a March 27, 1984, National Security Planning Group meeting devoted to arms control, Weinberger expressed skepticism that the United States could make progress on a Strategic Arms Reduction Treaty. He cited a department of defense paper entitled "What Is the Interest of the Soviet Union in Reaching an Agreement This Year?" It concluded: "There is very little evidence that they are interested in an agreement." The Soviets would accept nothing less than a recapitulation of SALT II, which Reagan had deemed unacceptable and which they were violating anyway. Weinberger saw no hurry to negotiate. "If we become too eager," he warned, "the Soviet Union will sense weakness."[95] Perhaps, Reagan acknowledged, but he still wanted to convey willingness. The president believed that his "letter to Chernenko offers an opportunity to get their attention." Temptation beckoned him to sign a bad deal just for the sake of having a deal, Reagan conceded; he pledged not to yield to it. "We want an agreement," he insisted, "but we want a good agreement. I do not intend to make unilateral concessions to get them back to the table, but I believe we must have a full credible agenda on arms control." The president was especially concerned that he might send the wrong message if he followed Weinberger's line. "Have we given enough attention to the fact that they have a climate of insecurity?" he asked.[96] Reagan informed Shultz that he wanted him "to be our public spokesman on arms control."[97]

Reagan always yearned for a man-to-man meeting with a Soviet leader. The 1983 meeting with Dobrynin had been a smashing success. On September 28, 1984, Reagan met with Gromyko for two hours in the Oval Office. Although Dobrynin had asked that Reagan not talk about human rights in this meeting, Shultz insisted that all topics would be on the table.[98] By the end of the meeting, neither man had acquitted himself particularly well. Gromyko's response evinced a belief in Marxism of near-religious proportions. Reagan countered with Lenin quotations of dubious origin. The two men employed selective evidence to argue that the other side was seeking superiority; they failed to reach a consensus on the origins of the Cold War.[99]

More important than the words exchanged was the slight humanization of Andrei Gromyko. During their joint press conference, Gromyko attempted to converse with Nancy Reagan, asking her to whisper "peace" in her husband's ear each night. "And I'll whisper it in yours too," Nancy responded. Gromyko was seen to blush.[100]

Gromyko said things that Reagan found outlandish—yet the president believed that he ultimately could persuade anyone. Hardliners within his administration saw naiveté behind his tremendous optimism and goodwill. They wanted to put an end to negotiations before Reagan gave away the store. Perhaps Gromyko would not be the Soviet man capable of change, Reagan conceded, but each time he met a Soviet person, interacted with him on a human level, discussed children and grandchildren, and shared visions of the future, he left optimistic that he could eventually win the Russians over to his point of view. And his confidence was growing.

The American people boosted Reagan's confidence to even greater heights by reelecting him in one of the biggest landslides in American history. Immediately after Americans went to the polls, rifts within the administration came to the fore. "We have trouble," Reagan wrote in his diary on November 14. "Cap & Bill Casey have views contrary to George's on S. Am., the middle East & our arms negotiations. It's so out of hand George sounds like he wants out. I cant let this happen. Actually George is carrying out my policy. I'm going to meet with Cap & Bill & lay it out to them. Wont be fun but has to be done."[101]

Reagan never did "lay it out" to Weinberger and Casey. Had he been less averse to personal confrontation and less committed to a personal sense of loyalty, he might well have dropped them after the 1984 election. But they were two of his oldest political associates and friends; he could not fire them. Thus, when it came to pursuing Soviet strategies, Shultz fought a war with Weinberger and Casey that lasted until the fall of 1987. By the start of 1985, however, the secretary of state was winning the battles.

George Shultz believed that the United States was negotiating from strength; Reagan's reelection demonstrated his administration's political strength. Deployment of INF projected America's renewed military strength and the cohesiveness of the NATO alliance. Shultz's burgeoning relationship with the president and the departure of William Clark garnered the secretary a position of bureaucratic strength. The crafting of strategy with the help of Jack Matlock harnessed strength to the purpose of changing how the Soviets behaved—not to overthrow the regime.

Shortly after the election, word came of Moscow's interest in resuming nuclear arms talks. Shultz was prepared for this. He selected his team and flew to Geneva to engage the adversary. The proposals the United States put on the table were those of the secretary of state and the president. The Soviet proposals would be those of a new man in the Kremlin.

# CHAPTER 4

# Gorbachev Adapts

*November 1984–October 1986*

On November 17, 1984, Ronald Reagan received a letter from General Secretary Konstantin Chernenko congratulating the president on his reelection and calling for a new round of arms negotiations on "both the issue of non-militarization of space and the questions of strategic nuclear arms and medium-range nuclear systems." Negotiations should go even further: "We are prepared to seek most radical solutions which would allow movement toward a complete ban and, eventually, liquidation of nuclear arms."[1] Neither Reagan nor his top advisers were inclined to believe this last part. The Soviets had stormed out of negotiations fourteen months earlier—now they were proposing to get rid of all nuclear weapons? When Shultz met Gromyko in Geneva on January 7, 1985, he heard the same message. Negotiations could resume in that city after they left, Gromyko told Shultz; these talks "must have as their ultimate objective the elimination of nuclear arms." The Soviet minister reiterated: "We are speaking of a common objective: both sides agree to the goal of completely eliminating nuclear arms."[2]

Navigating a path to zero nuclear weapons bedeviled U.S.-Soviet relations during Reagan's second term. The point of contention was nearly always SDI. Strategic missile defenses, "if they proved feasible, could contribute to the goal of eventually eliminating all nuclear weapons," Shultz asserted at Geneva. This was the president's position as well. "Let us not mince words, even if they are harsh ones," Gromyko replied. SDI "would be used to blackmail the USSR."[3]

Mikhail Sergeyevich Gorbachev proved to be the critical agent of change in breaking this impasse. He pressed forward not because of SDI but in spite of it. He made concessions because he deferred to ideas over power. His ideas were often little more than slogans, but Gorbachev believed in them more than missiles. In the period of November 1984 to October 1986, he made decisions to adapt to the international environment he inherited from Brezhnev, Andropov, and Chernenko in ways that arrested the nuclear arms race.

## General Secretary Gorbachev

"Entire families would accompany their men, profusely shedding tears and voicing parting wishes all the way," Gorbachev described the day his father was conscripted along with the other men in his village near Stavropol, in southern Russia. "We said goodbye at the village center. Women, children, and old men cried their hearts out, the weeping merging into one heart-rending wail of sorrow."[4] One time, fourteen-year-old Gorbachev and his friends came upon the remains of Red Army soldiers revealed by the melting snow. "There they lay, in the thick mud of the trenches and craters, unburied, staring at us out of black, gaping eye-sockets."[5] After his family mistakenly received an official letter of condolence, Gorbachev spent nearly a year thinking that his father had been killed by the Germans.

The wartime years of his youth led Gorbachev to believe in communism—"the war was not only a great victory over fascism but proof that our country's cause was the right one."[6] He joined the communist youth group, the Komsomol; studied law at Moscow State University; and rose through the ranks of the Communist Party. Gorbachev was affable and hardworking, and he enjoyed the good fortune to become the political boss of Stavropol at a time when Politburo members often vacationed there. Yuri Andropov took notice and brought him to Moscow. By 1978, Gorbachev was heading agriculture planning for the party secretariat. Two years later, he was a full member of the Politburo.

Gorbachev prided himself on being a citizen of the Soviet Union. When he visited Italy, Belgium, and West Germany in the 1970s, it stung his pride to see the disparity between the Soviet standard of living and that of Western Europe.[7] And he could not comprehend the anti-Soviet hostility he encountered when he traveled to Prague after 1968. Yet he possessed a sense of humor. "Gorbachev arrived with some delay to the official reception in the

Kremlin," a French senator in François Mitterrand's delegation later recalled an occasion in the summer of 1984. "When he sat down at our table he apologized, saying that he had been busy trying to solve some urgent problem of the agricultural sector. I asked when the problem had arisen, and he replied with a sly smile:'In 1917.'"[8]

In his high-profile trip to London that December, Gorbachev delivered a message: "The Soviet side is ready for new negotiations seeking radical arrangements toward the complete prohibition and elimination of nuclear weapons."[9] He surprised everyone to be seen standing with his wife, Raisa, who was glamorous and intelligent. She had a Ph.D. in sociology from Moscow State University; accordingly, Gorbachev took his wife's opinions seriously. As with Nancy, Raisa wanted her husband to be remembered as a man of peace. Furthermore, she was outspoken. In the Soviet Union, "we are all working class," her husband began explaining to the Thatchers over dinner. "No, we are not," Raisa interjected. "You are a lawyer."[10] Indeed, the Gorbachevs neither looked nor spoke like typical communists. "Whatever is dividing us," Mikhail Sergeyevich told Thatcher when they got down to business, "we live on the same planet and Europe is our common home."[11] He quoted Lord Palmerston's dictum that nations had neither permanent friends nor permanent enemies, only permanent interests. Thatcher was delighted to hear this shibboleth of realpolitik. At some point in his visit, Gorbachev showed Thatcher a map of Soviet missile targets in the United Kingdom, saying "Prime Minister, we need to stop with all this, as soon as possible."[12]

"I am cautiously optimistic," Thatcher told the BBC after the visit. "I like Mr. Gorbachev. We can do business together."[13] She was also a bit suspicious. "The more charming the adversary, the more dangerous," Thatcher reported to Reagan at Camp David after Gorbachev's visit.[14]

On March 11, 1985, the Politburo elected Gorbachev as general secretary. He inherited a Soviet Union in stagnation. Historian Vladislav Zubok has compared this moment to FDR and the coming of the New Deal (only Gorbachev wanted to save communism—not capitalism—without any knowledge of just how to do it).[15] At home, nothing exemplified stagnation so much as the rampant alcoholism. In one of the first Politburo meetings he chaired, Gorbachev was informed that "in 1913, although drinking was widespread, about half of men in Russia did not drink; 9 out of 10 women and 9 out of 10 boys of draft age did not consume any alcoholic drinks." In 1985, the report estimated, 99 percent of the adult population drank. "We have approached the threshold, after which, as they say, there is nowhere to retreat."[16] "I played tennis for two hours in the morning," Anatoly Chernyaev, who was to become Gorbachev's closest adviser on foreign policy, wrote in his diary that summer. "On the way home I stopped by the grocery store to get some vegetables. Everyone there, from the manager to the saleswomen, is drunk."[17] He was pleased when Gorbachev launched an anti-alcohol campaign that spring. So was Vadim Medvedev, another key adviser, who could now gracefully decline the cocktails foisted upon him whenever he traveled on government business.[18]

There were no such easy answers when it came to foreign policy. Traditional Soviet rallying cries no longer resonated. The Chinese were headed in their own direction, as were other communists. By 1985, indigenous communist parties were looking not to Moscow but to themselves. "The Eurocommunists have absolutely defeated the faithful, i.e., the people faithful to us," Chernyaev wrote in his diary. The "Communist Movement" had become obsolete. Eurocommunists still espoused the same language, but "they do not need us, the CPSU; do not need us at all. They see in us neither a model, nor an example, ideal, brother, trusted friend, not even someone who would save them from a nuclear catastrophe."[19] Gorbachev tried to win back their support. In 1984, he had attended the funeral of Enrico Berlinguer, the longtime leader of the Italian communist party who had rarely listened to anything Moscow told him. The tributes had so impressed Gorbachev that at Chernenko's funeral, he skipped over many others to meet with Berlinguer's successor, Alessandro Natta. His preference garnered attention. With "so many" good communist leaders in attendance, lamented Boris Ponomarev, head of the International Department, why did Gorbachev insist on meeting with the "bad one"?[20]

Gorbachev ignored old thinkers like Ponomarev. He listened to individuals such as Alexander Yakovlev. A standout among his Komsomol peers, Yakovlev had studied at Columbia University after distinguishing himself in the Great Patriotic War. Crafting official Soviet propaganda in his subsequent career, Yakovlev liked to remind everyone that he had once been mugged on the streets of New York City. In the early 1970s, Yakovlev wrote an article criticizing Brezhnev for tolerating anti-Semitism in the Kremlin.[21] He was sent to Canada, where Gorbachev found him in 1983.[22] "Mikhail Sergeyevich did not know what he wanted to do but our idea was to stop the cold war before it led to catastrophe," Yakovlev later recalled. "We had to do something."[23]

Chernyaev and Yakovlev had vivid memories of the siege of Leningrad; inefficiencies and incompetence during the postwar era also shaped their worldview. New thinkers accepted the ideals of Marxism-Leninism but could not deny that their system lagged behind the West. Nor could they pin the blame solely on the capitalist world. They were cosmopolitan in their outlook and had traveled abroad. And they disdained the provincial Soviet attitudes—particularly the rampant anti-Semitism that pervaded everyday discourse even at the highest levels.

New thinking sometimes originated outside the Soviet Union. Gorbachev admired the work of slain Swedish Prime Minister Olof Palme, whose strategic thinking was imbued with a notion of "common security." Gorbachev also read political works by Einstein and Gandhi and discussed ideas with Spanish Prime Minister Felipe González and former German chancellor Willy Brandt. Gorbachev also imputed new meaning to old terms. He championed the Leninism of the New Economic Policy of the 1920s, when the founder of the Soviet state wrote of complex and contradictory ideas in favor of experimentation. He did not, however, look to the economic reforms that Deng Xiaoping had set into motion in the People's Republic of China.

Since Khrushchev's attempts at "reform" had failed, Gorbachev embarked on "reconstruction," or perestroika. He called for a huge investment in heavy industry, setting the goal of a 20 percent increase in industrial production over fifteen years; administrative controls to reduce waste and corruption; and a leaner, more efficient communism. Uskorenie, or "acceleration," was his slogan for 1985.[24] The scope was relatively modest: replacing ineffective party officials, increasing discipline, and enacting the anti-alcohol campaign.

Gorbachev had two fundamental foreign policy motives. The first was to reassess Soviet military strategies and foreign commitments in light of his stated intention of restoring economic growth at home. The second was to halt the nuclear arms race, as Gorbachev abhorred these weapons just as much as Reagan did. "Never before has such a terrible danger hung over the heads of humanity as in our times," he told the Central Committee on his first day as general secretary. "The only rational way out of the current situation is for the opposing forces to agree to immediately stop the arms race—above all, the nuclear arms race—on the earth's surface and not allow it into outer space."[25]

The new Soviet leader was no saint, however. He escalated the Soviets' brutal campaign in Afghanistan. He hoped to win the war quickly, but on a human level, he differed not only from his predecessors but also from many leaders outside the Soviet Union. Brezhnev had relished his medals and his Orders of Lenin. Gorbachev was not interested in such trophies, nor in guns. He hated them, and he had no use for martial bravado. He had seen firsthand the horror of Nazi occupation: "The war touched us with its flame and made an impact on our characters and our entire worldview."[26] He was stuck with Afghanistan. He did not know how to end a war, but he knew he would not start another one.

## Engagement

"You can be assured of my personal commitment to work with you and the rest of the Soviet leadership in serious negotiations," Reagan wrote Gorbachev on March 11, 1985. "In that spirit, I would like to invite you to visit me in Washington at your earliest convenient opportunity."[27] A month later, he reiterated to Gorbachev his enthusiasm for direct engagement: "I believe that new opportunities are now opening up in U.S.-Soviet relations," the president wrote. "We must take advantage of them. You know my view that there are such opportunities in every area of our relations, including humanitarian, regional, bilateral and arms control issues."[28]

Privately, Reagan remained cautious. He was not going to let down his guard. A meeting with Ambassador Arthur Hartman confirmed what the president expected: that "Gorbachev will be as tough as any of their leaders. If he wasn't a confirmed ideologue he never would have been chosen" by the Politburo.[29] After a visit from Armand Hammer, the flamboyant Russian-born industrialist who had now met every Soviet leader since Lenin, Reagan expressed skepticism. "He's convinced 'Gorby' is a different type than past Soviet leaders & that we can get along," Reagan recorded in his diary. "I'm too cynical to believe that."[30] For his part, Gorbachev was also skeptical. Reagan's team at Chernenko's funeral had failed to impress him. "The general impression that the American delegation left is, I tell you honestly, quite mediocre. This is not a very serious team," he informed the Conference of Secretaries of the Communist Party. "When I touched upon questions that were outside of the text [Vice President George] Bush had, he got lost. The only issue the Americans kept pushing was that President Reagan wishes to meet with the Soviet leadership [and] wishes to conduct negotiations."[31]

Notwithstanding the "amorphous and general" content of Reagan's message, Gorbachev looked forward to meeting the president.[32] He summoned his advisers to help prepare for a summit; they reported back swiftly. Yakovlev acknowledged that the balance of power favored the United States. He advised Gorbachev to adapt to this reality while also convincing Reagan that the Soviet leader was not to be bullied. Hectoring the president would only antagonize him; Gorbachev's chief priority should be "not to lose real opportunities in terms of improving relations with the USA, because in the next quarter of a century the USA will remain the strongest power in the world."[33]

In earlier Soviet times, Yakovlev's candor would certainly have cost him his job. It was the old guard whose jobs were on the line under Gorbachev, however. On June 25, 1985, Marshal Sergei Sokolov attended a conference at the Chautauqua Institute and told a State Department official not to waste any more time with the current Soviet foreign policy team. The American passed this message on to Jack Matlock, who wrote Deputy National Security Advisor John Poindexter that Gromyko's days were numbered and that his underlings were positioning themselves "not to get burned in the fallout."[34]

On July 3, 1985, Gorbachev selected Eduard Shevardnadze—the political boss of Georgia who professed to know absolutely nothing about foreign policy—to be his foreign minister. Gorbachev had known Shevardnadze since the early 1970s. "He is a fully formed public figure, a principled person, who understands the interests of the party," the general secretary announced to the Politburo. "Eduard Amvrosievich has shown himself as an experienced, resilient person, capable of finding needed approaches to solving problems."[35] The swiftness with which Gorbachev consolidated power impressed Jack Matlock. It was a "brilliant tactical move which puts [Gorbachev] in direct charge of foreign policy," he wrote McFarlane, who forwarded the message to the president.[36] "We're all agreed the new Soviet Foreign Minister is there to hold the fort for Gorbachev," Reagan wrote in his diary the next day.[37]

Shevardnadze indicated that he might be more forthcoming than his predecessor, Andrei Gromyko. A few weeks after the new appointment, Matlock met with Larry Horowitz, a legislative aide to Senator Edward Kennedy and occasional back channel to the Soviets. Horowitz had just returned from Moscow. "In regard to Afghanistan, if the U.S would suspend temporarily and publicly assistance to the resistance, there would be a solution," Shevardnadze had admitted to him. "Gorbachev has decided to solve the problem."[38]

First impressions of Shevardnadze boded well. "Perhaps," Gromyko had once replied to an American diplomat who asked whether he had enjoyed his breakfast. "I like it when a person does business with a smile and gets the point of a witty remark," Shevardnadze wrote in his memoir. "We achieve little with dour solemnity and immobile facial muscles."[39] When, on July 31, 1985, Shevardnadze and Shultz met for the first time in Helsinki, it pleased Shultz that Shevardnadze assented to use simultaneous translation (suspicious of technology, Gromyko had always refused), which allowed each side to read the body language of the other. He liked that Shevardnadze did not drone on for hours about arcane details and procedure and that their wives toured the city together as the two men negotiated.[40]

Shultz assured Shevardnadze that his country bore no hostility toward the Soviet Union. He acknowledged that history had led Soviets to fear invasion and shared the story of his visit to a Leningrad war cemetery. Possibly some fringe elements in the United States did wish to see more Soviets die, but the vast majority of Americans did not. Nor did Washington desire an Afghanistan that threatened the Soviet Union; it sought to arrange a peaceful settlement.[41] The gravest threat lay not in the ideological struggle between capitalism and communism, Shultz contended, but rather in the very existence of nuclear weapons. He reiterated the "common purpose" of January 1985. "Both sides have set as a goal no nuclear weapons," he stated, but "we have to take a radical step to get there." That step was to put aside ideology. If significant reductions could be achieved, then the two sides could approach the United Kingdom, France, and China and tell them "that they must join us if we are to proceed to zero nuclear weapons."[42]

Although Shevardnadze seemed to like Shultz, he was not yet prepared to stake out new positions. "To be honest, the performance was ok," the Georgian later recalled.[43] His tone differed from Gromyko's, but their positions were not all that far apart. "It is clear that U.S. medium-range missiles are an addition to the U.S. strategic arsenal," Shevardnadze recited, using words Shultz had heard Gromyko say before. "Their purpose is not only to upset the regional balance but to gain global superiority and a first-strike capability on the part of the U.S. and its allies."[44]

Shultz was prepared to bargain, but not everybody within the Reagan administration supported him. Hardliners wanted Reagan's second term to begin the same way as the first. Chernenko's letter and the arrival of Gorbachev did not alter their thinking.

On December 17, 1984, National Security Council staffer John Lenczowski prepared a think piece that assailed any moderation. "The principal theme of Soviet strategic deception is to convince us that the political transformation of the U.S. is not a Soviet objective," Lenczowski asserted. The Kremlin was trying to trick the world into thinking that the Soviet people shared its fears; in fact, they were seeking the destruction of capitalism: "The very act of sitting at a negotiating table accomplishes this task by leading us to believe that a live-and-let-live policy . . . is acceptable to the Soviets, when in fact it is not acceptable whatsoever."[45] McFarlane forwarded this think piece to the president. The national security advisor did not necessarily agree with it, "but I believe that we must not dismiss the possibility that this analysis is correct," he wrote in the margin.[46] McFarlane was more pragmatist than hardliner, but he possessed neither Shultz's stature nor a relationship with the president to inoculate himself against the charge that he was soft.

Caspar Weinberger would not have doubted the essence of Lenczowski's memo. The more Weinberger heard Gorbachev talk about change, the more dangerous the Soviet leader sounded. The American people tended to be peace-loving and trusting; they might easily forget the true nature of communism when the Kremlin's leader exuded such charisma. Weinberger had various motivations for his assessment. He despised communism in any form; he also needed to secure votes in Congress. The emergence of Gorbachev accentuated Weinberger's fears that Democrats would kill funding for defense programs he deemed essential. If Gorbachev was truly a different kind of Soviet leader, they asked, what was the rationale for spending billions of dollars on new weapons and an extravagant missile shield?

Weinberger's concerns were understandable. Although Reagan won a decisive victory in 1984, the president no longer wielded the political capital of his first administration. Because he had cut taxes without reducing spending, the federal deficit was soaring. Fiscal conservatives needed to be convinced that the Soviet Union remained threatening enough to justify keeping the government's balance sheet in the red. Weinberger feared that domestic politics might pressure Reagan to agree to a bad deal, since he could not be assured a continuation of the U.S. arms buildup. Reagan vowed to resist such pressure, however, and he remained an ally to Weinberger. He was not convinced that America had rebuilt its strength. "In spite of some of the misinformation that has been spread around," Reagan stated publicly in September 1985, "the United States is still well behind the Soviet Union in literally every kind of offensive weapon, both conventional and in the strategic weapons."[47] The Soviet Union had "the most and greatest nuclear weapons arsenal in the world," he said on another occasion; it had "the world's only operational antiballistic missile system, the world's only operational anti-satellite system" as well as "the world's most extensive strategic air defense network."[48] While politicians in the United States dawdled over whether to fund SDI, Reagan alleged that the Soviet Union had "tested and deployed sophisticated air defense systems which we judge may have capabilities against ballistic missiles."[49]

Gorbachev had his own hardliners to deal with. Hearing the invective of Weinberger and his allies substantiated their fears that the United States was out to destroy communism. Even those voices receptive to change recoiled at Reagan and Shultz's insistence on talking about human rights. Defensiveness, ingrained anti-Semitism, and, in some cases, genuine concerns over national security helped substantiate the charge of an American crusade; Reagan's public rhetoric reinforced it.

These sentiments converged at a Politburo meeting in August 1985, where Gorbachev broached the matter of Andrei Sakharov, the great nuclear physicist-turned-dissident who had been exiled internally to the city of Gorky. Sakharov was requesting that his wife be allowed to travel abroad to receive medical treatment. Out of the question, Shevardnadze and the head of the KGB, Viktor Chebrikov, agreed. She would denounce the Soviet Union just like Aleksandr Solzhenitsyn and divulge secrets about its nuclear arsenal. Others in the room spoke with less refinement. "You can't expect any kind of decency from Bonner," declared Party Secretariat Mikhail Zimyanin. "She's a beast in a skirt, an imperialist plant."[50]

The difference between Gorbachev and Reagan was that Gorbachev was determined to get rid of the hardliners. Years of evidence collected on drinking habits and assorted indiscretions dealt Gorbachev a strong hand. And, unlike Reagan, he did not shy away from personal confrontation. In January 1987, Zimyanin resigned "for health reasons"—he lasted longer than most. Gorbachev replaced Brezhnev's longtime prime minister, Nikolai Tikhonov, with Nikolai Ryzhkov. He dismissed two potential rivals, Grigory Romanov and Viktor Grishin, replacing them with Yegor Ligachev and Boris Yeltsin.[51]

As Gorbachev cleaned house, Reagan prepared to meet him. He yearned to learn more about the Russian people and grasp why they tolerated a way of life he found so abhorrent. A summit appeared to be on the horizon, according to a memo that Bud McFarlane circulated, for which "it will be important for the President to develop a much more thorough knowledge of the Soviet Union, their history, culture, bureaucratic process, Gorbachev, the man and the survivor as leader, [and] their negotiating style."[52] Matlock responded by compiling "Soviet Union 101," consisting of twenty-one papers, roughly eight to ten pages each, on the country's history and the psychology of its people. As he had done in the Ivan and Anya speech, Matlock crafted a more conciliatory message to attract Reagan's interest and appeal to his sensibilities.

"Yes, they lie and cheat," Matlock's paper on Soviet psychology began. "And they can stonewall a negotiation [even] when it seems in their interest to strike a deal. They have a sense of pride and 'face' that makes the proverbial oriental variety pale in comparison." Superficialities belied a more complex Soviet psyche: "In private, with people he trusts, the Russian can be candid to a fault—groveling in his nation's inadequacies—and so scrupulously honest that it can be irritating, as when he makes a big deal over having forgotten to return a borrowed pencil."[53] Matlock beseeched Reagan to understand that Russian insecurities spanned centuries. Even as the Soviet Union built itself into a superpower, its leaders retained the suspicion that they were not taken seriously. "We recognize that you are a great country and have great achievements," Gorbachev told Secretary of Commerce Malcolm Baldrige that May, "but you ignore what we have achieved. You won't treat us as equals."[54]

The portrait of Soviet man that Matlock sketched out possessed few of the traits the hardliners presumed. Richard Pipes, Matlock's predecessor, had written that the Soviets were prepared to fight and survive a nuclear war. In a paper entitled "Russia's Place in the World," Matlock turned that view on its head. World War II was "a much more recent event in the Soviet Union than it is in the United States," he wrote. It had not steeled them for war; its legacy was "an abiding fear of war." When the prospect of nuclear war appeared in 1962, the Soviet people had acted just as ordinary Americans did: "During the Cuban missile crisis in 1962 and again during the invasion of Czechoslovakia in 1968 we heard that rural stores ran out of matches, kerosene and soap as peasant women hoarded in fear of war."[55] Matlock also sought to disabuse Reagan of the notion that Marxism-Leninism dictated every Soviet action. He summarized a book written by a Soviet defector describing how the Kremlin operated. "Everything is decided ad hoc," Matlock paraphrased. "They don't know themselves what they are going to do next. But they will always claim that they had it in mind all along." Matlock recalled instances when Soviets had told him privately that none of them actually believed the official rhetoric. They said certain things publicly because they had to. If "ideological deceptions" were ever jettisoned, Matlock wrote, "the Soviet Union would cease to be the Soviet Union [and] no party leader is likely to want to commit suicide."[56] In the meantime, the president should take everything he heard from Moscow with a grain of salt.

Reagan read these papers and absorbed the major themes, if not always the details. He also took a keen interest in visits by Suzanne Massie, the author of several popular books about tsarist Russia. Massie professed insight into the Russian soul, but she knew little about the Soviet era. She held the conviction that Sovietism had obscured, yet not extinguished, the inner Russian soul.[57] Reagan liked this distinction between Soviets and Russians. It comported with his broader political philosophy. Speaking about taxes and spending in his first inaugural address, he declared that "government is not the solution to our problem; government is the problem."[58] The same held true in foreign affairs. "People don't start wars," Reagan said repeatedly. "Only governments do that."[59] Reagan grew enamored of Massie's visits. "She is the greatest student I know of the Russian people," he wrote in his diary. "She's convinced the Russians are going through a spiritual revival & are completely tuned out on Communism."[60] The prospect excited Reagan; already, Billy Graham had described for him "a wave of religious revival, particularly on the part of young Russians."[61]

Reagan had hope that the Soviets might again be Russians one day. Writers who had impressed Reagan before his presidency—James Burnham, Aleksandr Solzhenitsyn, and Jeane Kirkpatrick—all rejected the prospect that totalitarian states were capable of reform. Reagan was more optimistic. He believed in transformation because he had twice experienced conversion in his lifetime—first as a child who asked for baptism, and then as an adult who became a Republican after voting for FDR four times.[62]

Reagan was eager to meet Gorbachev in Geneva that November. As the date of the summit neared, Reagan prepared to bargain, but not if that meant giving up SDI. "I won't trade our SDI off for some Soviet offer of weapons reductions," he wrote in his diary on September 11, 1985.[63] Integrating missile defense into "our respective arsenals would put international relations on a more stable footing," he told a meeting of the National Security Council on September 20, 1985. The Soviets claimed that SDI would lead to another arms race; the president deemed this bogus. "In fact," Reagan insisted, "this could even lead to a complete elimination of nuclear weapons." The president even said that he was "ready to internationalize these systems."[64]

Reagan was confident in his negotiating skills. He was ready to prod Gorbachev, cajole him, and persuade him that SDI was something to be supported. He saw no reason for Gorbachev to doubt his sincerity to share SDI. His optimism and confidence transcended the fact that this technology, much talked about and feared, did not yet exist.

## Geneva

On November 19, 1985, in Geneva, Reagan bounded down the steps in front of the American embassy to greet his Soviet counterpart. The hours and days that followed saw no meeting of the minds. The two men sometimes locked horns in a battle of pride. Reagan responded defensively when Gorbachev told him that Soviet scientists were predicting a large-scale earthquake in California sometime in the next two to three years.[65] On the way to one of their private meetings, Reagan suggested that Gorbachev ask the head of the U.S.A. Institute in Moscow to concede that Reagan had made not just "B movies" but also some very good ones.[66] When the two men put their emotions aside, however, they reaffirmed their mutual goal of eliminating nuclear weapons. "Nuclear war cannot be won and must never be fought," read

**FIGURE 4.1.**   Reagan and Gorbachev, 1985. The two leaders meet for the first time. Courtesy of the Ronald Reagan Library.

the joint declaration at the summit's conclusion. Contention remained over the means but not the ultimate end. Each man envisioned a way forward. Gorbachev proposed that the two sides cut their nuclear arsenals in half and repeat until they reached zero. Reagan insisted that only SDI could insure that both sides disarmed. He pleaded with Gorbachev, raising the additional specter that a "madman" like Mu'ammar Al-Qadhafi might someday obtain nuclear weapons.

"We have it in our power to start the world again," Reagan proclaimed in his toast at the last night's dinner. He desired a new world free of nuclear weapons, but he could convince Gorbachev neither that SDI was essential to this new world nor that he truly intended to share SDI with the Soviets. Reagan "wondered why the Soviets should object to research," as if Gorbachev meant all research, when in fact Gorbachev was insisting on restricting testing to the laboratory.[67]

During the summit, Reagan consistently came across as if participating in a televised debate. He delivered talking points and told one-liners to win over an audience that did not exist. And despite the tremendous confidence he placed in his persuasive abilities, his devotion to an idealized and mythic understanding of the United States detracted from his broader objectives. Once again, he told the story of how the proof of America's noble intentions lay in its foreign policies after World War II; once again, this story produced nothing. After one of the sessions, Deputy Foreign Minister Georgii Kornienko inquired of McFarlane and Shultz whether the president actually believed his explanation that the Cold War began when Stalin denied FDR landing rights in Soviet territory for bombing runs against Nazi Germany. If Reagan truly believed that, Kornienko later recalled asking his American counterparts, how could the Soviets possibly trust his judgment about something like SDI?[68]

Gorbachev did not appear to be enamored of Reagan. Their very first encounter had been awkward. The coatless president took pride in bounding down the steps. "You're lightly dressed. Don't catch cold, or I won't have anyone to hold talks with," Gorbachev told Reagan, who had outpaced his translator and had no clue what he was hearing.[69] The language barrier bridged, Gorbachev remained skeptical. "Reagan appeared to me not simply a conservative, but a political dinosaur," he told the Soviet team afterward.[70] "The man does not seem to hear what I am trying to say," he told Yakovlev.[71] At the airport, he told Ponomarev about having seen, at first, "only the blank, uncomprehending eyes of the President, who mumbled certain banalities from his paper."[72]

Gorbachev was disappointed. He also had little incentive to speak kindly. Projecting the image that Reagan was a dinosaur might allow the Soviet leader broader latitude to implement his reforms. He slammed Reagan's "crude primitivism, caveman views and intellectual impotence," when he returned to Moscow. Occasionally, the president gave hints at being reasonable, but "the essence of his policy—the policy of the military-industrial complex—has not changed."[73]

More promising were the conclusions Reagan drew from his meeting with Gorbachev. At Geneva, the president and first lady became John and Sally from Reagan's "Ivan and Anya" speech. The two couples spoke not about differences but shared values and affection for their children and grandchildren. At dinner, Gorbachev expressed "his belief that the family was the foundation of society" and his fear that this foundation might be eroding. Too many unwed couples now lived together in the Soviet Union, Gorbachev explained to Reagan; he planned to deliver a speech on family values when he returned to Moscow. Gorbachev then paraphrased from the New Testament. The two men shared a tremendous responsibility to the future; they should seize the moment to gather stones, not throw them. Perhaps, he mused, they should stay in Geneva until Christmas if it took that long to come to an agreement.[74]

Up to that moment, Reagan doubted whether the Soviets celebrated Christmas. He may not have understood Gorbachev's communist policies—and those few that he did understand, he rejected—but he approved of Gorbachev's language. As with Thatcher, Reagan liked hearing Gorbachev invoke Lord Palmerston's dictum that "every country has certain constant or permanent interests."[75]

"I don't know, Mike," Reagan told his former aide, Michael Deaver, after Geneva. "I honestly think he believes in a higher power."[76] Gorbachev seemed a polite and reasonable man who demonstrated neither Stalin's imperiousness nor Khrushchev's juvenile antics, about which Reagan had heard and read. His retort that Reagan should not criticize his country because America had its own problems such as drugs and race relations stung Reagan's pride, but they sounded like the complaints of ordinary American liberals and media tricksters—not tales about capitalist oppression and the inevitability of class conflict. Gorbachev "is a somewhat different breed even though he solidly believes in their system," Reagan wrote a supporter. "Strangely enough in those meetings he twice invoked God's name."[77]

Reagan's warming to Gorbachev did not mean he intended to make concessions. It inspired his confidence that eventually he could bring the Soviet leader around to his point of view. And the president began to think that the Soviets could indeed be trusted to uphold their end of a grand bargain on nuclear weapons.

On January 15, 1986, Gorbachev delivered a speech in which he called for the abolition of nuclear weapons by the year 2000. Two weeks earlier, he had gathered his top arms negotiators. Come up with bold new initiatives, he told them; report back in a few months.[78] But Gorbachev proved unable to wait that long. Even though Shultz and Gromyko had agreed one year earlier to set the goal at zero, Gorbachev's speech established a sense of urgency. And it very publicly put the ball in America's court.

"The proposal was intended to be 'revolutionary' enough to satisfy the ambitions of the new young Party leaders while unrealistic enough to be rejected by the West," wrote Andrei Grachev, a young foreign policy aide at the time. The Soviet propaganda machine could then accuse the West of obstructionism, just as the Americans had the Soviets on INF. Hardliners assumed it was a deadly gambit, because the idea came directly from Marshal Sergei Akhromeyev, chief of the General Staff of the Soviet Armed Forces.[79] Soviet hardliners were in for a surprise: Akhromeyev meant business. He and his peers on the General Staff grasped the danger posed by the "accumulation of a huge nuclear arsenal." Serving as a commanding officer in the Warsaw Pact had heightened his sensitivity to the fact that thousands of strategic missiles with tens of thousands of warheads were standing on hair-trigger alert. "This unimaginable nuclear power," Akhromeyev understood, could "incinerate all life on Earth within ten minutes."[80]

Gorbachev was serious about abolishing nuclear weapons and transforming Soviet foreign policy. He sought to adapt the country's founding principles to fit the modern era. Drawing upon the intellectual ferment within think tanks and academic institutes and consulting with advisers Alexander Yakovlev and Valery Boldin at a Black Sea retreat, Gorbachev prepared to announce further new thinking at the upcoming Party Congress. He wanted to "present a 'fresh' vision of the international scene," he told Yakovlev, and to articulate what role the Soviet Union should play.[81]

On February 1, 1986, Gorbachev fired Brezhnev's longtime foreign policy aide Alexei Aleksandrov-Agentov and promoted Chernyaev, who was already part of his circle. Chernyaev had distinguished himself in the Great Patriotic War, but he disdained martial activities. He had no formal background in security affairs, yet his priorities were Gorbachev's priorities. "My impression is that he's really decided to end the arms race no matter what," Chernyaev wrote in his diary after Gorbachev called for the abolition of nuclear weapons. "He is taking this 'risk' because ... nobody would attack us even if we disarmed completely. And in order to get this country on solid ground, we have to relieve it of the burden of the arms race."[82]

Chernyaev's first task as Gorbachev's national security advisor was to draft a paper that eliminated the Stalinist doctrine of "two camps," replacing it with a variation on the refrain from Geneva: "a nuclear war cannot be won and must never be considered." In so doing, Chernyaev eschewed the stated purpose of the Soviet state ever since 1917: safeguarding the process through which "international class struggle" led to a communist future while consigning capitalism to the dustbin of history.[83] "Notwithstanding all the ambiguity in our relations with the United States," Gorbachev told the Politburo that spring, hewing to what was now his common theme with Chernyaev, "reality is such that we cannot do anything without them, nor they without us. We live on one planet. And we cannot preserve peace without America."[84] He elaborated on interdependence before the 27th Congress of the Communist Party on February 25, 1986. "The course of history, of social progress, requires ever more insistently that there should be constructive and creative interactions between states and peoples," he said. History continued to favor socialism and communism, but it need not lead to confrontation. The "realistic dialectics" of the era consisted of a "growing tendency towards interdependence of the countries of the world community."[85] The danger was not that capitalism would attack, Gorbachev went on to say. If the Soviet Union did not accelerate its reforms, he warned, communism would fail.

Capitalism appeared more resilient than it had been a generation earlier: "The present stage of the general crisis does not lead to any absolute stagnation of capitalism and does not rule out possible growth of its economy and the mastery of new scientific and technical trends."[86] "Interdependence" thus replaced "two camps." "Regional conflicts" replaced "national liberation movements." With regard to Afghanistan, "security" trumped "revolution." "We don't seek socialism there," Gorbachev told the Politburo. Instead, the objectives were "to have a friendly neutral neighbor so that we can get out" and to keep the Americans out. "If there are no U.S. airfields or military camps, anything else they can decide on their own."[87]

This all amounted to a seismic shift—rhetorically. Action remained another matter. Shevardnadze was initially rebuffed when he proposed scrapping the longtime Soviet position that British and French forces be included in any INF deal. The replacement of 40 percent of the full members of the central committee during the party congress in February and March strengthened his hand, though. "It must be said directly that the nuclear weapons of France and Britain would not be counted," he announced on March 12, 1986. "This, of course, is a compromise version that does not follow the customary logic of the arms race."[88]

On February 11, 1986, Gorbachev settled one of the outstanding human rights disputes by allowing Anatoly Shcharansky to immigrate to Israel. The general secretary believed he was demonstrating his good faith, and wondered why Reagan did not reciprocate. "The President of the United States ... recalled similar statements of his own" in responding to his January 15, 1986, call to abolish nuclear weapons, Gorbachev told an Algerian reporter. But in the arms talks under way in Geneva "we simply can't get out of deadlock ... to begin real movement toward this objective."[89] Gorbachev kept trying. "More than four months have passed since the Geneva meeting," he wrote Reagan on April 2, 1986. "We ask ourselves. ... Where is the real turn for the better?" Perhaps the two men should select a European capital, he suggested, one where they could restore the spirit of Geneva and devote themselves to abolishing nuclear weapons.[90]

Reagan interpreted these initiatives with skepticism. It annoyed the president that Gorbachev got credit for nuclear abolitionism. The letter he received from Gorbachev after the January 1986 speech "has a couple of zingers in there which we'll have to work around," Reagan wrote in his diary.

"But at the very least it is a h—l of a propaganda move. We'd be hard put to explain how we could turn it down."[91] Reagan did not want to turn it down. "I want our children and grandchildren particularly to be free of these terrible weapons," he told one of his generals.[92] After discussing Gorbachev's letter with his national security team, Reagan was inclined to call the Soviet leader's bluff. "Some [in the meeting] wanted to tag it a publicity stunt," he wrote. "I said no. Let's say we share their overall goals & now want to work out the details. If it is a publicity stunt this will be revealed by them."[93]

"By noting apparent Soviet agreement to our objective of substantial nuclear reductions and by elaborating our own steps forward for achieving that end," Reagan wrote the other heads of NATO countries, "we can challenge the Soviet leadership to see whether their proposal advances the process of achieving substantial mutual reductions and limits which are equitable, verifiable, and stabilizing."[94] But this process could move forward only with unrestricted U.S. research into SDI, Reagan insisted. At a National Security Planning Group (NSPG) meeting devoted to arms control, he reminded his team that SDI would provide insurance so that each side stuck to its agreements. If the defensive system worked, not only did Reagan still intend to sign an arms agreement, he would even share this technology with both America's allies and its adversaries. "We should point out that SDI is not for the U.S. alone—we seek a mutual shift from sole reliance on offensive weapons to an offense–defense mix," Reagan said. "We should remember the principle of sharing SDI at the deployment stage."[95] He would consider stationing it under the authority of an international organization: "As we continue to develop SDI we need to find a way for SDI to be a protector for all." He pondered the "concept of a 'common trigger' where some international group, perhaps the UN, could deploy SDI against anyone who threatened use of nuclear weapons. Every state could have this guarantee."[96]

No U.S. leader but Ronald Reagan could ever have gotten away with saying these things. Who could conceive of a more extraordinary prospect than an American president sharing a nuclear shield with the Soviet Union? Someone who wanted to vest America's national security in the United Nations, perhaps, while the world embarked upon eliminating nuclear weapons. Reagan proposed doing the first one, hinted strongly at the second, and contemplated these schemes just three years after calling the Soviet Union an "evil empire."

In order to realize his vision, Reagan needed to establish real trust with his Soviet counterpart. Trustworthiness was his *own* greatest virtue, Reagan was sure. His integrity and honor endeared him to the American people—especially to his conservative base. Even those Americans who did not share

Reagan's political values seemed grudgingly to trust him. His two most prominent political critics, House Speaker Tip O'Neill and Senator Edward Kennedy, were routinely disarmed by presidential anecdotes playing up their common Irish ancestry.[97] Yet Reagan could not comprehend why the personal qualities that elicited the trust of the American people failed to have the same effect on Gorbachev. Neither could he disassociate himself from his idealized conception of America. "I do not understand the reasoning behind your conclusion that only a country preparing a disarming first strike would be interested in defenses against ballistic missiles," Reagan wrote Gorbachev on February 16, 1986. The United States had never borne ill toward anyone, the president insisted; he repeated the same history lesson about U.S. foreign policy after World War II that he recounted to Gorbachev in Geneva, and to every Soviet official he ever met.[98]

## Chernobyl

Reagan hoped to meet Gorbachev again. The venue set for the next summit was to be the United States, but neither side could foresee when that might occur. The timing depended on the ongoing negotiations in Geneva. Both sides waited for a breakthrough that might produce a document that Reagan and Gorbachev could sign. Until then, fate conspired against them.

On April 26, 1986, reactor number four at the Chernobyl nuclear power plant exploded. The fallout from the explosion left an immense swath of Ukraine uninhabitable; an entire ghost city was left standing. Gorbachev was horrified by the human toll, the incompetence of the Soviet bureaucracy's response, and the physical devastation the explosion wrought. And as the resulting radioactive cloud wafted across national boundaries, he realized the potential disaster it could spell for his efforts to improve his country's standing in the world. So fierce was the outrage in Scandinavia that Gorbachev immediately sent Akhromeyev to the Stockholm conference on conventional arms reductions and ordered him to cut through years of Soviet stonewalling and agree to on-site arms inspections.[99]

Chernobyl heightened Gorbachev's antipathy to nuclear weapons and reinforced his conviction that they should be abolished. "We need negotiations," he told the Politburo on May 8, 1986. The Americans were dragging their feet, but "even with this 'gang' we need to negotiate. If not, what remains? Look at the Chernobyl catastrophe. Just a puff and we can all feel what nuclear war would be like." A month later, he discussed the tragedy with Warsaw Pact leaders in Budapest. "It was like war," Gorbachev told them. "People were evacuated, families were separated and only slowly found their way back to each other." Fortunately, there were doctors to help. "Medical experts all over the world clearly state that there would be no medical help in case of a nuclear war."[100]

"Everybody was shocked" by Chernobyl, Gorbachev reported to the Politburo when he returned home. "Imagine what a nuclear war would mean for Europe with its concentration of population!" He ordered his team to make up for its shameful initial response. "We bear an enormous responsibility to evaluate the consequences, draw conclusions and prescribe further actions," he told them. "Our behavior will be scrutinized not only by our own people but by the entire world. We owe them all the full information on what has happened. A cowardly position—would be unworthy politics."[101] Over the next few months, the full weight of the Soviet bureaucracy focused on treating the sick and easing the fears of a population for whom "abstract nuclear danger suddenly turned out to be a menacing reality."[102]

Chernobyl was not the only disastrous event that spring. On April 5, 1986, two hundred people perished when a bomb exploded in a Berlin disco popular among American servicemen. Evidence pointed to Qadhafi, a constant thorn in Reagan's side ever since the Libyan strongman's actions provoked American airstrikes in the summer of 1981. Fed up with Qadhafi's harassment of American ships and fighter jets in the Gulf of Sidra and in retaliation for the disco bombing, Reagan ordered an extensive air assault on Libya on April 15, 1986. Gorbachev had no use for Qadhafi, who had been a Soviet patron. Still, it annoyed him that instead of reciprocating his own new thinking, Reagan concentrated on punishing this relatively minor thug. In retaliation, Gorbachev canceled a meeting between Shevardnadze and Shultz scheduled for the following month.[103]

The showdown with Qadhafi stiffened Reagan's resolve to build SDI. Not only might it potentially replace mutual assured destruction and insure that both sides stick to agreements, it might also protect the civilized world from rogue leaders like the Libyan strongman. "My own view is that we may be able to develop a defensive shield so effective that we can use it to rid the world once and for all of nuclear missiles," the president wrote his old friend Laurence Beilenson that summer. "Then—since we all know how to make them we preserve SDI as we did our gas masks in the event a madman comes along some day and secretly puts some together."[104]

Reagan may have distinguished between the "madman in Libya" and the adversary in the Kremlin, but his intelligence agencies drew few distinctions. Regardless of what Gorbachev said, the CIA discerned little change in its perception of Soviet threat. "During the next five year plan we expect ICBM production to increase substantially over the 1981–1985 plan, submarine production to be up about 20–25 percent, and tank production to jump well over 50 percent," stated a January 30, 1986, briefing. The CIA was predicting four thousand new Soviet fighters and helicopters about to come online, in addition to several hundred new heavy bombers. The briefing concluded, "The prospect is for continuation of the steady 20-year expansion and modernization of Soviet strategic and conventional forces."[105] Gorbachev did not intend to use this vast military power, according to the CIA assessment, so long as vital Soviet interests were not at stake. The Kremlin's military superiority threatened in other ways, however: "The mere existence of this force not only validates the Soviet Union as a superpower, but has an intimidating effect on countries around the world helping the Soviets expand their presence, influence, and power."[106]

"There is every indication that Gorbachev has adopted and is applying [the Brezhnev Doctrine] vigorously with renewed and increased weapons and Soviet and Cuban involvement against the growing effectiveness of the Mujahedin in Afghanistan, Savimbi in Angola, and the contras in Nicaragua," the CIA report asserted. The Soviets had their sights set as well on the Philippines and the horn of Africa. "Stronger Libyan and Soviet influence and presence in Sudan would face Egypt with a hostile force on the west and the south—and pro-Soviet elements in the Sudan, Ethiopia, and South Yemen would command the southern approaches to the Suez Canal."[107]

The CIA's dire assessment of Soviet capabilities and intentions arrived at a time when the Reagan administration was crafting the first defense budget of the Gorbachev era. New thinking posed a unique challenge for U.S. national security planning. A kinder and gentler general secretary might lessen the perception of a Soviet threat and complicate the Reagan administration's ability to support insurgencies in Central America and Afghanistan and to aid governments of dubious stature on several continents. If Soviet negotiators in Geneva anticipated budget cuts, moreover, their American counterparts feared, they might dig in to await a better deal. And, to no one's surprise, SDI stood out as the most contentious program. Bud McFarlane saw it in jeopardy unless the president clarified its purpose and created a bipartisan commission to support it. The Gramm-Rudman-Hollings deficit reduction act, which Reagan signed the previous December, had turned off the faucet that had allowed billions of dollars to flow into new defense systems in the first term. Although McFarlane had left his post as national security advisor around that time, he provided opinions to his former deputy and now successor, John Poindexter, using a newfangled "email" terminal from his home. "Unless this concept [of a bipartisan commission] or something like it which gets the initiative back in the White House is tried," McFarlane emailed Poindexter on March 5, 1986, "by September we will be watching the investment of the past five years go down the tubes, the victim of congressional preoccupation with the deficit (thanks to Don Regan and Gramm Rudman). With it goes arms control and before long, we will be seeing a more ambitious Soviet Union a la the late 70's."[108]

Even if the perceived Soviet threat had abated, Reagan would never have sacrificed SDI. In order to sustain momentum for it in the spring of 1986, his administration needed to play up the Soviet threat. Pessimistic CIA assessments helped justify a record $320 billion military budget. Hardliners were pleased that intelligence agencies buttressed what they had believed all along. "There was no line between policy advocacy and intelligence for Bill Casey," Deputy Director of the CIA Robert Gates later recalled.[109] The assertion could easily have applied to Gates himself while he was helping to formulate the agency's evaluation of Gorbachev. "Bob Gates has assembled a nice amt of intel on the Soviet threat—most of which is real," Oliver North emailed McFarlane on March 3, 1986.[110] Using such intelligence, the administration attempted to shore up support for keeping defense spending high. On February 26, 1986, Reagan delivered a televised address in which he cited a "long history of Soviet brutality toward those who are weaker."[111] The next month, Attorney General Ed Meese traveled to the Khyber Pass to accuse the Soviet Union of "torture, rape and toxic gas, of famine, of scorched earth and genocide"—all part of "a drive to dominate the entire world."[112]

Even with Gorbachev in charge, Reagan informed a group of teenagers, the Soviets pursued global domination. "They have a belief that their purpose must be to bring about world revolution to a one-world Communist State," he stated at a high school on May 21, 1986. "Karl Marx said that the only way it would succeed [was] when the whole world was that way."[113] Reagan also publicly accused Gorbachev of ramping up aid to the left-wing regime in Nicaragua. He denounced the "brutal and totalitarian nature of the Sandinista regime" and extolled those who had taken to the hills to fight for freedom. "Just as the men and women of the resistance have decided what they must do," he went on to say, "so, too, have Gorbachev, Castro, Arafat, and Qadhafi." Soviet military advisers numbered in the hundreds, Cuban troops swarmed the streets of Managua, and the Sandinistas possessed advanced helicopters "that represent, in effect, flying tanks," the president asserted, and the Palestinian Liberation Organization "has established an embassy there."[114]

As Gorbachev struggled to come to grips with the impact of Chernobyl, reduce arms, and implement domestic reforms, the Reagan administration fixated on continued Soviet support for Nicaragua. The prospect that the Sandinistas might hold on to power struck fear into the administration after Congress narrowly rejected aid to the Contras that March. Hardliners around the president searched for ways to direct money and arms to them. "Try everything," Weinberger implored his colleagues at a May 16, 1986, NSPG meeting. "We should try every country we can find, the committees, and the people of the United States. If the Contras are out of business in July, we will have to fight there ourselves someday."[115] One week later, Reagan sent a message to Congress: "The policies and actions of the Government of Nicaragua continue to pose an unusual and extraordinary threat to the national security and foreign policy of the United States."[116]

George Shultz reacted to this rhetorical assault with trepidation. He wanted to seize the opportunity to reduce nuclear weapons. An INF agreement was in reach, Dobrynin told him in April, but the moment might soon pass.[117]

Shultz sent Reagan a memo on May 19, 1986, prodding him to take a more active role. "I noted in my recent discussions with you that, as a result of Chernobyl and other events since last year's summit," the secretary wrote, "the Soviets are becoming increasingly defensive and withdrawn."[118] The other side had only itself to blame, Shultz assured the president, yet the purpose of the four-part framework was to prevent mistakes in one area from inhibiting agreements in another. America's allies counted on the president to lead. "A prolonged deadlock in U.S.-Soviet relations also may increase the electoral difficulties facing such strong supporters of yours as Mrs. Thatcher and Helmut Kohl," Shultz warned. "An American act of statesmanship now could go a long way to helping us on both these scores in the months ahead."[119]

Shultz urged the president to be bold. Begin with an INF treaty, he said, and then move on to make headway on a Strategic Arms Reduction Treaty. Recalling his days as an economics professor, Shultz spoke in terms of comparative advantage. "You know, the Soviet Union is not in our class economically or in terms of human values," he told Reagan. "Maybe there are some things they can produce like ballet dancers ... [and] there's one thing they do better than we do and that is produce ballistic missiles." This was not because their scientists and engineers were any smarter, "it's because our political system has a hard time with it."[120] Shultz also conveyed optimism that Gorbachev wanted to reduce Soviet land-based ballistic missiles like the SS-18 "Satan." Given the Soviets' strategic orientation, he was certain that, were these missiles to be reduced, Soviet relative losses would far exceed those of the United States. What Shultz did not realize was that nuclear strategy had almost no bearing on Gorbachev's thinking that summer. "Chernobyl opened my eyes like nothing else," Gorbachev later recalled. "One could now imagine much more clearly what might happen if a nuclear bomb exploded. According to scientific experts, one SS-18 rocket could contain 100 Chernobyls."[121] The human factor, in his mind, outweighed the ghastly strategies of nuclear war-fighting.

Gorbachev began to doubt whether he had a genuine partner in Reagan. Meeting with Mitterrand in July 1986, he spoke candidly. Hardliners in Washington alleged that the Soviet Union was still acting as if Stalin were in charge, he complained, while "the real threat to the United States, and to the Western world, according to those people, would arise if the Soviet Union successfully carries out its plans of acceleration of socio-economic development, if it can demonstrate its new economic and political capabilities." Gorbachev had not thought Reagan to be one of these people, but he was beginning to reconsider.[122]

Few might have expected Mitterrand to defend the conservative American president. Earlier that year, after all, the French president had denied the U.S. Air Force use of its airspace in the raid on Libya. Sensing a potential rift, Gorbachev came to France, in part, to encourage a more independent French Cold War stance in the tradition of de Gaulle. Yet Mitterrand resisted the temptation to bash the U.S. administration. Instead, he attempted to allay Gorbachev's fears: "As far as the assessment of the actions of the present U.S. administration, I am not inclined to be so pessimistic as you are." The military-industrial complex put significant pressure on the White House, he conceded, but that was not actually how policies were formulated. "I do not judge the American administration as harshly as you do," Mitterrand asserted; Reagan "is not without common sense and intuition." He was indeed stubborn, but "in contrast to other American politicians, Reagan is not an automaton. He is a human being."[123]

Gorbachev listened to Mitterrand's praise for Reagan. "This is extremely important," the Soviet leader replied, "and I am taking special note of it."[124] Gorbachev also listened to voices at home and decided to act even more boldly. It was madness to fear that the United States would attack the Soviet Union, he decided. It was insane that the Red Army was still rehearsing plans to invade Western Europe. Most of all, it was foolish to think that the Soviets could restructure their economy while continuing to produce weapons that neither side could ever afford to use. "Our super-goal is to avoid a new round of the arms race," Gorbachev told the Politburo on October 8, 1986. Another arms race would mean diverting resources to the modernization of nuclear weapons, which would lead to the "deterioration of our ecological, strategic and political security." It would result in the exhaustion of the Soviet economy, he predicted. "And this is not acceptable."[125]

Gorbachev decided that after forty years of pursuing nuclear weapons, the Soviet Union's strategic arsenal was sufficient. He followed this decision by recalibrating his negotiating positions. In a September 15, 1986, letter to Reagan, Gorbachev proposed restricting SDI research to laboratories for fifteen years. He would also strongly consider U.S. on-site inspections in his country. And he reiterated: a deal between the U.S. and Soviet Union would not count British and French nuclear forces.[126] The Soviet leader still planned to travel to the United States the following year, but why not meet sooner? Gorbachev repeated an idea he had suggested earlier that year: that the two meet in a European capital where they could talk man-to-man.

Shultz advised that Reagan accept Gorbachev's proposal. "We should take a positive, self-confident and commanding approach to this meeting," he wrote the president. That Gorbachev wanted to meet sooner rather than later and that he was willing to cut Soviet land-based missiles confirmed, in Shultz's opinion, that the president's policy of peace through strength was paying off. Shultz urged Reagan to include human rights in the discussion. He wrote, "Gorbachev must go home with a clear sense that Moscow's continuing insensitivity to the humanitarian dimension of the relationship will assume greater significance as prospects open up in areas of mutual concern."[127]

Reagan received more concessions from a Soviet leader in advance of this meeting than in the entirety of his presidency up to that time. It meant that for Gorbachev the stakes were enormous. "The United States has an interest in keeping the negotiations machine running idle, while the arms race overburdens our economy," he told Chernyaev on October 8, 1986. "That is why we need a breakthrough; we need the process to start moving."[128]

## Reykjavik

With the "non-summit" scheduled to begin on October 11, 1986, in Reykjavik, Iceland, there was little time to prepare. The papers that Reagan received were hastily written, admittedly, and did not acknowledge Gorbachev's concessions. The gist of the president's official briefing book was that his Soviet experts did not know what to expect.

Matlock's memo said not to worry. He advised Reagan: sit down alone with Gorbachev and engage him on a human level. The most recent letter from Moscow indicated that he wanted as many one-on-one meetings as possible. Weinberger and other hardliners presumed that this meant

Gorbachev was out to trick Reagan. Matlock deemed that conclusion nonsense. The Soviet leader "knows enough from dealing with you in Geneva to realize that you are not the sort of person who would buy a used car sight unseen from a fast-talking salesman without having your mechanic check it out." Matlock crafted his message in a way he knew Reagan would appreciate. "Despite all the propaganda attacks they previously levied against you, one thing is absolutely clear: both Gorbachev and the Soviet people as a whole respect you as a real leader," he wrote. And in "Soviet eyes, a real leader does not need to be propped up by a lot of 'advisers.'"[129]

Reagan took Matlock's advice. When he met Gorbachev on the weekend of October 10–12, 1986, the president engaged the general secretary in human terms. Nuclear weapons were horrible and should be abolished, he said. Let the advisers haggle over the details of different missile systems—in the end, what difference did it make how these terrible weapons were delivered? The two men needed to trust each other, Reagan emphasized. They needed also to verify that trust. Someone had taught Reagan the Russian expression for "trust, but verify." "Doveryai, no proveryai," Reagan stated over and over again. Verification meant inspections. Reagan wanted an insurance policy in case inspections broke down. SDI was to be that insurance policy.

Gorbachev's briefing book warned that the swifter the United States developed SDI, the more likely Washington might be tempted to wring all sorts of concessions from the Soviet Union. Were the linkage between the ABM treaty and strategic arms control to be broken, "it would be impossible for the Soviet Union to reduce its strategic nuclear forces because that would objectively help the United States to achieve a decisive military advantage over us. There will be one result: an uncontrolled arms race."[130] This did not mean that SDI was a deal breaker for Gorbachev. He just needed to slow it down. "A radical reduction (by 50%) of strategic offensive arms would be possible under the four conditions," his briefing read, "the most important being: if the USSR and the USA do not withdraw from the 1972 ABM Treaty for a period of up to 15 years and observe all of its provisions including the ban on development (except in laboratories), testing, and deployment of space-based missile defense systems and components."[131]

The objective Gorbachev carried to Reykjavik was *not* to strangle SDI in the cradle, in other words, but rather to prevent the United States from harnessing its technological superiority quickly: "If the United States does not test these weapons [SDI] over the next 10 years, that will allow us to decrease our lag behind them in creating the space-based echelon of ABM defense. Unless they observe the requirement to ban not only deployment but also testing, the aforementioned periods of non-withdrawal from the Treaty—whether 10 years or 15 years—will make no real sense."[132]

In Iceland, Gorbachev prodded Reagan to compromise on SDI. He proposed a 50 percent reduction over five years, to be followed by the remaining 50 percent over the subsequent five years. During this time, SDI testing in space was to be excluded.[133] After that, the two sides could reflect, reassess, and tackle the divisive issue once more. Reagan pleaded with Gorbachev. "While it would do no good to tell Gorbachev he was wrong, since it would only be the President's word (which the President knew to be true)," read the minutes of their encounter, "the President could say that we harbored no hostile intentions toward the Soviets." There were vast differences between the two systems. "But the President felt that we could live as friendly competitors."[134]

The two leaders could haggle about numbers, Reagan went on to tell Gorbachev; it "would be better to eliminate missiles so that our populations could sleep in peace." They could argue over the details of grim military strategies, or they could "give the world a means of protection that would put the nuclear genie back in his bottle."[135] Gorbachev became increasingly exasperated. How could he trust Reagan to share SDI with the Soviets when America would not even share the latest technology for milking cows? Reagan was insisting that neither he nor the American people harbored any malice toward the Soviet Union, but had not he only recently reiterated the essence of his Westminster speech calling for a "crusade against socialism in order to relegate it to the ash heap of history"? Gorbachev asked. The Soviet leader could not comprehend why the president spoke this way: "What would the outcome be if the U.S. sought to act according to these principles? Would we fight one another?"[136]

Reagan implored Gorbachev to accept his sincerity. He repeated the example he used with conservative friends who were also skeptical of his nuclear abolitionism. "As the oldest person in the room," Reagan noted, "he was the only one who could remember how, after World War I, poison gas had been outlawed. But people kept their gas masks. And it was a good thing, because poison gas came back. The same could happen with nuclear weapons: if, after their elimination, someone were to bring them back, we would need something to deal with that."[137]

The two sides did not break the impasse. The image of Reagan slumped over in his car headed for the airport encapsulated Reykjavik's apparent failure. Expectations had reached astronomical heights during the meetings, as both delegations felt tantalizingly close to eliminating nuclear weapons. An emotional crash ensued. Gorbachev had tried to delay SDI, but Reagan was convinced that the Soviets meant to block it. "He wanted language that would have killed SDI," the president wrote in his diary. "The price was high but I wouldn't sell & that's how the day ended. All our people thought I'd done exactly right. I'd pledge I wouldn't give away SDI & I didn't but that meant no deal on any of the arms reductions."[138]

As disappointment subsided, moderates on the U.S. side realized what they had gained without any sacrifice. "Suddenly the Soviets were human beings," Shultz's executive assistant, Charles Hill, later remembered the fall of 1986:

> I mean, they weren't before. I mean, visibly, they were people who were autonomized. You knew you were talking to someone who wasn't a real human being. You were talking to a programmed mind of some-one who was basically doing something for some reason other than what an individual human being would do on their own. And sud-denly somebody at the top said "It's ok to be a human being again." And their officials from top to bottom changed. Their personalities changed, their approach changed, their scathing wit changed. It was just a complete transformation on almost a whole body of people—officials—and maybe the whole nation changed.[139]

Shultz conveyed this message to the president. He worked to buoy the president's spirits, to transfigure the memory of Reykjavik from disappoint-ment to triumph. The Soviets appeared ready for an INF treaty and pre-pared for an intrusive verification regime. Hardliners like Weinberger and Casey recoiled in horror at the talk of eliminating nuclear missiles. Shultz fought back. He kept nudging the president toward more negotiations and was instrumental in the period from Gorbachev's ascent to the Reykjavik summit.

Reykjavik was the apogee of arms control during the Cold War. Reagan and Gorbachev had both articulated their long-term positions on nuclear weapons well in advance. Still, the drama and emotions were real, prob-ably a result of the mutual acknowledgment—for the first time—that the one leader shared an incredibly ambitious goal but would not accept a path forward that seemed eminently reasonable to the other. Neither man was prepared to give up.

Reagan wanted to achieve a grand bargain on nuclear arms before the end of his presidency. The more he got to know Gorbachev, the more he trusted the new Soviet leader. The experience at Reykjavik crystalized his vision for world security: the United States would build SDI, share it with the Soviet Union, and then eliminate nuclear missiles from the planet.

Reagan was adapting to the prospect of a new type of Soviet leader, but he was not altering his basic positions on strategic defenses and the overall need for American strength. He was at the height of his capabilities from November 1984 to October 1986.

Yet the indispensable agent of change was Gorbachev. The childhood memory of war shaped his worldview, but Chernobyl had disturbed Gorbachev to the core. He would jettison longstanding Soviet positions on land-based missiles, the independent British and French forces, and SDI. After Reykjavik, the world looked to him to banish the specter of nuclear annihilation and find a way out of the Cold War.

# CHAPTER 5

# Recovery and Statecraft

*October 1986–December 1988*

Mikhail Gorbachev returned from Iceland determined as ever to adapt his ideology to tackle the challenges of his era. He outlined his ideas in a book, *Perestroika: New Thinking for Our Country and the World,* that was published in the fall of 1987.[1] Perestroika—restructuring—aimed to retool communism in order to harness technological advancements in communications and industry and to preserve the superpower status of the Soviet Union, even as the country was undergoing wrenching changes at home. Gorbachev sensed that the capitalist economies were improving at a faster pace than communist economies. Perestroika was meant to give the Soviet Union a chance to share in prosperity. Unlike the economic reforms under way in the People's Republic of China in the mid-1980s, Gorbachev's initiatives included a political component: "glasnost."

In Washington, Secretary of State George Shultz encouraged Soviet reforms and mutual gains. The prospect of perestroika's turning the Soviet Union into a more formidable adversary did not disturb him. Shultz believed that the United States and its allies were operating from a position of renewed economic and military strength and sought to employ that strength to negotiate. Reagan encouraged this approach even as his presidency experienced turbulence and his own performance wavered.

## A Changing International Environment

As Gorbachev, Reagan, and Shultz pondered how they might eliminate nuclear weapons, changes were brewing that affected how hundreds of millions of ordinary people lived. Nearly every change favored the fundamental characteristics of the capitalist world: individualism, openness, and nationalism. By the start of 1987, the capitalist economies of the United States and its allies had recovered from the malaise and stagnation inherited from the 1970s. Developing countries were no longer putting faith in the communist model. While the Internet was to come a short time later, the world had already entered an information age that revolutionized how people communicated, vastly improved the efficiency with which financial firms operated, and eased the flow of capital between domestic and international markets.

These changes accorded with Reagan's optimism. The economic rebound substantiated what he had said all along about the vibrancy of American institutions of free enterprise and open markets. The economy was recovering, the president believed, because his administration had cut taxes and slashed regulations to encourage investment and entrepreneurialism. It was an incomplete assessment of a nation where millions remained impoverished in urban areas, rural Appalachia, and elsewhere, but many Americans were indeed better off than when Reagan had entered office. The so-called misery index (the sum of unemployment and inflation), which peaked above 20 during Reagan's campaign against Jimmy Carter, dropped below 9 in 1986, and did not rise above 10 until Reagan left office.[2]

One factor that sustained U.S. growth worked against the Soviet Union. Fluctuation in the global price of oil threatened to disrupt everything Gorbachev was hoping to achieve. Shortly after he returned from Geneva in the fall of 1985, Saudi Arabia announced that it would ramp up oil production. OPEC had relied on Western government controls like the British National Oil Company to enforce its prices. When Margaret Thatcher abolished the BNOC in the spring of 1985, the cartel could no longer reign in those countries that cheated.[3] The increase in supply precipitated a global price war, and the price of oil fell from $31.75 a barrel in November 1985 to $10 by the spring of 1986.[4] The Saudis' decision had little to do with U.S. pressure. Western energy companies traded oil on "spot markets" for cash on hand after the fall of the Shah of Iran in 1979. From 1979 to 1982, these types of exchanges rose from 10 percent of all internationally traded oil to 50 percent. With oil futures traded on the New York Mercantile Exchange, Saudi Arabia and its allies in OPEC found their pricing power subordinated to manic Wall Street traders and flamboyant corporate raiders.[5] These market and economic actors were beyond the purview of Cold War strategists.

"Lost oil revenue [during 1985 and 1986] called into question Moscow's ability to buy tens of millions of tons of grain, pay its foreign debt, and finance its army and military industrial complex," wrote Russian economist Yegor Gaidar.[6] It amounted to a loss of 9 billion rubles (some $7 billion), Gorbachev estimated at a Politburo meeting in July 1986.[7] Without hard currency, Gorbachev cautioned, the Soviet Union would struggle to purchase basic commodities. It was already purchasing millions of tons of grain and meat and each year was importing nine million tons of steel as well as chemicals and raw materials vital to support industry. "In general, we need all of that," Gorbachev acknowledged. "We have to buy it because we cannot live without it."[8] He lamented the disparity between the two sides: "In the United States, 160 million hectares are planted, feeding the country and the world."[9] The Soviet Union could not even feed itself.

Nor did it reap economic rewards from the anti-alcoholism campaign. Vodka sales constituted roughly one quarter of all trade in 1985. One year later, Gorbachev estimated that lost income because of restrictions on the sale of alcohol had cost the central planning agency 22 billion rubles (some $17 billion).[10] The program also failed to alleviate the scourge of substance abuse. The citizens of Moscow sought other ways to appease their need to drink: sales of cologne jumped 150 percent in 1986, and demand for window washing fluid and glue rose as well.[11] "You can't fool the people," Gorbachev's chief of staff, Valery Boldin later recalled. "They started to distill sugar and make moonshine. The result was a terrible shortage of sugar."[12]

Gorbachev sensed that the world economy was improving and hoped to share in the recovery. At the 27th Congress in February 1986, he called for doubling Soviet economic output by 2000. Progress in the first five years afterward was maddeningly slow. In the period from 1983, when capitalism's recovery took hold, to 1990, when the economics of the United States and Western Europe entered a mild recession, per capita GDP of the Soviet Union and its Eastern European bloc went from $6,407 to $6,446. In the Soviet Union itself, per capita GDP never rose above $7,098 during the years Gorbachev was in power.[13] West of Moscow, the economies in Europe were picking up: in the United Kingdom, per capita GDP went from $13,406 in 1983 to $16,411 in 1990; in France, from $15,567 to $18,093; and in West Germany, from $14,329 to $15,932. Even in Portugal, historically the least prosperous country in Western Europe and the one most stubborn to hold on to its overseas colonies, per capita GDP increased from $8,186 to $10,852.[14] East and south of Vladivostok, the same pattern played out: Japanese per

capita GDP increased from $14,308 to $18,789; in China, from $1,265 to
$1,858; in South Korea, from $5,007 to $8,704; in Thailand, from $2,850
to $4,645; in Taiwan, from $7,114 to $9,910; in Indonesia, from $1,878 to
$2,516; in Hong Kong, from $11,797 to $17,491; in Malaysia, from $4,095
to $5,131; and in Singapore, from $10,710 to $14,258.[15] The Soviet Union
remained mired in the stagnant growth of the 1970s and early 1980s, in other
words, as countries around it moved forward.

On the other side of the world, the American economy returned to the
pattern of sustained growth that predated Vietnam, oil shocks, and stagflation. From 1983 to 1990, per capita GDP in the United States increased
from $18,920 to $23,214.[16] Americans went from paying an average price
of $1.38 for a gallon of gasoline in 1981 to $0.95 in 1986. Cheap oil,
lower taxes, deregulation, increased government spending, and specialization
in high-technology exports fueled this growth. After his "shocks" tamed
inflation, Federal Reserve Chairman Paul Volcker lowered interest rates, and
central banks in Japan and Western Europe responded in kind. The U.S.
stock market responded favorably. On the day of Reagan's inauguration in
1981, the Dow Jones Industrial Average opened at 970. From November
1982 to January 1987 it rose steadily from 1,000 to 2,000. By August 1987,
an investment of $1,000 on inauguration day in General Electric, the com-
pany that had hired Reagan in the 1950s to pitch their consumer products
and the American way of life, was worth some five times that.[17]

For many Americans—not just stockholders—prosperity was returning.
In the 1982–1988 period, average yearly unemployment fell from 9.7 percent to 5 percent. Between 1983 and 1988, Americans purchased 105 million televisions, 88 million cars and trucks, 63 million VCRs, 62 million
microwave ovens, 57 million washers and dryers, 46 million refrigerators and
freezers, 31 million phones, and 30 million answering machines.[18] In 1985,
there were six times as many household phones in the United States as in
the Soviet Union, whose population exceeded that of the United States by
18 percent. Americans made some 37 billion intercity domestic calls that
year, compared to 1.7 billion in the Soviet Union.[19] There were 30 million
personal computers in the United States, compared to some fifty thousand
in the Soviet Union.[20]

On January 22, 1984, an estimated 77.6 million Americans watched Super
Bowl XVIII between the Los Angeles Raiders and the Washington Red-
skins.[21] "On January 24th, Apple Computer will introduce Macintosh,"
read the closing frame of an advertisement featuring a woman hurling an
oversized sledgehammer at Big Brother. "And you'll see why 1984 won't
be like *1984*."[22] George Orwell would have been astonished to see these

personal computers—and at the efforts under way to connect them. By 1987, Bloomberg L. P. had installed five thousand terminals at the top trading houses, giving brokers nearly instantaneous information on the trading floors. Another prototype had emerged from the Defense Advanced Research Projects Agency (DARPA), which in the 1950s had tackled the grim scenario of how to protect U.S. command and control structures during a nuclear war. By the 1980s this project, known then as WORLDNET, came online—fortunately, for a far less dire purpose. Through it, USIA Director Charles Wick used military relay stations to ramp up public diplomacy campaigns. In July 1987, representatives from the State Department, the CIA, the NSC, and the USIA met to develop "a strategy for enhancing the use of WORLDNET as an instrument for furthering U.S. policy objectives in Eastern Europe."[23] The U.S. Chamber of Commerce adopted a version called "Biznet," which Reagan employed in April 1986 to address the International Forum of Chamber of Commerce. The president marveled at this prototype of the Internet.[24]

The Soviet leader also sensed exciting technological breakthroughs. Even before becoming general secretary, Gorbachev had attempted to call a meeting of the Central Committee to address the "scientific-technical revolution" propelling Western economies. When he finally got his meeting in the summer of 1985, neither he nor anyone else in the room knew quite where to begin.[25] "There is closer and closer interconnection and interdependence among countries and continents," Gorbachev told Mitterrand later that year. "This is an inevitable condition for the development of the world economy, for scientific and technical progress, for the accelerated exchange of information, and for the movement of people and goods on the earth's surface and even in outer space—in short, for the overall development of human civilization."[26]

A "scientific-technical revolution" was under way. Unfortunately for Gorbachev, he did not get to witness the assembly line of the postindustrial age. When it seemed that Gorbachev might visit the United States sometime in 1986, Reagan's aides drew up plans to show off American technological and scientific know-how. These plans included taking the Soviet leader to Stanford University, whose licensing of software and other technology to corporate America brought in millions, or perhaps another of the "high-tech future oriented colleges & universities" that, according to the CIA, did not even appear on the radar of Soviet intelligence. Several of these institutions—Cornell, the University of Illinois, and the University of California at San Diego—had just received portions of a $200 million National Sciences Foundation grant to build supercomputer centers "to expand access to state-of-the-art equipment among university researchers and thus maintain U.S. supremacy in computer technology." Two of the nine "outstanding young Americans" considered—Steve Jobs and Michael Dell—exemplified the intersections between creativity and entrepreneurship that would usher in a fantastic new era, but the Soviet leader did not get to meet any of them.[27]

Instead, Gorbachev saw "progress" on display in the summer of 1987 when he visited Zelenograd—the Soviet effort to replicate Silicon Valley. The technology dazzled, he reported to the Politburo on July 30, 1987, and the amount of information held on a single computer was truly astounding. "We have all manner of computers," he boasted, plenty to "satisfy our needs."[28] Yet Gorbachev had no idea what this actually meant. The products of Zelenograd fell below Western standards. The only output for microprocessors was the guidance systems on ballistic missiles. Work began on Zelenograd-II next door—to produce "suitable equipment based on the parts made in Zelenograd-I."[29] According to historian Barry Eichengreen, at most three hundred thousand computers were in use in the Soviet Union by the end of the decade, "whereas Western experience suggested that a country of its size and wealth should have had more than twenty million."[30]

Far more attuned than Gorbachev to technological changes and how societies might adapt to them was George Shultz. "A worldwide revolution in economic thought and economic policy is under way," Shultz wrote in the spring of 1985. "And it is coming just in time, because it coincides with yet another revolution—a revolution in the technological base of the global economy." This revolution, "the onrushing age of information technology," had the potential to change the world. "The combination of microchip computers, advanced telecommunications—and a continuing process of innovation—is not only transforming communication and other aspects of daily life," Shultz wrote, "but is also challenging the very concepts of national sovereignty and the role of government in society."[31]

Shultz was right. The nascent information revolution was challenging the traditional notions of sovereignty and role of government. Western institutions proved extraordinarily capable of adapting. In June 1985, Jacques Delors, the new president of the European Commission, unveiled a plan for the expansion of Europe's common market. In a short time, France, West Germany, Belgium, Luxembourg, and the Netherlands signed the Schengen Agreement, which effectively ended passport controls for travel between these countries. An era of porous borders and greater dissemination of information ensued.

Gorbachev pondered the implications of increased movement across borders as well as economic and cultural interdependence. The radioactive cloud of Chernobyl made it clear that nuclear devastation, and pollution more broadly, knew no borders. Neither did disease. The AIDS virus, the "disease of the twenty-first century," Gorbachev told the Politburo, was "connected with the movement of foreigners to us and vice versa."[32] Mutual security from these challenges should drive international relations, Gorbachev speculated. "We must discard the old, outdated standards and principles that guided states in their relations in the past," he told former president Jimmy Carter on July 1, 1987. "We must see the world as it is, with all its complexities and problems. We are all tied with problems that did not exist before—the nuclear threat, environmental threats. And now, this new problem: information imperialism."[33]

Danger lurked (though Gorbachev never really elaborated on what "information imperialism" entailed). Opportunity existed as well. Gorbachev aspired to share in the new technologies and the newfound wealth they had helped to accumulate. He perceived that the Soviet economy was inextricably linked to the American juggernaut. "Remember," he told the Politburo on February 5, 1987, "without trade there would be no [U.S.-Soviet] relations."[34] While acknowledging this reality, he still hoped that perestroika would inspire all nations—especially the United States—to think and act differently. "The broader meaning of perestroika is that it reflects urgent problems not only in our country," he told the Colombian writer Gabriel Garcia Márquez that summer. "It seems that the whole world needs restructuring."[35]

## Gorbachev Improvises

The American president "bears full responsibility for the defeat of the [proposed] agreement," Gorbachev complained to the Politburo after Reykjavik; Reagan was "undertaking fraudulent maneuvers in order to distort the facts and to confuse the public."[36] "What is it that America wants?" Gorbachev queried his team on October 30, 1986. "I have more and more doubts about whether we can achieve anything at all with this administration."[37] "We are dealing with political scum," he complained privately a few weeks later. "One can expect anything from them."[38] He declined to record a New Year's greeting to the American people.[39]

Gorbachev refocused his energies toward home. "Return to patriotic works," Gorbachev told Andrei Sakharov on December 19, 1986, "you [and your wife] can return to Moscow."[40] At the January 1987 plenum of the

Communist Party, Gorbachev announced glasnost ("giving voice to"), a political component to his economic reforms. "Whoever doesn't like this and cares about only about their own interests—feel free to go, we can do without you," he said. "And we won't have to stock up on machine guns."[41] Gorbachev spoke more eloquently in his closing address: "We need democracy like air." He quoted one of Lenin's rally cries, but this time with a completely different meaning: "More light: let the Party know everything!"[42]

On February 4, 1987, a delegation of U.S. elder statesmen including former secretaries of state Henry Kissinger and Cyrus Vance arrived at the Kremlin. "If we speak realistically," Vance told Gorbachev and his advisers, "nuclear missiles will be in our arsenals for many years to come." Given the nature of American politics, the bipartisan group impressed upon its host, drastic policy shifts were rare. And no proposal could be more drastic than the dismantling of America's nuclear arsenal.[43]

Aleksandr Yakovlev received the message. Linking INF to START, he wrote Gorbachev on February 25, 1987, risked achieving neither one before Reagan left office. "In principle," he wrote, "there exists an opportunity to achieve agreement on disarmament but only if we 'untie' the Reykjavik package."[44] Just as Matlock did with Reagan, Yakovlev understood how to reach his boss. He knew that Gorbachev coveted his role as the world's leading spokesman for nuclear disarmament. Shortly after Vance and Kissinger had departed, Gorbachev hosted a conference in Moscow with the slogan, "For a Nuclear-Free World, for the Survival of Humanity." His country was "prepared to give up its status as a nuclear superpower," Gorbachev declared. Changes under way in his country were "essentially revolutionary [and of] immense significance for our society, for socialism as a whole, and for the entire world," Gorbachev proclaimed, before mingling with Gregory Peck, Graham Greene, and Yoko Ono.[45] Yakovlev knew that the reality was more complicated. The Soviets were about to resume nuclear testing, he reminded Gorbachev. The Reagan administration would seize upon this fact to denounce Gorbachev as a hypocrite. He prodded Gorbachev to recapture the initiative.

"No matter how difficult it is to do business with the United States, we are doomed to it," Gorbachev informed the Politburo on February 26, 1987. It was an article of faith for every other Soviet leader for seventy years that capitalism would collapse; Gorbachev acknowledged that it would not. "Do not assume there will be an economic collapse of capitalism."[46] "They used to tell us that the United States was in crisis," he had confided in his top advisers earlier. "But it seems like there is no crisis there."[47] Nor would a deal to trade the SS-20s for Pershing II missiles and cruise missiles leave the Soviet Union vulnerable to attack. Gromyko had once ruled out any agreement that did not compensate for the independent arsenals of the United Kingdom and France. Gorbachev considered this approach nonsense. "There will be no war with Britain or France," he chastised Marshal Sokolov. "It is not possible."[48]

SDI influenced Gorbachev's thinking—but not in the ways Washington hardliners presumed. "We were not afraid of SDI," Gorbachev later recalled, "first of all, because our experts were convinced that this project was unrealizable, and secondly, we would know how to neutralize it."[49] A report Gorbachev received in February 1987, compiled by a leading Soviet physicist, placed the technology needed actually to deploy SDI at decades in the future. Even then, it predicted that the Soviet nuclear arsenal could smash whatever shield the U.S. intended to deploy. The author of the report, Evgeny Velikhov, based his conclusions on the Soviets' own unsuccessful attempts to build a missile defense system.[50]

A different Soviet leader might have leapt at the chance to catch and surpass the Americans—many in the defense apparatus would have savored the fight—but Gorbachev took perestroika and other ideas more seriously than traditional concepts of security. "To put it simply," historian Vladislav Zubok has written, "Gorbachev took ideas too seriously."[51] He could have chosen a path of retrenchment, of holding the line while waiting out Reagan's lame-duck presidency. Frustration sometimes pointed him in that direction. "What can realistically be done with the current [U.S.] administration in the time remaining?" Gorbachev mused during a meeting with the Italian foreign minister the day after he had "untied the package." The Soviet leader expressed "serious doubts."[52]

Gorbachev turned his attention to Europe. He had impressed Margaret Thatcher in London in 1984 with his talk of a "common European home." When Thatcher came to Moscow in March 1987, however, she chided him for being a poor tenant. Thatcher liked new thinking but, on the whole, felt that too much old thinking lingered. "We do not believe you," Thatcher retorted, after Gorbachev denied that the Soviet Union had ever started a war. "You take grave actions irresponsibly. ... We could not imagine that you'd send troops to Czechoslovakia, but you did. The same again with Afghanistan. We are afraid of you."[53] In order for Thatcher and other Western leaders to trust Gorbachev, he needed to come clean about Soviet history. Gorbachev took this reproach seriously. "I must admit ... that our policy towards developing countries had been highly ideological and that, to a certain extent, Mrs. Thatcher had been right in her criticisms."[54] During her visit, Thatcher appeared on Soviet television, where she delivered a similar message. "Our T.V. journalists, three men, piled on top of her, and behaved very rudely, in their typical manner," Gorbachev recounted to his team afterward. "But she was not intimidated, and in general, won the battle on the screen."[55]

"Remember, I told you about my meeting with Thatcher," Gorbachev told the Politburo on May 8, 1987. "She said they were afraid of us, that we invaded Czechoslovakia, Hungary, and Afghanistan." This perception of fear "persists in the minds of many people" throughout the West. The Kremlin needed to find a way to counter the anti-Soviet propaganda based on it—"to strengthen our policy for the humanization of international relations with our actions."[56] Humanization meant reiterating the doctrine of strategic sufficiency. Gorbachev scoffed at the figures of the intricate war strategies that his generals propounded. "Strategic parity means that we have a reliable guarantee of defense of our country," he asserted. Were they to get hung up on "a gun there, and a gun here," then socialism was lost. In Vienna, mutual balanced force reduction talks had been ongoing for thirteen years. Gorbachev was calling for a breakthrough, but "we should not allow this to look like a retreat."[57]

Humanization also meant acknowledging that the world was changing and that Europe was changing. For centuries, Russian intellectuals and tsars alike had grappled with whether they inhabited a European nation. The Russian Revolution of 1917 had transposed the question: could Europe ever become a Soviet continent? By the 1980s, no serious person was asking this question. Changes in European civilization, its survival and economic miracle in the two decades after the end of the World War II, shaped Gorbachev's thinking. Capitalism had restored its strength in Europe, but not by preparing for war. "We are confident in our mutual power to overcome that which we are prevented from doing," Yakovlev told West German Foreign Minister Hans-Dietrich Genscher on July 7, 1987. "And history itself proves that we can be good neighbors in Europe."[58] As the "German threat" abated, Eastern Europe was no longer the defense in depth required to protect Russia. "Europe from the Atlantic to the Urals is ... a historical and cultural category in a high, spiritual sense," Gorbachev wrote in April 1987. "Here world civilization has been enriched with the ideas of the Renaissance and the Enlightenment."[59]

Not everyone in Moscow agreed with the man in charge. Even after the "promotions" and retirements, Gorbachev faced hardliners—especially in the military. Calls in Washington for quick deployment of SDI played into the hands of these "old thinkers." Military officers and representatives of the Soviet military industrial complex played up the threat of SDI.

In August 1987, the scientist who designed the SS-20 missile warned the Central Committee that Reagan's talk of a defensive system masked SDI's actual purpose: "to deliver an instant nuclear strike against the Soviet Union" from space.[60] "Never forget that we have class enemies," Gromyko reminded the Politburo on October 15, 1987. "Were it not for socialism, with all its might and muscles, U.S. and British missiles would have struck."[61] Gorbachev deflected these criticisms with help from key advisers, however. Marshal Sergei Akhromeyev lent his stature to talk of radical reductions in nuclear weapons. And Alexandr Yakovlev proved to be a wily tactician. When hard-line general Dmitri Volkogonov began writing articles opposed to nuclear disarmament, Yakovlev redirected the energies of this potential nuisance by inviting him to write a comprehensive biography of Stalin, giving him full access to the classified documents and a generous deadline.[62]

## A Weakened Presidency

Ronald Reagan did not match Gorbachev's dynamism in 1987 and 1988. Two weeks after Reagan returned from Reykjavik, an article in a Lebanese magazine alleged that the administration had sold weapons to Tehran in the hopes of freeing Americans taken hostage in Beirut. The same day, Attorney General Ed Meese confirmed the convoluted scheme and revealed further details. The administration had directed arms to Iran—at inflated prices— and then siphoned profits into private bank accounts made available to the Contras in Nicaragua. The first component of the Iran-Contra scandal contradicted Reagan's assertions that he did not negotiate with terrorists. The second appeared to violate the 1982 Boland Amendment forbidding U.S. assistance to the Contras.[63] Only after Meese's admission did Reagan act to contain the damage. He selected Senator John Tower to form an independent commission that ultimately substantiated many of the allegations and called for a reorganization of the National Security Council. On March 4, 1987, Reagan delivered a carefully scripted, televised confession from the Oval Office. "A few months ago, I told the American people I did not trade arms for hostages. My heart and my best intentions still tell me that's true, but the facts and evidence tell me it is not."[64] Reagan said what he had to. The American people accepted it. His presidency survived.

Reagan needed to make a public confession because of new political realities. Democrats had taken control of the U.S. Senate after the November 1986 midterm elections. Two of Reagan's most tenacious critics on Latin America over the previous six years—Senators John Kerry and Christopher Dodd—now chaired subcommittees empowering them to call members of

**FIGURE 5.1.** Regan and Baker, 1985. An example of Reagan's administrative style: the White House chief of staff and the treasury secretary inform him they are switching jobs. Courtesy of the Ronald Reagan Library.

the administration to testify under oath. Many southern Democrats in the House of Representatives, once supportive of the president's tax cuts and arms buildup, now balked at the skyrocketing national debt. For these and other reasons, Reagan was not, on the domestic front, negotiating from a position of political strength. Firsthand accounts of those around him suggest that six years in the Oval Office had taken a toll. On the whole, Reagan's physical stamina defied comprehension. Bounding down the steps to meet Gorbachev in Geneva, Reagan made everyone forget that he was the oldest president ever elected and that, after just a few months in office, he had taken a bullet in the chest. "This man has the insides of a forty-year-old," quipped the doctor who removed a tumor from the colon of the seventy-four-year-old president in March 1985.[65]

By 1987, however, several of his top advisers were expressing concern. In February, Shultz confided in his executive assistant, Charles Hill, about a conversation with White House Chief of Staff Don Regan. Regan was "frustrated and alarmed" that the president refused to read the administration's legislative proposals, was working shorter hours than usual, and seemed to absorb only what he had seen on the evening news. "He's not really working at the job and not in touch with reality," Regan lamented.[66] Historians can only speculate whether, as his son now claims, Reagan displayed symptoms of Alzheimer's disease while still in the White House.[67] No one will ever be able to say for sure.

Speculation aside, defeat in the midterm elections, Iran-Contra, the sheer physical toll of the office, and the perception that he had misled the American people conspired to make the first months of 1987 the lowest point of Reagan's presidency. His political fortunes down, Reagan played up the threat of communism. He suggested at the State of the Union on January 3, 1987, that Gorbachev had done nothing to alleviate perceptions of the Soviet threat. He conflated new thinking with old, accusing the Kremlin of having outspent the United States on military forces to the tune of half a trillion dollars since 1970. "With 120,000 Soviet combat and military personnel and 15,000 military advisers in Asia, Africa, and Latin America, can anyone still doubt their single-minded determination to expand their power?"[68]

No one should doubt the threat the communists posed to the free world, Reagan explained at a meeting of the National Security Council on March 13, 1987. "Lenin discussed their approach to world communism and said they would first take Eastern Europe, which they have already done," the president recounted for his team. "Then, they would organize the hordes of Asia." Perhaps Moscow did not yet control "hordes of Asia" in 1987, but "they have made great progress there." He expected Soviets to shift their focus to the Western hemisphere. "In taking Latin America, the United States, the last bastion of imperialism, would be isolated and fall into their hands like overripe fruit," Reagan concluded. "These are the stakes we are talking about today."[69]

Iran-Contra may have stung his administration, but only because its members had gotten caught. The president retained the same overall objective: support the Contras in their struggle against the Sandinistas. A Gallup poll in March 1987 found that 100 percent of administration officials favored giving military and economic aid to rebels fighting communist governments around the world, while just 24 percent of the public favored the same policy.[70] Reagan knew his stance was unpopular, and he blamed the media for distorting the facts. "Our foreign policy," he declared in the summer of 1987, "has been an attempt both to reassert the traditional elements of America's postwar strategy while at the same time moving beyond the doctrines of mutual assured destruction or containment." It sought "to break the deadlock of the past, to seek a forward strategy—a forward strategy for world peace, a forward strategy for world freedom." It aimed not to transform but to transcend. "We have not forsaken deterrence or containment," he assured the crowd, "but working with our allies, we've sought something even beyond these doctrines. We have sought the elimination of the threat of nuclear weapons and an end to the threat of totalitarianism."[71]

When it came to dealing with Moscow, Reagan had shifted the goalposts. In meetings with Gorbachev, he had implored the Soviet leader to withdraw from Afghanistan, promising that relations between their two countries would improve immediately thereafter. Around the same time that he decoupled INF from START, Gorbachev sent word through Reagan's friend Suzanne Massie that U.S. assistance for "national reconciliation" and support for Soviet withdrawal could lead to a "breakthrough" on arms control. Now withdrawal alone would not suffice. "I don't think we can say yes—if they plan to withdraw troops but leave a Communist government," Reagan informed Shultz.[72]

"I have not changed my belief that we are dealing with an 'evil empire,'" Reagan wrote his old friend William F. Buckley in the spring of 1987.[73] His hardline advisers encouraged him stay tough on communism. The romantic who had spoken at Reykjavik about eliminating nuclear weapons was not the genuine Reagan, they insisted, but a man spellbound—whether by Shultz's flattery, Gorbachev's charm, or Nancy's desire that he be remembered as a "man of peace." Indeed, the enemy still lurked, Weinberger and his allies assured the president at a February 1987 NSPG meeting. Robert Gates, a career CIA officer who knew Russian and doubted Gorbachev's sincerity, told the president that agents of the Soviet Union and their East European allies, as well as Cubans and Palestinians, had all penetrated Nicaragua with their sights set on spreading communism throughout Latin America. "The ghost of Vietnam must be exorcised," Attorney General Ed Meese declared. "We must show to [the American people] the Soviet threat to our security which will surely emanate from a communist Nicaragua."[74]

What was the threat to America's security? Meese did not, perhaps could not, elaborate. According to the National Security Strategy of the United States the White House issued at the start of 1987, the Soviets directed Cuba, North Korea, Nicaragua, Syria, and Libya to forward revolutionary goals. Despite everything Gorbachev had said, "evidence of the relationship between the Soviet Union and the growth of world-wide terrorism is now conclusive." And the fundamental nature of the Cold War had not changed: "Moscow seeks to alter the existing international system and establish Soviet global hegemony."[75]

The Democratic takeover of the Senate renewed hardliners' fears that SDI could be on the chopping block. They applauded the president for refusing to "sacrifice" missile defense at Reykjavik but feared that his fortitude would not hold indefinitely. Caspar Weinberger led the charge to save SDI. "I didn't, frankly, ever trust Gorbachev or believe that he was fully committed" to change, he later recalled.[76]

Because of the "astonishing success of the SDI program," Weinberger declared at a February 3, 1987, meeting of the NSPG, further progress required that the president immediately sign off on testing outside the laboratory. This meant embracing the "legally correct interpretation" of the ABM treaty, the "LCI"—an Orwellian-sounding neologism coined by an outside counsel for the defense department.[77] Successful tests of "space-based Kinetic Kill Vehicles" pointed to 1993 as a feasible starting date for phased deployment. The Joint Chiefs expressed skepticism over this rosy forecast; Weinberger did not care. "We should think of the concept of phased SDI deployments like building a house," he elaborated. "The 1st phase of deployment is like laying the foundation of the house. The 2nd phase can be like putting up the walls; the 3rd, the ceiling."[78]

Weinberger played political hardball. At the same February NSPG meeting, he told the president how to handle Congress: "You don't need to ask them [to adopt the so-called legally correct interpretation]; but in order to support your action, you do need to tell them."[79] In the version of the meeting leaked to the conservative *Washington Times* immediately afterward, this line was transcribed as Reagan himself commanding his team to issue ultimatums to the Soviets: "Don't ask them; tell them."[80]

Weinberger's attitude toward the Soviets was to take everything, give nothing, and ask for more. Fear of American power had compelled Gorbachev to yield on INF; why concede anything? Paul Nitze later summed up this mentality: "Soviet willingness to sever the linkage between INF and START indicated that the Soviets might be willing also to sever the link between reductions in offensive strategic systems and space and defense."[81] The Soviets "want a START agreement and I believe we will get a good one if we'll just hold," Weinberger declared at an NSPG meeting that September. In the meantime, he urged Reagan to outfox the Soviet leader by shutting down negotiations. "No talks for two years or more, no negotiations, no six month notification, none of that."[82]

When Reagan responded by suggesting that the United States might share SDI with the Soviets at each phase of deployment, Weinberger replied, "I don't believe that we could ever do that." He warned against anyone considering SDI merely to determine the "feasibility of deploying defenses," even though Reagan frequently stated in public that that was his goal. "That's not the program I see," Weinberger snapped at Max Kampelman.[83]

Weinberger knew that Reagan lacked patience for the intricacies of arms control. So he spoke in ways that accentuated and magnified every potential

Soviet advantage. When he warned that the Soviets "have mobile missiles now and we don't," he would have known that this statement would evoke "missile gap" rather than elicit questions from the president such as whether America's massive nuclear submarine fleet or its B-52s outfitted with air-launched cruise missiles might qualify as "mobile missiles." When Weinberger spoke of superior Soviet "air defenses," he provided figures relating to defense against aircrafts in the context of Soviet research into an equivalent of SDI. He did not mention that a nineteen-year-old German had recently penetrated these formidable air defenses before landing in Red Square. And Weinberger kept stoking the president's fears. In an NSPG on October 14, 1987, Frank Carlucci cut short his presentation on different arms control options after Reagan displayed bewilderment over which "sub-limits" of missile counts to endorse.[84] Weinberger summarized: the Soviets were ahead on air defense and long-range missiles; the United States needed to achieve a "level playing field"; and if scientists had been operating under the type of restrictions the ABM treaty placed on SDI, "we would never have had the auto or the cinema industry."[85]

It was imperative to settle this matter, Weinberger warned, because "we also need modernization of conventional forces after an INF agreement to ensure we have proper deterrence." He left Reagan convinced that the Soviets already possessed their own formidable version of SDI and that the clock was ticking. "We may have only 5 years to prepare, since the Soviets are already installing battle management radars," Reagan was saying by the end of the meeting.[86]

Iran-Contra boded ill for Shultz's future in the Reagan administration. Ironically, he and Weinberger found themselves on the same side on the key decisions that led to Iran-Contra: they opposed the swashbuckling of Bud McFarlane and Oliver North. Conservatives forgave Weinberger but sensed an opportunity to oust his rival. When Shultz balked at letting the White House edit his testimony to Congress, Casey urged Reagan to fire him for insufficient loyalty.[87] One of the contenders for the 1988 Republican presidential nomination, Congressman Jack Kemp, publicly called for Shultz to resign.[88] A more influential one, Vice President George H. W. Bush, advised Reagan to fire Shultz soon after news of Iran-Contra first broke.[89]

Shultz persevered. He bore tremendous responsibility for the improvement in U.S.-Soviet relations yet ascribed the credit to Reagan. He knew when to cajole the president, when to flatter. He cultivated a warm relationship with Nancy Reagan, took her views seriously, and encouraged her to share her thoughts with the president. Don Regan had not been so shrewd.

He quarreled with the First Lady in early 1987, hung up the phone on her, and lost his job.[90]

Regan's departure put to rest any talk of Shultz's political demise. The new chief of staff, former Senate Majority Leader Howard Baker, exuded personal integrity and professionalism. He thought highly of Shultz. One of his objectives, he later recalled, was "to try to reinforce what I perceived to be the President's basic desire to have an accommodation with the Soviets."[91]

No sooner had Senator Baker arrived than another scandal emerged. After a Marine guard at the U.S. Embassy in Moscow confessed that he had allowed his girlfriend, who turned out to be a KGB agent, access to the building, fear spread that the entire mission had been compromised. While the American press had a field day with the story of the hapless sergeant Clayton Lonetree, whose travails read like a John le Carré novel, Gorbachev invited Shultz to Moscow.[92]

As Shultz planned to travel to Moscow in April 1987, seventy U.S. senators expressed the view that he should stay home. Henry Kissinger spoke out against the trip. The head of the National Security Agency advocated closing the U.S. Embassy; Caspar Weinberger concurred.[93] The secretary of state brushed his critics aside. If "we still had had the same notion of linkage as in the past," he later recalled, "everything really would have just shut down."[94] Shultz arrived in Moscow on April 13, 1987, and met with Shevardnadze the next morning. At lunch, the American delegation sang "Georgia on My Mind" to a beaming Soviet foreign minister. That evening, Shultz attended a Passover Seder, where he assured Russian Jews: "You are in our minds and hearts. ... Never give up."[95]

The following day, Shultz met with Gorbachev. The two men jousted over human rights and other subjects. Gorbachev made a key concession: he would include a shorter-range Soviet missile (the SS-23) in an INF agreement. At their second meeting, Shultz transcended typical Cold War dialogue. He declared the negotiations over, walked around the table, sat down next to Gorbachev, and showed the Soviet leader charts about how different states were adapting their political economies to meet the challenges of the modern era as well as graphs projecting the GDP of the United States and the Soviet Union to the year 2000. By then, he predicted, advances in biotechnology, crop cultivation, and computers would change the nature of work and quality of life in a "post-industrial era." Governments needed to adapt so that their citizens would benefit from globalization, new economies of scale, and Walter Wriston's concept of an information standard that connected financial and media markets around the world almost instantaneously. Distinctions between capital and labor no longer applied; the deployment of "human capital" would drive economies.[96] At the end of this presentation, he left the charts with Gorbachev.

Shultz advocated Soviet reforms based on his own conception of capitalism. Distinctions between Milton Friedman and John Kenneth Galbraith were less important than an American secretary of state's message of two states confronting common challenges, aspiring for common results, and establishing greater trust. Gorbachev and those around him began to sense that the most conservative and anticommunist presidential administration of the Cold War was actually out to help them.

Shultz's trip made the prospect of the elimination of INF a reality. Not everyone regarded this as a universal good. In a May 21, 1987, meeting of the NSC, Shultz expressed concern that some Europeans were questioning whether large military budgets needed to be sustained to deter a foe that might actually no longer exist.[97] Talk that the Cold War was over, in turn, led others to fear a denuclearized continent vulnerable to Soviet penetration. The prospect emerged that the only nuclear weapons left in Europe might be stationed in—and targeted at—East and West Germany. "The shorter the missile, the deader the German," quipped the FRG's defense spokesman, Volker Rühe.[98] Expending tremendous political capital, governments in Western Europe had made INF deployment a reality. Four years later, their inclination was not necessarily to give them up.

"I'm afraid I can't agree with one of his views," Reagan wrote in his diary after meeting with Henry Kissinger in March 1987. "He doesn't think we should go for zero option we're negotiating with Soviets on INF."[99] After meeting with the outgoing NATO Supreme Commander, Reagan recorded: "He has a [nuclear] missile theory a little different than mine."[100] Hearing about Gorbachev's inclusion of the SS-23, Weinberger deemed the concession part of an elaborate deception. "He and I disagree on this one," Reagan wrote.[101] Not even Margaret Thatcher, over a very late dinner in Venice, could dissuade the president from taking the deal: "She says no & I had to differ with her."[102]

Besides simply repeating his INF position, however, Reagan gave no instructions for how he wanted his team to proceed. Shultz had grown accustomed to this style of leadership, managing to coexist with hardliners so long as he retained a clear channel to the Oval Office and so long as whoever was national security advisor minded his own business. Iran–Contra had threatened this arrangement. When National Security Advisor Frank Carlucci conceived of his own mission to West Germany to mediate concerns over INF that August, Shultz threatened to resign.[103] Take a vacation, the president advised Shultz. Hearing of Shultz's distress, Carlucci offered his own resignation. "No, I want you and George to get together," Reagan responded.[104] He didn't elaborate any further.

Reagan was taking a step backwards in leadership. One of the Tower Commission's criticisms was that the president had not realized the multiplicity of actors conducting foreign policy on his behalf during Iran-Contra, yet he proved no more willing to give clear orders in light of the report.[105] In a May 21, 1987, NSC meeting devoted to West Germans' anxieties over INF as well as the international economy, terrorism, and polls showing Gorbachev more firmly committed to reducing nuclear weapons than the president, Reagan gave a brief introduction and then did not utter a single word for the rest of the meeting, which lasted nearly an hour.[106] More new faces joined the NSC over the course of 1987 than during the changeover to Reagan's second term, and these staff changes added to the confusion. Many of the newcomers had military backgrounds and expected to hear decisions and then follow clear orders. "I can't tell whether I'm really helping him or not because he listens and I don't get a sense that he disagrees with me or agrees with me or what," the new CIA Director William Webster confided in Carlucci's military attaché, Lieutenant General Colin Powell. "Listen, I'm with him a dozen times a day and I'm in the same boat," Powell replied.[107]

On May 28, 1987, a single-engine aircraft landed in front of St. Basil's Cathedral; once the craft came to a stop, out onto Red Square stepped its pilot. Faulty radar, primitive computers, and the coincidence that many border guards were home celebrating national "Border Guards Day" allowed the plane to penetrate Soviet airspace. In the aftermath of KAL 007, no one wanted to shoot it down.[108] The stunt, pulled off by a troubled nineteen-year-old German named Mathias Rust, did not amuse Gorbachev.[109] At first, he scolded his subordinates for their levity, but he soon realized how to use the incident to his advantage. Senior officers in the military were chafing at Gorbachev's talk of strategic sufficiency, so he decided to act in the wake of the landing. For their incompetence at failing to defend the motherland against the young German invader, he "retired" some 150 senior officers, beginning with his minister of defense, Marshal Sokolov. According to William Odom, Gorbachev's bloodless "purge" amounted to an elimination of a greater percentage of Soviet military leadership than Stalin's execution of his generals on the eve of World War II.[110]

On October 21, 1987, Gorbachev endured a challenge to his domestic reforms. Boris Yeltsin launched a stinging critique of Yegor Ligachev in a meeting of the Central Committee. Gorbachev was the real target, of course. In the months that followed, Yeltsin would move to Gorbachev's left, Ligachev to his right. As potential rivals positioned themselves around

Gorbachev, U.S. and Soviet negotiators worked tirelessly in Geneva, Shultz traveled to Moscow, Shevardnadze came to Washington, and the first agreement to eliminate an entire class of nuclear weapons neared completion. During this period, Caspar Weinberger stepped down as secretary of defense.

## INF Treaty

When Gorbachev traveled to Washington in December 1987 to sign the INF Treaty, he and Raisa electrified the American public. "All I had ever seen of Soviet leaders was Khrushchev banging his shoe on the table and some old men in drab uniforms all looking like Mao Zedong, you know, had no personality and looked like they were zombies," recalled one Reagan supporter. "But here comes Gorbachev: he's wearing a good, well-cut Brooks Brothers suit and tie; he even had on a white shirt! He was outgoing, he was meeting people, he was joking and he was getting along with people in Washington, D.C."[111] Gorbachev chatted with Steven Spielberg and signed a baseball for Joe DiMaggio. On the last day of the summit, he ordered his limousine to stop and got out and worked the crowd. "The people I saw this morning were not the people I had been told I would see in America," he told Ambassador Jack Matlock at lunch. "I want you to know that I will never again think of America as I used to."[112] The night before, Vice President Bush joked to Raisa at dinner that he might be falling in love with her. "This is an election year, you shouldn't do that," she responded, before making a quip about Gary Hart, a presidential aspirant who had suffered a campaign-crippling sex scandal earlier that year.[113]

Deputy CIA Director Robert Gates warned of the consequences of Gorbachev's charm. "It is hard to detect fundamental changes, currently or in prospect, in the way the Soviets govern at home or in their principal objectives abroad," he wrote the president one week prior to the summit. Notwithstanding Gorbachev's "new thinking," Gates predicted that the Communist Party would remain unopposed well into the future and that "the basic structures of the Stalinist economy will remain." To the extent, if any, that the Kremlin sought economic modernization, its purpose "remains to further increase Soviet military power and political influence." Gorbachev's "dynamic diplomacy," Gates contended, threatened "to make the USSR a more competitive and stronger adversary in the years ahead."[114] But the conclusions Gates drew were wrong. After he arrived in Washington, Gorbachev informed Reagan that back home he needed to explain "why the Soviets had been so generous toward the Americans." Soviet citizens knew that their leader was proposing to eliminate four times as many missiles as the Americans and could not understand "how Gorbachev could bow down to the U.S."[115] Gorbachev referred to a Gallup poll showing far more support for the INF treaty among Americans than among his own countrymen.[116]

It would be easier to justify his concessions if both sides dispensed with the rhetoric of the Cold War, the Soviet leader stated. His ego could withstand Reagan's disparagement of communism, "but pride was a matter for a nation."[117] The Soviet people were enduring wrenching changes. "It was people's greatest wish to go to bed and wake up in the morning to see everything changed for the better," Gorbachev went on to say. "But even in fairy tales the heroes had to go through trials, and in real life things were even harder."[118] Gorbachev thus bared his aspirations and anxieties.

Then Reagan delivered a dumbfounding response. The president "did not want to offend Gorbachev," but he recently had met with an American scholar just home from a trip to the Soviet Union. On his way to the airport in the United States, the professor chatted with his taxi driver, who was finishing school and earning money on the side. What did the young American want to be? "He had not yet decided." Upon arriving in the Soviet Union, the professor was driven from the airport to his hotel by a young man of similar circumstances. What did the young Soviet man want to be? "They haven't told me yet."[119]

No one laughed at Reagan's joke. Shultz was "disturbed and disappointed."[120] "It was offensive," Colin Powell later recalled. "The meeting was a disaster."[121] The U.S. team went into crisis mode, gathering early the next morning to revise talking points for the next round of meetings.

The next morning, Reagan refrained from telling jokes. He was "prepared to negotiate with Gorbachev a period during which neither side would deploy strategic defenses beyond those permitted by the ABM Treaty." He proposed a treaty to stand alongside START that would allow both sides to conduct research into missile defense.[122]

Gorbachev reiterated his philosophical objection to SDI as well as his willingness to compromise. Neither side should exercise its right to withdraw from the ABM Treaty for ten years. He no longer insisted, as he had at Reykjavik, that the U.S. side restrict SDI testing to the laboratory during this period. Only if the United States deployed SDI before the expiration date would it trigger a Soviet breakout.[123] Reagan listened to Gorbachev but apparently did not hear what the Soviet leader was saying. The record of this conversation suggests a man more intent on persuading the Soviet leader of the merits of SDI than one contemplating the deal Gorbachev proposed. The president repeated what he had told Gorbachev on previous occasions: "If the U.S. and Soviet Union ever reached the point where they had eliminated all their nuclear arms, they would have to face the possibility that a madman in one country or another could develop a nuclear capability for purposes of conquest or blackmail."[124] For his part, Gorbachev repeated that he opposed SDI in principle but was open to a deal that might only delay it. Shultz interjected that both sides shared common ground. The secretary did not understand why the Soviets opposed SDI, but he acknowledged that they did. Fears needed to be allayed, and such was the purpose of drafting a new treaty to go alongside START: to "give the Soviet side greater confidence that it understood what was going on on the U.S. side."[125]

Gorbachev still could not understand: why would the United States not accept the straightforward formula of a 50 percent reduction of heavy missiles and a ten-year period of nonwithdrawal? He offered to reduce the period to nine years and, at the end of the meeting, hinted at less.[126]

Shevardnadze intervened to say that a START deal was within reach. He hoped Reagan could come to Moscow the following year to sign a 50 percent reduction in strategic arms "in the context of the preservation of the ABM Treaty for an agreed period." Fixating on the distant future would mean that "the President's visit could not be crowned by signature of an agreement." He urged Reagan to define parameters for observance of the ABM Treaty: "If the question were consigned to experts, there would never be a decision."[127] Reagan responded by repeating his talking points. The Soviets were forgetting that "prior to Gorbachev's assuming office, there had been violations by the Soviet side of the ABM Treaty." Moreover, that agreement allowed for the type of research that SDI entailed. The real question was "when the Soviet side would begin to abide by the ABM Treaty."[128]

Reagan then grew impassioned. He wanted to make one thing clear: he "did not want to talk about links to SDI but about 50% reductions, about how the Hell the two sides were to eliminate half their nuclear weapons." He wanted another treaty like INF, "which had made everyone in the world so damned happy it could be felt in the room at dinner the night before."[129] He concluded, "Let's get started with it."[130]

Gorbachev also wanted to "get started with it." He asked Reagan to state the U.S. position on SLCMs, but the president did not know it. "The U.S. had no answer on this and other issues he had raised," Gorbachev scoffed, "only more demands of the Soviet side."[131] He recounted a Russian proverb: "If you respect me, don't make a fool of me. Tell me what you want."[132] Reagan wanted Gorbachev to agree with him that with 50 percent less missiles, both sides still needed missile defense. "It would be a long time before that was a problem," Gorbachev responded.[133]

## Trust but Verify

Notwithstanding his mediocre performance at the Washington Summit, Reagan had achieved something remarkable. Six years earlier, when he announced his "zero option," his critics presumed it was a cynical ploy. The INF Treaty eliminated more firepower than any previous agreement in history. Reagan had set its terms, and he never wavered from his position. The president wanted more reductions. On February 9, 1988, he summoned his national security team to determine whether an agreement could be reached before the Moscow Summit, scheduled for May. National Security Advisor Colin Powell expressed skepticism. It was not a question of Soviet willingness; the American side had not yet articulated its own position. The Joint Chiefs of Staff were dragging their feet, Powell told the president, and the lieutenant general did not necessarily blame them. Carlucci also warned that it would be exceedingly difficult to reach an agreement by the summit. A perception of haste on START might upset the Senate deliberation of the INF treaty, warned CIA Director Webster.[134]

Others in the room disagreed. Shultz exhorted his colleagues to "pledge to make an all-out effort" to get it done. Unless they could achieve a START agreement, Chief of Staff Howard Baker opined, the INF Treaty would have been a mistake. Unless Reagan took decisive action, "it's going to drift away from us." The president concurred: "We need to go for the gold."[135]

Shultz took the message of intent to Moscow on February 22, 1988. A tremendous amount of work needed to be accomplished to reach an agreement before May, he told Gorbachev, "but START was certainly possible, and the President was pushing in that direction." Gorbachev concurred. "We should lay the foundation for [START] while Reagan is in office," he instructed the Politburo a week later. "He is also striving for this."[136]

Reagan's aspirations met with resistance from America's NATO allies. The Red Army still loomed over Western Europe. The elimination of all medium-range nuclear weapons meant that the SS-20s no longer threatened Paris and Rome and all the great capitals of Western Europe, but the allies were potentially more vulnerable than ever to overwhelming Soviet conventional forces. And the prospect of a new agreement on ballistic missiles engendered fears that the United States might withdraw its protective nuclear umbrella. The president was undeterred. As he prepared to travel to Brussels for a NATO conference, Reagan pledged to do "all that he could to reach meaningful and useful understandings with Soviets—not for agreement's sake but for the security of the Alliance as a whole." The larger goal was to reverse the momentum that had led to more weapons. It did not particularly matter whether the two sides were talking about missiles or tanks—Reagan did not think that Gorbachev "wanted to engage in an arms race with the United States, but our task was to convince him not to try."[137]

Reagan could handle NATO, but had bigger trouble with the U.S. Senate. The body was still deliberating ratification of the INF Treaty, and although an overwhelming majority of senators favored it and some 79 percent of Americans expressed support, Senators Jesse Helms and Dan Quayle filibustered ratification.[138] "Believe it or not there are elements who are hinting it would be a bad treaty," he wrote in his diary after meeting with Republican leaders on the eve of Gorbachev's arrival.[139] The conservative movement, certainly, was "immune to 'Gorby fever,'" according to Lou Cannon.[140] In the judgment of one conservative activist who helped Reagan win the nomination in 1980 and whose support Republican presidential candidates were courting in 1988, Reagan was "weakened in spirit as well as clout, and not in a position to make judgments about Gorbachev at this time."[141] Another conservative activist declared: "It is tragic that we have a President who has made himself nothing more than an instrument of Soviet propaganda."[142] The columnist George Will, an icon of the conservative movement who had contributed to Reagan's 1982 Westminster Speech, asserted that the day Reagan signed the INF Treaty was the day the Cold War was lost.[143]

Attacks came as well from the self-professed "realists," to whom Soviet willingness to sign a treaty indicated it must not be in the U.S. interest. Haig, Nixon, and Scowcroft all expressed opposition.[144] Neoconservatives such as Richard Perle did not like the treaty, but "we were stuck with it, because the U.S. and its allies had invested a lot of political capital in launching that program and it was politically important for the alliance that we not fail to bring it to a conclusion."[145] The conservative revolt over INF provided a dose of reality for Reagan's dream of a world without nuclear weapons. All signals pointed to the president's taking this goal back to his ranch in California once he left the White House. In January 1988, the Commission on Integrated Long-Term Strategy released "Discriminate Deterrence," a report signed not only by several of Reagan's peers from the Committee on the Present Danger but also by Henry Kissinger and Zbigniew Brzezinski—two figures once reviled by the CPD. The report painted a dire picture of the nuclear balance. "We have depended on nuclear and other advanced weapons to deter attacks on our allies," it read, "even as the Soviets have eliminated our nuclear advantage. If Soviet military research continues to exceed our own, it will erode the qualitative edge on which we have long relied."[146]

One of the signatories was Reagan's former national security advisor William Clark, who was apparently disavowing the goals of his former boss.

"For the foreseeable future, it will not be realistic to pursue agreements to eliminate all nuclear weapons," the report stated. Gorbachev spoke in lofty tones, dressed well and smiled—but he did nothing to alter the perception of Soviet threat. "The [Warsaw] Pact is now well positioned to launch a surprise attack, and in the coming decade it could enhance this capability." Its forces "would be aiming for a blitzkrieg, expecting to break through forward defenses quite rapidly and destroy much of NATO's nuclear force before it could be used."[147] In other words, the American foreign policy elite did not take Reagan's nuclear abolitionism seriously. If the Cold War were to end, it would not be because the two sides had eliminated nuclear weapons. More than that, a broad spectrum of American cold warriors—ideologues, hardliners, and realists—were giving no indication in 1988 that the Cold War was going to end anytime soon.

Reagan spent four days in Helsinki in May 1988 preparing to visit Gorbachev in Moscow. During this layover, the American delegation received Gorbachev's agenda for the upcoming Party Conference. "The text came in fairly late in the evening, and I went to my room," Jack Matlock recounted. "I began to skim through the theses, and I was electrified." There was no reference to class conflict or any other standard trope. "For me, ideology was important and when I saw a Communist Party document that borrowed more from the American Constitution than from Marxism-Leninism," Matlock recalled thinking at the time, "I was impressed."[148]

When Reagan arrived in Moscow, the official conversations between Gorbachev and himself produced no formal agreements. Reagan attempted to discuss religion, but Gorbachev changed the subject. The president recounted a story about a Russian immigrant and his brownie business that did not arouse Gorbachev's interest; far more important was the public diplomacy.[149] After the meeting, Reagan and Gorbachev walked out of the Kremlin and made their way to Red Square. "Shake hands with Grandfather Reagan," Gorbachev told a small boy he took in his arms. "Do you still think you're in an evil empire, Mr. President?" asked ABC's Sam Donaldson, one of Reagan's most vociferous critics. "No, I was talking about another time and another era."[150]

The president was right. On previous occasions, Reagan loved to repeat Churchill's line that the Soviets respected "only strength." But Gorbachev did not respect only strength. He had no use for martial fervor. "We must get rid of any presence of chauvinism in our countries," Gorbachev later wrote.[151] In the nuclear era, excessive pride matched by strength led to "politics that are inadmissible." He was not Gandhi, but then no strict pacifist

**FIGURE 5.2.**    Reagan in Moscow, 1988. A Cold Warrior in Red Square. Courtesy of the Ronald Reagan Library.

could ever have survived atop the Soviet Union (or become president of the United States, for that matter). He took steps in 1988 that demonstrated his commitment to renounce the Brezhnev Doctrine. Gorbachev had originally escalated the war in Afghanistan in the hope of achieving a quick victory. It was now time to abandon that hope and to bring the Soviet troops home.

Gorbachev always faced choices. Soviet citizens had not rioted in the streets or clamored for popular representation. Nor had workers walked out of the factories. The Soviet people did not demand that Gorbachev call for a parliament, as he soon would at the Nineteenth Party Congress in June 1988. If Gorbachev was naive to be suspicious of the dogma of free enterprise, he was no more so than the people of Sweden and Norway or the millions of West Europeans who regularly elected social democrats. If he was wrong to think that the state should guarantee certain rights to the sick and the poor, he was no more so than the plurality of Americans who told pollsters that they opposed some of Reagan's individual policies but supported his presidency. Changes in the international economy and technological revolutions, in other words, did not dictate how Gorbachev would behave. He decided.

Reagan and Shultz frequently disappointed Gorbachev, but ultimately he trusted the Americans. He also wanted to seize the initiative before Reagan's successor was chosen. On October 31, 1988, he summoned his top advisers: Shevardnadze, Yakovlev, Dobrynin, Falin, and Chernyaev. Gorbachev planned to deliver a blockbuster speech at the upcoming annual meeting of the United Nations. In his 1946 speech to Westminster College in Fulton, Missouri, Winston Churchill had described an "iron curtain" descending upon Eastern Europe. "This speech should be an anti-Fulton," Gorbachev told his team. "Fulton in reverse."[152]

# CHAPTER 6

# Gorbachev's New World Order

*December 1988–December 1989*

"The history of the past centuries and millennia has been a history of almost ubiquitous wars, and sometimes desperate battles, leading to mutual destruction," Mikhail Gorbachev proclaimed at the United Nations General Assembly in New York on December 7, 1988. "They occurred in the clash of social and political interests and national hostility, be it from ideological or religious incompatibility." Gorbachev then spoke of a brighter future linked to "the emergence of a mutually connected and integral world." This future required new thinking, "a consensus of all mankind," and "a new world order." Over the next two years, he pledged, the Soviet Union was to cut its conventional arsenal by 500,000 personnel, 10,000 tanks, 8,500 artillery, and 800 combat aircraft.[1]

Gorbachev promised "freedom of choice"—a "universal principle to which there should be no exceptions." He urged fellow leaders to "search jointly for a way to achieve the supremacy of the common human idea over the countless multiplicity of centrifugal forces, to preserve the vitality of a civilization that is possibly the only one in the universe"; to renounce violence, because "force and the threat of force can no longer be, and should not be instruments of foreign policy"; and not to wait—"we have the preconditions for making 1989 the decisive year."[2]

"Perhaps not since Woodrow Wilson presented his Fourteen Points in 1918 or since Franklin Roosevelt and Winston Churchill promulgated

**Figure 6.1.** Gorbachev at the United Nations, December 1988. The General Secretary sets the stage for a year of revolutions. Courtesy of the United Nations.

the Atlantic Charter in 1941 has a world figure demonstrated the vision Mikhail Gorbachev displayed yesterday at the United Nations," read the editorial page of the *New York Times* the following day.[3] The incoming presidential administration of George Herbert Walker Bush was cautious yet encouraging. In the year of revolutions that followed, Gorbachev lived up to his vision of a new world order in 1989 as the Bush administration adapted to a rapidly changing environment with shrewdness and flexibility.

## Early Optimism

Hungary and Poland would test the two leaders' commitments and abilities in the early months of the Bush administration. Hungary was a country where change predated Gorbachev's proclamation of a new world order. Reforms tended to originate from the top. Dissatisfied with the performance of the longtime head of the Hungarian Socialist Workers Party, János Kádár, Gorbachev encouraged the younger Károly Grósz to take over in May 1988. "You should retire," Soviet Chairman of the Council of Ministers Nikolai Ryzhkov informed Kádár that spring.[4] Never having possessed the same cult of personality as a Nicolae Ceaușescu or an Erich Honecker, Kádár took Ryzhkov's advice. Kádár's ouster did not augur a dramatic shift. Lacking explicit instructions from Gorbachev, Grósz interpreted his promotion as a mandate to do more of what communist Hungary had already been doing. For much of the 1970s and 1980s, Kádár tolerated some independent thinking, did not imprison political opponents, and enjoyed a measure of popularity.[5] "There are no Marxists in the Institute of Sociology," a leading Hungarian sociologist quipped to an international meeting of academics in 1981.[6] The following year, the country joined the International Monetary Fund and the World Bank.[7] "Not capitalism—human nature," Kádár described Hungary's system to the American industrialist Armand Hammer.[8]

Grósz continued this pragmatic line. Before long, however, he found himself at odds with Ceaușescu. Fearing that the Romanian dictator aimed to clamp down on them, ethnic Hungarians began crossing over the border from Transylvania. After an August 1988 meeting, Grósz believed that they had reached a settlement; instead, Ceaușescu launched a publicity campaign trumpeting his defiance against "Hungary's intolerable interference in Romanian affairs."[9] Outflanked by the self-proclaimed "Genius of the Carpathians," Grósz made a series of economic concessions intended to shore up his standing at home. He signed off on measures that allowed foreign and domestic investors to purchase Hungarian companies. He brought new faces into the fold, among them Imre Pozsgay, a former culture minister who had called for political and economic liberalization several years earlier.[10] In a few years, Pozsgay told Western journalists, Hungary was to become "like Austria—or perhaps Sweden."[11] On November 24, 1988, Miklós Németh, a graduate of Harvard Business School, was appointed prime minister. The new Hungarian leadership sought to adapt the nation's political economy to share in the economic recovery of the countries west of it.

Grósz and Németh traveled to Moscow the following spring. "Now we are opening the way towards socialist pluralism," Gorbachev told Németh on March 3, 1989. Far from a "tragedy for the society," multiple opinions constituted a "real advantage." Németh agreed—yet why limit the exchange of ideas to a single-party system? "I see no difference between pluralism in a single-party system and in a multi-party system."[12] Németh probed cautiously. After the general secretary did not strenuously object, word found its way to the Hungarian foreign minister, Péter Várkonyi. "The Soviets are fully supportive" of Hungary's reforms, he told Secretary of State James Baker in Vienna on March 5, 1989.[13] The Soviet Union no longer reserved the right to intervene to rescue socialist regimes, Várkonyi publicly declared in London on March 17. The Brezhnev Doctrine, in other words, was "dead."[14]

The Hungarians found flexibility in Moscow. Gorbachev saw them as new thinkers cut from the same cloth as his own advisers. Later that March, Grósz again traveled to Moscow and broached a delicate subject. The country's evolving liberalism had led some Hungarians to reopen questions surrounding the tragedy of 1956. Were the events that had precipitated Soviet repression a counterrevolution or a rebellion? "The estimation of the 1956 events is entirely up to you," Gorbachev responded, confirming to many hopeful Hungarians that perhaps real change in the Kremlin had at last arrived.[15] Further changes advanced rapidly in Hungary. On June 16, 1989, some hundred thousand people gathered in Hero's Square to rebury Imre Nagy, the Hungarian leader executed for his role in the rebellion of 1956.[16] A month later, Németh declared that the government could no longer afford to pay for the vast electric border fence with Austria. In his meeting with Gorbachev that spring, he had alluded to a decision to "completely remove the electronic and technological defenses from the western and southern borders of Hungary." The Soviet leader had not objected.[17] On June 27, 1989, Németh and the new foreign minister, Gyula Horn, traveled to the border and dramatically cut sections of the fence.[18] Gorbachev did nothing to stop them.

In Poland, tensions eased slightly in the years immediately following the crisis period of 1980–1981, and Wojciech Jaruzelski lifted martial law in July

1983. The 1984 martyrdom of the popular priest Jerzy Popiełuszko at the hands of members of the Ministry of the Interior, as well as the rigged trials of the perpetrators one year later, however, reinvigorated the Polish Catholic Church's hostility toward the regime. Jaruzelski's government estimated that the number of priests openly "hostile to the state" more than doubled from 1983 to 1985. It hoped to curb the "threat" from the pulpit by launching a propaganda war against the Church. Accusing priests of fathering illegitimate children and engaging in pedophilia, the communists hoped to "roll back" the Catholic Church.[19]

They could not roll back Pope John Paul II. "Remember this: Christ will never agree to man being viewed only as a means of production, or agree to man viewing himself as such," he declared in Poland in June 1979. "He will not agree that man should be valued, measured, or evaluated only on this basis. Christ will never agree to that!"[20] The pontiff returned in 1983, just before the lifting of martial law, to meet with a beleaguered Lech Wałęsa. He implored the electrician and their fellow countrymen never to give up. "In the name of mankind and of humanity, the word 'solidarity' must be pronounced," the Pope proclaimed in front of an audience of ship workers, sailors, and fishermen in Gdansk in June 1987. "Today it fades away like the waves that extend across the world." The word *solidarity* "was uttered right here, in a new way and in a new context." The world cannot forget Solidarity, said the Pope. "This word is your pride."[21] Returning to Rome, he issued a decree calling for the "right of economic initiative" and denouncing any suppression of it under the pretenses of "equality."[22]

Pope John Paul II was perhaps the foremost enemy of communism in the world. He opposed it on spiritual, moral, and political grounds. He equated capitalism with freedom. Throughout the 1980s, his actions drew the support of the Reagan administration, which hoped to keep Solidarity alive by sending aid and providing moral support. Champions of these two men have written that they waged a "secret war" against communism. But it was not a war, and there was hardly anything secret about it.[23]

More consequential than U.S. rhetoric was the downward spiral to which the Polish economy returned in 1988. That April, in an effort to redress what historian Stephen Kotkin has called the regime's "crack cocaine–style borrowing from the West," Jaruzelski raised prices on most foods by some 40 percent.[24] The strikes that followed demonstrated Solidarity's renewed strength as well as Wałęsa's enduring popularity. On August 26, 1988, Jaruzelski reached out to his nemesis to propose a roundtable discussion to reconcile the communist regime with Solidarity. The opposition grew suspicious. Was Jaruzelski setting up Solidarity so that he could later blame them for Poland's ills? Ardent communists were also incensed; they retained the illusion that the people were on their side.

Television changed Polish history. On November 30, 1988, Alfred Miodo-wicz, head of the official Polish trade union, faced Wałęsa in a debate that was broadcast live all over the country. The communist veteran came off as arrogant and dismissive; the electrician was witty and implacable. "Let's give pluralism a chance," Wałęsa told an audience of 25 million Poles (in a country of 35 million). "I trust the people."[25] In the face of this televised humiliation of the communist leadership, Jaruzelski relented further. He set up a roundtable process in the spring of 1989 with the intent to share power with Solidarity. The fragile agreement that resulted called for two sets of elections: a lower house, or Sejm, in which 65 percent of the representatives were to be reserved for the communist government; and a Senate, in which 100 percent of the seats were to be openly contested. The plan was announced on April 4, 1989; elections were to be held two months later. As with Hungary, Gorbachev allowed the changes in Poland to play out, because they accorded with his call at the United Nations for a new world order.

## President Bush

President George H. W. Bush detected winds of change in Eastern Europe as he took office. He had no way of knowing where the changes were headed or at what point they might cease. His priority was to make sure they did not lead to widespread violence.

As a politician and leader, Bush did not resemble Ronald Reagan. He pledged, drolly, to try to hold "his charisma in check" and professed to lack "the vision thing."[26] "If you give me a ten, I'm going to send it back and say, 'Give me an eight,'" he told his speechwriters. "And you'll be lucky if I deliver like a six."[27] At times he spoke directly. "We know what works: freedom works. We know what's right: freedom is right." Other times, Bush sounded nothing like his predecessor. "We will always try to speak clearly," he stated during his inaugural address, "for candor is a compliment; but subtlety, too, is good and has its place."[28]

Bush brought to the White House a sterling résumé—congressman, ambassador to the United Nations, U.S. envoy to China, director of the Central Intelligence Agency, and, for the previous eight years, vice president. His father, Prescott Bush, one of the "wise men" of the Eastern establishment who had surrounded FDR and Truman, a Republican in the mold of Henry Stimson, Robert Lovett, and John McCloy, had imbued in his son a sense that duty to country comes before politics. George Bush had been the youngest aviator in the navy during World War II; he was the last veteran of that conflict to serve as president.

"For the common man and the intellectual alike, the direction of change today is not leftward," Bush proclaimed on the campaign trail. "The gloom of the West, the 'malaise' we heard so much about just a few years ago, is in retreat, replaced by a healthy confidence in our ability to cope, to change, and to grow." It was an assessment not necessarily shared by American intellectuals as 1989 began. Yet Bush remained optimistic. "If we continue on this course," he stated, "the revolutionary concept of freedom embodied in Western democracy will surely prevail."[29] While Bush aspired to prevail, he also understood that 1989 in Eastern Europe was a time and place for caution and subtlety. Whether change occurred peacefully depended on how the Kremlin reacted. Bush knew that verbal pronouncements could not change reality. He was not the person who had employed the phrase "evil empire" in 1983 or spoke of "another time, another era" in 1988. He was not a bellicose Cold Warrior, and he had not, in the course of the 1980s, become a naive optimist. "The Cold War isn't over," Bush told a reporter in the wake of Reagan's visit to Red Square.[30]

While the Soviet Union was changing, he told a joint session of Congress on February 9, 1989 "prudence and common sense dictate that we try to understand the full meaning of the change going on there, review our policies, and then proceed with caution."[31] Gorbachev's reforms notwithstanding, the "fundamental facts remain that the Soviets retain a very powerful military machine in the service of objectives which are still too often in conflict with ours." Moderation needed to be championed, illusions to be put aside. "So, let us take the new openness seriously, but let's also be realistic."[32]

The man Bush chose to be his national security advisor, Brent Scowcroft, saw plenty of Soviet objectives in conflict with American ones. "I think the Cold War is not over," Scowcroft told a *Washington Post* reporter shortly after returning to the position he had held during the Ford administration.[33] The Red Army was still casting a pall over central Europe; Soviet military aid was still flowing to Cuba and Nicaragua; a vast Soviet nuclear arsenal was still threatening the free world. "I was suspicious of Gorbachev's motives and skeptical of his prospects," Scowcroft later recalled. Were Gorbachev anything but a committed Marxist, he reasoned, Moscow's inner circle would have chosen someone else to lead the Soviet Union.[34] Scowcroft "believed that Gorbachev's goal was to restore dynamism to a socialist political and economic system and revitalize the Soviet Union domestically and internationally to compete with the West." This objective did not make him a friend of the United States. If anything, Gorbachev's popularity in the West made him "potentially more dangerous than his predecessors, each of whom, through some aggressive move, had saved the West from the dangers of its own wishful thinking about the Soviet Union."[35] The Soviet invasion of Afghanistan, according to this thinking, revealed the truth to an American public accustomed to détente. Unlike Brezhnev, Gorbachev had done nothing to shock the American people in a negative way—yet.

Scowcroft believed that enthusiasm on the part of Reagan and the men and women around him had outpaced sober calculations of U.S. national interest. The previous administration's "willingness to declare an end to the Cold War, without taking into consideration what that would require," troubled him. So did talk of eliminating nuclear weapons. However horrible, these weapons "were an indispensable element in the U.S. strategy of keeping the Soviets at bay, a compensation for their enormous superiority in conventional forces."[36] Scowcroft thus seconded Bush's inclination to be cautious about embracing Gorbachev. He ordered a comprehensive review of U.S.–Soviet relations. After a draft Soviet strategy review from the State Department, he entrusted Robert Blackwill, a highly regarded foreign service officer in charge of European and Soviet Affairs at the NSC, as well as a protégé of his own, Condoleezza Rice, to embark on a new study. Until its completion, Scowcroft ruled out an early summit, which he figured would only provide Gorbachev a propaganda victory.[37]

Scowcroft and Bush wanted to buy time. Not entirely sure how to proceed, they allowed former secretary of state Henry Kissinger to reassert himself at the highest levels. On January 17, 1989, Kissinger met Gorbachev in Moscow and spoke in terms of realpolitik. "I have said repeatedly that you do not change the seventy-year history of the Soviet Union, the four hundred year history of Russia, and the two hundred year history of the United States," Kissinger told Gorbachev. "If there is a conflict between our two countries, we will lose, and others will benefit." American foreign policy tended to be missionary in character, Kissinger went on to say; Soviet foreign policy, defensive. The two sides needed to move beyond these fundamental differences and beyond the "details" of arms control. The new administration in Washington was not interested in challenging Soviet "security interests," nor was Bush as allured by SDI as his predecessor.[38] Gorbachev "was prepared to send Dobrynin to the United States or receive Scowcroft in Moscow," Kissinger reported back to Washington. "Or an emissary could come if Scowcroft was unavailable. A note should be sent via the Soviet UN Ambassador, preferably from Scowcroft, although in order to preserve the privacy of the channel it would be best if the outside envelope were from me."[39]

Kissinger's ambitions probably foundered the moment that the new secretary of state, James Baker, underlined the words "would be best if the outside envelope were from me."[40] Baker, who owed nothing to Kissinger, was not about to share power. Like his longtime tennis doubles partner, George Bush, Baker had spent eight years as a "moderate" in the Reagan administration, nearly every day of which conservatives had viewed him with suspicion. During his confirmation hearings, critics pounced on Baker for his lack of traditional foreign policy experience and his background as a maestro of political campaigns. Yet Baker was no less qualified than George Shultz. Both men had graduated from Princeton, joined the Navy, and served as secretary of the treasury. Both men understood the principle articulated by Dean Acheson that a critical role of any secretary of state was to marshal and sustain domestic political will for foreign policy objectives. They believed in negotiations backed by strength and in the possibility of reaching a deal. And both men forged a personal bond with Eduard Shevardnadze.

In his Princeton days, Baker wrote an undergraduate thesis about the provisional government led by Alexander Kerensky that briefly ruled Russia between the collapse of the Romanov dynasty and the Bolshevik Revolution.[41] At the beginning of 1989, he joined Scowcroft in cautioning against wishful thinking. "Progress in arms control, human rights, [and] Afghanistan" were "reasons to be hopeful," read his notes for a January 23, 1989, cabinet meeting. "But, realism demands prudence"—despite the tremendous changes since 1981, when Baker served as chief of staff to President Reagan, the Soviet Union remained "a heavily-armed superpower hostile to American values and interests."[42] Baker was tough yet open-minded. The Soviets "have to make hard choices," he wrote Bush in February 1989. "We do Gorbachev no favors when we make it easier to avoid choices. ... He made a choice in arms control because there was a need for it."[43] The Bush administration's penchant for caution drew criticism, nearly from his first day in office, for being out of step, as changes in the Soviet Union seemed undeniable to so many observers. Reagan himself indicated in an interview that spring that he felt Bush was being too cautious in his dealings with Gorbachev.[44]

The patrician Bush would not say so, either publicly or privately, but Reagan had left behind a messy inheritance. The massive federal budget deficits that resulted from Reaganomics compelled the new president to do more with less.[45] Concern over the federal deficit reverberated throughout the 1988 presidential campaign. "Read my lips: no new taxes," Bush asserted at the Republican Convention. Yet promotion of liberty in Eastern Europe surely bore a hefty price tag. "A political solution in Poland cannot endure without economic assistance from the West," read a proposal by financier George Soros that wound up on the desk of Condoleezza Rice. "Indeed, both sides are entering into a social contract in the firm expectation of such assistance."[46] Emotions were running high in Poland, Bush acknowledged to Helmut Kohl on June 23, 1989, but it was "important to act carefully and to avoid pouring money down a rat-hole."[47]

Reagan also bequeathed to Bush a vision of the world that the latter did not regard as secure. Bush believed—as did Scowcroft and every other adviser surrounding him in 1989—that nuclear weapons served as an indispensable deterrent and should not be abolished. So long as the Red Army loomed over Central and Western Europe, these weapons protected the peace. Bush did not oppose strategic arms reductions, but he wanted to proceed carefully. He did not wish to antagonize the Navy, which balked at proposed inspections of submarines as part of a START agreement. And he knew that conservatives would insist that any arms deal be accompanied by unrestricted research on SDI. Although he supported missile defense, Bush was skeptical. He did not see how it could replace the doctrine of Mutual Assured Destruction, and he was not certain that the government had the resources to afford the technological research and development.

The president's position on nuclear weapons accordingly drew criticism from the Kremlin. Gorbachev saw it as a reproach to the spirit of Reykjavik. Simply by stepping away from a vision of nuclear abolition, Bush was bound to disappoint the Soviet leader. Whatever else the president could have done in the first few months in office, it probably would not have changed Moscow's basic sense of aggravation at the loss of the understanding and momentum achieved with the Reagan administration.

A former head of the CIA, Bush appreciated that American intelligence services could not decide quite what to make of Gorbachev. "Some analysts see current policy changes as largely tactical, driven by the need for breathing space from the competition," read a National Intelligence Estimate titled "Soviet Policy Toward the West: The Gorbachev Challenge." Adherents to this view "believe the ideological imperatives of Marxism-Leninism and its hostility toward capitalist countries are enduring. They point to previous failures of reform and the transient nature of past 'détentes.' They judge that there is a serious risk of Moscow returning to traditionally combative behavior when the hoped for gains in economic performance are achieved."[48] The same National Intelligence Estimate went on to say, "Other analysts believe Gorbachev's policies reflect a fundamental rethinking of national interests and ideology as well as more tactical considerations. They argue that ideological tenets of Marxism-Leninism such as class conflict and capitalist-socialist enmity are being revised. They consider the withdrawal from Afghanistan and the shift toward tolerance of power sharing in Eastern Europe to be historic shifts in the Soviet definition of national interest. They judge that Gorbachev's changes are likely to have sufficient momentum to produce lasting shifts in Soviet behavior."[49]

For all the billions of dollars poured into U.S. intelligence services, in other words, their assessment of Soviet behavior provided no resolution for policy choices. Even the most optimistic assessment went only so far as "lasting shifts in Soviet behavior" as a prospective goal. The mixed messages reinforced Bush's inclination to be cautious. Members of his administration did not consider radical nuclear arms reductions desirable, could not achieve consensus that Gorbachev meant the things he said, and could not guarantee that a reformed and strengthened Soviet Union would not rekindle Cold War tensions. "As the Cold War was ending in 1989," recalls Robert Zoellick, perhaps Secretary of State James Baker's closest adviser during this period, "U.S. officials were at a great disadvantage compared to subsequent scholars: we could not be sure that the Cold War was in fact ending!"[50]

Nor did they sense that the administration was negotiating from a position of political strength. Unlike Reagan's first administration, Bush faced a Senate filled with Democrats and a House of Representatives shorn of many of the "boll weevil" Democrats who had supported Reagan's arms buildup and tax cuts. Those who remained were particularly bitter over the nasty campaign Bush had conducted in the 1988 presidential election. It had been a far cry from "Morning in America" four years earlier, a contest in which candidate Bush had acted rather unlike Vice President Bush.[51]

The president's team recognized political reality. "Protocol and prudence had dictated that I consult with members of my own party first," Baker later wrote of his efforts to craft a new policy toward Nicaragua. "But as a practical matter, I understood that the support of the Democrats who were the majority was more critical."[52] So did the seasoned observers of American politics who traveled to Moscow in the first months of the administration. They told Gorbachev's aides that the new president did not enjoy the same popularity as Reagan and did not possess an abundance of political capital. "He has a delicate position with Congress," West German Chancellor Helmut Kohl told Alexander Yakovlev in January.[53] The new president's "position is very difficult," Senator Edward Kennedy's aide Larry Horowitz told Vadim Zagladin later that year. "He would like to make progress in arms control," but his own base was unhappy with his domestic legislation and his change in policy toward Central America. If anything, Horowitz went on to say, the Democrats in Congress were acting "as his real allies."[54]

Democrats were not Bush's allies, however. As if to flex their political muscles, Senate Democrats voted down Bush's nominee for secretary of defense, John Tower, notwithstanding his four terms in that same body. Bush's second choice, Richard Cheney, surmised of Gorbachev on NBC's *Meet the Press*: "If I had to guess today, I would guess he ultimately would fail. That is to say, he will not be able to reform the Soviet economy to turn it into an efficient modern society."[55] The administration swiftly distanced itself from Cheney. But the original comments and subsequent denials fueled suspicions that the Bush administration wanted Gorbachev to "stew in his own juices." From Moscow, Ambassador Jack Matlock again attempted to nudge a president toward negotiating with the Soviets. "The four-part agenda which we have successfully pursued over the past six years ... has been successful in the sense that it has finally produced significant Soviet positive movement" in bilateral relations, regional problems, arms reductions, and human rights, he wrote in one of three cables that February. "It has not yet exhausted its full potential, however, since much remains to be done in all four areas."[56]

Matlock tailored his message to the so-called realists in the new administration. "We of course have many specific interests which we must pursue," he went on to say, "but no long-term goals are more important than the transformation of the Soviet political system into one with effective structural constraints on the use of military force outside Soviet borders, along with the evolution of the Soviet military machine into one suitable primarily for defensive purposes." Many doubted whether, absent a "total collapse of the system," this would ever occur. Perhaps collapse might happen someday in the future, Matlock acknowledged; in the near term, "for the first time in at least sixty years," political reformation and military restraint were "consistent with avowed Soviet aspirations." The administration "would be remiss if we did not reinforce incentives for Soviet movement in this direction."[57]

Bush's advisers detected in Matlock's cable the language of Reaganism. They wanted more specificity. As Bush and Scowcroft waited for the results of the strategic review, they pondered alternatives to the ambitious dream of a world without nuclear weapons. In March, Scowcroft considered a public declaration to call on both the Soviets and the United States to withdraw all conventional forces from Europe.[58] Blackwill talked his boss out of this proposal, which he feared might undercut America's commitment to its European allies. Blackwill wanted to focus on Germany instead. "Today, the top priority for American foreign policy in Europe should be the fate of the Federal Republic of Germany," began a memo he and Philip Zelikow crafted for Scowcroft on March 20, 1989.[59] Within a year, Kohl faced reelection—a contest many expected him to lose. The prospect of the SPD's return to power jeopardized U.S. plans to modernize its Lance short-range tactical nuclear missile and, more broadly, the cohesion of NATO amidst Gorbymania on the streets of Western Europe. Scowcroft contributed to Blackwill and Zelikow's memo by linking Kohl's reelection to a "vision of Europe's future" that included "an approach to the 'German question.'" He advised the president to "send a clear signal to the Germans that we are ready to do more if the political climate allows." These ideas intrigued the president, who apparently wrote back to Scowcroft that he had read it "with interest!"[60]

Bush decided that spring to shift the focus of U.S.-Soviet diplomacy from nuclear disarmament to the long-term future of Europe with the fate of Germany potentially on the table. Western Europe appeared on a path toward economic and political integration, yet there was tremendous anxiety. What of the huge Soviet army that remained the largest force on the continent? Would a unified Western Europe be responsible for its own defense? These were the types of questions the Bush team thought that the Reagan administration, in its exuberance to reduce nuclear weapons and take Gorbachev at his word, had neglected. Indeed, Gorbachev had pledged to withdraw half a million troops from central and eastern Europe. "Even with these reductions," Bush wrote in a February 16, 1989, response to a Japanese newspaper, "the Warsaw Pact has far to go to correct the conventional forces imbalance in Europe."[61]

On May 15, 1989, Baker's deputy, Robert Zoellick, sent his boss a memo in advance of the upcoming NATO summit urging him to enunciate the "common values of the West"—democratization, market systems, individual rights, and free associations—in the context of drawing "Eastern Europe and the USSR into the 'community of nations.'" The goal should be to end "the division of Europe on our terms," to contrast "common values of the West" with "Gorbachev's more narrow, territorial concept of the Common European House."[62]

Zoellick saw Germany as "the real opportunity to get ahead of the curve and to exceed expectations." Official NATO documents dating back to the 1950s stated German reunification as a long-term goal. "And there's no doubt the topic is coming back," he wrote. "The real question is whether Gorbachev will grab it first." Or the Germans might grab it themselves— "especially after Honecker passes from the scene." Zoellick advocated an initiative built upon the "tear down the Wall" rhetoric, one that would include "freer and more open links between the two Germanies, in the areas of communications, flow of information, movement of people, aviation (building on our Berlin Air proposal so as to include German participation), and the environment." Why not call for a Berlin Olympics in 2000, he asked, where athletes from "the two Germanies" could compete on one team?[63]

Bush was already speaking out more forcefully. Three days before Zoellick's memo, the president delivered a speech in College Station at Texas A&M University. "Wise men—Truman and Eisenhower, Vandenberg and Rayburn, Marshall, Acheson, and Kennan—crafted the strategy of containment," he told the graduating Aggies. "They believed that the Soviet Union, denied the easy course of expansion, would turn inward and address the contradictions of its inefficient, repressive, and inhumane system. And they were right—the Soviet Union is now publicly facing this hard reality. Containment worked."[64] Opportunity beckoned the United States to go further. "Our goal is bold," Bush stated, "more ambitious than any of my predecessors could have thought possible. Our review indicates that 40 years of perseverance have brought us a precious opportunity, and now it is time to move beyond containment to a new policy for the 1990s—one that recognizes the full scope of change taking place around the world and in the Soviet Union itself." Bush raised the stakes from containing Soviet expansionism to something new: "We seek the integration of the Soviet Union into the community of nations." This could be achieved, Bush went on to say, if the Soviets reduced arms, tore down the Iron Curtain, gave up meddling in the Third World once and for all, expanded human rights and pluralism, and joined the international fight against the drug trade and environmental degradation.[65]

Two weeks later, Bush took this message to Europe. He now incorporated some of Zoellick's suggestions. The administration's "policy is to move beyond containment," he declared on May 31, 1989, in Mainz, Germany. "For 40 years, the seeds of democracy in Eastern Europe lay dormant, buried under the frozen tundra of the Cold War. And for 40 years, the world has waited for the Cold War to end. And decade after decade, time after time, the flowering human spirit withered from the chill of conflict and oppression; and again, the world waited. But the passion for freedom cannot be denied forever. The world has waited long enough. The time is right. Let Europe be whole and free."[66]

Tentatively, Bush was laying out the concrete terms on which the Cold War might end: when Europe was whole and freedom triumphed. And "the momentum for freedom does not just come from the printed word or the transistor or the television screen," he proclaimed in Mainz, "it comes from a single powerful idea: democracy." In other words, the Cold War could end when the Soviets withdrew from the GDR and Eastern Europe, when those countries became democracies. Bush hoped this process could occur peacefully, yet history gave no assurance that this was possible. Pressures had welled up against communist regimes in 1953, 1956, 1968, and 1981 only to be met by force. American presidents had tripped over themselves extolling the superiority of democratic capitalism. And yet, for forty years, the Cold War had persisted.

The bottom line was that only the Kremlin could ensure that the end of the Cold War happened peacefully. "OK, so long as the programs do not smack of fomenting revolution," Scowcroft wrote on a USIA proposal for a "democratic dialogue" with Eastern Europe in June.[67] At the same time, the Bush administration had no desire to broker a deal that conceded continued Soviet domination of Eastern Europe for peaceful liberalization. Facing a hostile congress and distrusting conservatives, Bush could not afford to be seen as concocting "Yalta II." His priorities were to insure that reforms in Eastern Europe continued peacefully; to broach the German question delicately; to seek conventional arms reductions; and to respond intelligently, imaginatively, and swiftly to events that no one could predict.

## Early Warning

Events on the other side of the world provided the Bush administration reasons for concern. In 1989, China commemorated not only the two-hundredth anniversary of the French Revolution (the "co-opted" proletarian revolution) and the seventieth anniversary of the cultural and spiritual revival after the humiliation of the Versailles Treaty (the "May 4th movement") but also, most importantly, the fortieth anniversary of Mao's proclamation of the People's Republic of China. The regime planned a number of festivities scheduled for May. Deng Xiaoping invited Gorbachev to celebrate these anniversaries and mark the apex of the Chinese leader's fifty-year political odyssey.

A bolt out of the blue struck the People's Republic of China on April 15, 1989, when Hu Yaobang died of a sudden heart attack. Three years earlier, Deng had dismissed Hu from his post as general secretary of the Chinese Community Party for taking too soft a line in response to a student protest movement. Hu remained incredibly popular among Chinese students, many of whom saw his death as an opportunity to revive a movement for political reform.[68] The CCP leadership was divided over how to proceed. The reform-minded Zhao Ziyang predicted that students would return to their campuses after the April 22 memorial scheduled for Hu. Premier Li Peng and other hardliners detected "well-planned and well-organized" activities whose underlying purpose was to destroy socialism and the Communist

Party. The roundtable processes under way in Eastern Europe weighed on their minds. "Indeed," the historian Chen Jian has written, "it was Deng's and his fellow party elders' determination not to allow Solidarity's story of success in Poland to be replayed in China that opened the door leading to the Tiananmen tragedy."[69]

On May 14, 1989, Gorbachev arrived in Beijing. Accompanying him was a sizable contingent of newspaper and television journalists from the West. Members of the press came to China to witness the first official visit from a Soviet leader in thirty years and to gauge the possibility of a rapprochement between these two countries. Instead, they reported on hundreds of thousands of students holding demonstrations and disrupting events Deng and Gorbachev planned to attend. "Young people besieged the building [in which they stayed] chanting 'Gorbachev! Gorbachev!'" Shevardnadze later recalled. "They demanded that Gorbachev speak with them. It was ruled out. We had to leave to Beijing immediately."[70] On May 15, Gorbachev called his adviser Vadim Medvedev in Moscow to report a "sticky situation."[71]

The media coverage generated by the students was unprecedented. When millions of Chinese students poured out their grief for the revered Zhou Enlai in 1976, the ruling Gang of Four had censored any mention of it. Thirteen years later, amidst the sea of foreign press and within range of satellite broadcasts, the PRC could still hide the truth from much of the country but not the rest of the world. Indeed, after Gorbachev left, Western journalists stayed. During the period between the declaration of martial law on May 20 and the crackdown on June 4, members of the press perceived a revolution unfolding before their eyes. So did the outside world. Surely one of the most evocative images ever captured on film was that of a lone Chinese man standing in front of an approaching column of tanks. Yet sympathetic protests did not spread throughout that vast country.

The Chinese government's actions galvanized world opinion against the PRC. Back in the United States, Congress unanimously passed a resolution sponsored by Rep. Nancy Pelosi to cut off all exchange programs with China. The reports of violence troubled Bush, as did what he viewed as the knee-jerk responses from Pelosi and others. "The reports from China are still crazy," the president wrote in his diary. He did not believe the number of casualties the newscasters projected. "There are rumors that 'Li Peng has been shot,' and rumors that 'Deng was dead,'" he wrote. "All of this tells me to be cautious, and be calm."[72] Bush thought that he understood China as well as any of his "experts." From his time as de facto ambassador to that country in 1973, he knew its current leaders on a first-name basis. "While angry rhetoric might be temporarily satisfying to some, I believed it would deeply hurt our efforts in the long term," Bush later recalled. "The Chinese are extremely sensitive to anything that might be interpreted as interference in their internal affairs, the legacy of many decades of damaging foreign intrusion."[73]

Bush feared that the Chinese students did not know what they had gotten themselves into. He welcomed the spread of liberty to communist countries, but change needed to happen gradually. Television cameras and heightened emotions stirred by Hu's death, Gorbachev's visit, and the dizzying array of anniversaries had inspired protestors to take undue risks. Similar circumstances in Eastern Europe could easily lead to further tragedy. "We Are With You," read the banner at a student demonstration in front of the Chinese embassy in Budapest.[74] This anxiety weighed on Bush's mind as he traveled to Eastern Europe in July. In Poland, he faced a delicate assignment. After Solidarity trounced the Polish Union Workers' Party in the June elections, its leaders figured that it needed Jaruzelski to remain head of state to prevent civil war breaking out between the old communist elites and the supporters of the new majority party. Bush shouldered the burden of convincing Jaruzelski to help Solidarity—which the Polish general had spent a decade trying to destroy—to dismantle communism.

During this time, Bush drew lessons from Tiananmen Square and applied them to Eastern Europe. He needed to deal with the forces of order, to appeal to the patriotism of the communists in power in Eastern Europe, and to convince them that they had a stake in reform. He needed to remain cautious about careless words that might incite violence and to ignore the recriminations of political opponents bound to criticize him in any case.

Bush sensed the intensity of the emotions; indeed, he shared them. When he arrived in Budapest on July 11, 1989, he stepped in front of the crowd and tore up his speech. He spoke from the heart: stick with the reformers, and do not give up. The next day, the president nearly wept when Németh presented him a plaque containing a piece of barbed wire from the dismantled border fence.[75] Yet Bush's emotions reinforced his sense of caution. He liked Németh and the other communist reformers, but his meeting with the noncommunist opposition did not go well.[76] Were these men really capable of leading Hungary down a better path? Perhaps, Bush surmised, it was more prudent to support slower reforms—even if that meant keeping the communists in power.

## Gorbachev's Frustration

Bush's penchant for caution annoyed Gorbachev, as did his speeches in College Station, Mainz, and Budapest. Gorbachev preferred Reagan's conception of "beyond containment": a world without nuclear weapons. He remembered Bush's candor following the INF agreement in 1987—the forthcoming presidential campaign was to feature tough talk about the Soviets, but Moscow should pay it no heed. "Pavel, I know that you could not take notes, but try to write a record of that conversation with Bush in the car," Gorbachev told interpreter Pavel Palazchenko.[77] The campaign indeed had been hot, but a visit from a well-regarded Democratic congressman in August 1988 led the Soviets to believe that a victory by either candidate meant continuity.[78] After Bush won, Dobrynin confided in Baker: "We're happy to be dealing with you guys. You are known quantities."[79]

In the time between the election and inauguration, Gorbachev attempted to seize the initiative. He regarded his UN speech in December 1988 as crucial. "Most of all," he later recalled, "I wanted to show the world community" that it was "entering a period of history when the old principles for relations between states, based on competition, gave way to co-development and co-creation."[80] "We wanted to show in words and deeds that we no longer considered the United States and the West to be our enemies," Shevardnadze later described the UN speech. "And we would also cease to be enemies of the United States."[81] But Gorbachev did not think his message was getting through to Washington. On Governor's Island in December 1988, shortly after he delivered the UN speech, Gorbachev beseeched the president-elect not to get hung up on whether perestroika would succeed. "I think that even Jesus Christ could not answer your question definitively," Gorbachev mused. "I can only guarantee that the Soviet Union is irrevocably embarked upon the path toward economic and political change."[82]

The deadly earthquake that struck Armenia on December 7, 1988, compelled Gorbachev to cut his New York visit short. When he convened the Politburo at the end of the month, the Soviet leader was weary. He did not like reading about the *Washington Times* and the Heritage Foundation calling on the new administration to sit on its hands. "The Soviet Union, so they say, as well as other socialist countries, have no way out ... [and] will give up its positions step by step."[83] He complained about Russian-language radio broadcasts in foreign countries, where "the emphasis is clearly on the difficulties of perestroika, on growing obstacles to the process in the economy, in relations among nationalities, in the process of democratization and glasnost."[84]

No one needed to remind Gorbachev of these challenges. Economic difficulties threatened to derail everything. The new thinkers surrounding him began to lose confidence. "The General Secretary doesn't focus on the issue, entrusting the job entirely to government officials who are not very competent in the financial field," Deputy Foreign Minister Anatoly Adamishin confided to his diary on New Year's Day. "They, in turn, don't heed any of the independent experts. The situation is close to a crisis: the gap between salaries paid to the workers and the availability of goods that could be bought for this money is widening. Unsatisfied demand is near to 80 billion rubles [$48.5 billion]."[85] "In three years of perestroika," Nikolai Ryzhkov estimated that "government spending exceeded budget revenue by 133 billion rubles [$82.5 billion]." Some 77 billion rubles ($47.75 billion) in losses resulted from the decline in oil prices and the reduced sales of vodka. An industrial surplus of 10 billion rubles ($6.2 billion) was offset by a loss of 15 billion rubles ($9.3 billion) per year—more than at any time since World War II.[86]

Still, Gorbachev pressed forward. "The essence of [our] change is that we want to depart from administrative command methods of economic management, and head toward greater decentralization ... and to use methods characteristic of a market economy," he told a group of British businessmen on April 6, 1989.[87] And here was the difference between China and the Soviet Union: Moscow's political changes accompanied economic reforms. Soviet citizens went to the polls that spring to elect a Congress of People's Deputies, which then chose a new Supreme Soviet—the first democratically elected body in Moscow since 1917. The results of these elections thrust into the spotlight an assortment of political neophytes. They included an ethnically German tractor operator from Kazakhstan who feared that the new body might turn around and overthrow Gorbachev. For his part, Chernyaev did not consider these fears unjustified. Gorbachev's response was to order that the proceedings of the Central Committee be published.[88]

In February 1989, the last Soviet troops withdrew from Afghanistan. There was no way for Gorbachev to atone fully for Soviet sins in Afghanistan, but he was trying. He felt, however, that the new American administration was not acknowledging his efforts. He told Henry Kissinger that he did not understand why the Jackson-Vanik amendment, which restricted trade with the Soviet Union, was still on the books, even after Gorbachev had liberalized his country and allowed many Jews to emigrate. "We are waiting for a signal from the administration," Gorbachev told Kissinger.[89]

When Gorbachev finally met James Baker in Moscow in May 1989, he left the meeting disappointed. Baker brought with him Robert Gates, the deputy national security advisor whose skepticism of Gorbachev's motives was well known to the Kremlin. "Whatever Baker's intention was in bringing him to the Kremlin to sit in on the meeting with Gorbachev," Palazchenko later recalled, "the effect was not good."[90] Neither was that of Baker's message: the United States intended to modernize the Lance missile, whose range of just under 500 kilometers excluded it from the INF Treaty. "We believe that a minimum number of nuclear weapons is essential to our strategy of flexible response, which ensures the preservation of peace in Europe," Baker told the Soviet leader. The secretary of state understood the "political appeal" of a "triple zero option." Yet progress could occur only when the Soviets reevaluated its massive conventional forces and decided, "We are ready to reduce our superiority."[91]

Gorbachev and his team suspected that the Americans either wanted to see the Soviet Union suffer or did not care. While Washington operated on the time horizon of a presidential administration, Moscow had only urgency. Implementing perestroika and constructing a new world order, in Gorbachev's mind, could not be postponed. "We probably have no more than two to three years to prove that socialism as formulated by Lenin can work," Yakovlev warned in a speech in December 1988. The failure of perestroika would likely lead to "a triumphant, aggressive, and avenging conservatism."[92] Gorbachev reiterated this concern. "We are walking on a razor blade," he told Vadim Medvedev the day of Kissinger's visit in January.[93] Later that month, he asked Yakovlev to coordinate with different agencies and think tanks to draft and submit reports on contingencies that might arise in Eastern and Central Europe.

"Crisis symptoms are visible in all spheres of public life inside the countries as well as in relations among them," read one of the reports. "In the economy the intensity of these symptoms varies from a slowdown of economic growth, a widening social and technological gap with the West, a gradual worsening of shortages in domestic markets and the growth of external debt (GDR, Czechoslovakia, Bulgaria) to a real threat of economic collapse (Yugoslavia, Poland)." (Of particular concern were the problem of inflation, the potential for 1920s-style "hyperinflation," and the prevalence of a "shadow economy" and accompanying corruption.)[94] Yakovlev prescribed that Moscow coopt the forces of reform in these countries. This was becoming increasingly difficult. The arrest of playwright and dissident Václav Havel had made him "a national hero," said one of Vadim Zagladin's friends in the Czech foreign ministry. "This is a priceless gift for the West."[95] Still, the priority Yakovlev set was to avoid the use of force should Czechoslovakia attempt to exit the Soviet Bloc. "These memoranda preached to the converted," writes Vladislav Zubok; Yakovlev, Shevardnadze, and Chernyaev were all disinclined to repeat the example of Czechoslovakia in 1968.[96]

Gorbachev did not want a repeat of 1968. He sensed fissures in the communist world, from Cuba to North Korea.[97] He was horrified when protestors clashed with Soviet troops on the streets of Tbilisi on April 9, 1989, leaving twenty Georgians dead. From now on, he told the Politburo on May

11, 1989, "use of force is excluded." It was not acceptable in foreign policy and "even more inadmissible against our own peoples."[98] The images beamed out of China that June agitated Gorbachev. So did the response of the communist "friends." Ceaușescu clamored for a Chinese approach in Eastern Europe, Gorbachev told Kohl on June 14, 1989; that was unacceptable. Such behavior did not befit the Soviet leader's conception of how Europeans should act. "It is certainly strange that this kind of family clan would be established in the center of civilized Europe, in a state with rich historical traditions," Gorbachev told the West German leader. One "could imagine something like that to emerge somewhere else, like it has in [North] Korea, but here, right next to us—it is such a primitive phenomenon."[99] Yet Gorbachev's own reforms led to unintended and sometimes threatening consequences. In May, an anti-Semitic group named Pamyat ("Memory") exploited glasnost to insinuate that perestroika was a Jewish plot; it emerged just as another group, Memorial, organized one hundred thousand people to rally in Moscow, many of whom supported an increasingly popular line of Russian nationalism.[100] Its chief proponent, Boris Yeltsin, demoted in late 1987 after criticizing Gorbachev, won a seat in the Congress of People's Deputies.

Tensions long kept at bay found their way to the fore. From the Caucasus to the Baltics, ethnic nationalism threatened to engulf Soviet socialist republics in separatism and violence. Nagorno-Karabakh, an ethnically Armenian enclave landlocked and fully within Azerbaijan, demanded either some form of autonomy or union with Armenia. In neighboring Georgia, the prospect of more violence weighed heavily on the minds of Gorbachev's team—Shevardnadze's above all. Far on the other side of Gorbachev's Stavropol, nationalists in Estonia and Lithuania began speaking openly about independence from the Soviet Union.

Just before Gorbachev's trip to the FRG, a railway accident in Bashkiria, caused by an explosion of a ruptured natural gas pipeline, killed hundreds and galvanized the nation.[101] The next month, a miners' strike broke out in West Siberia, further compounding economic difficulties.[102] Demoralization set in. "Inside me, depression and alarm are growing [about] the sense of crisis of the Gorbachevian idea," Chernyaev confided in his diary. "He has no concept of where we are going. His declaration about socialist values, the ideals of October, as he begins to tick them off, sound like irony ... behind them—emptiness."[103]

Amidst these setbacks, Gorbachev reiterated his theme of a common European home. The idea of a united Europe renewed his confidence and buoyed his spirits. On July 6, 1989, he delivered an impassioned speech to the Parliament of Europe in Strasbourg, France. "Victor Hugo said that the day would come when you, France, you, Russia, you, Italy, you, England, you, Germany—all of you, all the nations of the continent—will, without losing your distinguished features and your splendid distinctiveness, merge inseparably into some high society and form a European brotherhood." That day beckoned. Talk of European integration sounded a lot like a "common European home," his own idea "born out of the realization of new realities, of our realization of the fact that the linear continuation of the path, along which inter-European relations have developed until the last quarter of the twentieth century, is no longer consonant with these realities."[104]

"Differences between states cannot be eliminated," Gorbachev acknowledged. But competition needed to be relegated to each side's attempts to create "better material and spiritual conditions of life for people." Because perestroika was ultimately bound to succeed, Gorbachev proclaimed, "the Soviet Union will be in a position to take full part in such an honest, equal and constructive competition." Notwithstanding his country's shortcomings, "we know full well the strong points of our social system which follow from its essential characteristics."[105]

Gorbachev's litany of promises struck many as naive. Cautious members of the Bush administration had heard similar things from Leonid Brezhnev, Andrei Gromyko, and others who pledged peaceful coexistence. Scowcroft did not think Gorbachev was another Brezhnev, but he considered the timing of Gorbachev's disarmament proposals to be suspect. When Gorbachev announced after meeting with Baker that he would unilaterally reduce short-range nuclear weapons, Scowcroft did not take him seriously. Nor did he think that Gorbachev would ever allow East Germany to leave the Soviet Bloc peacefully. Even Pavel Palazchenko, Gorbachev's interpreter and confidante, remained skeptical. "I had friends in Eastern Europe," he later recalled, "and I knew that culturally and psychologically they did not belong in the quasi-Soviet system. But even many people my age were doubtful that Eastern Europe could just be allowed to go its own way. What about our security? And, some said, we won the war and there were millions of our soldiers buried in the soil of Eastern Europe. Had that been in vain?"[106]

Immediately after the Strasbourg speech, Gorbachev traveled to Bucharest to meet with military leaders of the Warsaw Pact. Western politicians were speaking about the Cold War being over, Gorbachev told them. Perhaps they were correct; perhaps "we are talking about the end of a period that has lasted over forty years, [and] about the beginning of a transition to a new international order."[107] Relaxation of tensions proceeded "in the favorable political atmosphere that was created by the process of the renewal of socialism." Cold

War institutions needed to be reconfigured to reflect new realities. The time had come for the Warsaw Pact to transform itself "from a military-political alliance into a politico-military one."[108]

Warsaw Pact leaders absorbed the message. Gorbachev "confirmed the readiness of the USSR to coordinate the size of the Soviet contingents and the order of their withdrawal from Eastern Europe with the leadership of the allied countries," Bulgaria's foreign minister wrote the Politburo in Sofia.[109] Countries in the Eastern bloc needed to pay careful attention to the integration of Western Europe and to consider establishing joint programs in areas such as transport, technology, and nuclear power safety. The host of the conference, Nicolae Ceauşescu, ridiculed talk of a "pan-European home," the Bulgarian foreign minister recounted. To everyone else, Gorbachev's message rang clear: renew socialism, look to the West.[110]

This message held true as Gorbachev met with the Hungarian communist leadership on July 24, 1989. Asked about plans to withdraw Soviet troops from Hungary, Gorbachev read a press release that stated: "In the course of negotiations, the issues of Soviet troops stationed in Hungary was brought up, and the parties decided that steps will be made to further reduce the number of Soviet troops, in accordance with the European disarmament process and with the continuation of the Vienna talks."[111]

By the end of July, Gorbachev's spirits were picking up. Chernyaev wrote him on July 26, 1989, to report Akhromeyev's successful visit to the Norfolk Naval Base. Given how well the Soviet Marshal had been treated, Chernyaev surmised that a "shift" was under way in Washington. "I take advantage of this opportunity to express satisfaction over the development of Soviet-U.S. dialogue," Gorbachev wrote Bush on July 29, 1989, "particularly on the key problems of strengthening security and reducing military confrontation."[112]

## Curtains

"The Hungarian government condemns Hungary's participation in the 1968 military intervention to Czechoslovakia," Prime Minister Németh publicly declared the following month. "And not only condemns it, but wishes to receive institutionalized guarantees through initiating the reform of the Warsaw Treaty against the recurrence of any such action." Németh hoped his words would bring greater harmony among the Hungarian, Czech, and Slovak people—perhaps even the Romanians. He did not care what outsiders had to say about it. "We are not to accept any lectures from others. We have had enough of that."[113]

On September 10, 1989, the Hungarian government allowed East German tourists to cross the border. Citizens of the GDR traveled a circuitous route to the FRG. Some made it only so far as Prague, where they set up camp in the West German embassy. To "resolve" the situation, Honecker ordered sealed trains to transport them through East Germany. Images of German security forces deporting families on trains conjured up appalling memories. For reasons only he could understand, Honecker regarded it as a triumph.[114]

Gorbachev distanced himself from Honecker and the other communist stalwarts. When Gorbachev traveled to East Germany that month for the fortieth anniversary of the GDR, a surreal scene unfolded. During a torchlit parade, a crowd of young Germans called out, "Gorbachev, help us!"[115] Wherever Gorbachev went that trip, the chant followed. "This is it," Gorbachev turned to Honecker and said. "This is the end."[116] Honecker's old thinking had failed; by the end of the year, the GDR was to owe the West some $26.5 billion.[117] Gorbachev could not comprehend the figures. Returning to Moscow, he shared with Chernyaev his assessment of the long-time GDR leader, calling him a "scumbag."[118]

Protest movements took hold in each of the major cities of the GDR that fall. They were led by clergy, physicians, and artists such as Bärbel Bohley. Bohley, a veteran of antinuclear protests earlier in the decade, helped found the Neues Forum dissident group after the rigged East German elections of May 1989. Some protestors wanted to leave permanently, others to stay and enjoy personal and political liberties. The right to travel became a crucible for reform.[119] East Germans tuned in to West German evening news broadcasts. In September and October, they saw images of their countrymen who had made it across the border being welcomed with cheers and open arms by other Germans.[120] On October 9, 1989, thousands of East Germans gathered to protest. Hospitals in Leipzig prepared for mass casualties.[121] The East German Politburo, led by Egon Krenz, saw the writing on the wall. On October 18, 1989, they forced Honecker to resign in a bloodless coup. Change at the top had little effect. On November 4, half a million people gathered in the Alexanderplatz in East Berlin to demand the right to travel.[122]

Five days later, Krenz convened a meeting of the East German Politburo. Afterwards, he handed a draft of a statement to Günter Schabowski, a communist official who had not attended. Schabowski proceeded to give a rambling press conference that included an inarticulate passage of unexpected consequence:

> What will happen to the Berlin Wall? Information has already been provided in connection with travel activities. ... The issue of travel, um, that ability to cross the Wall from our side, ... hasn't been answered yet

and exclusively the question in the sense ... , so this, I'll put it this way, fortified state border of the GDR. ... We have always said that there have to be several other factors, um, taken into consideration. And they deal with the complex of questions that Comrade Krenz, in his talk in the—addressed in view of the relations between the GDR and the FDR, in light of the, um, necessity of continuing the process of assuring peace with new initiatives.

And ... surely the debate about these questions, um, will be positively influenced if the FDR and NATO also agree to and implement disarmament measures in a similar manner to that of the GDR and other socialist countries. Thank you very much.[123]

As evening fell on the East Coast of the United States, NBC's Tom Brokaw, a witness to Shabowski's press conference, declared: "This is a historic night. ... The East German Government has just declared that East German citizens will be able to cross the wall ... without restrictions."[124] Within hours, Germans were dancing atop the Berlin Wall. Historian Mary Sarotte summed up this moment: "Television shaped reality."[125]

In 1989, an information revolution helped foster political revolution. Western radio and television speeded up history, exemplifying what historian David Reynolds called "the multiplier effect of modern technology."[126] In Poland, Wałęsa's televised besting of a high-ranking communist presaged his electoral triumph. In Hungary, images of its leader cutting the barbed wire fence border, and of the "Pan-European Picnic" held later that summer, circulated throughout Europe and inspired other reformers to take risks. In East Berlin, thousands of citizens went to the border crossings the evening of November 9 because television broadcasts had led them to believe they were to be opened. In Moscow, images from China earlier in the year presented Gorbachev the model of what not to do.

On October 23, with little fanfare, the Hungarian parliament formally jettisoned communism and established a republic; its first act was to tell the Soviet troops to go home. On November 10, Bulgaria's longtime dictator Todor Zhivkov quit; the communist party was gone by the following spring. On November 28, following ten days of largely peaceful protests, the Czech communist party announced it was relinquishing power; a month later, Václav Havel was president and Alexander Dubček, the great hero of 1968, was rehabilitated. In Bucharest on December 21, the crowd turned on Ceaușescu during a live televised broadcast; on Christmas Day, a military tribunal sent his wife and him to the firing squad. The violence in Romania was not replicated elsewhere.

People took risks because they did not think that Gorbachev would crack down on them. He proved them right. To intervene would have sacrificed the new world order Gorbachev hoped to construct. Ideas drove his decisions; frequently, these ideas were slogans. Gorbachev wanted more "spiritualization" and "rethinking the relationship between man and nature, other people, and with himself." He spoke of a "revolution in consciousness." The actual fall of the Berlin Wall and communist regimes in Eastern Europe reiterated the concrete need for "new thinking for the world," he told Italian Prime Minister Giulio Andreotti in December. "Common European home" was the answer to the German question. Developing tools to expand economic and political integration across Europe was their shared objective.[127]

"I am familiar with your addresses to the world, with your reflection upon its problems," Gorbachev informed the Pope. "I even noted that we often use similar expressions. This means that there is agreement at the source—in our thoughts."[128] Gorbachev appeared completely aloof from Pope John Paul II's crusade against communism. So long as he heard variants of peace, new thinking, and freedom to choose, he found commonality between the Catholic Church and his new world order.

As 1989 drew to a close, tough questions emerged. What was the future of the German people now that a physical barrier no longer separated them? What would replace the governments that had collapsed in Eastern Europe? Would the Soviets retain the largest and most powerful conventional army on the continent? What about the gigantic nuclear arsenals both sides still possessed? Gorbachev hoped these questions could be addressed through the framework he had introduced to the United Nations in December 1988. His new world order evolved from acceleration, perestroika, glasnost, new thinking, and a common European home. It included freedom to choose, nuclear abolitionism, a reduction of troops, common security, greater concern about environmental degradation, more effort to prevent the spread of pandemic disease. It called for greater reliance on institutions like the Commission on Security and Cooperation in Europe (CSCE) and the United Nations. New world order was the summation of Gorbachev's aspirations. "Universal human values and not the balance of power would be the foundation of the new home," writes historian Svetlana Savranskaya.[129]

Years later, Gorbachev's words do not always convey substance. If indeed universal values were a foundation to a new home, the house lacked clear blueprints. Yet Gorbachev was a phenomenon. The world subscribed to his "new thinking." On the streets of Eastern Europe, his words led people to take greater risks. The UN speech in January 1989, writes historian Marie-Pierre Rey, "helped to free Eastern Europeans from their fears, to question the Stalinist heritage in Eastern Europe that was based on constraint, and so consequently paved the way to the pacific revolutions of autumn 1989."[130] Of course, the distribution of international power mattered as well. The American economy could afford the Cold War. Capitalism survived the 1970s and empowered the West in the mid-1980s. It cast a spider's web upon Eastern Europe. Indebted beyond comprehension and no longer able to rely on Moscow for economic sustenance, every communist regime except Romania looked to the Federal Republic of Germany for cash.[131] Given the revitalization of the West German economy, along with the rest of Western Europe, its politicians and bankers were able to comply. In Germany and elsewhere, the revolutions of 1989 confirmed what Shultz had told Gorbachev in Moscow two years earlier—a closed system could not survive, given changes in the international economy and the information revolution, without resorting to uncivilized methods. It was harder to keep brutality a secret in the industrialized world. The revolutions of 1989 all depended in some measure on the rapid and direct dissemination of media that had not existed a generation earlier.

Economic factors and technological advances notwithstanding, Gorbachev still defied history. Twenty seven million Soviet citizens had died in World War II—the vast majority at the hands of Germans. For their sacrifice, the Soviet people got forty more years of hardship, repression, and unceasing threat of a nuclear war. The consolation for these losses was dominion over the lands of what had once been Prussia and control of the corridor through which Napoleon and Hitler had invaded Russia. Soviet occupation stifled liberty, violated human dignity, and extended the dark shadow of World War II for nearly half a century. The system was cruel and unjust, yet its greatest product was Gorbachev. In 1989, he sacrificed an empire for something he called a new world order.

# CHAPTER 7

# Bush's New World Order

*November 1989–January 1991*

"Time and again in this century," President George H. W. Bush declared on February 28, 1990, "the political map of the world was transformed. And in each instance, a new world order came about through the advent of a new tyrant or the outbreak of a bloody global war, or its end. Now the world has undergone another upheaval, but this time, there's no war." The Berlin Wall had fallen; so had the dictators of Eastern Europe. "Victor Hugo said that no army can match the might of an idea whose time has come. In the Revolutions of '89, an idea overcame armies and tanks, and that idea is democracy."[1] The president did not employ the phrase "new world order" again in public for several months. On September 11, 1990, he addressed a joint session of Congress laying out his rationale for confronting Saddam Hussein, the Iraqi strongman whose forces had invaded Kuwait and imperiled stability in the Middle East. He called for a "new world order": "a new era—freer from the threat of terror, stronger in the pursuit of justice, and more secure in the quest for peace."[2]

In the period between the fall of the Berlin Wall and the outbreak of the Persian Gulf War, a new world order was indeed taking shape. Democracy, capitalism, and an open world economy were integral components. It evolved neither by accident nor grand design but by improvisation. President Bush and his top advisers adapted to change and responded swiftly to the challenges emerging from the collapse of the Soviet empire. They did so despite political and economic constraints at home. Yet the Bush administration acted and emboldened its allies in ways that settled fundamental Cold War disputes on terms favorable to the United States. Mikhail Gorbachev's new world order had been a slogan; George Bush's new world order was becoming a reality.

## Support for Perestroika

On December 2, 1989, Bush met Gorbachev off the coast of Malta. "I do want to say that the world will be a better place if perestroika succeeds," the president affirmed. He remembered that Gorbachev had expressed doubt about U.S. intentions at their previous encounter. "You said some U.S. elements want to see perestroika fail," he recalled. "I can't say there are no such elements in the U.S.—but there are no serious elements, and most Americans don't feel that way."[3] Bush now wanted to discuss how his administration could help perestroika succeed. He pledged support for overturning the Jackson-Vanik amendment and boosting trade with the Soviet Union: "I believe we can get that done: not a program of assistance, but a program of cooperation."[4] He handed over a paper with suggestions for creating small businesses, breaking up monopolies, and establishing a stock exchange. "These are just suggestions," the president clarified. "You may think some are good, and some are bad." Previously, Bush had opposed Soviet observer status at the General Agreement on Tariffs and Trade. "I've changed," he acknowledged. "I believe GATT should accept the USSR as an observer, so that we can learn together."[5]

"I know it is difficult, but I want to have a frank discussion about Nicaragua and Cuba," the president went on to say. He regarded Soviet support for those regimes as "the single most disruptive factor to a relationship that is going in the right direction."[6] So long as Gorbachev was sending MiG-29s to Castro, the U.S. Congress would limit Bush's ability to dismantle Cold War trade restrictions.[7] Yet Bush wanted to avoid the impression that he was issuing demands to a defeated rival. The two leaders, he explained, could demonstrate joint leadership. "On the environment, I know you are getting hit hard," the president stated. "I am getting hit hard. Global climate change is a key issue. Some in the West want to shut down the whole world because of global climate change." Achieving sustainable growth without environmental degradation would not be easy. Why not plan a conference in which Moscow and Washington could lead the way in meeting this twenty-first century challenge? he asked.[8]

Gorbachev had other priorities. "Overall, my conclusion is that strategically and philosophically, the methods of the Cold War were defeated," he proclaimed. "We are aware of that defeat, and the man in the street is more aware than anyone."[9] Yet in American political discourse, he detected "one idea very present": U.S. strength had forced the Soviet Union to change course and the regimes in Eastern Europe to disintegrate. "The policies of the Cold War were right; these policies should not change," went this line of thought. "The only thing the U.S. needs to do is to keep its baskets ready to gather the fruit."[10] Bush assured Gorbachev that such thinking did not account for his own actions. The president drew criticism at home from both sides of the political spectrum for his lack of outward triumphalism. "I have been called cautious or timid," Bush acknowledged, when it came to the momentous events of that fall. "I am cautious, but not timid," he clarified. "But I have conducted myself in ways not to complicate your life. That's why I have not jumped up and down on the Berlin Wall."[11]

Gorbachev interpreted Bush's restraint as support for moving perestroika forward. "Our policy is to move more and more to adjust to the world economy," he declared.[12] Property and land reform would coincide with the full convertibility of the ruble. He hoped that the international political economy would adopt new thinking as well. "We must learn to take the world economy into perestroika," he stated.[13] It was not at all clear, then or now, what this meant.

Over lunch, Gorbachev spoke candidly of the challenges he faced. "In Italy, I saw a lot of products and few customers," he told the Americans.[14] "In our country, it is the opposite. Your shops have merchandise. Ours have none." Personal savings had created a "ruble overhang" threatening massive inflation if new goods were to flood the market too quickly. A psychological component also stood in the way of reforms. "We need to wean our people away from a leveling principle," Gorbachev admitted. "They need to learn how to work, to depend on themselves. Our society is changing and we must change our thinking."[15] Gorbachev elaborated upon ideas for economic reforms without much ideological or practical coherence. "We are reducing our volume of industrial investments to funnel them elsewhere," he stated. In one case, "we gave a government order to 325 military enterprises to produce food processing equipment."[16] Overall, the Soviets were "moving toward private property, but very small and with no big business." Gorbachev described efforts to pick and choose from the economic models of Italy, the United Kingdom, and Sweden. Even in the United States, he told Bush, "it is difficult to find pure genuine private property. . . . What counts is the degree of economic independence."[17]

George Bush, a former businessman, and James Baker, a former secretary of the treasury, were skeptical. "At Malta I was amazed at how little

Gorbachev really knows about Free Market economics," Bush recorded in his diary after returning home.[18] Yet he and the secretary of state wanted to help him find a successful formula. They did not debate ideology. "I was simply astonished when I heard Bush, and particularly Baker (acting as a professional economist), discussing the problems of our reforms with Gorbachev," Anatoly Chernyaev later recalled. "They spoke, if not as members of our leadership, then at least as experts sincerely interested in our success."[19]

Yet the fundamental point about Cuba remained. "I don't want to sound like a broken record," Bush told Gorbachev in a smaller session. "Let me express U.S. public opinion on you yourself. There is strong support for perestroika and for establishing pluralistic answers in Eastern Europe— strong support." The American people regarded his support for Castro "as an embarrassment. He is against the causes you are advocating."[20] Why not simply hang him out to dry?

Gorbachev was encouraged by Bush and Baker's spirit of cooperation. He was displeased by the tone of triumphalism he detected elsewhere. "What I dislike is when some U.S. politicians say unity of Europe should be on the basis of Western values," he complained. "We have long been accused of exporting ideology. That is what is now being proposed by some—not you." Bush offered compassion and candor but no commitments. He and Baker acceded to Gorbachev and Yakovlev's request that "universal values" replace "Western values."[21] They did not remark upon Gorbachev's intention to "bring the world economy into perestroika." Gorbachev complained about West German Chancellor Helmut Kohl. "Mr. Kohl is in too much of a hurry on the German question," he said. "That is not good." "We cannot be asked to disapprove of German reunification," Bush informed Gorbachev.[22] "I realize that this is a highly sensitive subject and we have tried to conduct ourselves with restraint." The Soviet leader was insistent: there were two German states "mandated by history. So let history decide the outcome."[23] This phrase, "let history decide," summed up Gorbachev's plan: he did not have one.

Gorbachev did not commit to abandon Moscow's Cold War allies. He did not provide a compelling answer on Cuba, and he did not provide specificity on how to transcend Cold War policies. Indeed, he even accepted one of its fundamental components. "I reject the remark that we are closer to Europe," he told the American delegation. "We are equally involved and integrated. We are well aware of your involvement and any approach that rejects the involvement and role for the U.S. would be unrealistic and unconstructive. ... Acceptance of your role is a basic point with us."[24] His predecessors had attempted to drive a wedge between the United States and its allies in Western Europe; Gorbachev foresaw an open-ended U.S. presence.

## Bush Improvises

Bush and his team were pleased with the Malta Summit, but they were not yet prepared to declare the Cold War over. That would have to wait for the establishment of new governments to replace communist regimes, some guarantee of European security, and a resolution of whether Germany was to be one country or two. Their preference for achieving these objectives was to retool and refurbish old institutions rather than construct new ones. There was neither a clamor at home nor pressure abroad for great innovations.

"From the Baltic to the Adriatic, an irresistible movement has gathered force—a movement of, by, and for the people," Baker declared in Berlin on December 12, 1989. "In their peaceful urgent multitude, the peoples of Eastern Europe have held up a mirror to the West and have reflected the enduring power of our own best values." Establishing stable, legitimate regimes based on the consent of the people stood as the next priority. "Free men and free governments are the building blocks of a Europe whole and free," he proclaimed.[25] Baker hoped that existing and evolving institutions would move democratization forward. He delivered a strong endorsement of European integration. At the start of the administration, neither the secretary nor the president was eager for the impending expansion of a Common European Market, which they feared might shut out American exports. "For President George H. W. Bush, 1992 would also be the year of his reelection campaign," Counselor to the Secretary of the State Robert Zoellick put it; no one looked forward to this potential "protectionist exercise."[26] The events of 1989 changed the minds of the president and his national security team. "We believe that the attraction of the European Community for the countries of the east depends most on its continued vitality," Baker declared in his Berlin speech.[27]

Baker proposed expansion of the Conference on Security and Cooperation to promote human rights and help "the transition from stalled, planned economies to free, competitive markets."[28] The most important institution, however, was to be NATO. Baker called for the alliance "to evolve" into "the forum where Western nations cooperate to negotiate, implement, verify, and extend agreements between East and West." NATO would "provide a clearinghouse for information contributed by national governments." NATO's charter had always transcended military affairs, Baker impressed upon his audience—particularly in the case of Germans and French. "The reconciliation of ancient enemies, which has taken place under the umbrella of NATO's collective security, offers the nations of Eastern Europe an appealing model of international relations."[29] Communities of nations who embraced democracy and capitalism could overcome the hatreds of the past. They could learn from NATO's example—especially as the alliance took on greater political responsibilities.

The overriding objective of NATO had been to deter the Red Army from invading Central Europe. As that threat dissipated, Bush and his team considered permanent reductions to conventional forces on both sides. "Why do we always need the same number of troops and bombs?" Bush challenged his top advisers. "We should test the Soviets. Ask them to do something we think they'll never do." The past decade taught the president that this approach worked. Reagan weathered relentless criticism for his "zero option" for intermediate-range missiles in Europe; six years later, Gorbachev accepted his terms. "We shouldn't be seen as begrudging change but acting boldly," Bush instructed his team. "We have an enormous opportunity to do something dramatically different."[30]

In his State of the Union message on January 30, 1990, Bush called for reducing American and Soviet forces in Central and Eastern Europe to 195,000 on each side.[31] The Soviets should consider the figures a "floor" for the United States and a "ceiling" for themselves, Scowcroft clarified after the speech—even though Soviet ground and air forces based in Central Europe outnumbered their American counterparts by 565,000 to 255,000. "Since the Soviets stationed troops on foreign territory only in the Central Zone, and we planned to have 30,000 additional troops in the rest of Europe," Baker later explained, "the practical effect would be ... [to turn] a Soviet advantage in conventional forces into a disadvantage."[32] Bush declared later that year that "the Conventional Forces in Europe Treaty which we have proposed would be the most ambitious conventional arms control agreement ever concluded."[33] CFE redressed one of the fundamental strategic dilemmas throughout the entire Cold War: the stark imbalance between the Red Army and the combined forces of the United States and its West European allies. America's Faustian bargain, struck by President Dwight Eisenhower and sustained by his successors, threatened "massive retaliation" so that the United States would not have to maintain a huge standing army in perpetuity.[34]

Nuclear weapons were meant to keep the country from becoming a "garrison state."[35] Bush's CFE proposal was an end run around nuclear weapons as a strategic concept. The administration continued to pursue START, notwithstanding the lingering debates over SLCMs, ALCMs, and other missile systems. The prospect of massive reductions in Soviet conventional forces, however, meant that the United States no longer needed a huge nuclear arsenal. Reductions in both nuclear and conventional forces presaged a potential "peace dividend" for the Bush administration at a time when the federal deficit and the long-term national debt dominated American political discourse.

As the Bush administration took the initiative on reducing conventional forces in Europe and preserving institutions of stability, Helmut Kohl took the lead on the question of German unification. Born within one year of Gorbachev, Kohl had also grown up amidst the horror of World War II. His brother, like Eduard Shevardnadze's, had died in the war.[36] Before entering politics, Kohl wrote a dissertation about postwar reconstruction. He revered Konrad Adenauer, the Christian Democratic leader of postwar West Germany who refused to accept the fate of permanent division.

Kohl did not always act with refinement. He incurred the wrath of Margaret Thatcher by cutting short a meeting in the early 1970s on account of "pressing business," only to be spotted eating a cream cake at a nearby bakery.[37] He drew an unproductive comparison between Gorbachev and Nazi propaganda minister Joseph Goebbels in a 1986 interview with Newsweek.[38] But Kohl's thinking evolved; he warmed to Gorbachev when the Soviet leader visited in June 1989 and joined him in a stroll along the Rhine.[39]

Gorbachev was more popular among West Berliners than Kohl, against whom they had mobilized during the lead-up to INF deployment in 1983. On November 10, 1989, they jeered and made obscene gestures as Kohl addressed the crowd immediately after his former political adversary, Willy Brandt.[40] Kohl reached beyond his critics to the audience watching on television: "I would like to call out to everyone in the GDR: You are not alone! We stand at your side! We are and will remain one nation, and we belong together!"[41] "I've just arrived from Berlin," Kohl reported to Bush over the telephone that day. "It is like witnessing an enormous fair."[42] In the subsequent two and half weeks, Kohl and his national security advisor, Horst Teltschik, plotted a strategy to unify their countrymen. The Chancellor delivered a speech on November 28, 1989, with the title "Overcoming of the division of Germany and Europe." Free and multiparty elections in the GDR topped his priorities. East German finances were abysmal, yet "economic assistance can only prove effective if fundamental reforms of the economic system follow." That alone might not suffice. "We are also prepared to take yet another decisive step, namely, to develop confederative structures between both states in Germany, with the aim of creating a federation, that is, a federal order, in Germany."[43]

To champions and critics alike, Kohl's speech was a first step toward German reunification. According to Anatoly Chernyaev, Gorbachev interpreted Kohl's speech as "a breach of his promise not to push events forward or try

**Figure 7.1.** Bush and Kohl, 1989. The president and the chancellor worked toward the reunification of Germany. Courtesy of the George Bush Presidential Library and Museum.

to extract one-sided political advantage, and ... a violation of their agreement to consult each other on every new move."[44] The Soviet leader had informed Bush of his apprehensions when they met off the coast of Malta. "Gorbachev said you are in too much of a hurry," Bush reported back to Kohl, who indeed was in a hurry.[45] A parliamentary election loomed before the end of 1990. West Germans did not credit his party with the collapse of the Berlin Wall. Kohl needed to shore up his party's base, and conservatives spoke of reincorporating lands east of the Oder-Neisse rivers that lay within the boundaries of Poland. Kohl made no mention of it in his 10 Point plan for German reunification, but he sympathized with Germans whose families had been expelled from their homes after World War II. "No, I will not guarantee anything," he told Thatcher after dinner at Strasbourg in December 1989. "I do not recognize the current borders."[46]

Rapid developments in East Germany changed the political calculus of West Germany. The man who replaced Erich Honecker, Hans Modrow, called for free elections to be held in March. Anticipating that success in the East in the spring would augur victory in the West in the fall, parties from the FRG established counterparts in the GDR and waged political campaigns.

The foreign minister and leader of the centrist Free Democrats, Hans-Dietrich Genscher, sensed opportunity. Born and raised in Halle, Genscher remained in East Germany until 1952. Suffering from severe heart disease and risking his own health, Genscher grew indignant that Germany's fate might again be decided by outsiders. He did not appreciate listening to Gorbachev and Shevardnadze hector him, as they did in December, about Kohl's 10 Points. Yet he discerned a lesson: a bold speech could set the terms of debate. In an effort to raise his stature and that of his party, Genscher spoke in Tutzing on January 31, 1990. He stated, among other things, that a NATO that incorporated a unified Germany would not expand eastward.[47] Genscher's speech created anxiety in Washington. The Bush administration, fearing separate deals between Germans and Soviets, supported Kohl in the forthcoming election. "Everything we've heard about [SPD leader Oskar] Lafontaine makes us anxious," the president stated.[48] Bush did not want limits on NATO, and his team did not want a neutral Germany. In January 1990, they allowed Kohl take the lead so long as a unified Germany was a part of NATO, the United States avoided commitments, and the Soviet Union participated in the diplomatic process.

Of German heritage, Robert Zoellick proposed a review of "how a confederated Germany would operate within the EC [European Community] and NATO" and advised Baker to press for a summit with Gorbachev so that the Soviets did not feel excluded.[49] "We must avoid any 'Congress of Vienna' effort to draw up rigid guidelines for a new European order," he wrote. The better option was to encourage democracy. "By insisting that free elections be a critical building block of any new rule in Europe, we secure a system on our terms."[50] Staffers on the National Security Council drew similar conclusions. Moscow's position toward Germany had yet to be determined, Robert Blackwill, a European specialist on the NSC, wrote Scowcroft on January 19, 1990. Dithering in Washington would allow Gorbachev time to ask for concessions in exchange for his assent. Promoting German reunification, from Blackwill's perspective, should be the overriding U.S. objective.[51]

Blackwill was correct that Gorbachev lacked a plan. The Soviet leader had only a vague notion that "restructuring" could be applied to East Germany. He blamed East Germany's woes on Honecker's aversion to change. When the head of the KGB predicted that the Social Democrats would probably win the East German elections that March, Gorbachev took comfort because the SPD was only marginally committed to reunification—and far less committed to NATO. Perhaps, he speculated, the communists might even pull off a surprise victory.[52] A visit from the new GDR leader, Hans Modrow, disabused him of this notion. Voters had branded the East German communist party a "criminal organization," Modrow acknowledged.[53] He estimated that 500,000 people might leave the GDR by the end of 1990—many of them highly educated youths and skilled workers. Strikes and work slowdowns were crippling the economy.

Modrow implored Gorbachev to come to East Germany. The communist party, officially called the Socialist Unity Party, needed his charisma because it no longer had any political infrastructure. Modrow estimated that out of the 2.2 million members of the Socialist Unity Party the previous summer, perhaps half a million remained. Meanwhile, Kohl and Brandt were attracting huge crowds at campaign rallies in Dresden and Leipzig, Modrow lamented. The communists simply could not compete with highly experienced political parties from the West.[54] Gorbachev sympathized with Modrow but could not offer him substantive help. Oil production had recently fallen by 17 million tons, Premier Nikolai Ryzhkov told him. "We are in a difficult position." Perestroika was entering a "turbulent phase," in Gorbachev's words. Events in Eastern Europe "are beginning to affect us."[55]

Gorbachev faced criticism from hardliners over Germany. He followed up Modrow's visit by sending Bush a letter of protest. "Unification sentiments are boiling over, which someone is clearly trying to exploit in order to create an uncontrollable situation," he wrote on February 2, 1990. "Any haste, leaping over stages, overly categorical conclusions and assessments can only result in chaos."[56]

Gorbachev's letter arrived in Washington shortly after Zoellick and Director of Policy Planning Dennis Ross sent Baker a memo outlining a negotiating strategy. The State Department labeled its proposal "Two Plus Four"—East Germany and West Germany plus the four occupying powers after World War II.[57]

On Thursday, February 8, 1990, Baker met Shevardnadze in Moscow. Baker had established a personal bond with Shevardnadze, taking him fly fishing in Jackson Hole, Wyoming, the previous fall. A neutral Germany might pose a threat to its neighbors, Baker told his friend; a unified one in NATO would not. "I realize that might be hard for you to believe," he acknowledged. "In effect it suggests that the risk comes not from the United States, which for a long time you've seen as your enemy, but instead it suggests that greater risk could come from a neutral Germany that becomes militaristic."[58] Baker told Gorbachev the next day: "We fought together, and together brought peace to Europe. Unfortunately, we poorly ordered the peace, and it led to a cold war."[59] The two sides should strive to do better in 1990. "I very much want you to know: neither the president nor I intend to extract advantages from the ongoing processes."[60] Baker went on to repeat what he had told Shevardnadze: a unified Germany within NATO was the surest guarantee of peace. He reiterated the U.S. position at Malta: the Bush administration could help Gorbachev far more easily if he ditched Castro.

Unification was not imminent, the Soviet leader insisted. Several prominent Germans, including the Nobel laureate writer Günter Grass, had predicted that West Germans would balk at costs of unification "An interesting mosaic of opinions" existed, according to the Soviet leader. They did not all point to reunification.[61] German reunification was certainly not Gorbachev's preference. The risk of German aggression sometime in the future could never be eliminated. Anchoring Germany in "European structures," however, might reduce it. That was a scenario Gorbachev could live with. If reunification was destined to come, the "presence of American troops could play a moderating role." He trusted Baker and Bush. He would go along with Two Plus Four. Again he accepted an open-ended U.S. presence on the continent—though he ruled out any expansion of NATO eastward.[62]

Baker wrote Kohl to say that Gorbachev was receptive to the idea of Two Plus Four and was possibly resigned to the inevitability of reunification.[63] A united Germany did not intend to seek lands east of the Oder-Neisse line, Kohl had pledged in his own meeting with Gorbachev. He also offered to procure massive loans from West German banks. By the end of the meeting with Kohl, Gorbachev had acceded to the American framework of Two Plus

Four.[64] "No one doubts the rights of the Germans in the GDR and the FRG to self-determination," Shevardnadze declared in a speech to the Canadian parliament the next week. "But equally certain is the right of Germany's neighbors and the European states to have guarantees that a united Germany, if it is created, will not be a threat to them, that it will not raise the question of a review of European borders, and that Nazism and fascism will not revive in it."[65]

"I don't know how the elections will turn out," Kohl confided in Bush on March 15, 1990. "The situation is very vague. ... The GDR still has to bear the consequences of 40 years of Communist rule, with its snooping, spying, and blackmailing."[66] Three days later, the chancellor's party won a smashing victory in East Germany. Kohl interpreted the results as mandate to reunite Germany as quickly as possible. The clearer it became just how much West Germans would have to pay to service the debt of their compatriots to the East and refurbish its economy, he reasoned, the harder it would be to maintain support. Kohl feared that "people in the FRG were unwilling to make sacrifices for unification," he confided in the British foreign minister.[67]

As the Two Plus Four negotiations got under way, Kohl arranged for Teltschik to accompany the heads of Deutsche Bank and Dresdner Bank on a flight to meet Gorbachev in Moscow.[68] "Behind us are 27 million Soviet victims [and] 18.5 million injured, and tens of millions orphaned," Gorbachev told the delegation. The entire nation had been "shaken to its foundation" during the Great Patriotic War; the same could certainly be said of the Germans. The past was behind them, and now the Soviet Union desperately needed help. "We need oxygen to survive two or three years"—15 to 20 billion rubles ($9 to 12 billion) and nearly 2 billion rubles ($1.2 billion) as soon as possible.[69] The Germans pledged their support.

## An Open World Economy

"The world before World War I was a very different world than that since," Brent Scowcroft said publicly in January 1990. "And ever since World War I we have been trying to put back together the pieces of the world which was destroyed by that war."[70] Scowcroft's words summed up the restorative quality of what the Bush administration hoped to achieve. A renewed enthusiasm for neoliberal economics, lower tariffs, and free trade zones was the dominant trend among industrialized economies by the start of the 1990s. The Single European Act of July 1987 created the largest and most prominent burgeoning free trade zone in the world. In 1988, the United States signed a comprehensive free trade agreement with its largest trading partner,

Canada. Coming shortly after the Caribbean Basin Initiative, the measure advanced the continent one step closer to the North American Free Trade Agreement, which would include Mexico.[71]

In South America, free trade found unexpected champions in the late 1980s. Brazil and Argentina developed a Southern Common Market—Mercosur—which would eventually include Uruguay, Paraguay, Bolivia, and Venezuela as well. In the case of Chile, opponents of General Augusto Pinochet had charged U.S. trade policies with emboldening human rights abuses. As Pinochet stepped down and democratic reforms came to Chile at the end of the 1980s, the new government kept many of the free trade policies its members had previously castigated. Other democrats in Latin America likewise jettisoned talk of Yankee imperialism and dependency theory.[72] The Bush administration responded by seeking ways to connect North and South America. "Throughout the region, nations are turning away from the statist economic policies that stifle growth and are now looking to the power of the free market to help this hemisphere realize its untapped potential for progress," the president declared as he unveiled the Enterprise for the Americas Initiative. Bush proposed "that we begin the process of creating a hemisphere wide free trade zone." The end result, he hoped, was "a free trade system that links all of the Americas ... a free trade zone stretching from the port of Anchorage to the Tierra del Fuego."[73]

On the other side of the Pacific Ocean, similar trends played out. In 1989, Australian Prime Minister Bob Hawke established the Asia–Pacific Economic Cooperation. Its members included Indonesia, Japan, Malaysia, the Philippines, Thailand, and Singapore as well as the United States and Canada. APEC was not an economic union along the lines of the European Economic Community, nor was it a binding set of free trade regulations in the mold of NAFTA. Yet it tightened the link between East Asia and North America, which, in turn, extended Europe around the world and bolstered the notion of a single world economy.

By the 1990s, burgeoning economic trading zones spanned from west of St. Petersburg to east of Vladivostok. Beginning in Uruguay in 1986, the 123 members of the General Agreement on Tariffs and Trade met annually to hammer out a comprehensive overhaul in trade barriers. Negotiators plodded through 1990, stuck on agricultural subsidies and patent protections; final agreement did not come until 1994. The drawn-out conclusion aside, the countries in negotiations shared basic assumptions about how their economies ought to be structured.[74] The combination of the collapse of communism in Eastern Europe, the rise of free trade zones, and the Uruguay Round of tariffs all suggested that the international economy was returning to an age of interconnectedness that arguably exceeded the system in place prior to World War I and the rise of communism and fascism. "By the 1990s global capitalism was again in full flower," writes historian Jeffry Frieden. "As before 1914, capitalism was global, and the globe was capitalist."[75]

Fervent nationalism and ethnic solidarity had brought down an era of globalization in 1914. On March 11, 1990, led by a musicologist named Vytautas Landsbergis, Lithuania's parliament approved a measure declaring the country's independence. To Moscow, the precedent was deeply troubling. "What could happen next?" Shevardnadze asked Baker when they met later that spring. "I'll tell you. The Moldavians say the same thing; the Georgians, the Armenians, the Azerbaijanis, the Ukrainians."[76] Gorbachev responded to Lithuania with an economic blockade that called into question his commitment to "new thinking."

Hundreds of thousands of ethnic Russians resided in Lithuania, comprising an unloved, powerful minority. "I've got telegrams from all over the country—maybe I'll show them to President Bush," Gorbachev told Baker. "Because what they do is protest and say American Presidents act very quickly to protect American citizens, why don't you, as the Soviet President, act quickly to protect Russian citizens in Lithuania?"[77]

President Bush did not wish to complicate Gorbachev's life. "The Baltics were an emotional issue for us," Bush and Scowcroft later put it.[78] In other words, the issue aroused passions among Americans and evoked memories of an earlier era; but the future of the Soviet republics was a distraction from the higher priority of integrating a unified Germany into NATO. It was simply not in America's interest for the Soviet Union to disintegrate. If the Baltic states broke away, which ones might go next? "Gorbachev has inherited an empire," Mitterrand told Bush that April. "It is now in revolt. If the Ukraine starts to move, Gorbachev is gone; a military dictatorship would result." Dictatorship would almost certainly spell doom to peaceful revolutions in Eastern Europe.[79]

The United States had no vital interest at stake in Lithuania. Nor was Gorbachev committing atrocities, although he did order crackdowns and impose an economic embargo. As in China the previous year, the twenty-four-hour news cycle magnified every aspect of the standoff. (It drew from a limited repository of historical analogies. CNN carried footage of Landsbergis expressing concern that the West had accepted "another Munich." When the Kremlin cut off energy sales, newscasters made comparisons to the only other quarantine they could recall: the U.S. Navy's quarantine of Cuba in 1962.) Meeting with

Shevardnadze in Windhoek, Baker stressed that "the Baltics were markedly different in American eyes" and that "there was strong support for them on Capitol Hill, and they resonated in the American psyche as little guys who had been taken over by a bully who now seemed poised to shed blood."[80] In truth, the problem was not American public opinion. A *Time Magazine*/CNN poll conducted that April revealed that only one quarter of those surveyed said that the United States "should pressure the Soviet Union to give Lithuania its independence," while nearly two thirds believed it was "none of our business."[81] American politicians from both parties were to blame: Democrats sensed an opportunity to chip away at the president's high popularity, while conservatives like Senator Jesse Helms could not resist attacking the Soviets.

Baker seemed embarrassed by the political sniping. On March 28, 1990, he sent Gorbachev a handwritten note: "I hope you know that the President and I are very aware of the pressures you face" and "want to help you succeed, not make it more difficult; have demonstrated this in our speeches and public statements; and have done so now for many months (almost one year) notwithstanding the fact that others—both in the administration and the congress—disagree with our approach."[82] Bush also grew frustrated by calls to exploit the growing turmoil. "They want us to ratchet up the pressure and announce a bunch of steps; yet if we did, the next criticism would be, well, why are you doing this when you have a whole bunch of other agenda items to worry about with the Soviet Union? It's almost a no-win situation," the president confided in his diary on April 17, 1990.[83] "We could have climbed on the bandwagon, recognized the Landsbergis government, and called for Lithuanian independence," Scowcroft later wrote. "It would have felt good and would have ended the barrage of criticism. ... The reality was that the only way the Baltic States could achieve lasting independence was with the acquiescence of the Kremlin. Our task was to bring Moscow to that point."[84]

With Bush constrained by domestic politics, Kohl took the lead. Meeting with Lithuanian prime minister, Kazimiera Prunskienė, on May 11, 1990, Kohl told her to back down because the independence fight threatened to topple Gorbachev. "With him, we know where we stand," Kohl told Prunskienė. "What comes afterward, we have no idea."[85]

## Freedom on the March

"Having Germany in NATO might be good for West Germany and the United States, but don't expect me to say that it would be good for the Soviet Union," Marshal Sergei Akhromeyev informed the head of the RAND Corporation on May 24; Defense Minister Dmitri Yazov concurred. "Don't treat us like kids," added Valentin Falin.[86] Gorbachev planned to arrive in Washington at the end of the month. "On the German Question, as it is called, I don't expect much breakthrough," Bush admitted to Kohl in advance of Gorbachev's visit.[87]

At the White House on May 31, 1990, Akhromeyev, Yazov, and Falin sat aghast as Bush pressed Gorbachev on the matter of Germany in NATO. Was it not an extension of the Helsinki Accords—and of all the principles Gorbachev stood for—that Germans could choose their associations and alliances? Bush asked. "To my astonishment," Bush later remarked, "Gorbachev shrugged his shoulders and said yes."[88] A little more than a month after the Washington Summit, Gorbachev provided his final assent. Kohl met the Soviet leader and his team in the Stavropol region. While Gorbachev and Shevardnadze hemmed and hawed over the future of NATO, they agreed that German NATO troops would not go into the GDR until Soviet troops had left.[89] Before Moscow had time to reconsider, Kohl called an immediate press conference and announced to the world: a reunified Germany was to be part of NATO.

Gorbachev made concessions in 1990 because he hoped that U.S. investment could provide the stimulus to rescue perestroika. Legacies of the Cold War hindered these aspirations. Moscow continued to sell arms to dubious clients who paid for them with Soviet aid—a type of military Keynesianism that made it nearly impossible for the Bush administration to ask Congress for direct aid to Gorbachev. "It would be advantageous to you, since we would pay in hard currency," Baker deadpanned after Shevardnadze's suggestion in February that Moscow sell MiG-29s to the United States instead of Cuba.[90] In all seriousness, Gorbachev interjected, he hoped that the United States could assist him to wean the Soviet economy off its dependence on military industries and to form collaborative ventures to convert Soviet military technology to civilian use. Restrictions on trade did, however, need to be lifted; if not, the Soviets were "talking about the technology of yesterday."[91]

The administration was reviewing the restrictions, Baker assured Gorbachev. Yet nothing could happen until the Soviets stopped selling arms to countries like Cuba. Meeting with Baker that spring, Soviet Finance Minister Valentin Pavlov asked for a loan of $10 to $12 billion to make up for deficits in agricultural and consumer spending. "Domestic political considerations in the Soviet Union do not permit the Soviet government to request or receive a U.S. government loan openly on the governmental level," Pavlov told Baker. Political elements in the Soviet Union "would connect such a loan with various Soviet-U.S. agreements which are being worked out." But he wanted the money all the same.[92]

Baker paid lip service to providing substantial aid. The underlying message was that Washington could not pick up the bill for rebuilding Eastern Europe—let alone the Soviet Union. "We must integrate the new market democracies into the international economic system," Baker declared in Prague in February 1990. "You need access to IMF and World Bank resources. You need barriers to trade removed bilaterally and through GATT, so potential investors will know they can export to other markets. You need access to high technology."[93] "The Marshall Plan of the '90s should rely on private capital and the help of those who were rebuilt by the first Marshall Plan," Zoellick had written Baker even before the Iron Curtain ascended.[94] Eastern Europe, in other words, needed access to an open world economy to seek capital investment to rebuild after forty years of inefficiency and neglect.

Provided that Gorbachev demonstrated his sincerity to allow outside investment and committed to respect the rights of private property, he too could seek a place in an open international economy. Yet he would have to compete with newly elected leaders in Czechoslovakia, Poland, and Hungary—individuals whose zeal for capitalism the Soviet leader could not rival. When Lech Wałęsa came to Washington in late 1989, he sounded like a disciple of Milton Friedman. "Realistically," read Bush's talking points for one of his meeting with Gorbachev during the 1990 Washington Summit, trade and investment between the two countries "will remain marginal" until Gorbachev took "the necessary steps to open the Soviet economy to the outside world."[95] If Gorbachev complained that Moscow was not receiving "its full share" from the European Bank of Reconstruction and Development set up to facilitate loans, Bush was prepared to respond: "Frankly, it concerned us that an economy of your size might have absorbed most of the bank's resources at the expense of East European countries that have made a commitment to market reform."[96]

The failure to produce a blockbuster U.S.-Soviet trade deal at the Washington Summit disappointed Gorbachev. The Soviet leader had counted on one "to solve most of his internal problems."[97] Given the Soviet economic embargo of Lithuania, Moscow's continued arms sales to Cuba, and the priority to refurnish Eastern Europe using limited resources, the Bush administration faced limited options. "There is no way we will be able to conclude our Trade Agreement, and thus MFN [most favored nation status], unless dialogue with the Lithuanians begins," Bush wrote Gorbachev in advance of the Washington Summit. "Here is the basic reality—there is no way Congress will approve MFN under existing circumstances—no way at all."[98]

Even after Gorbachev lifted the economic blockade of Lithuania, he was to learn a harsh lesson of capitalism. In an open world economy, the Soviets had to compete for investment with not only Eastern Europe but also developing nations around the world. As it happened, 1990 was the same year that India liberalized rules governing foreign trade and outside investment. Indonesia, Malaysia, and Vietnam were fast becoming the new "Asian Tigers." And China's economic reforms continued, unhindered by the turmoil of Tiananmen Square. Driven by new opportunities for profit, direct foreign investment skyrocketed. After a decade of capital flows mainly between "first world" nations, the 1989–1996 period saw a massive uptick in investment in emerging markets—from some $36 billion to $243.8 billion in total. By 1996, 75 percent of these dollars ended up in east Asia or Latin America.[99] The billions that Gorbachev received from German banks for his assent over German reunification would have to suffice. By and large, Western banks, corporations, and pension funds were finding better opportunities elsewhere.

"Freedom is on the march," Bush's budget director, Richard Darman, wrote the president. "The wall has come down. The Soviet empire is collapsing. The new competition for global influence and primacy will be among market-oriented powers. U.S. economic strength and primacy—if sustained—hold unprecedented promise for the shaping of a better world order. But at the moment, the U.S. growth agenda is stalled."[100] Given the automatic spending cuts triggered by the Gramm-Rudman-Hollings Balanced Budget Act, the monetary tightening on the part of Alan Greenspan at the Federal Reserve, and the slowing U.S. economy, Darman was convinced that delaying a budget deal to reduce the federal deficit would retard U.S. economic growth. The president concurred. He signed off on an ongoing budget summit with congressional leaders that would continue into the fall and culminate with his breaking the pledge of "no new taxes." His aspiration to cut the federal deficit ruled out aid to Moscow on a massive scale.

At the Houston Economic Summit of the G7 shortly after Gorbachev lifted the Lithuanian embargo, the Bush administration reiterated that Moscow should join the open world economy. "We commit ourselves to working with the Soviet Union to assist its efforts to create an open society, a pluralistic democracy, and a market-oriented economy," read one of the summit's declarations.[101] The president and his team wanted to educate Moscow about "the concept of the worldwide movement toward democracy and free markets," but the last thing in the world the administration could countenance in the summer of 1990 was a massive loan to shore up the foundering Soviet economy.[102]

## The Cold War Ends

On August 2, 1990, the Iraqi Army invaded Kuwait. Baker heard about the invasion while in Irkutsk with Shevardnadze. He departed for Mongolia, as his two assistants, Robert Zoellick and Dennis Ross, traveled to Moscow to work on a joint statement with their Soviet counterpart, Sergei Tarasenko. On the evening on August 3, 1990, Baker and Shevardnadze held a joint press conference at Vnukovo Airport outside Moscow. The Soviet foreign minister denounced Saddam's behavior. "Let me tell you that it was a rather difficult decision for us ... because of the long-standing relations that we have with Iraq," Shevardnadze told the press. But "this aggression is inconsistent with the principles of new political thinking and, in fact with the civilized relations between nations."[103]

Baker was awestruck. He recalled Reagan's proclamation in January 1981 that the Soviets "have openly and publicly declared that the only morality they recognize is what will further their cause, meaning they reserve unto themselves the right to commit any crime, to lie, to cheat, in order to attain that."[104] In August 1990, the secretary of state "couldn't help remembering those words with a sense of irony."[105] The Soviet Union was "actively engaging in joining the United States in condemning one of its staunchest allies." It was as if "the world had just turned upside down."[106]

"My personal judgment is that the stakes in this for the United States are such that to accommodate Iraq should not be a policy option," Scowcroft declared at a meeting of the National Security Council two days later. "This is the first test of the post war system," Deputy Secretary of State Lawrence Eagleburger added. "As the bipolar contest is relaxed, it permits this, giving people more flexibility because they are not worried about the involvement of the superpowers." Moscow had "come down hard" on Saddam but could do little to rein him in. "Saddam Hussein now has greater flexibility because the Soviets are tangled up in domestic issues. If he succeeds, others may try the same thing. It would be a bad lesson."[107] Bush and his team discussed whether they believed that Saddam would send his forces on to Saudi Arabia. The scenario would be disastrous to regional stability and the health of an international economy dependent on access to Saudi oil. Ousting Manuel Noriega from Panama had been a smashing success, acknowledged Colin Powell, the chairman of the Joint Chiefs of Staff. The Iraq Republican Guard possessed far more experience: "This would be the NFL, not a scrimmage."[108]

"U.S. interests in the Persian Gulf are vital to the national security," read National Security Directive 45, which the president signed on August 20,

1990. "These interests include access to oil and the security and stability of key friendly states in the region. The United States will defend its vital interests in the area, through the use of U.S. military force if necessary and appropriate, against any power with interests inimical to our own."[109] The directive defined vital U.S. interests without reference to ideology or the Soviet Union.

In the days and weeks that followed, President Bush ramped up America's military presence in Saudi Arabia, crafted a United Nations resolution backed by the threat of a U.S.-led force, and sent Secretary of State Baker around the world to procure financial backing for a possible invasion. The president spoke of "drawing a line in the sand." In Moscow, Shevardnadze took the invasion personally. "You know, people sometimes rarely mentioned Kuwait at this time," Alexander Bessmertnykh later recalled. "But to Shevardnadze himself, it was a huge psychological shock that a small country just could be a victim of a larger neighbor; and he felt that someone should do something to protect this small country."[110] Shevardnadze also wanted to help his friend James Baker. "For your information I would like to just say that yesterday at the end of the day we sent a very high level message from the Soviet leadership to Saddam Hussein," he told Baker on the phone on August 6, 1990. "And in it we made a very strong demand that there has to be a massive withdrawal and it must begin now."[111] He called in Iraqi diplomats to inform them that Moscow would not protect them.[112] "An act of terrorism has been perpetrated against the emerging new world order," Shevardnadze declared at the United Nations on September 25, 1990. "This is a major affront to mankind."[113]

In his copy of Shevardnadze's speech, Baker underlined the words "new world order." Gorbachev had employed the phrase in his UN speech of December 1988. "I think we do have a chance at a new world order," George Bush stated at a press conference on August 30—provided that Saddam's aggression was checked.[114]

On September 9, 1990, Bush and Gorbachev met in Helsinki. Saddam's actions portended ill for the region, the two men agreed, and imperiled the prospect of peace between Israelis and Palestinians. "If you look at the situation more broadly," Bush told Gorbachev in their one-on-one meeting, "I see a real possibility of a new world order," repeating his sentiment from two weeks earlier. Out of the crisis and tragedy new opportunities might emerge. The United States and the Soviet Union could not allow the precedent to be set that someone like Saddam Hussein stood to benefit from aggression. "I do not want to use military force," Bush reiterated, but Saddam needed to understand that if he did not leave Kuwait, the United States and its allies were prepared to resort to force.[115]

The president wanted "to put all my cards on the table." Throughout the Cold War, the United States had opposed any Soviet involvement in the Middle East. Bush assured Gorbachev that those days were over. Both sides should work toward a comprehensive Middle East peace. But first, Saddam needed to be turned back. The closer the cooperation between Washington and Moscow in achieving that goal, the more favorable Bush saw the prospects for the "new world order."[116] Saddam's behavior was abhorrent, Gorbachev acknowledged. The Soviet leader supported the UN Security Council resolutions and would abide by them, but he was aggrieved that Bush had not consulted him before sending American troops to Saudi Arabia.[117] Hearing these words, Bush expressed regret. He accepted Gorbachev's remarks as "constructive criticism." Deployment of U.S. troops resulted from an urgent request from Saudi Arabia, the president explained. His administration, he assured Gorbachev, would never act behind the Soviet leader's back.

Gorbachev was mollified, but he still wanted to dissuade Bush from using force. Perhaps the Americans could redraw the line in the sand—to consider force only if Saddam attacked Saudi Arabia or Jordan. He kept insisting that there needed to be a peaceful resolution to the crisis as well as an international conference on the Middle East.[118] "You can't do that," Dennis Ross told Baker, upon hearing talk of a conference. "This will absolutely undercut what we're trying to do. We'll put the moderate Arabs in a position where Saddam is delivering for the Palestinians and they're not. If we created linkage, [Saddam] can claim victory."[119] Ross and his Soviet counterpart, Sergei Tarasenko, worked toward a compromise. The final statement made no reference to a conference, which Baker quietly assured the Soviets he would seek after Saddam was defeated. Dealing with a team they had grown to trust, Gorbachev and Shevardnadze took the Bush administration at its word. They continued to oppose the use of force, yet would not filibuster the campaign to wrest Saddam from Kuwait.

Gorbachev had no use for Saddam or his henchmen. "We will not sacrifice our alliance with the U.S. for this," he instructed Georgy Arbatov to tell his contacts in the Arab world.[120] "You may have received instruction from God, but I still would like to give you advice," Gorbachev told Iraqi foreign minister Tariq Aziz on September 5, 1990, "and you can decide whether to take it or not."[121] That advice was to seek a political settlement with the United States. Neither Aziz nor Saddam heeded it. Still, Gorbachev wanted desperately to prevent a war. He allowed Yevgeny Primakov, an ambitious foreign policy aide, to make a quixotic attempt to broker a deal with Saddam.[122]

In Washington, Scowcroft was impressed. Throughout the Cold War, "any time there was a big international crisis, the United States was on one side and the Soviet Union was on the other," he later recalled. The two countries now found themselves on the same side, which "spawned on our side the hope for what we began to call the New World Order, with the United States and the Soviet Union standing shoulder to shoulder."[123]

"We stand today at a unique and extraordinary moment," Bush declared at a joint session of Congress on September 11, 1990. "The crisis in the Persian Gulf, as grave as it is, also offers a rare opportunity to move toward an historic period of cooperation. Out of these troubled times . . . a new world order— can emerge: a new era—freer from the threat of terror, stronger in the pursuit of justice, and more secure in the quest for peace." All civilized nations, he hoped, could find a place in this order to live together. "A hundred generations have searched for this elusive path to peace, while a thousand wars raged across the span of human endeavor. Today that new world is struggling to be born, a world quite different from the one we've known. A world where the rule of law supplants the rule of the jungle. A world in which nations recognize the shared responsibility for freedom and justice. A world where the strong respect the rights of the weak."[124]

The Bush administration strove to confront Saddam while encouraging Gorbachev's reforms. Immediately following Bush's speech to Congress, James Baker traveled to Moscow to promote investment in the Soviet Union. He brought with him the U.S. secretary of commerce as well as a group of American CEOs representing Chevron, ADM, Pepsico, and other large corporations. New economic thinking was flourishing, Gorbachev told the American delegation. He extolled the virtues of a market-based economy. "We have reached a real turning point in our economy," Gorbachev proclaimed—he had signed off on the Shatalin Plan, which set "500 days" to transform the Soviet economy—but he needed more outside investment. Two of his goals were "financial stabilization" and the convertibility of rubles to dollars.[125] The delegation was not impressed. They considered "financial stabilization" a prerequisite for foreign direct investment—not merely an incentive. The chaotic scenes the Americans encountered in Moscow were troubling. "Privately, I made a number of mental notes about my experiences in the Soviet Union, which only hardened my resolve never to do any business there in the region myself," Secretary of Commerce Robert Mosbacher, a close associate of George Bush from their days in the oil business, later recalled.[126]

After the businessmen had left, Gorbachev pressed his case to Baker. "Could you provide us an interest-free loan of between $1 and 1.5 billion?" Gorbachev asked. When Baker attempted to change the subject, Gorbachev reformulated his question: perhaps one of the Saudi princes who was close with the United States might have a few billion to spare? Baker attempted to lighten the mood: "Just please don't ask Israel—because, like with any good marriage: their money is our money too."[127]

"Difficult time of transition," Baker jotted down during the meeting. "Critical—help us now."[128] He and the president wanted to help Gorbachev. Their hands were tied by the ongoing budget negotiations. At the end of September, the government shut down all nonessential federal offices until an agreement could be reached. "I think this week has been the most unpleasant, or tension filled of the Presidency," Bush confided in his diary on October 6. "It's the damnedest pounding I've ever seen."[129]

Given U.S. budgetary constraints, the administration believed that promoting economic openness was the best way for Gorbachev to procure the loans he needed to modernize the Soviet economy. Part of their vision for the end of the Cold War was a system where developing nations did not have to rely on direct government assistance. The problem for Gorbachev was not that Washington neglected to take steps for him to succeed but that he lacked the imagination to ditch Castro, resolve the Baltics crisis without the use of coercion, or pursue economic openness with the same vigor as the political openness of glasnost.

"The U.S.-Soviet relationship is finally beyond containment and confrontation," Bush declared at the United Nations in October. "The long twilight struggle that for 45 years has divided Europe, our two nations, and much of the world has come to an end." The United Nations, Bush hoped, would "no longer be frozen by the divisions that plagued us during the cold war, that at last—long last—we can build new bridges and tear down old walls, that at long last we will be able to build a new world based on an event for which we have all hoped: an end to the cold war."[130] The president indicated that the United States and its allies would seek a UN resolution to use force to repel Saddam Hussein from Kuwait.

The following month, Bush traveled to Prague. He elaborated on what a new world order entailed. "The United States welcomes the new democracies of central and eastern Europe fully into the commonwealth of freedom, a moral community united in its dedication to free ideals." Every "new nation that joins the ranks of this commonwealth of freedom," he went on to say, "advances us one step closer to a new world order, a world in which the use of force gives way to a shared respect for the rule of law." Europe was on a path toward integration and unity; the spread of freedom need not stop "at the edge of this continent." Aggression in the Persian Gulf, if not confronted, threatened to do just that. At the same time, the "first crisis of the post–cold war era" might also provide "the opportunity to draw upon the great and growing strength of the commonwealth of freedom and forge for all nations a new world order far more stable and secure than any we have known."[131]

The showdown with Saddam coincided with the resolution of the other components of Washington's new world order. The economic merger of the two Germanies followed the Stavropol meeting. On August 31, both parliaments ratified a treaty setting up the process of political union. On September 12, representatives of the four wartime powers relinquished their rights; as of October 3, 1990, the GDR no longer existed.[132] In November 1990, the Charter of Paris for a New Europe laid out a vision of free speech and association, economic liberty, and protection of human rights. It was a realization of the Atlantic Charter—of the principles for which the United States had fought World War II. The Treaty on Conventional Armed Forces in Europe, signed on November 19, 1990, reduced dramatically troop levels on the continent. On November 9, one year after the breach of the Berlin Wall, Germans celebrated peaceful unification.

"The hope," recalls Robert Hutchings, a staffer on the National Security Council, "was that the end of the Cold War would create the conditions not only for a continued transatlantic relationship but a stronger and more natural one, freed from the unnatural imbalances of roles and responsibilities that the Cold War had imposed."[133] The Bush administration aspired to a more peaceful world through institutions such as the United Nations, NATO, the CSCE, the EU, the IMF, GATT, and the World Bank as well as through ideas like freedom and democracy. In his speech to the United Nations in December 1988, Gorbachev renounced the use of force. Bush's conception of a new world order did not renounce force, however. Sanctified by the United Nations and the U.S. Congress, the administration threatened force to drive Saddam from Kuwait. It built a huge coalition army in Saudi Arabia, gave the Iraqi strongman a deadline of January 15, 1991, and prepared for war.

Gorbachev did not agree with Bush's approach. Ultimately, however, he trusted the president. He hoped that that trust would translate into financial assistance. The problems he faced at home were becoming insurmountable. In November 1990, at perhaps the lowest point of his political career, he received the Nobel Peace Prize. The next month, fed up with the attacks against him from the military and annoyed that Gorbachev had allowed Primakov to try to outflank him, Shevardnadze resigned, complete with gloomy predictions of a coming dictatorship. Around this time, Baker arranged for the Saudis to provide a loan to Moscow to get Gorbachev through the winter.[134] As stock markets plummeted amidst the prospect of a war in the Middle East, Western banks that might otherwise have lent to Moscow lost all appetite for risk.[135] Gorbachev could not understand why the United States

**FIGURE 7.2.**   Bush announces Operation Desert Storm, 1991. The president addresses the American people on January 17, 1991. Courtesy of the George Bush Presidential Library and Museum.

would spend billions preparing for war rather than invest in him to make peace. The Persian Gulf War confounded the Soviet leader. Yet he could not stop it.

As the January 15, 1991, deadline approached, Saddam showed no signs of compliance. On January 11, Bush and Gorbachev spoke on the phone. He had received a letter from Saddam, Gorbachev told Bush. Based on his reading of it, the Iraqi strongman was willing to negotiate. He beseeched Bush to give diplomacy just one more chance.

The president thanked Gorbachev for his cooperation. He wanted "to be frank." He took seriously Gorbachev's reservations and preferred to avoid the use of force, "but the final assessment is not optimistic."[136] It was not too late, Gorbachev responded. "Let's work together." A diplomatic solution would be difficult, he acknowledged. "But we must do everything possible—also, the impossible. And let's not lose hope. The Soviet Union and the United States mean something in the world."[137] The January 15 deadline was firm, Bush responded. The United Nations and a coalition of nations supported him.

Gorbachev and Bush spoke again on January 18, 1991, after allied bombing had already begun. Saddam had brought the war on himself, Gorbachev declared. Perhaps Bush would consider a ceasefire—or at least a scaling back of the bombing—and refrain from using the massive land force built up in Saudi Arabia. Bush listened politely but remained firm. A ceasefire would only allow Saddam to snatch "victory from the jaws of defeat."[138] It would legitimize Saddam's aggression and make him a hero in the Middle East. This would surely challenge the "new order" they both sought.[139] Bush told Gorbachev that he held the Soviet leader in his thoughts. He considered the challenges the Soviet Union faced with great sympathy. The president intended to make every effort to resolve any problems arising from the CFE Treaty and to work finally to sign a START treaty. "Call me anytime, day or night," Bush told him. "I wish you success, and best of luck in all things, in resolving your problems."[140]

The previous evening, Operation Desert Storm rained destruction on Baghdad. One of the many planes used that evening was the F-117 Nighthawk. Classified throughout the 1980s, the F-117 was a product of Lockheed Martin's "Skunk Works" advanced research design program. It was originally built for a much different purpose: to evade Soviet air defenses in central Europe, destroy critical targets, and degrade Soviet capabilities to wage war against NATO. Instead, the U.S. Air Force used the plane to demolish Saddam's air defense network, strike critical targets in Baghdad, and erode Iraq's capacity to resist an internal coalition reflecting Bush's new world order. Meanwhile, Apache helicopters designed to fend off an approaching Soviet army, now stationed at the Fulda Gap in Germany, headed to liberate Kuwait, and Patriot Missiles attempted to shoot down medium-range ballistic missiles designed by Soviet scientists.

The Bush administration launched the Persian Gulf War to rid Kuwait of Saddam's forces and to usher in a new world order. It was a war fought for ideals and self-interest by a mighty coalition, legitimized by the United Nations, against a ruthless tyrant. It came after a year in which America's Cold War dreams had come true: Germany unified; Europe whole and free; an open world economy; and a Soviet Union that no longer threatened the existence of the United States. The great dilemmas and agonies of U.S. foreign policy did not end. Nor did history. Yet on January 17, 1991, as the bombs fell on Baghdad, the Cold War was over.

# Conclusion

## Individuals and Strategy

What marked the period from approximately 1978 to 1991 was the sustained attempt on the part of powerful officials to revitalize capitalism and on the part of brilliant entrepreneurs to improve productivity and reshape consumer habits. Paul Volcker's interest rate hikes caused tremendous pain in the short term. They hindered Jimmy Carter's prospects for reelection and produced setbacks for Reagan in the first two years of his presidency, but the rate hikes ultimately tamed inflation. The stimulus of Reagan's tax cuts and ramped-up government spending, combined with deregulation, selective liberalization of trade, low inflation, technological advancements, higher productivity, and the nascent information revolution, fostered an economic recovery for international capitalism sustained by a drop in the global price of oil.[1] Capitalism's recovery, in turn, boosted the strength and appeal of the West. Communism's persistent stagnation undermined the cohesion of the Eastern bloc and undercut the Soviet challenge to capitalist and democratic institutions. By themselves, these developments were not enough to end the Cold War. Individuals in power ended the Cold War through unscripted actions. The four critical individuals in that final decade were Ronald Reagan, George Shultz, George H. W. Bush, and Mikhail Gorbachev.

Rather than perform as was expected of them, Reagan, Shultz, Bush, and Gorbachev improvised. In the last years of the conflict, improvisation mattered more than any master plan. Ascribing important events to wise decisions laid out in a clear set of directives might be more comforting to historians as they seek to find coherence amidst change, but such interpretations do not explain the swift and peaceful end to the Cold War.[2]

Grand strategies did not shape the end of the Cold War. Reagan's "rhetorical offensive" had little impact on the decisions and events that ended the conflict. Yes, Reagan called the Soviet Union an "evil empire" in 1983. That had no bearing on the coming of Mikhail Gorbachev. Yes, Reagan stood in Berlin in the summer of 1987 and proclaimed: "Mr. Gorbachev, tear down this wall!" But Gorbachev never gave an order to tear down the Berlin Wall. Demolition occurred by accident.[3]

Triumphalist histories of the end of the Cold War do not accept that anything was accidental or, more curiously, that Gorbachev played a key role. They regard NSDD-32 and NSDD-75 as comprising a roadmap to victory and point to Reagan's rhetoric as part of that campaign.[4] As I describe in chapter 1, NSDD-32 set forth these objectives: foster pluralism and promote nationalism in the Soviet Union; curtail its meddling abroad; and force that nation's leaders to "bear the brunt of its shortcomings." In short, the document called for the United States "to prevail" in the Cold War.[5] As I describe in chapter 3, NSDD-75 called for the United States "to contain and over time reverse Soviet expansionism by competing effectively on a sustained basis with the Soviet Union in all international arenas."[6] These objectives were scarcely different from those put forward by previous U.S. presidential administrations. Starting with George Kennan's Long Telegram and Mr. X article, the long-term goal of the Truman administration and those that followed was always more than containment: it was victory.[7] The "responsibility of world leadership," read NSC-68, "demands that we make the attempt, and accept the risks inherent in it, to bring about order and justice by means consistent with the principles of freedom and democracy."[8] President Dwight Eisenhower accepted the goals of his predecessor yet called for a more proactive "New Look" to achieve them. "In the end he rejected the objective of coercive rollback and the concept of a time of peak danger from the Soviet threat," write Robert Bowie and Richard Immerman. "In his view the task of preventing war and Soviet expansion, seeking to induce and encourage change in Soviet hostility, and mitigating the risk of war would require cooperative actions by a vigorous free world over many years before the eventual decline of the Soviet system and threat."[9]

While the objectives of Reagan's national security decision directives were of long standing, their strident tone was not. Yet Gorbachev's reforms went far beyond the aspirations of these strategy statements and were not caused by them. Soviet economic and political life changed dramatically. Increased "pluralism" and resurgent "nationalism" within the USSR accompanied change. In 1990, the Bush administration might very well have preferred they had not. Bush, Baker, and Scowcroft did not want to deal with Boris Yeltsin. While they all sympathized with Lithuanians, they feared "suicidal nationalism," as Bush put it, in Ukraine the following year. If NSDD-32 indeed was responsible for "nationalism" and "pluralism" in the Soviet Union, it proved to be a tremendous headache for the Bush administration at precisely the time Washington was defining and implementing a Cold War victory.

U.S. policies, as scripted in NSDD-32 and NSDD-75, were not responsible for pluralism and nationalism in the Soviet Union. Gorbachev was. Moreover, by the time of Gorbachev's selection, the individuals who crafted these statements had departed the Reagan administration. Hardliners like Caspar Weinberger, to be sure, continued to invoke them, but Reagan relied more on those who thought differently. The document that mattered most of all between 1984 and 1988 was not NSDD-32 but the one championed by George Shultz and Jack Matlock. Shultz and Matlock's four-part framework was not a grand strategy; it was a blueprint for pursuing strength and diplomacy simultaneously.[10] It outlined procedures meant to rationalize U.S.-Soviet relations. It ensured that diplomacy would not stop on account of events that no one could foresee. It helped transcend Reagan's contradictions and ambivalence, which persisted even after the fall of 1983—a point that some historians have identified as a clear shift in his thinking.[11] And it proved to be far more important than NSDD-32, NSDD-75, and other formal strategy statements.

So did the concept of nuclear abolitionism, which was nowhere in the two NSDDs. That Reagan and Gorbachev shared this vision was incredible. At Reykjavik, the president articulated a plan unlike any other: The two sides would agree to eliminate all nuclear missiles. The United States would pursue SDI without restrictions and share it with the Soviet Union once the system worked. Mutual missile defense would ensure that both sides upheld their end of the bargain. SDI would provide protection in case a madman like Qadhafi ever got his hands on an ICBM. Surely, no American president in history ever conceived of a grander strategy than that! But Reagan's proposal was not a grand strategy; it was a fantasy. Indeed, the president "was as skillful a politician as the nation had seen for many years," John Lewis Gaddis writes, but he was not "one of its sharpest grand strategists ever."[12] Still, one should not dismiss Reagan's dream—as Caspar Weinberger and other hardliners did at the time. Reagan believed in SDI, and his sincerity elicited Gorbachev's trust.[13]

Rather than comprising a grand strategy or a "triumph of imagination," Reagan's outlook was defined by his ebullient optimism.[14] The president could not quite comprehend that anyone could see the world differently than he did. Unbounded optimism led him to dream of a world without nuclear weapons and without communism. Unbounded optimism inspired him to proclaim that the United States had the power to cast the world anew. One reason historian Sean Wilentz can regard the period from 1974 to 2008 as "the Age of Reagan" is that the president's words encapsulated Americans' idealized view of themselves and their role in the world.[15] The United States, Reagan loved to proclaim, was too great for small dreams.[16] But with this aspiration for big dreams came contradictions, ambivalence, ambiguity, and potential blowback. From 1981 to 1988, the country paid a small price; it paid a big price from 2001 to 2008, when efforts to change the world wrought more havoc and destruction than resultant democracy and freedom.[17]

Reagan believed in "peace through strength" as much as he believed in a "crusade for freedom." Even after the huge arms buildup, as described in chapters 3 through 5, Reagan did not think that the United States had redressed the nuclear imbalances that he insisted still favored the Soviet Union. In the nuclear era, strength was subjective. Hardliners could always accentuate "inferiority" in one category of weapons in a way that ignored "superiority" in another. In the summer of 1987, Caspar Weinberger did precisely that. He wanted Reagan to cut off all nuclear negotiations with the Soviets until Washington could deploy SDI. Only then could the United States truly negotiate from a position of strength. Henry Kissinger and other prominent U.S. statesmen agreed; they urged the president and America's allies to keep the Pershing II and cruise missiles in Western Europe.[18]

Weinberger and Kissinger did not prevail; George Shultz did. Shultz believed in negotiating while building strength. He believed that INF deployment signaled U.S. strength. It demonstrated the cohesion of the Western alliance and illustrated that the Atlantic community would not be rent apart by protests and strikes. After the Soviet invasion of Afghanistan in 1979 and 1980 and the withdrawal of SALT II, no arms treaty could proceed through the U.S. Senate absent a dramatic demonstration of Western strength. Just as importantly, INF deployment empowered Shultz to best Weinberger in internal debates. As described in chapter 3, Shultz submitted to Reagan the four-part framework before INF deployment. He testified to Congress in June 1983 that it was time to negotiate. Time and again after INF deployment, he reminded the president that the United States and its allies were now negotiating from strength. Shultz was willing to negotiate both before and after the fall of 1983; he never wanted to wait until the United States had achieved maximal strength. Shultz's role is a key to understanding the end of the Cold War, a point overlooked in many scholarly accounts, especially among Reagan triumphalists.[19] He ought to be regarded as one of the great secretaries of state in American history.[20]

Conversations between Secretary of State Alexander Haig and Foreign Minister Eduard Shevardnadze would also have gone very differently than the ones that actually did take place between Shultz and Shevardnadze. Had Haig stayed in the administration, he would have loathed hearing about Ivan and Anya and Jim and Sally. Haig would have given his own speech calling for more linkage and more talk of interests and reciprocity. Human rights, according to his view of the world, was not something to be discussed in politics among nations.[21]

Shultz was secretary of state when Reagan prepared to give a speech on U.S.-Soviet relations in January 1984. The president's top Soviet adviser at that time, Jack Matlock, drafted the "Ivan and Anya" speech and, a year and a half later, the "Soviet Union 101" tutorials for Reagan before the meeting with Gorbachev in Geneva.[22] Matlock was also the U.S. ambassador to the Soviet Union when George H. W. Bush entered the Oval Office. The Soviet specialist lamented the "pause" that ensued—as have many historians since then.

Yet the Cold War was not over in January 1989. And, as I describe in chapter 6, the new administration was more active than critics have alleged. George Bush and his top advisers could not predict the future, so they improvised. Their overriding priority in 1989 was to minimize the prospect of violence. When walls came down, Bush was better suited than Reagan to set the terms for a Cold War victory. Scowcroft and Baker were personally close to Bush, just as Shultz and Weinberger had been to Reagan. The difference was that Bush was capable of intervening to resolve disputes. Principals left the Cabinet Room confident that they knew what the commander-in-chief wanted. Because he set clear priorities for his administration, his national security team seldom needed the president to intervene. (In his eight years in office, Reagan had six national security advisors. In his four years in office, Bush had only one—Brent Scowcroft.)[23] Even those accounts that praise the skill of Bush's national security team still fault it for failing to construct an enduring Cold War strategy.[24] "Bush offered no concrete vision of America's future international role now that containment . . . was no longer relevant," writes George Herring.[25]

As chapters 6 and 7 demonstrate, however, Bush and his advisers acted with clarity of purpose, thoughtfulness, and prudence amidst formidable political and economic constraints. When German chancellor Helmut Kohl seized the initiative on German reunification, Bush's national security team reacted skillfully.[26] In their approach to Europe after the Cold War they adjusted old institutions to new realities. Their pursuit of free trade and globalized markets were premised on old ideas. They wanted to adjust these old ideas to new realities.[27]

Gorbachev also wanted to adjust old ideas to new realities. He sought to reconfigure communism to meet the social and economic challenges of the 1980s. He rejected the status quo upon taking office in 1985 and embarked upon radical reform. William Wohlforth and Stephen Brooks have written that changes in the nature of the international economy meant that Gorbachev did not have much choice. Economic constraints during this era, they aver, necessitated reform and strategic retrenchment on the part of whatever dignitary happened to occupy the Kremlin.[28] The structural changes that Wohlforth, Brooks, and others describe were important. I hope this book has provided a more textured account of both structure and agency than recent works that emphasize personal diplomacy alone.[29] Yet leaders always faced choices, and structural conditions did not dictate outcomes. Economic factors did not shape the Soviet decision to invade Afghanistan in 1979, nor did material factors impel Gorbachev to resist using force in 1989.

Evolving notions of how to reform communism and changing perceptions of threat led Gorbachev to make decisions that ended the Cold War. If he did not possess a grand strategy, he did know how to learn and improvise.[30] He sought nuclear arms reductions because he hated these weapons and wanted to reallocate resources to spur economic growth inside the USSR, harness new technologies, reverse environmental degradation, create a consumer culture, allow freedom of expression, and rekindle pride in the Soviet way of life.[31] Gorbachev certainly did not regard his foreign policies as retrenchment. In 1987, he called for perestroika not only for the Soviet Union but also "for the world." He did so not because he actually possessed a master plan for the world but because he wanted to retain a leadership role for the Soviet Union. The big developments of the mid-1980s—the recovery of the industrialized global economy, the economic and political integration of Europe, China's new trajectory—did not need Soviet leadership, but Gorbachev perceived that he had a stake in them. He was committed to personal relationships with Reagan, Shultz, Thatcher, and Mitterrand, and, later, to Bush and Kohl. Reagan's devotion to SDI aggravated Gorbachev, as did Bush's strategic review in 1989 and his promotion of German unification in 1990. Yet Gorbachev never walked away from his counterparts in Washington. He would not take action that risked alienating them. This was not the attitude of his predecessors, who approached the world after the destruction of World War II and the malaise of the 1970s.

A different Soviet leader could easily have returned to Moscow after Reykjavik in 1986, halted all reforms, and mobilized his countrymen to fend off the capitalist world's quest for nuclear inviolability. Or, in light of the Reagan administration's decision to free itself of SALT II limitations, Gorbachev, as Vladislav Zubok points out, could have decided at the start of 1987 "to give up on Reagan and wait for future opportunities."[32] Gorbachev took neither approach. He did not believe that Reagan—or any other Western leader—was out to destroy the USSR.

"A different person could have taken a very different course of action," Zubok sums up his critique of Gorbachev, "and perhaps as a result the Soviet Union would not have collapsed as disastrously as it did, creating so many problems for the future."[33] Indeed, in his mission to revive and recalibrate Soviet communism, Gorbachev failed. Ironically, his failure to conceive of a new form of socialism opened the floodgates for a torrent of capitalism. His foreign policies sacrificed Moscow's superpower status and led to the triumph of the Soviet Union's Cold War adversary. Gorbachev's idealism may indeed have destroyed the Soviet Union, but it allowed 1989 to happen. Gorbachev believed that John Paul II promoted the same agenda. He did not see reformers in Poland and Czech as threatening, because he naively believed all were working toward a common purpose: a common European home within a new world order.

Revolutions could not have played out peacefully in 1989 had it not been for the personal courage of such individuals as Lech Wałęsa, Václav Havel, Pope John Paul II, and the leaders of the East German protest movements, all of whom renounced violence.[34] But it was Gorbachev who empowered and enabled them. He was the independent variable that distinguished 1989 from 1956 and 1968. These were heroic individuals who risked their lives, while Gorbachev and Reagan risked their political legacies.

The Politburo would never have chosen Gorbachev to lead the country in 1985 had its members possessed any inkling of the reforms he would adopt—especially if they had known that so many of these reforms were destined to fail! Gorbachev attempted to adapt his beliefs to new realities whether he understood them fully or not. Improvisations worked abroad because they arrested the nuclear arms race, and his concepts of a common European home and a new world order based on common human values rather than class conflict led to peaceful revolutions that opened closed societies. Improvisations failed at home because communism did not work without the authoritarianism and coercion that Gorbachev was seeking to abandon. The failed coup in August 1991 made him a lame duck to Yeltsin. By the start of the next year, Gorbachev was out of power, and the Soviet Union no longer existed.

Gorbachev's reforms led to the collapse not only of the Soviet empire but also of much of the Russian empire dating back for centuries. Although he lost an empire, he did not believe that he lost the Cold War. But he did. And because he did, a generation of human beings in the United States, Russia, and elsewhere on this planet grew up innocent of the specter of a nuclear holocaust.

# Notes

## Introduction

1. Robert M. Gates, *From the Shadows: The Ultimate Insider's Story of Five Presidents and How They Won the Cold War* (New York: Simon and Schuster), 114. See also National Security Archive, "The 3 A.M. Phone Call," available at www.gwu.edu/~nsarchiv/nukevault/ebb371/, accessed February 20, 2013.

2. See CNN, *Cold War,* Episode 23, "The Wall Comes Down."

3. In one of the most discussed history books of the past thirty years, Paul Kennedy wrote (even after the emergence of Gorbachev), "There is nothing in the character or tradition of the Russian state to suggest that it could ever accept imperial decline gracefully." Kennedy, *The Rise and Fall of the Great Powers: Economic Change and Military Conflict from 1500 to 2000* (New York: Random House, 1987), 514.

## Chapter 1

1. Reagan, "The President's News Conference," January 29, 1981, available at www.reagan.utexas.edu/archives/speeches/1981/12981b.htm, accessed February 19, 2013.

2. Stuart Spencer, quoted in Thomas C. Reed, *At the Abyss: An Insider's History of the Cold War* (New York: Presidio Press/Ballantine Books, 2004), 234.

3. "Excerpts From an Interview with Walter Cronkite of CBS News," March 3, 1981, available at www.reagan.utexas.edu/archives/speeches/1981/30381c.htm, accessed February 19, 2013.

4. Ibid.

5. Reagan, "Address to British Parliament," June 8, 1982, available at www.reagan.utexas.edu/archives/speeches/1982/60882a.htm, accessed February 19, 2013.

6. James A. Baker, interviewed in "Reagan," *The American Experience,* television documentary produced by PBS, WGBH-TV Boston, 1998.

7. George Church, Dean Brelis, and Gregory Wierzynski, "Alexander Haig: The Vicar Takes Charge," *Time,* March 16, 1981.

8. Ibid. "He's like a Greek god," his wife observed the first time she saw him, according to *Time.*

9. See Timothy Naftali, *Blind Spot: The Secret History of American Counterterrorism* (New York: Basic Books, 2005), 117.

10. Kissinger was less enamored of Haig. "We should all have such protégés," he bemoaned to Arthur Schlesinger, upon hearing of Haig's appointment. Arthur M. Schlesinger Jr., February 4, 1981, in *Journals, 1952–2000* (New York: Penguin Press, 2007), 512.

11. Alexander M. Haig Jr., *Caveat: Realism, Reagan, and Foreign Policy* (London: Weidenfeld and Nicolson, 1984), 32.

12. "Memorandum for the Record: Record of National Security Council Meeting," February 11, 1981, box 91282, Executive Secretariat, NSC: National Security Council Meeting Files, Ronald Reagan Library, Simi Valley, California (hereafter RRL).

13. Raymond L. Garthoff, *The Great Transition: American-Soviet Relations and the End of the Cold War* (Washington, DC: Brookings Institution Press, 1994), 15–16.

14. Quoted in Lou Cannon, *President Reagan: The Role of a Lifetime,* 1st ed. (New York: PublicAffairs, 2000), 162.

15. *NBC Evening News,* March 24, 1981, available at http://tvnews.vanderbilt.edu/program.pl?ID=515842, accessed February 19, 2013.

16. Ibid.

17. Ronald Reagan, *An American Life* (New York: Simon and Schuster, 1990), 36.

18. Ronald Reagan, February 4, 1981, in Douglas Brinkley, ed., *The Reagan Diaries* (New York: HarperCollins, 2007), 2.

19. "Memorandum of Conversation with Dutch Prime Minister," March 31, 1981, William Clark Files, RRL.

20. Reagan, *American Life,* 272–73.

21. Ibid., 272.

22. Reagan, "A Time for Choosing," October 27, 1964, available at www.reagan.utexas.edu/archives/reference/timechoosing.html, accessed February 19, 2013.

23. Reagan, "Will They Say We Kept Them Free?" August 19, 1976, available at www.reagan.utexas.edu/archives/reference/8.19.76.html, accessed February 19, 2013.

24. Paul Kengor, *God and Ronald Reagan: A Spiritual Life* (New York: Harper, 2004), 18.

25. Ibid., 34.

26. Nancy Reagan, *My Turn* (New York: Random House, 1989), 63.

27. "1980 Presidential Debate between Jimmy Carter and Ronald Reagan," available at www.reagan.utexas.edu/archives/reference/10.28.80debate.html, accessed February 19, 2013.

28. Reagan, "Communism, the Disease," radio broadcast, May 1975, in Kiron K. Skinner, Annelise Anderson, and Martin Anderson, eds., *Reagan, In His Own Hand* (New York: Free Press, 2001), 11–12.

29. Reagan to Severin Palydowycz, June 1980, in Kiron K. Skinner, Annelise Anderson, and Martin Anderson, eds., *Reagan: A Life in Letters* (New York: Free Press, 2003), 374–75.

30. Reagan, "SALT Talks II," radio broadcast, July 31, 1978, in Skinner et al., eds., *Reagan, In His Own Hand,* 84.

31. Reagan, "PEACE," August 18, 1980, in ibid., 484.

32. Reagan, "Two Worlds," radio broadcast, August 7, 1978, in ibid., 15.

33. Reagan, "Announcement to Seek the Republican Nomination for President," November 13, 1979, available at www.reagan.utexas.edu/archives/reference/11.13.79.html, accessed February 19, 2013.

34. Reagan, "PEACE," August 18, 1980, in Skinner et al., eds., *Reagan, In His Own Hand,* 482.

35. Reagan, "Soviet Workers," radio broadcast, May 25, 1977, in Skinner et al., eds., *Reagan, In His Own Hand,* 146–47.

36. Reagan, "Neutron Bomb," radio broadcast, February 20, 1978, box 19, "Speeches and Writings: Radio Taping," RRL.

37. Reagan, "Russians," radio broadcast, May 25, 1977, in Skinner et al., eds., *Reagan, In His Own Hand,* 33–34; "Spaceships," radio broadcast, February 20, 1978, box 19, "Speeches and Writings: Radio Taping," RRL.

38. Reagan, "Farewell Speeches," radio broadcast, January 19, 1977, in Skinner et al., eds., *Reagan, In His Own Hand,* 65.

39. Reagan, "The Military," radio broadcast, September 27, 1977, in ibid., 69–70.

40. Reagan to "Ed," after June 1976, in Skinner et al., eds., *Reagan: A Life in Letters,* 516.

41. Reagan to Charles Burton Marshall, April 8, 1980, in ibid., 398–99.

42. Quoted in Paul Lettow, *Ronald Reagan and His Quest to Abolish Nuclear Weapons* (New York: Random House, 2005), 23.

43. Reagan, "War," radio broadcast, March 13, 1978, in Skinner et al., eds., *Reagan, In His Own Hand,* 99–100.

44. Reagan, "Defense IV," radio broadcast, September 11, 1979, in ibid., 120

45. David Stockman, *The Triumph of Politics: How the Reagan Revolution Failed* (New York: Harper and Row, 1986), 281.

46. Reagan, "Commencement Address at West Point," May 27, 1981, available at www.reagan.utexas.edu/archives/speeches/1981/52781c.htm, accessed February 19, 2013.

47. "Memorandum for the Record: Record of National Security Council Meeting," July 7, 1981, Box 91282, Executive Secretariat, NSC: National Security Council Meeting Files, RRL.

48. William Odom, quoted in Naftali, *Blind Spot,* 119.

49. Cannon, *President Reagan,* 158.

50. William Clark, quoted in Paul Kengor, *The Judge: William P. Clark, Ronald Reagan's Top Hand* (San Francisco: Ignatius Press, 2007), 105.

51. Ibid., 116.

52. See Stockman, *Triumph of Politics,* 116–19.

53. "Memorandum for the Record: Record of National Security Council Meeting," May 22, 1981, box 91282, Executive Secretariat, NSC: National Security Council Meeting Files, RRL.

54. Caspar W. Weinberger, *In the Arena: A Memoir of the 20th Century* (Washington, DC: Regnery, 2001), 23.

55. Ibid., 273–74.

56. "Memorandum for the Record: Record of National Security Council Meeting," February 6, 1981, box 91282, Executive Secretariat, NSC: National Security Council Meeting Files, RRL.

57. Colin L. Powell and Joseph E. Persico, *My American Journey* (New York: Random House, 1995).

58. Michael K. Deaver, *A Different Drummer: My Thirty Years with Ronald Reagan,* 1st ed. (New York: HarperCollins, 2001), 77.

59. See Jeane Kirkpatrick, "Dictatorships and Double Standards," *Commentary* (November 1979), available at www.commentarymagazine.com/viewarticle.cfm/dictatorships-double-standards-6189, accessed February 19, 2013.

60. See Richard Pipes, "Why the Soviet Union Thinks It Could Fight and Win a Nuclear War," *Commentary* 64 (July 1977): 21–34.

61. Ofira Seliktar, *Politics, Paradigms, and Intelligence Failures: Why So Few Predicted the Collapse of the Soviet Union* (Armonk, NY: M.E. Sharpe, 2004), 118–19.

62. Richard Pipes, "Inside Reagan's Bid for Détente," August 22, 2004, available at http://articles.latimes.com/2004/aug/22/books/bk-pipes22, accessed November 13, 2012.

63. Memo, Charles Z. Wick to David R. Gergen, "Countering Soviet Disinformation," August 7, 1981, RRL.

64. For an overview of Wick's initiatives, see Nicholas J. Cull, *The Cold War and the United States Information Agency: American Propaganda and Public Diplomacy, 1945–1989* (New York: Cambridge University Press, 2009).

65. William Casey, quoted in John Prados, *Safe for Democracy: The Secret Wars of the CIA,* 1st ed. (Chicago: Ivan R. Dee, 2006), 495. See also Joseph E. Persico, *Casey: The Lives and Secrets of William J. Casey: From the OSS to the CIA* (New York: Viking, 1990).

66. David Arbel and Ran Edelist, *Western Intelligence and the Collapse of the Soviet Union, 1980–1990: Ten Years That Did Not Shake the World* (London: Frank Cass, 2003), 152.

67. Richard Perle, quoted in Roy Gutman, "The Nay-Sayer of Arms Control," *Newsday,* February 18, 1983, p. 6.

68. "Memorandum for the Record: Record of National Security Council Meeting," March 19, 1981, box 91282, Executive Secretariat, NSC: National Security Council Meeting Files, RRL.

69. Reagan, June 21, 1981, in Brinkley, ed., *Reagan Diaries,* 24.

70. Letter, Ronald Reagan to John O. Koehler, July 9, 1981, in Skinner et al., eds., *Reagan: A Life in Letters,* 375.

71. Reagan, "The President's News Conference," June 16, 1981, available at www.reagan.utexas.edu/archives/speeches/1981/61681b.htm, accessed February 19, 2013.

72. Reagan, July 14, 1981, in Brinkley, ed., *Reagan Diaries,* 30.

73. Richard Pipes, quoted in Laurence I. Barrett, *Gambling with History* (New York: Penguin, 1984).

74. "Memorandum for the Record: Record of National Security Council Meeting," October 13, 1981, box 91283, Executive Secretariat, NSC: National Security Council Meeting Files, RRL.

75. Ibid.

76. Reagan, "Remarks to Members of the National Press Club on Arms Reductions and Nuclear Weapons," November 18, 1981, available at www.reagan.utexas.edu/archives/speeches/1981/111881a.htm, accessed February 19, 2013.

77. This wholly skeptical interpretation of the "zero option" is laid out in Strobe Talbot, *Deadly Gambits: The Reagan Administration and the Stalemate in Arms Control* (New York: Alfred A. Knopf, 1984).

78. Reagan, "Remarks to Members of the National Press Club on Arms Reductions and Nuclear Weapons," November 18, 1981, available at www.reagan.utexas.edu/archives/speeches/1981/111881a.htm, accessed February 19, 2013.

79. Ibid.

80. Letter, Ronald Reagan to Leonid Brezhnev, November 17, 1981, box 38, U.S.S.R.: General Sec. Brezhnev, Head of State Correspondence File, RRL.

81. Ibid.

82. "Memorandum for the Record: Record of National Security Council Meeting," October 16, 1981, box 91282, Executive Secretariat, NSC: National Security Council Meeting Files, RRL.

83. See, for example, "The Haig vs. Allen Dispute," *Washington Post,* November 8, 1981, L20.

84. Reagan, November 1, 1981, in Brinkley, ed., *Reagan Diaries,* 47.

85. Reagan, November 5, 1981, in ibid.

86. Reagan to Brezhnev, April 3, 1981, box 38, U.S.S.R.: General Sec. Brezhnev, Head of State Correspondence File, RRL.

87. "Memorandum for the Record: Record of National Security Council Meeting," p. 4, December 21, 1981, box 91283, Executive Secretariat, NSC: National Security Council Meeting Files, RRL.

88. Ibid., 4.

89. Ibid., 6.

90. Ibid., 7.

91. Ibid., 11.

92. "Memorandum for the Record: Record of National Security Council Meeting," pp. 7–9, December 22, 1981, box 91283, Executive Secretariat, NSC: National Security Council Meeting Files, RRL.

93. Reagan, December 22, 1981, in Brinkley, ed., *Reagan Diaries,* 58.

94. See Memo, Norman A. Bailey to James Nance, December 23, 1981, Nance Chron., box 2, James Nance Files, RRL. A full accounting of the measures adopted can be found in Haig's cable one week later. See Cable, Alexander M. Haig Jr. to Andrei Gromyko, December 30, 1981, RAC box 5, Norman A. Bailey Files, RRL.

95. Ronald Reagan, "Interview with the President," December 23, 1981, available at www.reagan.utexas.edu/archives/speeches/1981/122381f.htm, accessed November 13, 2012.

96. "Memorandum for the Record: Record of National Security Council Meeting," pp. 5, 9, January 5, 1982, box 91283, Executive Secretariat, NSC: National Security Council Meeting Files, RRL.

97. Ibid., 7.

98. Ibid., 9.

99. Cannon, *President Reagan,* 158. Following a minor scandal, Richard Allen had submitted his resignation on the eve of the Polish crisis.

100. Roger Robinson, quoted in Kengor, *Judge,* 148.

101. William Clark, interviewed in *In the Face of Evil: Reagan's War in Word and Deed.* DVD. Directed by Stephen K. Bannon (Los Angeles: Bannon Films, 2004).

102. Pipes, quoted in Kengor, *Judge,* 150.

103. NSDD-32, available at www.fas.org/irp/offdocs/nsdd/nsdd-032.htm, accessed February 19, 2013.

104. "Memorandum for the Record: Record of National Security Council Meeting," April 16, 1982, box 91284, Executive Secretariat, NSC: National Security Council Meeting Files, RRL.

105. Letter, Thomas Reed to William Clark, "Release Plan, NSDD-32 (with attachment)," May 8, 1982, box 32, NSDD-32, RRL.

106. Ibid.

107. Richard Pipes to William Clark, "Your Georgetown Speech," May 27, 1982, quoted in Kengor, *Judge,* 168.

108. Quoted in ibid., 169.

109. "The Neo-Conservative Anguish over Reagan's Foreign Policy," *New York Times,* May 2, 1982.

110. Reagan, "Address at Commencement Exercises at Eureka College," May 9, 1982, available at www.reagan.utexas.edu/archives/speeches/1982/50982a.htm, accessed February 19, 2013.

111. Ibid.

112. Ibid.

113. Letter, Leonid Brezhnev to Ronald Reagan, May 20, 1982, box 38, "U.S.S.R.: General Sec. Brezhnev," Head of State Correspondence File, RRL.

114. "Memorandum for the Record: Record of National Security Council Meeting," May 24, 1982, box 91284, Executive Secretariat, NSC: National Security Council Meeting Files, RRL.

115. Ibid.

116. Reagan, May 25, 1982, in Brinkley, ed., *Reagan Diaries,* 86.

117. Reagan, "Address to British Parliament," June 8, 1982, available at www.reagan.utexas.edu/archives/speeches/1982/60882a.htm, accessed November 13, 2012.

118. Ibid.

119. Robert Schlesinger, *White House Ghosts: Presidents and Their Speechwriters: From FDR to George W. Bush,* 1st ed. (New York: Simon and Schuster, 2008), 327.

120. Richard Pipes, *Vixi: Memoirs of a Non-Belonger* (New Haven, CT: Yale University Press, 2003), 199.

121. Ibid.

122. Reagan, June 25, 1982, in Brinkley, ed., *Reagan Diaries,* 90–91.

123. Reagan, December 3, 1981, in ibid., 52.

124. Reagan, February 18, 1982, in ibid., 70.

## Chapter 2

1. See Philip Zelikow, "The Suicide of the East? 1989 and the Fall of Communism," *Foreign Affairs* 88, no. 6 (November/December 2009), available at www.foreignaffairs.com/articles/65628/philip-d-zelikow/the-suicide-of-the-east (accessed March 20, 2011); see also *Time,* 106, no. 2 (July 14, 1975) and *Time,* 115, no. 16 (April 21, 1980).

2. See Giovanni Arrighi, "The World Economy and the Cold War," in *The Cambridge History of the Cold War,* ed. Melvyn P. Leffler and Odd Arne Westad (New York: Cambridge University Press, 2010), 3:27. Arrighi identified "the crisis of U.S. hegemony which became the dominant event of the 1970s."

3. Charles S. Maier, "'Malaise': The Crisis of Capitalism in the 1970s," in *The Shock of the Global: The 1970s in Perspective,* ed. Niall Ferguson, Charles S. Maier, Erez Manela, and Daniel J. Sargent (Cambridge, MA: Harvard University Press, 2010), 37.

4. Jeffry A. Frieden, *Global Capitalism: Its Fall and Rise in the Twentieth Century* (New York: W. W. Norton, 2006), 373.

5. For a recent account of Reagan's involvement with General Electric and its effect on his political outlook, see Thomas W. Evans, *The Education of Ronald Reagan: The General Electric Years and the Untold Story of His Conversion to Conservatism* (New York: Columbia University Press, 2008).

6. See Niall Ferguson, "Introduction: Crisis, What Crisis?" in *Shock of the Global,* ed. Ferguson et al., 1–21.

7. Tony Judt, *Postwar: A History of Europe since 1945* (New York: Penguin Press, 2005), 537.

8. John W. Young, "Western Europe and the End of the Cold War, 1979–1989," in *Cambridge History of the Cold War,* ed. Leffler and Westad, 3:300.

9. Helmut Schmidt, "The 1977 Alastair Buchan Memorial Lecture," *Survival,* Jan./Feb. 1978.

10. Maynard Glitman, *The Last Battle of the Cold War* (New York: Palgrave, 2006), 22–23.

11. See Jeffry Herf, *War by Other Means: Soviet Power, West German Resistance, and the Battle of the Euromissiles* (New York: Free Press, 1991).

12. Memorandum of Conversation, "Secretary Haig's Breakfast Meeting with FRG Chancellor Schmidt," January 6, 1982, available at http://foia.state.gov/documents/foiadocs/31b3.PDF, accessed November 22, 2010.

13. Herf, *War by Other Means,* 158–63.

14. See Frédéric Bozo, *Mitterrand, the End of the Cold War, and German Unification,* translated from the French by Susan Emanuel (New York: Berghahn Books, 2009), 9–12.

15. N. Artemov, "Difficult Legacy," January 20, 1981, *Sotsialisticheskaya Industria.* Translated and included in *Current Digest of the Post-Soviet Press,* vol. 33, no. 3, February 18, 1981, p. 1.

16. Alexander Bessmertnykh, quoted in William Wohlforth, ed., *Witnesses to the End of the Cold War* (Baltimore: Johns Hopkins University Press, 1996), 106.

17. Nikolai Tikhonov, quoted in Raymond L. Garthoff, *The Great Transition: American-Soviet Relations and the End of the Cold War* (Washington, DC: Brookings Institution Press, 1994), 56.

18. Anatoliy Fedorovich Dobrynin, *In Confidence: Moscow's Ambassador to America's Six Cold War Presidents (1962–1986),* 1st ed. (New York: Random House, 1995), 455.

19. Ibid., 486.

20. See V. M. Zubok, *A Failed Empire: The Soviet Union in the Cold War: From Stalin to Gorbachev* (Chapel Hill: University of North Carolina Press, 2007).

21. Pyotr Fedoseev, quoted in ibid., 106

22. Oleg Grinevskii, *Perelom: ot Brezhneva k Gorbachevu* (Moscow: Olma, 2004), 12.

23. Sergei Nikolaevich Semanov, *Brezhnev: Pravitel "zolotogo veka"* (Moscow: Veche, 2004), 9.

24. Anatoly Chernyaev, quoted in Zubok, *Failed Empire,* 231.

25. Georgii Kornienko, *Kholodnaia Voina: Svidetel'stvo ee uchastnika* (Moscow: Mezhdunarodnye otnosheniya, 2001), 236. According to Kornienko, the Soviets knew by the end of the 1960s that Pershing II and cruise missiles lay on the horizon and that British and French nuclear forces would also be upgraded.

26. Grinevskii, *Perelom,* 19.

27. Colin L. Powell and Joseph E. Persico, *My American Journey* (New York: Random House, 1995), 355.

28. Oleg Kalugin, interviewed in *1983: The Brink of Apocalypse.* DVD. Directed by Henry Chancellor, 2007.

29. Andrei Aleksandrov-Agentov, *Ot Kollontai do Gorbacheva: Vospominaniia diplomata, sovetnika A.A. Gromyko, Pomoshchnika L.I. Brezhneva, Iu.V. Andropova, K.U. Chernenko i M.S. Gorbacheva* (Moscow: Mezhdunarodnye Otnosheniia, 1994), 272; See also interview with Andrei Aleksandrov-Agentov, January 24, 1990, p. 37; Don Oberdorfer Papers, box 1, folder 2; Public Policy Papers, Department of Rare Books and Special Collections, Princeton University Library, Princeton, New Jersey.

30. Transcript of CPSU CC Politburo Discussions on Afghanistan, March 19, 1979, *Cold War International History Project Bulletin* 11 (Winter 1996): 143.

31. Ibid.

32. Meeting of Kosygin, Gromyko, Ustinov, and Ponomarev with Taraki in Moscow, March 20, 1979, in ibid., 146–50.

33. See Transcript of CPSU CC Politburo Session on Afghanistan, March 22, 1979, in ibid., 150–51.

34. Gregory Feifer, *The Great Gamble: The Soviet War in Afghanistan,* 1st ed. (New York: HarperCollins, 2009), 38–54.

35. Diego Cordovez and Selig S. Harrison, *Out of Afghanistan: The Inside Story of the Soviet Withdrawal* (New York: Oxford University Press, 1995), 19.

36. Kornienko, *Kholodnaia Voina,* 243.

37. Valentin Varennikov, *Nepovtorimoe. 5. Chast' 7: Afganistan I doblest', i pechal' Chernobyl'* (Moscow: Sovetskii pisatel', 2001), 52.

38. Quoted in Aleksandr Liakhovskii, "Inside the Soviet Invasion of Afghanistan and the Seizure of Kabul," December 1979, Cold War International History Project Working Paper 51, 23.

39. Kornienko, *Kholodnaia Voina,* 193–95; for analyses of the Soviet invasion of Afghanistan, see Amin Saikal, "Islamism, the Iranian Revolution, and the Soviet Invasion of Afghanistan," in *Cambridge History of the Cold War,* ed. Leffler and Westad, 3:121–29; Vladislav Zubok, "Soviet Foreign Policy From Détente to Gorbachev, 1975–1985, in ibid., 102–4; Artemy M. Kalinovsky, *A Long Goodbye: The Soviet Withdrawal from Afghanistan* (Cambridge, MA: Harvard University Press, 2011), 13–23; Odd Arne Westad, *The Global Cold War: Third World Interventions and the Making of Our Times* (Cambridge: Cambridge University Press, 2005), 316–26; Zubok, *Failed Empire,* 259–64; and Melvyn P. Leffler, *For the Soul of Mankind: The United States, the Soviet Union, and the Cold War,* 1st ed. (New York: Hill and Wang, 2007), 319–34.

40. Aleksandr Liakhovskii, quoted in Jan Hoffenaar and Christopher Findlay, eds., *Military Planning for European Theatre Conflict during the Cold War: An Oral History Roundtable, Stockholm, 24–25 April 2006* (Zurich: Center for Security Studies, ETH Zurich, 2007), 87–88.

41. Raymond L. Garthoff, *Détente and Confrontation: American-Soviet Relations from Nixon to Reagan,* rev. ed. (Washington, DC: Brookings Institution, 1994), 1022.

42. Matthew J. Ouimet, *The Rise and Fall of the Brezhnev Doctrine in Soviet Foreign Policy* (Chapel Hill: University of North Carolina Press, 2003), 95.

43. Steve Coll, *Ghost Wars: The Secret History of the CIA, Afghanistan, and Bin Laden, from the Soviet Invasion to September 10, 2001* (New York: Penguin Press, 2004), 65.

44. Feifer, *Great Gamble,* 104.

45. James Earl Carter, "The State of the Union Address Delivered Before a Joint Session of the Congress," January 23, 1980, available at www.presidency.ucsb.edu/ws/index.php?pid=33079, accessed February 19, 2013.

46. "Reagan Raps Carter's Handling of Crises in Iran, Afghanistan," *Miami News,* January 10, 1980.

47. William F. Endicott, "Reagan Says Iran May Be Next Soviet Target," *Los Angeles Times,* January 17, 1980, B19.

48. Caspar Weinberger, interviewed in CNN, *Cold War,* Episode 20, "Soldiers of God," available at www.gwu.edu/~nsarchiv/coldwar/interviews/episode-20/weinberger1.html, accessed November 14, 2012.

49. Richard Pipes, "Soviet Global Strategy," *Commentary,* April 1980, 39.

50. Zubok, *Failed Empire,* 263.

51. "Directive from the CPSU Secretariat, January 14, 1981, with Supporting Cables" January 14, 1981, History and Public Policy Program Digital Archive, TsKhSD, F. 89, Op. 42, D. 49, first published in CWIHP Special Working Paper 1. http://digitalarchive.wilsoncenter.org/document/112740.

52. "Transcript of the CPSU Politburo Session, January 22, 1981 (excerpt)," in Mark Kramer, Cold War International History Project, Special Working Paper 1, available online at http://digitalarchive.wilsoncenter.org/document/112744, accessed February 19, 2013.

53. Ibid.

54. Ibid.

55. Stephen Kotkin with Jan Gross, *Uncivil Society: 1989 and the Implosion of the Communist Establishment* (New York: Modern Library, 2009), 113.

56. "Session of the CPSU CC Politburo, March 26, 1981 (excerpt)" March 26, 1981, History and Public Policy Program Digital Archive, TsKhSD, F. 89, Op. 42, D. 38, first published in CWIHP Special Working Paper 1. http://digitalarchive.wilsoncenter.org/document/112757, accessed May 4, 2013. Ruble conversions are based on Bank of Russia historical figures, available at http://cbr.ru/currency_base/OldDataFiles/USD.xls, accessed May 4, 2013.

57. Ibid.

58. "Session of the CPSU CC Politburo, April 2, 1981 (excerpt)," in ibid.

59. "Session of the CPSU CC Politburo, April 9, 1981 (excerpt)," in ibid.

60. Transcript of the Meeting Between Comrade L. I. Brezhnev and Comrade E. Honecker at the Crimea on August 3, 1981 (excerpt), available at http://digitalarchive.wilsoncenter.org/document/111229 (accessed February 19, 2013).

61. Transcript of Brezhnev's Phone Conversation with Kania, September 15, 1981, available at http://digitalarchive.wilsoncenter.org/document/112799, accessed February 19, 2013.

62. "Session of the CPSU CC Politburo, December 10, 1981," available at http://digitalarchive.wilsoncenter.org/document/110482, accessed February 19, 2013.

63. "The Anoshkin Notebook on the Polish Crisis, December 10, 1981," available at http://digitalarchive.wilsoncenter.org/document/112001, accessed February 19, 2013.

64. Ibid.

65. See Vojtech Mastny, "How Able Was 'Able Archer'? Nuclear Trigger and Intelligence in Perspective," *Journal of Cold War Studies* 11, no. 1 (2008): 108–23.

66. Oleg Kalugin with Fen Montaigne, *The First Directorate: My 32 Years in Intelligence and Espionage against the West* (New York: St. Martin's Press, 1994), 302.

67. Vladimir Kryuchkov, interviewed in *1983: The Brink of Apocalypse*. Elsewhere, Kryuchkov has written that Andropov contracted chickenpox while visiting Afghanistan in the winter of 1980–1981 and that this illness affected his judgment. See Vladimir Kryuchkov, *Lichnoye Dyelo* (Moscow: Eksmo, 2003), 158–59.

68. Vojtech Mastny and Malcolm Byrne, *A Cardboard Castle? An Inside History of the Warsaw Pact, 1955–1991* (Budapest: Central European University Press, 2005), 469–71.

69. Quoted in B. Heuser, "The Soviet Response to the Euromissiles Crisis," in *Crisis of Détente in Europe*, ed. Leopoldo Nuti (New York: Routledge, 2008), 143–45.

70. See Pavel Podvig, "The Window of Vulnerability That Wasn't," *International Security* 33, no. 1 (Summer 2008): 118–38; David Hoffman, *The Dead Hand: The Untold Story of the Cold War Arms Race and Its Dangerous Legacy* (New York: Random House, 2009); these works draw on the Vitalii Leonidovich Kataev Papers, 10 boxes, Hoover Institution, Stanford University, Palo Alto, California.

71. Quoted in National Security Archive, *Soviet Intentions 1965–1985, Volume II: Soviet Post–Cold War Testimonial Evidence: Vitalii Leonidovich Kataev*, available online at www.gwu.edu/~nsarchiv/nukevault/ebb285/vol%20II%20Kataev.PDF (accessed February 19, 2013)

72. Brezhnev to Reagan, May 5, 1981, box 38, U.S.S.R.: General Sec. Brezhnev, Head of State Correspondence File, RRL.

73. Ibid.

74. Brezhnev to Reagan, December 2, 1981, box 38, U.S.S.R.: General Sec. Brezhnev, Head of State Correspondence File, RRL.

75. Georgi Arbatov, *Cold War or Détente? The Soviet Viewpoint* (London: Zed Books, 1983), 17.

76. Henry Kissinger, *White House Years* (New York: Little, Brown, 1979), 788–89.

77. Gromyko, quoted in Grinevsky, "The Crisis that Didn't Erupt: The Soviet-American Relationship, 1980–1983," in *Turning Points in the End of the Cold War*, ed. Kiron K. Skinner (Stanford, CA: Hoover Institution Press, 2007), 65.

78. Memorandum of Conversation between Alexander Haig and Andrei Gromyko, September 23, 1981, p. 5, box 3, William P. Clark Files, Haig/Gromyko Meetings 09/23/1981 and 09/28/1981, RRL.

79. Ibid.

80. Ibid.

81. Memorandum of Conversation between Alexander Haig and Andrei Gromyko, September 23, 1981, box 3, William Clark Files, RRL.

82. Vladislav Zubok and Konstantin Plešakov, *Inside the Kremlin's Cold War: From Stalin to Khrushchev* (Cambridge, MA: Harvard University Press, 1996).

83. Stephen E. Hanson, "The Brezhnev Era," in *The Cambridge History of Russia, Vol. 3: The Twentieth Century*, 1st ed., ed. Ronald Grigor Suny (Cambridge, U.K.: Cambridge University Press, 2006), 314.

84. See Piero Gleijeses, *Conflicting Missions: Havana, Washington, and Africa, 1959–1976* (Chapel Hill: University of North Carolina Press, 2002).

85. Quoted in National Security Archive, *Soviet Intentions 1965–1985, Volume II: Soviet Post–Cold War Testimonial Evidence: Adrian A. Danilevich,* available online at www.gwu.edu/~nsarchiv/nukevault/ebb285/vol%20iI%20Danilevich.pdf (accessed February 19, 2013)

86. Garthoff, *Great Transition,* 684.

87. Westad, *Global Cold War,* 298; see also Saikal, "Islamism, the Iranian Revolution, and the Soviet Invasion of Afghanistan," 3:112–21.

88. Grinevskii, *Perelom,* 77.

89. Brezhnev, Dinner Speech, Foreign Broadcast Information Service, May 13, 1981.

90. Bao Pu, Renee Chiang, and Adi Ignatius, eds., *Prisoner of the State: The Secret Journal of Zhao Ziyang* (New York: Simon and Schuster, 2009), 111–13.

91. See Chen Jian, "China and the Cold War after Mao," in *Cambridge History of the Cold War,* ed. Leffler and Westad, 3:186–95; Westad, "The Great Transformation," in *Shock of the Global,* ed. Ferguson et al., 65–79.

92. This meeting is recounted by Brzezinski's military attaché, William Odom, in Hoffenaar and Findlay, eds., *Military Planning for European Theatre Conflict,* 121.

93. Aleksandr Liakhovskii, quoted in ibid., 119.

94. Cable, "China Essays No. 9: The Evolving Chinese Worldview," January 7, 1981, on file at RRL.

95. William Clark to Ronald Reagan, September 23, 1982, William Clark Files, RRL.

96. "Memorandum for the Record: Record of National Security Council Meeting," September 20, 1983, box 91284, Executive Secretariat, NSC: National Security Council Meeting Files, RRL.

97. Westad, "Great Transformation," 76.

98. Timothy Garton Ash, *The Polish Revolution* (New York: Scribner, 1984), 17; for an overview of the debt crisis in Eastern Europe, see Stephen Kotkin, "The Bloc Goes Borrowing," in *Shock of the Global,* ed. Ferguson et al., 80–93.

99. Frieden, *Global Capitalism,* 381; see also Arrighi, "The World Economy and the Cold War," 3:23–44.

100. See Alan P. Dobson, "The Reagan Administration, Economic Warfare, and Starting to Close Down the Cold War," *Diplomatic History* 29 (May 2005): 531–55.

## Chapter 3

1. George Pratt Shultz, *Turmoil and Triumph: My Years as Secretary of State* (New York: Scribner's, 1993), 119.

2. The selection of Shultz is described in detail in Lou Cannon, *President Reagan: The Role of a Lifetime,* 1st ed. (New York: PublicAffairs, 2000), 59–61.

3. Interview with George Shultz; July 11, 1989, Seg. III–IV-10; Don Oberdorfer Papers; box 3, folder 2; Public Policy Papers, Department of Rare Books and Special Collections, Princeton University Library, Princeton, New Jersey.

4. Shultz, *Turmoil and Triumph*, 30.

5. Ibid., 31.

6. Interview with George Shultz, July 11, 1989, Seg. II-17-18, Don Oberdorfer Papers, box 3, Public Policy Papers, Department of Rare Books and Special Collections, Princeton University Library, Princeton, New Jersey; after Reagan's nomination of Shultz, Henry Kissinger bemoaned privately, on August 19, 1982: "George has no knowledge of foreign policy, none at all; worse than that, he has no feel for it. In the dozen years I have known him we have never had a conversation about foreign policy. He just doesn't think in terms of foreign policy." Quoted in Arthur M. Schlesinger Jr., *Journals, 1952–2000* (New York: Penguin Press, 2007), 537.

7. Shultz, *Turmoil and Triumph*, 122–23.

8. Ibid., 123.

9. Ronald Reagan, "Remarks and a Question-and-Answer Session with Rockwell International Employees," May 25, 1982, available at www.reagan.utexas.edu/archives/speeches/1982/52582b.htm, accessed February 19, 2013.

10. "Reagan to Ann Landers," May 20, 1982, in Kiron K. Skinner, Annelise Anderson, and Martin Anderson, eds., *President Reagan: A Life in Letters* (New York: Free Press, 2003), 406.

11. Memo, Dick Boverie and Sven Kraemer to Bud McFarlane, November 11, 1982, Executive Secretariat: Confidence Building Measures, box 25, RRL.

12. Cannon, *President Reagan*, 196.

13. Memo, Charles Hill to William Clark, "Public Speaking Themes on Arms Control and Nuclear Issues During the Next Few Months," December 4, 1982, box 20, Arms Control—USSR, Jack Matlock Files, RRL.

14. Bud McFarlane, quoted in documentary, "The Reagan Legacy: Star Wars."

15. Memo, William Clark to Ronald Reagan (drafted by John Lenczowski), "The Truth and The Strength of America's Deterrent," January 5, 1983, William Clark Files, RRL.

16. NSDD-75, available at www.fas.org/irp/offdocs/nsdd/nsdd-075.htm, accessed February 19, 2013.

17. Ronald Reagan, "Address Before a Joint Session of the Congress on the State of the Union," January 25, 1983, available at www.reagan.utexas.edu/archives/speeches/1983/12583c.htm, accessed February 19, 2013.

18. Ronald Reagan, January 7, 1983, in Douglas Brinkley, ed., *The Reagan Diaries* (New York: HarperCollins, 2007), 124.

19. Shultz, *Turmoil and Triumph*, 162.

20. Cable, "Arthur Hartman to George Shultz," January 25, 1983, William Clark Files, box 8, U.S.-Soviet Relations Papers Working File, RRL.

21. Shultz, *Turmoil and Triumph*, 164.

22. Ronald Reagan, *An American Life* (New York: Simon and Schuster, 1990), 558.

23. Reagan, February 15, 1983, in Brinkley, ed., *Reagan Diaries*, 131.

24. "Memorandum for the Record: Record of National Security Council Meeting," February 25, 1983, Executive Secretariat, NSC: National Security Council Meeting Files, box 91285, RRL.

25. Reagan, *American Life,* 568.

26. Reagan, March 7, 1983, in Brinkley, ed., *Reagan Diaries,* 134–35.

27. Reagan, Remarks at the Annual Convention of the National Association of Evangelicals in Orlando, Florida, March 8, 1983, Public Papers of the Presidents: Ronald Reagan, 1983, Book 1, 364.

28. Quoted in Robert Schlesinger, *White House Ghosts: Presidents and Their Speechwriters: From FDR to George W. Bush,* 1st ed. (New York: Simon and Schuster, 2008), 329.

29. See Aram Bakshian Jr. Interview, Miller Center, University of Virginia, Ronald Reagan Presidential Oral History Project, January 14–15, 2002, 31, available at http://millercenter.org/scripps/archive/oralhistories/detail/3211, accessed February 19, 2013.

30. Schlesinger, *White House Ghosts,* 329.

31. Ronald Reagan, "Reagan to Reverend Stephen Majoros," March 15, 1983, in Skinner, ed., *Reagan: A Life in Letters,* 378.

32. Ronald Reagan, "Address to the Nation on Defense and National Security," available at www.reagan.utexas.edu/archives/speeches/1983/32383d.htm, accessed February 19, 2013.

33. Ibid.

34. Martin Anderson, *Revolution: The Reagan Legacy* (Stanford, CA: Hoover Institution Press, 1990), 106.

35. Edward Teller to Ronald Reagan, July 23, 1982, Keyworth Files, box 94705, Teller, Edward, RRL.

36. Reagan, September 14, 1982, in Brinkley, ed., *Reagan Diaries,* 100.

37. Lance Gay, "U.S. Speeds Up 'Star Wars' Laser Plan," *Pittsburgh Press,* September 29, 1982.

38. Anderson, *Revolution,* 97.

39. Reagan to Patrick Mulvey, June 20, 1983, in Skinner et al., eds., *Reagan: A Life in Letters,* 425.

40. Reagan, Remarks and a Question-and-Answer Session with Reporters on Domestic and Foreign Policy Issues, March 25, 1983, available at www.reagan.utexas.edu/archives/speeches/1983/32583b.htm, accessed February 19, 2013.

41. Reagan, Question-and-Answer Session with Reporters on Domestic and Foreign Policy Issues, March 29, 1983, www.reagan.utexas.edu/archives/speeches/1983/32983a.htm, accessed February 19, 2013.

42. Oleg Grinevskii, *Perelom: ot Brezhneva k Gorbachevu* (Moscow: Olma, 2004), 28.

43. Shultz, *Turmoil and Triumph,* 268.

44. Don Oberdorfer, *From the Cold War to a New Era* (Baltimore: Johns Hopkins University Press, 1998), 35. Vice President Bush later told Shultz that a series of "absolutely vicious memos" flowed from the National Security Council staff to Reagan in the aftermath of this meeting.

45. Shultz to Reagan, March 16, 1983, William Clark Files, RRL.

46. Handwritten Note, William Clark to Ronald Reagan, March 1983, William Clark Files, RRL.

47. Reagan, April 6, 1983, in Brinkley, ed., *Reagan Diaries,* 142.

48. Jeane Kirkpatrick, quoted in Jay Winik, *On the Brink: The Dramatic Behind-the-Scenes Saga of the Reagan Era and the Men and Women Who Won the Cold War* (New York: Simon and Schuster, 1996), 258.

49. Reagan, June 26, 1983, in Brinkley, ed., *Reagan Diaries,* 163.

50. "Secretary Shultz's Statement before the Senate Foreign Relations Committee," June 15, 1983, *Department of State Bulletin,* vol. 83 (July 1983).

51. Oberdorfer, *From the Cold War to a New Era,* 40.

52. Ibid., 41–42.

53. Paul Kengor, *The Judge: William P. Clark, Ronald Reagan's Top Hand* (San Francisco: Ignatius Press, 2007), 343; Laurence I. Barrett, Gregory H. Wirzynski, and Maureen Dowd, "The Man with the President's Ear," *Time,* August 8, 1983, available at www.time.com/time/magazine/article/0,9171,955165,00.html, accessed February 19, 2013.

54. Reagan, May 4, 1983, in Brinkley, ed., *Reagan Diaries,* 150.

55. Quoted in Peter Schweizer, *Victory: The Reagan Administration's Secret Strategy That Hastened the Collapse of the Soviet Union* (New York: Atlantic Monthly Press, 1996), 8–9.

56. Ronald Reagan, Remarks to Reporters on the Soviet Attack on a Korean Civilian Airliner, September 2, 1983, available at www.reagan.utexas.edu/archives/speeches/1983/90283c.htm, accessed November 15, 2012.

57. Christopher Andrew, *For the President's Eyes Only: Secret Intelligence and the American Presidency from Washington to Bush* (New York: Harper Perennial, 1996), 473.

58. Reagan, Address to the Nation on the Soviet Attack on a Civilian Airliner, September 5, 1983, available at www.reagan.utexas.edu/archives/speeches/1983/90583a.htm, accessed February 19, 2013.

59. Memo, McFarlane to Shultz, December 10, 1983, box 2, Matlock Chron., December 1984, Jack Matlock Files, RRL.

60. "Time/Yankelovich, Skelly & White Poll," December 1983.

61. Jack F. Matlock, Summary of meeting with Vishnevsky, October 11, 1983, Jack Matlock Files, RRL.

62. Memo, Jack Matlock to Bud McFarlane, box 2, Matlock Chron., October 1983, Jack Matlock Files, RRL.

63. See Curtis Peebles, *Shadow Flights: America's Secret Airwar against the Soviet Union: A Cold War History,* new ed. (New York: Presidio Press, 2001).

64. "Time/Yankelovich, Skelly & White Poll," December 1983.

65. For a description of the circumstances leading to Clark's resignation, see David Rothkopf, *Running the World: The Inside Story of the National Security Council and the Architects of American Power* (New York: PublicAffairs, 2005), 236.

66. Interview with George Shultz; July 11, 1989; Don Oberdorfer Papers; box 3, folder 2; Public Policy Papers, Department of Rare Books and Special Collections, Princeton University Library, Princeton, New Jersey.

67. Shultz, *Turmoil and Triumph,* 377.

68. Jack F. Matlock, *Reagan and Gorbachev: How the Cold War Ended,* 1st ed. (New York: Random House, 2004), 76.

69. Memo, Jack Matlock to Robert McFarlane, "U.S.-Soviet Relations: Toward Defining a Strategy," February 6, 1984, box 3, Matlock Chron., February 1984, Jack Matlock Files, RRL.

70. Ibid., 2.

71. "Memorandum of Conversation between George Shultz and Andrei Gromyko," January 18, 1984, box 42, U.S.-USSR Relations, Jack Matlock Files, RRL.

72. Memo, Jack Matlock to Robert McFarlane, "U.S.-Soviet Relations: Toward Defining a Strategy," February 6, 1984, box 3, Matlock Chron., February 1984, Jack Matlock Files, RRL.

73. Interview with Robert McFarlane; October 9, 1989, p. 3; Don Oberdorfer Papers, box 2, folder 22, Public Policy Papers, Department of Rare Books and Special Collections, Princeton University Library, Princeton, New Jersey.

74. Memo, Robert C. McFarlane to Ronald Reagan, February 18, 1984, box 3, Matlock Chron., February 1984, Jack Matlock Files, RRL.

75. For the most comprehensive account of Reagan's friendship with Massie, see James Mann, *The Rebellion of Ronald Reagan: A History of the End of the Cold War* (New York: Viking Press, 2009).

76. Letter, Reagan to Andropov, December 23, 1983, Executive Secretariat, NSC: Head of State File, RRL.

77. Reagan, January 4, 1984, in Brinkley, ed., *Reagan Diaries,* 211.

78. Ronald Reagan, "Address to the Nation and Other Countries on United States-Soviet Relations," January 16, 1984, available at www.reagan.utexas.edu/archives/speeches/1984/11684a.htm, accessed February 19, 2013.

79. Reagan, February 1, 1984, in Brinkley, ed., *Reagan Diaries,* 216–17.

80. Matlock, quoted in William Wohlforth, ed., *Witnesses to the End of the Cold War* (Baltimore: Johns Hopkins University Press, 1996), 113.

81. "Memorandum of Conversation between Jack Matlock and Vadim Zagladin," February 15, 1984, box 3, Matlock Chron., February 1984, Jack Matlock Files, RRL.

82. Ibid.

83. Reagan, February 22, 1984, in Brinkley, ed., *Reagan Diaries,* 220.

84. Memorandum of Conversation of Ronald Reagan and Helmut Kohl, March 5, 1984, box 3, Matlock Chron., March 1984, Jack Matlock Files, RRL.

85. Reagan, March 2, 1984, in Brinkley, ed., *Reagan Diaries,* 223.

86. Memo, Shultz to Reagan, March 14, 1984, box 3, Matlock Chron., March 1984, Jack Matlock Files, RRL.

87. Dobrynin reported to Assistant Secretary of State Richard Burt that Gromyko refused any encroachment on his authority. See Memo, Richard Burt to George Shultz, March 28, 1984, box 3, Matlock Chron., March 1984, Jack Matlock Files, RRL.

88. Letter, Ronald Reagan to Konstantin Chernenko, April 7, 1984, General Secretary Chernenko, box 39, Executive Secretariat, NSC: Head of State File, RRL.

89. Letter, Konstantin Chernenko to Ronald Reagan, June 6, 1984, General Secretary Chernenko, box 39, Executive Secretariat, NSC: Head of State File, RRL.

90. Quoted in Benjamin B. Fischer, *A Cold War Conundrum: The 1983 Soviet War Scare* (Central Intelligence Agency: Center for the Study of Intelligence, 1997), available online at www.cia.gov/library/center-for-the-study-of-intelligence/csi-publications/books-and-monographs/a-cold-war-conundrum/source.htm, accessed February 19, 2013.

91. Reagan, June 14, 1984, in Brinkley, ed., *Reagan Diaries,* 247.

92. Memo, Jack Matlock to Robert McFarlane, August 24, 1984, box 5, Matlock Chron., August 1984, Jack Matlock Files, RRL.

93. "Address to the Nation on U.S. Policy in Central America," May 9, 1984, available at www.reagan.utexas.edu/archives/speeches/1984/50984h.htm, accessed November 17, 2013.

94. Memo, John Lenczowski to Robert McFarlane, February 10, 1984, box 3, Matlock Chron., February 1984, Jack Matlock Files, RRL.

95. "Minutes of National Security Planning Group," March 27, 1984, Executive Secretariat, NSC: National Security Council Meeting Files, box 91303, RRL.

96. Ibid.

97. Ibid.

98. Memo, George Shultz to Ronald Reagan, September 17, 1984, box 6, Matlock Chron., September 1984, Jack Matlock Files, RRL.

99. "Memorandum of Conversation between Andrei Gromyko and Ronald Reagan," September 28, 1984, box 58, Meetings with USSR Officials, 1983–1986, Jack Matlock Files, RRL.

100. Melvyn P. Leffler, *For the Soul of Mankind: The United States, the Soviet Union, and the Cold War,* 1st ed. (New York: Hill and Wang, 2007), 364.

101. Reagan, November 14, 1984, in Brinkley, ed., *Reagan Diaries,* 277.

## Chapter 4

1. Letter, Chernenko to Reagan, November 17, 1984, General Secretary Chernenko, box 39, Executive Secretariat, NSC: Head of State File, RRL.

2. Memorandum of Conversation, George Shultz and Andrei Gromyko, January 7, 1985, pp. 3, 9, box 60, Meetings with USSR Officials, 1983–1986, Jack Matlock Files, RRL.

3. Ibid., 1, 4.

4. Mikhail Gorbachev, *Memoirs* (New York: Doubleday, 1995), 28.

5. Ibid., 34.

6. Mikhail Gorbachev and Zdenek Mlynar, *Conversations with Gorbachev on Perestroika, the Prague Spring, and the Crossroads of Socialism,* trans. George Shriver (New York: Columbia University Press, 2002), 17.

7. See Melvyn P. Leffler, *For the Soul of Mankind: The United States, the Soviet Union, and the Cold War,* 1st ed. (New York: Hill and Wang, 2007), 367–68.

8. Claude Estier, *Dix Ans Qui Ont Changé le Monde: Journal, 1989–2000* (Paris: B. Leprince, 2000), 62.

9. Iz besedy s premier-ministrom Velikobritanii M. Tjetcher, December 16, 1984, in Mikhail Gorbachev, *Sobranie sochinenii,* Tom 2 (Moscow: Ves' Mir, 2008), 118.

10. "The Rise and Rise of Raisa Gorbachev," *Time,* January 4, 1988, available at www.time.com/time/magazine/article/0,9171,966396,00.html, accessed February 19, 2013.

11. Gorbachev, *Memoirs,* 212.

12. Quoted in Aleksandr Yakovlev, *Omut Pamiati,* vol. 1 (Moscow: Bagrius, 2000), 236.

13. Thatcher BBC Interview with John Cole, December 17, 1984, available online at www.margaretthatcher.org/archive/displaydocument.asp?docid=105592, accessed February 19, 2013.

14. "Memorandum for the Record: Meeting with British Prime Minister Margaret Thatcher," December 22, 1984. NSC: Thatcher Visit—Dec. 1984, box 90902, RRL.

15. Vladislav Zubok, *A Failed Empire: The Soviet Union in the Cold War: From Stalin to Gorbachev* (Chapel Hill: University of North Carolina Press, 2007).

16. "Session of the Politburo of the CC CPSU, April 4, 1985," National Security Archive, available at www.gwu.edu/~nsarchiv/NSAEBB/NSAEBB172/Doc8.pdf, accessed February 19, 2013.

17. Diary of Anatoly S. Chernyaev, July 6, 1985, National Security Archive, available at www.gwu.edu/~nsarchiv/NSAEBB/NSAEBB192/Chernyaev_Diary_translation_1985.pdf, accessed February 19, 2013.

18. Vadim Medvedev, *V komande Gorbacheva: Vzgliad iznutri* (Moscow: Bylina, 1994), 40.

19. Diary of Anatoly S. Chernyaev, May 22, 1985, National Security Archive, available at www.gwu.edu/~nsarchiv/NSAEBB/NSAEBB192/Chernyaev_Diary_translation_1985.pdf, accessed February 19, 2013; see also Silvio Pons, "The Rise and Fall of Eurocommunism," in *The Cambridge History of the Cold War,* ed. Melvyn P. Leffler and Odd Arne Westad (New York: Cambridge University Press, 2010), 3:45–65.

20. Diary of Anatoly S. Chernyaev, March 15, 1985, National Security Archive, available at www.gwu.edu/~nsarchiv/NSAEBB/NSAEBB192/Chernyaev_Diary_translation_1985.pdf, accessed February 19, 2013.

21. For a recent overview of Yakovlev's life, see Christopher Shulgan, *The Soviet Ambassador: The Making of the Radical behind Perestroika* (Toronto: McClelland and Stewart, 2008).

22. Yakovlev was especially disgusted by the tales of Brezhnev's alleged heroism. "He was as gray as a soldier's tunic," he later wrote. "He was a farcical trick of history. Marshal of 'the little land,' he won the war while everybody else, Georgy Zhukov included, sat it out in the trenches of Stalingrad, and then the Battle of Kursk." A. N. Yakovlev, *The Fate of Marxism in Russia* (New Haven, CT: Yale University Press, 1993), 81.

23. Yakovlev, quoted in Janice Gross Stein, "Political Learning by Doing: Gorbachev as Uncommitted Thinker and Motivated Learner," *International Organization* 48, no. 2 (Spring 1994): 174.

24. Archie Brown, *The Gorbachev Factor* (New York: Oxford University Press, 1996), 122.

25. Mikhail Gorbachev, *On My Country and the World* (New York: Columbia University Press, 2000), 180.

26. Quoted in Zubok, *Failed Empire,* 283.

27. Letter, "Reagan to Gorbachev, March 11, 1985," available at www.gwu.edu/~nsarchiv/NSAEBB/NSAEBB172/Doc2.pdf, accessed February 19, 2013.

28. Letter, "Reagan to Gorbachev, April 4, 1985," available at www.gwu.edu/~nsarchiv/NSAEBB/NSAEBB172/Doc7.pdf, accessed February 19, 2013.

29. Ronald Reagan, April 19, 1985, in Douglas Brinkley, ed., *The Reagan Diaries* (New York: HarperCollins, 2007), 317.

30. Reagan, June 24, 1985, in ibid., 337.

31. "Conference of Secretaries of the CC CPSU," March 15, 1985, National Security Archive, available at www.gwu.edu/~nsarchiv/NSAEBB/NSAEBB172/Doc5.pdf, accessed February 19, 2013.

32. Ibid.; see also Zubok, *Failed Empire,* 284.

33. Alexander Yakovlev, "About Reagan," March 12, 1985, National Security Archive: To The Geneva Summit, available at www.gwu.edu/~nsarchiv/NSAEBB/NSAEBB172/Doc3.pdf, accessed February 19, 2013.

34. Memo, Jack F. Matlock to John Poindexter, June 27, 1985, box 10, Matlock Chron., June 1985, Jack Matlock Files, RRL.

35. Session of the Politburo of the CC CPSU, June 29, 1985, National Security Archive: To The Geneva Summit, available at www.gwu.edu/~nsarchiv/NSAEBB/NSAEBB172/Doc11.pdf, accessed February 19, 2013.

36. Memo, Jack F. Matlock to Robert McFarlane, July 2, 1985, box 10, Matlock Chron., July 1985, Jack Matlock Files, RRL.

37. Reagan, July 3, 1985, in Brinkley, ed., *Reagan Diaries,* 340.

38. Memo, Jack F. Matlock to Robert McFarlane, July 19, 1985, box 10, Matlock Chron., July 1985, Jack Matlock Files, RRL.

39. Eduard Shevardnadze, *The Future Belongs to Freedom* (New York: Free Press, 1991), 74.

40. William Wohlforth, ed., *Witnesses to the End of the Cold War* (Baltimore: Johns Hopkins University Press, 1996), 117.

41. "Memorandum of Conversation between George Shultz and Eduard Shevardnadze," July 31, 1985, box 47, Memcons-Shultz/Shevardnadze Meetings Helsinki and New York, Jack Matlock Files, RRL.

42. Ibid., 13.

43. Eduard Shevardnadze, "O Proshedshem i Budushchem," Druzhba Narodov 2006, 11, available at http://magazines.russ.ru/druzhba/2006/11/zi10-pr.html, accessed February 19, 2013.

44. Ibid., 5.

45. Memo, Robert McFarlane to Ronald Reagan, December 17, 1984, box 6, Matlock Chron., December 1984, Jack Matlock Files, RRL.

46. Ibid.

47. Reagan, "The President's News Conference," September 17, 1985, available at www.reagan.utexas.edu/archives/speeches/1985/91785c.htm, accessed February 19, 2013.

48. Reagan, "Interview with Foreign Journalists," April 29, 1985, available at www.reagan.utexas.edu/archives/speeches/1985/42985g.htm; Reagan, "Radio Address to the Nation on the Strategic Defense Initiative," July 13, 1985, available at www.reagan.utexas.edu/archives/speeches/1985/71385a.htm, accessed February 19, 2013.

49. Ibid.

50. "Excerpt from Minutes of the Politburo Session, August 29, 1985," National Security Archive: To the Geneva Summit, available at www.gwu.edu/~nsarchiv/NSAEBB/NSAEBB172/Doc12.pdf, accessed November 25, 2012.

51. Brown, *Gorbachev Factor,* 109.

52. Memo, Robert McFarlane to Jack F. Matlock, May 28, 1985, box 9, Matlock Chron., May 1985, Jack Matlock Files, RRL.

53. Jack Matlock, "Soviet Russian Psychology," p. 6, box 45, Series III: U.S.-USSR Summits, 1985–1986, Jack Matlock Files, RRL.

54. Ibid.

55. Jack Matlock, "Russia's Place in the World," box 45, Series III: U.S.-USSR Summits, 2, 1985–1986, Jack Matlock Files, RRL.

56. Jack Matlock, "USSR: A Society in Trouble," p. 4, box 45, Series III: U.S.-USSR Summits, 1985–1986, Jack Matlock Files, RRL.

57. For a thorough exposition of Reagan's friendship with Suzanne Massie, see James Mann, *The Rebellion of Ronald Reagan: A History of the End of the Cold War* (New York: Viking, 2009).

58. Reagan, Inaugural Address, January 20, 1981, available at www.reagan.utexas.edu/archives/speeches/1981/12081a.htm, accessed February 19, 2013.

59. Reagan to Mr. and Mrs. Ronald D. Paton, July 16, 1984, in Kiron K. Skinner, Annelise Anderson, and Martin Anderson, eds., *Reagan: A Life in Letters* (New York: Free Press, 2003), 379.

60. Reagan, May 20, 1986, in Brinkley, ed., *Reagan Diaries,* 412.

61. Reagan, December 14, 1984, in ibid., 287.

62. For more background on Reagan's conversions, see Thomas W. Evans, *The Education of Ronald Reagan: The General Electric Years and the Untold Story of His Conversion to Conservatism* (New York: Columbia University Press, 2008).

63. Reagan, September 11, 1985, in Brinkley, ed., *Reagan Diaries,* 352.

64. "Memorandum for the Record: Record of National Security Council Meeting," September 20, 1985, Executive Secretariat, NSC: National Security Council Meeting Files, box 91303, RRL.

65. "Memorandum of Conversation, November 19, 1985, 10:30 a.m–11:20 a.m.," National Security Archive: To the Geneva Summit, available at www.gwu.edu/~nsarchiv/NSAEBB/NSAEBB172/Doc15.pdf, accessed February 19, 2013.

66. "Memorandum of Conversation, November 19, 1985, 11:27 a.m.–12:14 p.m.," National Security Archive: To the Geneva Summit, available at www.gwu.edu/~nsarchiv/NSAEBB/NSAEBB172/Doc16.pdf, accessed February 19, 2013.

67. "Memorandum of Conversation, November 20, 1985, 11:30 a.m.–12:40 p.m.," National Security Archive: To the Geneva Summit, available at www.gwu.edu/~nsarchiv/NSAEBB/NSAEBB172/Doc21.pdf, accessed February 19, 2013.

68. Sergei Akhromeyev and Georgii Kornienko, *Glazami marshala i diplomata: Kriticheskii vzgliad na vneshniuiu politiku SSSR do i posle 1985 goda* (Moscow: Mezhdunarodnye otnosheniia, 1992), 82.

69. "The Fleur D'eau Villa, Geneva," *Izvestia,* November 21, 1985, translated and included in *Current Digest of the Post-Soviet Press,* vol. 37, no. 47, December 18, 1985.

70. Gorbachev, *Memoirs,* 404.

71. Yakovlev, quoted in Andrei Grachev, *Gorbachev's Gamble: Soviet Foreign Policy and the End of the Cold War* (Cambridge, U.K.: Polity, 2008), 64.

72. Anatoly Chernyaev, "Excerpt from Anatoly Chernyaev's Diary: November 24, 1985," National Security Archive: To the Geneva Summit, available at www.gwu.edu/~nsarchiv/NSAEBB/NSAEBB172/Doc26.pdf, accessed November 25, 2012.

73. Conference at the Central Committee of the Communist Party of the Soviet Union in preparation for the 27th Congress of the CPSU, National Security

Archive, available at www.gwu.edu/~nsarchiv/NSAEBB/NSAEBB172/Doc27.pdf (February 19, 2013).

74. "Memorandum of Conversation," November 19, 1985, 8:00–10:30 pm, National Security Archive: To the Geneva Summit, available at www.gwu.edu/~nsarchiv/NSAEBB/NSAEBB172/Doc20.pdf, accessed November 25, 2012.

75. Gorbachev, *On My Country and the World,* 181.

76. Michael K. Deaver, *A Different Drummer: My Thirty Years with Ronald Reagan,* 1st ed. (New York: HarperCollins, 2001), 118.

77. Ronald Reagan, "Reagan to Mrs. Elsa Sandstrom," November 25, 1985, in Skinner et al., eds., *Reagan: A Life in Letters,* 414.

78. Zubok, *Failed Empire,* 285.

79. Grachev, *Gorbachev's Gamble,* 68.

80. Akhromeyev and Kornienko, *Glazami marshala i diplomata,* 87–88.

81. Falin, quoted in Grachev, *Gorbachev's Gamble,* 71–72.

82. Quoted in Leffler, *For the Soul of Mankind,* 388.

83. Robert English, *Russia and the Idea of the West: Gorbachev, Intellectuals, and the End of the Cold War* (New York: Columbia University Press, 2000), 210.

84. Quoted in Anatoly Chernyaev, *My Six Years with Gorbachev,* trans. and ed. Robert English and Elizabeth Tucker (University Park: Pennsylvania State University Press, 2000), 57.

85. Political Report of the CPSU Central Committee, February 25, 1986, Foreign Broadcast Information Service, March 28, 1986, O8.

86. Quoted in F. Stephen Larrabee and Allen Lynch, "Gorbachev: The Road to Reykjavik," *Foreign Policy,* no. 65 (Winter 1986–1987): 7.

87. Grachev, *Gorbachev's Gamble,* 104.

88. "Speech by Comrade E. A. Shevardnadze, USSR Minister of Foreign Affairs," in *Current Digest of the Post-Soviet Press,* March 12, 1986.

89. "M. S. Gorbachev's Replies to the Algerian Magazine Revolution Africaine," March 31, 1986, translated and available in *Current Digest of the Post-Soviet Press,* vol. 38, no. 14, May 7, 1986, 19–21.

90. Gorbachev to Reagan, April 2, 1986, Executive Secretariat, NSC: Head of State File, USSR, box 40, RRL.

91. Reagan, January 15, 1986, in Brinkley, ed., *Reagan Diaries,* 383.

92. Edward Rowny, quoted in Leffler, *For the Soul of Mankind,* 388.

93. Reagan, February 3, 1986, in Brinkley, ed., *Reagan Diaries,* 388.

94. "Wright and Linhard to Poindexter," February 4, 1986, Poindexter Chron., February 1986, box 1, John Poindexter Files, RRL.

95. "Memorandum for the Record: Record of National Security Planning Group," February 3, 1986, Executive Secretariat, NSC: National Security Council Meeting Files, box 91308, RRL.

96. Ibid.

97. See Edward M. Kennedy, *True Compass: A Memoir* (New York: Twelve/Hachette Books, 2009).

98. Reagan to Gorbachev, February 16, 1986, Executive Secretariat, NSC: Head of State File, USSR, box 40, RRL.

99. Zubok, *Failed Empire,* 289.

100. Minutes of the Political Consultative Committee Party Secretaries' Meeting in Budapest, June 11, 1986, available at www.gwu.edu/~nsarchiv/NSAEBB/ NSAEBB154/doc115.pdf, accessed February 19, 2013.

101. Grachev, *Gorbachev's Gamble,* 81.

102. Akhromeyev and Kornienko, *Glazami marshala i diplomata,* 107.

103. Anatoly Chernyaev notes from Politburo Session, April 15, 1986, Opus 1, Fond 1, Archive of the Gorbachev Foundation.

104. Letter, Ronald Reagan to Laurence W. Beilenson, August 1, 1986, in Skinner, ed., *Reagan: A Life in Letters,* 428.

105. "CIA Worldwide briefing," January 30, 1986, p. 5, box 14, Matlock Chron., January 1986, Jack Matlock Files, RRL.

106. Ibid., 6.

107. Ibid., 12.

108. Robert C. McFarlane to John Poindexter, March 5, 1986, in Thomas Blanton, *White House E-Mail: The Top-Secret Messages the Reagan/Bush White House Tried to Destroy* (New York: The New Press, 1995), diskette.

109. Robert M. Gates, *From the Shadows: The Ultimate Insider's Story of Five Presidents and How They Won the Cold War* (New York: Simon and Schuster, 1996), 332.

110. Oliver North to Robert C. McFarlane, March 3, 1986, in Blanton, *White House E-Mail,* diskette.

111. Address to the Nation on National Security, available online at www.reagan. utexas.edu/archives/speeches/1986/22686b.htm, accessed February 19, 2013.

112. "Meese Accuses Soviet Union of Afghan War Crimes," *New York Times,* March 27, 1986, A5.

113. "Remarks and a Question-and-Answer Session With High School Students From the Close Up Foundation," May 21, 1986, available at www.reagan.utexas.edu/ archives/speeches/1986/52186a.htm, accessed February 19, 2013.

114. Ronald Reagan, "Remarks to the Georgetown University Center for Strategic and International Studies on United States Assistance for the Nicaraguan Democratic Resistance," June 6, 1986, available at www.reagan.utexas.edu/archives/ speeches/1986/60986b.htm, accessed February 19, 2013.

115. "National Security Planning Group Meeting," box 90318, Executive Secretariat, NSC: National Security Planning Group (NSPG) Records, 1981–1987, RRL.

116. "Message to the Congress Reporting on the National Emergency With Respect to Nicaragua," May 23, 1986, available at www.reagan.utexas.edu/archives/ speeches/1986/52386a.htm, accessed February 19, 2013.

117. George Pratt Shultz, *Turmoil and Triumph: My Years as Secretary of State* (New York: Scribner's, 1993), 709.

118. Memo, "Shultz to Reagan," May 19, 1986, box 16, Matlock Chron., May 1986, Jack Matlock Files, RRL.

119. Ibid.

120. Interview with George Shultz; July 11, 1989, Seg. VI-3; Don Oberdorfer Papers; box 3, folder 2; Public Policy Papers, Department of Rare Books and Special Collections, Princeton University Library, Princeton, New Jersey.

121. Mikhail Gorbachev, "The Nuclear Disaster that Opened Our Eyes to the Truth," *The Australian,* April 19, 2006.

122. Chernyaev, *My Six Years with Gorbachev,* 76.

123. Ibid.

124. Ibid.

125. Quoted in Grachev, *Gorbachev's Gamble*, 84.

126. Gorbachev to Reagan, September 15, 1986, National Security Archive: The Reykjavik File, available at www.gwu.edu/~nsarchiv/NSAEBB/NSAEBB203/Document01.pdf, accessed February 19, 2013.

127. George Shultz, "Memorandum to the President," October 2, 1986, National Security Archive: The Reykjavik File, available at www.gwu.edu/~nsarchiv/NSAEBB/NSAEBB203/Document04.pdf, accessed February 19, 2013.

128. "Anatoly Chernyaev: Notes from the Politburo Session," National Security Archive: The Reykjavik File, available at www.gwu.edu/~nsarchiv/NSAEBB/NSAEBB203/Document08.pdf, accessed February 19, 2013.

129. Memo, "Poindexter to Reagan" (prepared by Matlock), October 3, 1986, p. 3, box 18, Matlock Chron., October 1986, Jack Matlock Files, RRL.

130. "The Soviet Preparation for Reykjavik: Four Documents," in *Hoover Institution on War, Revolution, and Peace, Implications of the Reykjavik Summit on Its Twentieth Anniversary: Conference Report* (Stanford, CA: Hoover Institution Press, 2007), 64.

131. Ibid., 77.

132. Ibid.

133. "Memorandum of Conversation: October 12, 1986, 3:25–4:30 PM and 5:30–6:50 PM," October 12, 1986, National Security Archive: The Reykjavik File, available at www.gwu.edu/~nsarchiv/NSAEBB/NSAEBB203/Document15.pdf, accessed February 19, 2013.

134. Ibid., 10.

135. Ibid.

136. "Memorandum of Conversation, October 12, 1986, 10:00 am–1:35 pm," National Security Archive: The Reykjavik File, available at www.gwu.edu/~nsarchiv/NSAEBB/NSAEBB203/Document13.pdf, accessed February 19, 2013.

137. Ibid., 16

138. Reagan, October 12, 1986, in Brinkley, ed., *Reagan Diaries,* 482.

139. Charles Hill; Don Oberdorfer Papers; box 2, folder 17; Public Policy Papers, Department of Rare Books and Special Collections, Princeton University Library, Princeton, New Jersey, 14.

## Chapter 5

1. Mikhail Gorbachev, *Perestroika: New Thinking for Our Country and the World* (New York: Harper and Row, 1987).

2. See "Misery Index by Year," available at www.miseryindex.us/indexbyyear.aspx, accessed February 19, 2013.

3. Daniel Yergin, *The Prize: The Epic Quest for Oil, Money, and Power* (New York: Free Press, 1991), 727.

4. Ibid., 731.

5. Ibid., 709–23.

6. Yegor Gaidar, *Collapse of an Empire: Lessons for Modern Russia* (Washington, DC: Brookings Institution Press, 2007), 109.

7. The minutes of this meeting are recounted in Yegor Ligachev and Stephen Cohen, *Inside Gorbachev's Kremlin: The Memoirs of Yegor Ligachev* (Boulder, CO: Westview Press, 1996), 133.

8. Ibid.

9. "Iz Vystuplenij na Zasendanii Politbjuro CK K PSS, 11 July 1986," in Mikhail Gorbachev, *Sobranie sochinenii,* Book 4 (Moscow: Ves' Mir, 2008), 308.

10. Gaidar, *Collapse of an Empire,* 134.

11. Ibid., 136.

12. Valery Ivanovich Boldin, interview by Oleg Igorevich Skvortsov, Moscow, February 24, 1999, available at https://kb.osu.edu/dspace/bitstream/handle/1811/31647/Interview?sequence=6, accessed February 19, 2013.

13. Angus Maddison, *The World Economy: Historical Statistics,* vol. 673 (Paris: OECD Publishing, 2003), 481.

14. Ibid., 279–80.

15. Ibid., 304–5.

16. Ibid., 89.

17. See "Technical Analysis: General Electric Company Common (NYSE)," Yahoo! Finance, available at http://finance.yahoo.com/q/ta?s=GE, accessed February 19, 2013.

18. Lou Cannon, *President Reagan: The Role of a Lifetime,* 1st ed. (New York: Public Affairs, 2000), 23.

19. David Reynolds, "Science, Technology, and the Cold War," in *The Cambridge History of the Cold War,* ed. Melvyn P. Leffler and Odd Arne Westad (New York: Cambridge University Press, 2010), 3:391.

20. Joseph S. Nye, "Gorbachev and the End of the Cold War." *New Straits Times,* April 5, 2006.

21. http://tvbythenumbers.com/2009/01/18/historical-super-bowl-tv-ratings/11044, accessed February 19, 2013.

22. Steven Hayward, *The Age of Reagan: The Conservative Counterrevolution: 1980–1989* (New York: Random House, 2010), 344.

23. Memorandum from National Security Council (NSC) executive secretary Grant Green, Jr., July 2, 1987, Document CK3100532137, Declassified Documents Reference System (Farmington Hills, MI: Gale, 2010).

24. Ronald Reagan, April 23, 1986, in Douglas Brinkley, ed., *The Reagan Diaries* (New York: HarperCollins, 2007), 407.

25. William E. Odom, *The Collapse of the Soviet Military* (New Haven, CT: Yale University Press, 2000), 99.

26. Mikhail S. Gorbachev, *On My Country and the World* (New York: Columbia University Press, 2000), 183.

27. Memo, Frederick Ryan to William Henkel, March 3, 1986, box 15, Matlock Chron., March 1986, Jack Matlock Files, RRL.

28. "Zatsedanie Politbyuro tsk kpss 30 iyulya goda," in Mikhail Gorbachev, *Sobranie sochinenii,* Book 9 (Moscow: Ves' Mir, 2008), 342–43.

29. Valery Ivanovich Boldin, interview by Oleg Igorevich Skvortsov, Moscow, February 24, 1999, available at https://kb.osu.edu/dspace/bitstream/handle/1811/31647/Interview?sequence=6, accessed February 19, 2013.

30. Barry Eichengreen, *The European Economy since 1945: Coordinated Capitalism and Beyond* (Princeton, NJ: Princeton University Press, 2007), 295.

31. George Shultz, "New Realities and New Ways of Thinking," *Foreign Affairs* 63, no. 705 (January 1985).

32. "Iz Vystuplenij na Zasendanii Politbjuro CK KPSS," March 5, 1987, in Gorbachev, *Sobranie sochinenii,* Book 6, 160–61.

33. "Iz Besedy s Byvshim Prezidentam SSha Dzh. Karterom," July 1, 1987, in Gorbachev, *Sobranie sochinenii,* Book 7, 214–15.

34. "Iz Vystuplenij na Zasendanii Politbjuro CK KPSS," February 5, 1987, in Mikhail Gorbachev, *Sobranie sochinenii,* Book 5 (Moscow: Ves' Mir, 2008), 483.

35. "Beseda s Gabrijelem Garsia Markesom," July 15, 1987, in Gorbachev, *Sobranie sochinenii,* Book 7, 286.

36. Svetlana Savranskaya, trans., "Session of the Politburo of the CC CPSU, October 22, 1986," p. 2, available at www.gwu.edu/~nsarchiv/NSAEBB/NSAE BB203/Document22.pdf, accessed February 19, 2013.

37. Quoted in David Hoffman, *The Dead Hand: The Untold Story of the Cold War Arms Race and Its Dangerous Legacy* (New York: Random House, 2009), 274.

38. Anatoly Chernyaev, "Anatoly Chernyaev: Notes from the Conference with Politburo Members and Secretaries of the Central Committee, December 1, 1986," trans. Svetlana Savranskaya, December 1, 1986, National Security Archive, available at www.gwu.edu/~nsarchiv/NSAEBB/NSAEBB203/Document28.pdf accessed February 19, 2013

39. Jack F. Matlock, *Reagan and Gorbachev: How the Cold War Ended,* 1st ed. (New York: Random House, 2004), 251.

40. "Telephone Call to Andrei Sakharov," in Mikhail Gorbachev, *Sobranie sochinenii,* Book 5 (Moscow: Ves' Mir, 2008), 324.

41. Anatoly Chernyaev, *My Six Years with Gorbachev,* trans. and ed. Robert English and Elizabeth Tucker (University Park: Pennsylvania State University Press, 2000), 98.

42. "Zakljuchitel'noe Slovo N Plenume TsK KPSS," in Mikhail Gorbachev, *Sobranie sochinenii,* Book 5 (Moscow: Ves' Mir, 2008), 455.

43. Record of Conversation of Chief of General Staff of the USSR Armed Forces Marshal of the Soviet Union S.F. Akhromeev and H. Brown, C. Vance, H. Kissinger, and D. Jones, National Security Archive: The INF Treaty and the Washington Summit: 20 Years Later, available at www.gwu.edu/~nsarchiv/ NSAEBB/NSAEBB238/russian/Final1987-02-04Akhromeev-Americans.pdf accessed February 19, 2013

44. Aleksandr Yakovlev, Memorandum for Gorbachev, "Toward an Analysis of the Fact of the Visit of Prominent American Political Leaders to the USSR," February 25, 1987, National Security Archive, available at www.gwu.edu/~nsarchiv/ NSAEBB/NSAEBB238/russian/Final1987-02-25%20Yakovlev%20memo.pdf, accessed February 19, 2013

45. For a description of Gorbachev's interaction with his famous guests, see Dusko Doder and Louise Branson, *Gorbachev: Heretic in the Kremlin* (New York: Viking, 1990), 209.

46. "Iz Vystuplenij na Zasendanii Politbjuro" CK KPSS February 26, 1987, in Gorbachev, *Sobranie sochinenii,* Book 6 (Moscow: Ves' Mir, 2008), 125.

47. Anatoly Chernyaev, "Anatoly Chernyaev: Notes from the Conference with Politburo Members and Secretaries of the Central Committee," December 1, 1986, trans. Svetlana Savranskaya, National Security Archive, available at www.gwu.edu/~nsarchiv/NSAEBB/NSAEBB203/Document28.pdf, accessed November 25, 2012

48. "Iz Vystuplenij na Zasendanii Politbjuro CK KPSS, February 26, 1987," in Gorbachev, *Sobranie Sochinenii,* Book 6 (Moscow: Ves' Mir, 2008), 125. Most Soviet strategic planners had determined that the independent nuclear forces of Great Britain and France were inconsequential and would be "leveled" by the aggregate power of the strategic nuclear arsenal of the USSR. See Aleksandr G. Savel'yev and Nikolay N. Detinov, *The Big Five: Arms Control Decision-Making in the Soviet Union* (Greenwood, CT: Praeger, 1995), 138.

49. Andrei Grachev, *Gorbachev's Gamble: Soviet Foreign Policy and the End of the Cold War* (Cambridge, U.K.: Polity Press, 2008), 84. Gorbachev said these words to Grachev in an interview conducted in 1999.

50. See Elizabeth Charles, *The Game Changer: Reassessing the Impact of SDI on Gorbachev's Foreign Policy, Arms Control, and U.S.-Soviet Relations,* Ph.D. dissertation, George Washington University, 2010.

51. V. M. Zubok, *A Failed Empire: The Soviet Union in the Cold War: From Stalin to Gorbachev* (Chapel Hill: University of North Carolina Press, 2007), 309.

52. "Iz Besedy S Ministram Inostrannyh Del Italii Dzh. Andeotti," in Gorbachev, *Sobranie Sochinenii,* Book 6, 130.

53. Chernyaev, *My Six Years with Gorbachev,* 104.

54. Michael Gorbachev, *Memoirs* (New York: Doubleday, 1995), 434.

55. "Iz Razgovora s Je.A Shevardnadze, AF. Dobryninym, AN Jakovlevym, V.A. Medvedevym, As. Chernjaevym," April 1, 1987, in Gorbachev, *Sobranie sochinenii,* Book 6, 219.

56. "Anatoly Chernyaev's Notes from the Politburo Session (Soviet Union)," May 8, 1987, National Security Archive, available at http://chnm.gmu.edu/1989/archive/files/gorbachev-demilitarization_f59533ed51.pdf, accessed February 19, 2013.

57. Ibid.

58. "Zapis' Besedy A.N Jakovleva S Zamestitelem Federal'nogo Kanslera, Ministrom Inostrannykh Del FRG G.D. Genscherom," July 7, 1987, in Aleksandr Yakovlev, *Perestroika: 1985–1991. Neizdannoe, maloizvestnoe, zabytoe* (Moscow: MGD, 2008), 129.

59. Gorbachev, quoted in *Pravda,* April 11, 1987, translated in Jerry Hough, *Democratization and Revolution in the USSR, 1985–1991* (Washington, DC: Brookings Institution Press, 1997), 195; see also Svetlana Savranskaya, "The Logic of 1989: The Soviet Peaceful Withdrawal from Eastern Europe," in *Masterpieces of History: The Peaceful End of the Cold War in Europe,* ed. Svetlana Savranskaya, Thomas Blanton, and Vladislav Zubok (Budapest: Central European University Press, 2010).

60. Alexander Nadiradze, quoted in Hoffman, *Dead Hand,* 292.

61. "Zatsedanie Politbyuro tsk kpss 15 oktyabrya goda," in Mikhail Gorbachev, *Sobranie Sochinenii,* Book 9 (Moscow: Ves' Mir, 2008), 505.

62. Doder and Branson, *Gorbachev,* 214.

63. For an overview of the Iran-Contra scandal, see Peter Kornbluh and Malcolm Byrne, eds., *The Iran-Contra Scandal: The Declassified History* (New York: New Press, 1993); see also Lawrence E. Walsh, *Firewall: The Iran-Contra Conspiracy and Cover-up* (New York: Norton, 1998).

64. Reagan, "Address to the Nation on the Iran Arms and Contra Aid Controversy," March 4, 1987, available at www.reagan.utexas.edu/archives/speeches/1987/030487h.htm, accessed February 19, 2013

65. Quoted in Don Regan, *For the Record: From Wall Street to Washington* (New York: St. Martin's Press, 1989), 9.

66. Shultz recounted this conversation to his executive secretary, Charles Hill, whose notes appear in Molly Worthen, *The Man on Whom Nothing Was Lost: The Grand Strategy of Charles Hill* (New York: Houghton Mifflin Harcourt, 2006), 214.

67. Ron Reagan, *My Father at 100* (New York: Viking, 2011).

68. Ronald Reagan, "Address Before a Joint Session of Congress on the State of the Union," January 3, 1987, available at www.reagan.utexas.edu/archives/speeches/1987/012787a.htm, accessed February 19, 2013

69. "Memorandum for the Record: Record of National Security Council Meeting," March 13, 1987, box 91304, Executive Secretariat, NSC: National Security Council Meeting Files, RRL.

70. Frances Fitzgerald, *Way Out There in the Blue: Reagan, Star Wars, and the End of the Cold War* (New York: Simon and Schuster, 2000), 415.

71. Reagan, "Remarks on Soviet—United States Relations at the Town Hall of California Meeting in Los Angeles," August 26, 1987, available at www.reagan.utexas.edu/archives/speeches/1987/082687a.htm, accessed February 19, 2013.

72. George Pratt Shultz, *Turmoil and Triumph: My Years as Secretary of State* (New York: Scribner's, 1993), 872.

73. Ronald Reagan, "Reagan to William F. Buckley," May 5, 1987, in William F. Buckley, *The Reagan I Knew* (New York: Basic Books, 2008), 201–2.

74. "Memorandum for the Record: Record of National Security Planning Group," February 20, 1987, p. 7, box 91308, Executive Secretariat, NSC: National Security Planning Group Records, RRL.

75. Cited in Raymond L. Garthoff, *The Great Transition: American-Soviet Relations and the End of the Cold War* (Washington, DC: Brookings Institution Press, 1994), 308.

76. Caspar Weinberger Interview, p. 29, Miller Center, University of Virginia, Ronald Reagan Presidential Oral History Project, November 19, 2002, available at http://millercenter.org/president/reagan/oralhistory/caspar-weinberger, accessed February 19, 2013

77. "Memorandum for the Record: Record of National Security Planning Group," February 3, 1987, p. 3, box 91308, Executive Secretariat, NSC: National Security Planning Group Records, RRL.

78. Ibid.

79. "Memorandum for the Record: Record of National Security Planning Group," February 3, 1987, p. 12, box 91308, Executive Secretariat, NSC: National Security Planning Group Records, RRL.

80. Gregory A. Fossedal, "NSC Minutes Show President Leaning to SDI Deployment," *Washington Times,* February 6, 1987, 10A.

81. Paul Nitze, *From Hiroshima to Glasnost: At the Centre of Decision, A Memoir* (London: Weidenfeld and Nicolson, 1989), 449.

82. "Memorandum for the Record: Record of National Security Planning Group," September 8, 1987, p. 7, box 91308, Executive Secretariat, NSC: National Security Planning Group Records, RRL.

83. Ibid., 11.

84. "Memorandum for the Record: Record of National Security Planning Group," October 14, 1987, p. 6, box 91309, Executive Secretariat, NSC: National Security Planning Group Records, RRL.

85. Ibid., 8.

86. Ibid.

87. Don Oberdorfer, *From the Cold War to a New Era* (Baltimore: Johns Hopkins University Press, 1998), 212.

88. Phil Gailey, "Conservatives Pressing 1988 G.O.P. Contenders for a Rigid Foreign Policy Agenda," *New York Times,* February 23, 1987, available at www.nytimes.com/1987/02/23/us/conservatives-pressing-1988-gop-contenders-for-a-rigid-foreign-agenda.html, accessed February 13, 2013

89. Timothy Naftali, *George H. W. Bush,* 1st ed. (New York: Times Books, 2007), 48.

90. Interview with Frank Carlucci, p. 25, August 28, 2001, Miller Center, University of Virginia, Ronald Reagan Presidential Oral History Project, available at http://millercenter.org/president/reagan/oralhistory/frank-carlucci accessed February 13, 2013

91. Interview with Howard Baker; June 26, 1990, p. 1; Don Oberdorfer Papers; box 2, folder 4; Public Policy Papers, Department of Rare Books and Special Collections, Princeton University Library, Princeton, New Jersey.

92. Shultz, *Turmoil and Triumph,* 880–81.

93. Oberdorfer, *From the Cold War to a New Era,* 220.

94. Quoted in William Wohlforth, ed., *Witnesses to the End of the Cold War* (Baltimore: Johns Hopkins University Press, 1996), 94.

95. Shultz, *Turmoil and Triumph,* 886–87.

96. Ibid., 887.

97. "Memorandum for the Record: Record of National Security Council Meeting," May 21, 1987, p. 3, box 91304, Executive Secretariat, NSC: National Security Council Meeting Files, RRL.

98. Quoted in Hugh Faringdon, *Strategic Geography: NATO, the Warsaw Pact, and the Superpowers* (London: Routledge, 1989), 30.

99. Reagan, March 12, 1987, in Brinkley, ed., *Reagan Diaries,* 486.

100. Reagan, April 21, 1987, in ibid., 490.

101. Reagan, April 30, 1987, in ibid., 716.

102. Reagan, June 8, 1987, in ibid., 505.

103. David Rothkopf, *Running the World: The Inside Story of the National Security Council and the Architects of American Power* (New York: PublicAffairs, 2005), 255.

104. Frank Carlucci Interview, August 28, 2001, Miller Center, University of Virginia, Ronald Reagan Presidential Oral History Project, available at http://millercenter.org/president/reagan/oralhistory/frank-carlucci accessed February 13, 2013.

105. See John Tower, *The Tower Commission Report* (New York: Bantam, 1987)

106. "Memorandum for the Record: Record of National Security Council Meeting," May 21, 1987, box 91304, Executive Secretariat, NSC: National Security Council Meeting Files, RRL.

107. William Webster Interview, August 21, 2011, Miller Center, University of Virginia, Ronald Reagan Presidential Oral History Project, available at http://millercenter.org/president/reagan/oralhistory/william-webster accessed February 19, 2013 Even before the fallout from Iran-Contra, top military officers found Reagan puzzling. In an NSPG meeting on October 27, 1986, Reagan's generals expressed concern over his proposal to eliminate all ballistic missiles. The president responded by stating how proud he was of the nation's armed forces, the Chairmen of Joint Chiefs of Staff Admiral William Crowe later recalled. "If the President was angry [at the admiral], it was not obvious to me," Crowe wrote in his memoir. "If he had heard my remarks, it was not obvious to me. If he simply did not wish to respond, that was not clear to me either." Listening to Reagan's response was "the most incredible thing in my life"; it led the admiral to question whether, when it came to nuclear weapons, Reagan truly "understood the horrendousness of what he was sitting on." See Crowe, *In the Line of Fire: From Washington to the Gulf, the Politics and Battles of the New Military* (New York: Simon and Schuster, 1993), 269; interview with William Crowe; November 16, 1989, p. 16; Don Oberdorfer Papers; box 2, folder 9; Public Policy Papers, Department of Rare Books and Special Collections, Princeton University Library, Princeton, New Jersey.

108. For a discussion of the technological impediments see Hoffman, *Dead Hand,* 288.

109. Rust's post–Red Square travails are described in Victor Sebestyen, *Revolution 1989: The Fall of the Soviet Empire* (London: Weidenfeld and Nicolson, 2009), 191.

110. Odom, *Collapse of the Soviet Military* 110.

111. Raymond "Doc" Frasier, quoted in CNN, *Cold War,* Episode 22, "Star Wars."

112. Jack F. Matlock Jr., *Autopsy on an Empire: The American Ambassador's Account of the Collapse of the Soviet Union* (New York: Random House, 1995), 151.

113. George Bush, *All the Best, George Bush: My Life in Letters and Other Writings* (New York: Scribner, 1999), 371.

114. Webster to Reagan (written by Gates), "Gorbachev's Gameplan: The Long View," November 24, 1987, National Security Archive: The INF Treaty and the Washington Summit, available at www.gwu.edu/~nsarchiv/NSAEBB/NSAEBB238/usdocs/Doc%2011%20%28Memo%20from%20Webster%2011.24.87%29.pdf, accessed November 25, 2012, p. 3.

115. "Memorandum of Conversation: Meeting with General Secretary Mikhail Gorbachev of the USSR," December 8, 1987, 10:45 am to 12:30 pm, available at www.gwu.edu/~nsarchiv/NSAEBB/NSAEBB238/usdocs/Doc%2011%20 (Memo%20from%20Webster%2011.24.87).pdf, accessed February 19, 2013.

116. Ibid.

117. "Memorandum of Conversation: Meeting with General Secretary Mikhail Gorbachev of the USSR," December 8, 1987, 2:30 p.m. to 3:15 p.m., National Security Archive, p. 8, available at www.gwu.edu/~nsarchiv/NSAEBB/NSAEBB238/usdocs/Doc%2015%20%28Memcon%20Gorby%20Reagan%2012.08.87%29.pdf accessed February 19, 2013.

118. Ibid.

119. Ibid., 8–9.

120. Shultz, *Turmoil and Triumph,* 1011.

121. Powell, quoted in Cannon, *President Reagan,* 776.

122. "Memorandum of Conversation: Meeting with General Secretary Mikhail Gorbachev of the USSR," December 9, 1987, 10:55 am to 12:35 pm, National Security Archive, p. 3, available at www.gwu.edu/~nsarchiv/NSAEBB/NSAEBB238/usdocs/Doc%2017%20(Memcon%20Gorby%20Reagan%2012.09.87).pdf accessed February 19, 2013.

123. Ibid.

124. Ibid.

125. Ibid.

126. Ibid.

127. Ibid.

128. Ibid., 11.

129. Ibid., 12.

130. Ibid.

131. Ibid., 13.

132. Ibid., 14.

133. Ibid.

134. "Memorandum for the Record: Record of National Security Planning Group," February 9, 1988, Executive Secretariat, NSC: National Security Council Meeting Files, RRL.

135. Ibid.

136. Memorandum of Conversation, "The Secretary's Meeting with Gorbachev," February 22, 1988, 11:05 a.m.–2:40 p.m., Declassified Documents Reference System (Farmington Hills, MI: Gale, 2010).

137. "Memorandum for the Record: Record of National Security Planning Group," February 26, 1988, pp. 2–3, Executive Secretariat, NSC: National Security Council Meeting Files, RRL.

138. Cannon, *President Reagan,* 780.

139. Reagan, December 3, 1987, in Brinkley, ed., *Reagan Diaries,* 544.

140. Cannon, *President Reagan,* 778.

141. Ibid.

142. Howard Phillips, quoted in Susan F. Rasky, "Treaty Critics Lash Back at Reagan," *New York Times,* December 5, 1987, available at www.nytimes.com/1987/12/05/world/treaty-critics-lash-back-at-reagan.html accessed February 19, 2013.

143. Richard Reeves, *President Reagan: The Triumph of Imagination* (New York: Simon and Schuster, 2005), 489.

144. For a vivid description of a clandestine meeting between Nixon and Reagan after the Washington Summit, see James Mann, *The Rebellion of Ronald Reagan: A History of the End of the Cold War* (New York: Viking, 2009), 3–8.

145. Quoted in Cannon, *President Reagan,* 699.

146. *Discriminate Deterrence: Report of the Commission on Integrated Long-Term Strategy* (Washington, DC: Government Printing Office, 1988), 1.

147. Ibid., 2.

148. Jack Matlock, quoted in Savranskaya, Blanton, and Zubok, eds., *Masterpieces of History,* 110.

149. Accounts of these meetings are available at the National Security Archive, "The Moscow Summit 20 Years Later," available at www.gwu.edu/~nsarchiv/ NSAEBB/NSAEBB251/index.htm accessed February 19, 2013

150. See Mann, *Rebellion of Ronald Reagan,* 304.

151. Gorbachev, *Perestroika,* 204.

152. Document 31: Notes of a Meeting between Mikhail Gorbachev and Foreign Policy Advisors, in Savranskaya, Blanton, and Zubok, eds., *Masterpieces of History,* 312.

## Chapter 6

1. "Excerpts of Address by Mikhail Gorbachev to the 43rd U.N. General Assembly Session," December 7, 1988, available at http://legacy.wilsoncenter.org/coldwar files/files/Documents/1988-1107.Gorbachev.pdf, accessed February 19, 2013

2. Ibid.

3. "Gambler, Showman, Statesman," *New York Times,* December 8, 1988, available at www.nytimes.com/1988/12/08/opinion/gambler-showman-statesman.html, accessed February 19, 2013.

4. Victor Sebestyen, *Revolution 1989: The Fall of the Soviet Empire* (London: Pantheon Books, 2009), 214.

5. Jacques Lévesque, "The East European Revolutions of 1989," in *The Cambridge History of the Cold War,* ed. Melvyn P. Leffler and Odd Arne Westad (New York: Cambridge University Press, 2010), 3:320.

6. Archie Brown, *The Rise and Fall of Communism* (New York: Ecco, 2009), 528.

7. William Hitchcock, *The Struggle for Europe: The Turbulent History of a Divided Continent* (New York: Anchor Books, 2004), 359.

8. David D. Newsom, *Private Diplomacy with the Soviet Union* (Lanham, MD: University Press of America, 1987), 56.

9. Sebestyen, *Revolution 1989,* 240.

10. Hitchcock, *Struggle for Europe,* 360.

11. Sebestyen, *Revolution 1989,* 213.

12. Record of Conversation between President M.S. Gorbachev and Miklós Németh, March 3, 1989, Gorbachev Foundation Archive, Moscow, translated by Csaba Farkas, Cold War International History Project, available at http://digital archive.wilsoncenter.org/document/112492 accessed February 19, 2013

13. James A. Baker III with Thomas M. DeFrank, *The Politics of Diplomacy: Revolution, War, and Peace, 1989–1992* (New York: G.P. Putnam's Sons, 1995), 63–64.

14. B-Wire, "Varkonyi Says the Brezhnev Doctrine is Dead," on file at Radio Free Europe Archive: International Relations: Great Britain, 1982–89, Open Society Archive, Budapest, Hungary.

15. Memorandum of Conversation between President M.S. Gorbachev and Karoly Grósz, March 23–24, 1989, MOL M-KS-288-11/4458 o.e., translated by

Csaba Farkas, Cold War International History Project, available at www.wilsoncenter.
org/sites/default/files/EotCW_Part2.pdf, accessed February 19, 2013

16. Henry Kamm, "Hungarian Who Led '56 Revolt Is Buried as a Hero," *New York Times,* June 16, 1989, Opinion section, available at www.nytimes.com/1989/06/17/world/hungarian-who-led-56-revolt-is-buried-as-a-hero.html, accessed February 19, 2013

17. William Taubman and Svetlana Savranskaya, "If a Wall Fell in Berlin and Moscow Hardly Noticed, Would It Still Make a Noise?" in *The Fall of the Berlin Wall: The Revolutionary Legacy of 1989,* ed. Jeffrey A. Engel (New York: Oxford University Press, 2009), 83.

18. The removal of the fence had actually begun weeks earlier, and when Horn suggested a fence-cutting ceremony, Németh later recalling saying, "Gyula, do it, but hurry up—there isn't much barbed wire left." Quoted in Walter Mayr, "Cutting the Fence and Changing History," *Der Spiegel,* available at www.spiegel.de/international/europe/0,1518,627632,00.html, accessed February 19, 2013

19. For a description of the Polish authorities failure to do so, see Gregory F. Domber, "The Catholic Church and the Cold War's End in Europe: Vatican Ostpolitik and Pope John Paul II, 1985–1989," in *Europe and the End of the Cold War: A Reappraisal,* ed. Frédéric Bozo, Marie-Pierre Rey, N. Piers Ludlow, and Leopoldo Nuti (New York: Routledge, 2008).

20. Pope John Paul II, quoted in Matthew J. Ouimet, *The Rise and Fall of the Brezhnev Doctrine in Soviet Foreign Policy* (Chapel Hill: University of North Carolina Press, 2003), 114–15.

21. Robert Suro, "Pope Calls Solidarity a Rights Model," June 12, 1987, *New York Times,* available at www.nytimes.com/1987/06/12/world/pope-calls-solidarity-a-rights-model.html, accessed February 19, 2013

22. George Weigel, *Final Revolution: The Resistance Church and the Collapse of Communism* (New York: Oxford University of Press, 1992), 153.

23. See, most recently, John O'Sullivan, *The President, the Pope, and the Prime Minister: Three Who Changed the World* (Washington, DC: Regnery, 2006).

24. Stephen Kotkin with Jan Gross, *Uncivil Society: 1989 and the Implosion of the Communist Establishment* (New York: Modern Library, 2009), 102.

25. Ibid., 125–26. For a vivid depiction of these developments, see Timothy Garton Ash, *The Magic Lantern: The Revolution of '89 Witnessed in Warsaw, Budapest, Berlin, and Prague* (New York: Random House, 1990).

26. George H. W. Bush, "Acceptance Speech at the Republican National Convention," August 18, 1988, available at http://millercenter.org/scripps/archive/speeches/detail/5526, accessed February 19, 2013.

27. Robert Schlesinger, *White House Ghosts: Presidents and Their Speechwriters: From FDR to George W. Bush,* 1st ed. (New York: Simon and Schuster, 2008), 363.

28. George H. W. Bush, "Inaugural Address," January 20, 1989, available at http://bushlibrary.tamu.edu/research/public_papers.php?id=1&year=1989&month=01, accessed February 19, 2013

29. Excerpts of Remarks for Vice President George Bush, National Press Club, Washington, D.C., January 5, 1988, on file at George H. W. Bush Presidential Library.

30. Alessandra Stanley, "More Worldly Than Wise," *Time,* August 15, 1988, available at www.time.com/time/magazine/article/0,9171,968127,00.html, accessed February 19, 2013

31. "Address on Administration Goals Before a Joint Session of Congress," February 9, 1989, available at http://bushlibrary.tamu.edu/research/public_papers.php?id=51&year=1989&month=2, accessed February 19, 2013

32. Ibid.

33. Quoted in David Hoffman, "Gorbachev Seen as Trying to Buy Time for Reform," *Washington Post,* January 23, 1989, A1.

34. George H. W. Bush and Brent Scowcroft, *A World Transformed,* 1st ed. (New York: Alfred A. Knopf, 1998), 13.

35. Ibid.

36. Ibid., 12.

37. Ibid., 46.

38. "Zapis' besedy M. S. Gorbacheva s H. Kissingerom, Yanvarya 17, 1989 goda," Fond 1, Opis 1, Archive of the Gorbachev Foundation.

39. "Kissinger's Report on Meeting with Gorbachev"; January 17, 1989; James A. Baker Papers, box 108, Public Policy Papers, Department of Rare Books and Special Collections, Princeton University Library, Princeton, New Jersey.

40. Ibid.

41. "Proposed Agenda for Meeting with the President"; July 13, 1990; James A. Baker Papers, box 115, Public Policy Papers, Department of Rare Books and Special Collections, Princeton University Library, Princeton, New Jersey.

42. "Talking Points for Jan. 23 1989 Cabinet Meeting," James A. Baker Papers, box 108, Public Policy Papers, Department of Rare Books and Special Collections, Princeton University Library, Princeton, New Jersey.

43. "Baker's notes on U.S.-Soviet relations," February 1989, James A. Baker Papers, box 108, Public Policy Papers, Department of Rare Books and Special Collections, Princeton University Library, Princeton, New Jersey.

44. Lou Cannon, "Reagan Is Concerned about Bush's Indecision," *Washington Post,* May 6, 1989, A21.

45. As Giovanni Arrighi puts it: "The mobilization of the world's financial resources to rescue the U.S. economy from the deep recession of the early 1980s, and simultaneously to escalate the armaments race with the USSR, transformed the United States into the greatest debtor nation in world history, increasingly dependent on cheap East Asian credit, labor, and commodities for the reproduction of its wealth and power." Giovanni Arrighi, "The World Economy and the Cold War," in *Cambridge History of the Cold War,* ed. Leffler and Westad, 3:41.

46. George Soros, "International Economic Assistance for Poland," March 24, 1989, in Condoleezza Rice Files, Aid to Poland and Hungary, George H. W. Bush Presidential Library.

47. "Memorandum of Conversation: Telephone Call from the President to Chancellor Helmut Kohl of West Germany," June 23, 1989, available at www.margaretthatcher.org/document/B1E15262B42B47749865ACF3306DE0AB.pdf, accessed November 25, 2012.

48. National Intelligence Estimate, "Soviet Policy toward the West: The Gorbachev Challenge," April 1989, available at www.gwu.edu/~nsarchiv/NSAEBB/NSAEBB261/us11.pdf, accessed November 25, 2012.

49. Ibid.

50. Robert B. Zoellick, "An Architecture of U.S. Strategy after the Cold War," in *In Uncertain Times: American Foreign Policy after the Berlin Wall and 9/11,* Melvyn P. Leffler and Jeffrey Legro (Ithaca, NY: Cornell University Press, 2011), 28.

51. For a vivid description of this campaign, see Sidney Blumenthal, *Pledging Allegiance: The Last Campaign of the Cold War* (New York: Harper, 1991).

52. Baker with DeFrank, *Politics of Diplomacy,* 55.

53. Zapis' Besedy A.N Jakovleva S federal'nym kantslerom FRG G. Kolem, January 9, 1989, in Aleksandr Yakovlev, *Perestrojka: 1985–1991. Neizdannoe, maloizvestnoe, zabytoe* (Moscow: MGD, 2008), 302.

54. Zagladin to Gorbachev, June 22, 1989, Fond 5, Document 7223, Archive of the Gorbachev Foundation.

55. Quoted in Ann Devroy, "Bush and Baker Disclaim Cheney's Gorbachev View," *Washington Post,* May 1, 1989, A15.

56. Cable from Jack Matlock to State Department, "U.S.-Soviet Relations: Policy Opportunities," February 22, 1989, in *Masterpieces of History: The Peaceful End of the Cold War in Europe,* ed. Svetlana Savranskaya, Thomas Blanton, and Vladislav Zubok (Budapest: Central European University Press, 2010), 401.

57. Ibid.

58. Philip Zelikow and Condoleezza Rice, *Germany Unified and Europe Transformed: A Study in Statecraft* (Cambridge, MA: Harvard University Press, 1995), 27.

59. Ibid., 28.

60. Ibid.

61. "Written Responses to Questions Submitted by the Kyodo News Service of Japan," February 16, 1989, available at http://bushlibrary.tamu.edu/research/public_papers.php?id=65&year=1989&month=2, accessed February 19, 2013.

62. Zoellick to Baker, "NATO Summit—Possible Initiatives (Zoellick draft for Baker)"; May 15, 1989; James A. Baker Papers, box 108, Public Policy Papers, Department of Rare Books and Special Collections, Princeton University Library, Princeton, New Jersey.

63. Ibid.

64. George H. W. Bush, "Remarks at the Texas A&M University Commencement Ceremony in College Station," May 12, 1989, available at http://bushlibrary.tamu.edu/research/public_papers.php?id=413&year=1989&month=5, accessed February 19, 2013.

65. Ibid.

66. George H. W. Bush, "Remarks to the Citizens in Mainz, Federal Republic of Germany," May 31, 1989, available at http://bushlibrary.tamu.edu/research/public_papers.php?id=476&year=1989&month=5, accessed February 19, 2013.

67. Memo, Nancy Bearg Dyke to Brent Scowcroft, June 27, 1989, 1, OA/ID 91124-009, Brent Scowcroft Collection, George Bush Presidential Library.

68. See Chen Jian, "China and the Cold War After Mao," in *Cambridge History of the Cold War,* ed. Leffler and Westad, 3:181–200.

69. Chen Jian, "China's Path Toward 1989," in *Fall of the Berlin Wall,* ed. Engel, 111–12.

70. Eduard Shevardnadze, *Kogda Rukhnul Zheleznyi Zanaves: Vstrechi i Vospominaniia* (Moscow: Evropa, 2009), 143.

71. "Razgovor s Myedvyedyevim po tyelyefonoo iz Pyekina 15 maya 1989 goda," in *Otvechaia na vyzov vremeni: vneshniaia politika perestroiki: documental'nye svidetel'stva: po zapisiam besed M.S. Gorbacheva s zarubezhnymi deiateliami i drugim materialam* (Moscow: Ves' Mir, 2010), 880.

72. Bush and Scowcroft, *World Transformed,* 98.

73. Ibid., 38

74. Business Wire, "Hungarian Students Proclaim Solidarity with Chinese Colleagues," May 25, 1989, on file at International Relations: China, 1976–89, Open Society Archive, Budapest.

75. Bush and Scowcroft, *World Transformed,* 124–25.

76. "It was like, 'Who is this strange guy with a beard who looks like Woody Allen?'" U.S. Ambassador to Hungary Mark Palmer later recalled. Interview with Mark Palmer, Foreign Affairs Oral History Collection, October 30, 1997, Frontline Diplomacy, Manuscript Division, Library of Congress, Washington, D.C., available online at http://hdl.loc.gov/loc.mss/mfdip.2004pal02, accessed November 25, 2012.

77. Pavel Palazchenko, *My Years with Gorbachev and Shevardnadze: The Memoir of a Soviet Interpreter* (University Park: Pennsylvania State University Press, 1997), 80.

78. Zagladin to Gorbachev, August 18, 1988, Fond 3, Document 7154, Archive of the Gorbachev Foundation. Zagladin is reporting on a meeting he had with Congressman Stephen Solarz.

79. Baker with DeFrank, *Politics of Diplomacy,* 62.

80. Mikhail Gorbachev, *Ponyat' perestroiku…Pochemu eto vazhno seichas* (Moscow: Alpina Books, 2006), 177.

81. Shevardnadze, *Kogda Rukhnul Zheleznyi Zanaves,* 117.

82. Visit of Gorbachev to New York, December 7, 1988, in Mikhail Gorbachev, *Sobranie Sochinenii,* Book 13 (Moscow: Ves' Mir, 2008), 42.

83. Transcript of CC CPSU Politburo Session, in *Masterpieces of History,* ed. Savranskaya, Blanton, and Zubok, 333.

84. Ibid., 334.

85. Anatoly Adamishin and Richard Schifter, *Human Rights, Perestroika, and the End of the Cold War* (Washington, DC: USIP, 2009), 215.

86. Taubman and Savranskaya, "If a Wall Fell in Berlin," 72–73.

87. Vistooplyeniye v Lankastyer-haoozye na vstryechye s pryedstavityelyami dyelovih kroogov Vyelikobritanii, 6 April 1989," in Gorbachev, *Sobranie Sochinenii,* Book 14, 54.

88. The Diary of Anatoly Chernyaev, April 30, 1989, National Security Archive, available at www.gwu.edu/~nsarchiv/NSAEBB/NSAEBB275/1989%20for%20posting.pdf, accessed November 25, 2012.

89. "Zapis' besedy M. S. Gorbacheva s H. Kissingerom, 17 yanvarya 1989 goda," Fond 1, Opis 1, Archive of the Gorbachev Foundation.

90. Palazchenko, *My Years with Gorbachev and Shevardnadze,* 131.

91. "Iz byesyedi s gossyekryetaryem Jyeymsom Byeykyerom," in *Otvechaia na vyzov vremeni,* 230.

92. Translated from a Perm newspaper by Paul Quinn-Judge, *Christian Science Monitor*, December 29, 1988.

93. "Razgovor M.S. Gorbachyeva s Pomoshshnikami i V.A. Myedvyedevim," January 17, 1989, in Gorbachev, *Sobranie Sochinenii*, Book 13, 170.

94. "Memorandum to Alexander Yakovlev from the Bogomolov Commission," The Cold War International History Project, available at www.wilsoncenter.org/sites/default/files/EotCW_Part2.pdf (accessed February 19, 2013).

95. "Report of Vadim Zagladin on his conversation with Chairman of the Czechoslovak Association for U.N., Deputy Chairman of the Committee for European Security, Jan Pudlak," The Cold War International History Project, available at www.wilsoncenter.org/sites/default/files/EotCW_Part2.pdf, accessed February 19, 2013.

96. V. M. Zubok, *A Failed Empire: The Soviet Union in the Cold War: From Stalin to Gorbachev* (Chapel Hill: University of North Carolina Press, 2007), 322.

97. The Diary of Anatoly Chernyaev, January 15, 1989, National Security Archive, p. 4, available at www.gwu.edu/~nsarchiv/NSAEBB/NSAEBB275/1989%20for%20posting.pdf, accessed February 19, 2013.

98. Quoted in Taubman and Savranskaya, "If a Wall Fell in Berlin," 76.

99. "Third Conversation between M. S. Gorbachev and FRG Chancellor Helmut Kohl (West Germany)," June 14, 1989, The Cold War International History Project, p. 2, available at www.wilsoncenter.org/cwihp/documentreaders/eotcw/890614.pdf, accessed February 19, 2013.

100. The Diary of Anatoly Chernyaev, May 21, 1989, National Security Archive, available at www.gwu.edu/~nsarchiv/NSAEBB/NSAEBB275/1989%20for%20posting.pdf, accessed February 19, 2013.

101. Palazchenko, *My Years with Gorbachev and Shevardnadze*, 140.

102. Mikhail Gorbachev, *Memoirs* (New York: Doubleday, 1995).

103. The Diary of Anatoly Chernyaev, May 2, 1989, National Security Archive, available at www.gwu.edu/~nsarchiv/NSAEBB/NSAEBB275/1989%20for%20posting.pdf, accessed February 19, 2013.

104. Address given by Mikhail Gorbachev to the Council of Europe, July 6, 1989, available at www.ena.lu/address-given-mikhail-gorbachev-council-europe-july-1989-020003958.html,5, accessed February 19, 2013.

105. Ibid., 4.

106. Palazchenko, *My Years with Gorbachev and Shevardnadze*, 144.

107. "Document No. 146: Records of the Political Consultative Committee Meeting in Bucharest, July 7–8, 1989," in *A Cardboard Castle? An Inside History of the Warsaw Pact, 1955–1991*, ed. Vojtech Mastny and Malcolm Byrne (Budapest: Central European University Press, 2005), 644.

108. Ibid., 645.

109. "Memorandum from Foreign Minister Petar Mladenov to the Politburo of the Central Committee of the Bulgarian Communist Party," July 12, 1989, Diplomatic Archive, Sofia, Opis 46–10, File 29, pp. 4–12, document obtained by Jordan Baev, available at http://legacy.wilsoncenter.org/coldwarfiles/files/Documents/Bulgaria12July1989.pdf. accessed February 19, 2013.

110. Ibid.

111. "Negotiation between Mikhail S. Gorbachev and Rezso Nyers," National Security Archive, available at www.gwu.edu/~nsarchiv/news/19991105/24jul89.htm, accessed February 19, 2013.

112. Gorbachev to Bush; July 29, 1989; James A. Baker Papers, box 115, Public Policy Papers, Department of Rare Books and Special Collections, Princeton University Library, Princeton, New Jersey. Gorbachev was replying to condolences Bush had sent him after a Soviet submarine was lost in the Norwegian Sea.

113. Quoted in Magyar Távirati Iroda in English, "Németh Says Hungary Condemns Czechoslovakia Invasion," August 20, 1989, on file at Radio Free Europe Files: International Relations: Czechoslovakia, 1985–89, Open Society Archive, Budapest.

114. Michael Meyer, *The Year That Changed the World: The Untold Story behind the Fall of the Berlin Wall* (New York: Scribner, 2009), 123.

115. Gorbachev, *Ponyat' Perestroiku,*. 215.

116. Gorbachev, in CNN, *Cold War,* Episode 23, "The Wall Comes Down."

117. Ibid.

118. "Excerpt From the Diary of Anatoly Chernyaev," National Security Archive, available at www.gwu.edu/~nsarchiv/NSAEBB/NSAEBB275/1989%20for%20posting.pdf, accessed February 19, 2013.

119. Elizabeth Pond, *Beyond the Wall: Germany's Road to Unification* (Washington, DC: Brookings Institution, 1993), 96.

120. Mary Elise Sarotte, *1989: The Struggle to Create Post–Cold War Europe* (Princeton, NJ: Princeton University Press, 2009), 33.

121. Charles Maier, *Dissolution: The Crisis of Communism and the End of East Germany* (Princeton, NJ: Princeton University Press, 1997), 142.

122. Maier, *Dissolution,* 159.

123. Translated in Cold War International History Project Bulletin, Issue 12/13, available at www.wilsoncenter.org/sites/default/files/cover-toc-intro.pdf, accessed February 19, 2013.

124. Quoted in Melvyn P. Leffler, "Dreams of Freedom, Temptations of Power," in *Fall of the Berlin Wall,* ed. Engel, 136.

125. Sarotte, *1989,* 38.

126. David Reynolds, "Science, Technology, and the Cold War," in *Cambridge History of the Cold War,* ed. Leffler and Westad, 3:389.

127. Gorbachev, *Ponyat' perestroiku,* 225.

128. "Record of Conversation of M.S. Gorbachev and John Paul II, National Security Archive, available at www.gwu.edu/~nsarchiv/NSAEBB/NSAEBB298/Document%208.pdf (February 19, 2013).

129. Svetlana Savranskaya, "The Logic of 1989: The Soviet Peaceful Withdrawal from Eastern Europe," in *Masterpieces of History,* Savranskaya, Blanton, and Zubok, eds., 46.

130. Marie-Pierre Rey, "The End of the Cold War: Soviet-American Relations and the Radical Changes in Europe," in *From Fulton to Malta: How the Cold War Began and Ended,* ed. Pavel Palazhchenko and Olga Zdravomyslova (Moscow: Gorbachev Foundation, 2008), 60.

131. See Stephen Kotkin, "The Bloc Goes Borrowing," in *The Shock of the Global: The 1970s in Perspective,* ed. Niall Ferguson, Charles S. Maier, Erez Manela, and Daniel J. Sargent (Cambridge, MA: Harvard University Press, 2010).

## Chapter 7

1. George H. W. Bush, "Remarks at a Fundraising Dinner for Gubernatorial Candidate Pete Wilson in San Francisco, California," February 28, 1990, available at http://bushlibrary.tamu.edu/research/public_papers.php?id=1598&year=1990&month=2, accessed February 19, 2013.

2. George H. W. Bush, "Address Before a Joint Session of the Congress on the Persian Gulf Crisis and the Federal Budget Deficit," September 11, 1990, available at http://bushlibrary.tamu.edu/research/public_papers.php?id=2217&year=1990&month=9, accessed February 19, 2013.

3. Memorandum of Conversation, First Expanded Bilateral Session with Chairman Gorbachev of the Soviet Union, December 2, 1989, 10:00–11:55 a.m., 2, OA/ID CF00718-066, Condoleezza Rice Files, George Bush Presidential Library.

4. Ibid.

5. Ibid., 4.

6. Ibid.

7. Ibid., 5.

8. Ibid., 6.

9. Ibid., 7.

10. Ibid., 7–8.

11. Ibid.

12. Ibid., 10.

13. Ibid.

14. Memorandum of Conversation, Luncheon Meeting with Chairman Gorbachev of the USSR, December 2, 1989, 1:30 p.m.–2:45 p.m., 3, OA/ID CF00718-006, Condoleezza Rice Files, George Bush Presidential Library.

15. Ibid., 3.

16. Ibid., 4.

17. Ibid., 5.

18. George Bush, *All the Best, George Bush: My Life in Letters and Other Writings* (New York: Scribner's, 1999), 459.

19. Anatoly Chernyaev, *My Six Years with Gorbachev*, trans. and ed. Robert English and Elizabeth Tucker (University Park: Pennsylvania State University Press, 2000), 234.

20. Memorandum of Conversation, First Restricted Bilateral Session with Chairman Gorbachev of Soviet Union, December 2, 1989, 12:00–1:00 p.m., OA/ID CF00769-005, Arnold Kanter Files, George Bush Presidential Library, 3.

21. Ibid., 10.

22. Memorandum of Conversation, Second Expanded Bilateral Session, December 3, 1989, 4:35–6:45 p.m., OA/ID CF00718-006, Condoleezza Rice Files, George Bush Presidential Library, 6.

23. Memorandum of Conversation, First Restricted Bilateral Session with Chairman Gorbachev of Soviet Union, December 2, 1989, 12:00–1:00 p.m., OA/ID CF00769-005, Arnold Kanter Files, George Bush Presidential Library, 5.

24. Memorandum of Conversation, Second Expanded Bilateral Session, December 3, 1989, 4:35–6:45 p.m., OA/ID CF00718-006, Condoleezza Rice Files, George Bush Presidential Library, 6.

25. James Baker, "A New Europe, a New Atlanticism: Architecture for a New Era," U.S. Department of State Bureau of Public Affairs, Current Policy no. 1233 (December 12, 1989).

26. Robert Zoellick, "An Architecture of U.S. Strategy after the Cold War," in *In Uncertain Times: American Foreign Policy after the Berlin Wall and 9/11,* ed. Melvyn P. Leffler and Jeffrey W. Legro (Ithaca, NY: Cornell University Press, 2011), 30.

27. James Baker, "A New Europe, a New Atlanticism: Architecture for a New Era," in U.S. Department of State, *Current Policy,* no. 1233 (December 1989).

28. Ibid.

29. Ibid.

30. George H. W. Bush and Brent Scowcroft, *A World Transformed,* 1st ed. (New York: Alfred A. Knopf, 1998), 212.

31. George Bush, "Address Before a Joint Session of the Congress on the State of the Union," January 31, 1990, available at http://bushlibrary.tamu.edu/research/public_papers.php?id=1492&year=1990&month=01, accessed February 19, 2013.

32. James A. Baker III with Thomas M. DeFrank, *The Politics of Diplomacy: Revolution, War, and Peace, 1989–1992* (New York: G. P. Putnam's Sons, 1995), 212.

33. George H. W. Bush, "Remarks at the Oklahoma State University Commencement Ceremony in Stillwater," May 4, 1990, available at http://bushlibrary.tamu.edu/research/public_papers.php?id=1853&year=1990&month=5,    accessed February 19, 2013.

34. For a brief overview of the role of nuclear weapons from the end of World War II to the Cuban Missile Crisis, see David Holloway, "Nuclear Weapons and the Escalation of the Cold War, 1945–1962," in *The Cambridge History of the Cold War,* ed. Melvyn P. Leffler and Odd Arne Westad (New York: Cambridge University Press, 2010), 1:376–97.

35. See Aaron L. Friedberg, *In the Shadow of the Garrison State: America's Anti-Statism and Its Cold War Grand Strategy* (Princeton, NJ: Princeton University Press, 2000).

36. In 1944, at aged fourteen, Kohl was sent to training to be an assistant to an anti-aircraft battery. See Helmut Kohl, *Erinnerungen: 1930–1982* (Munich: Droemer, 2004), 35–38.

37. For more information on the "cream cake incident," see Mary Elise Sarotte, *1989: The Struggle to Create Post–Cold War Europe* (Princeton, NJ: Princeton University Press, 2009), 146.

38. Almost immediately, Kohl regretted the words. But they probably reflected his thinking at the time. "No matter how many times one may re-read and twist and turn the remark," writes historian Hannes Adomeit, "one is left to conclude that Kohl did believe, or profess to believe, that a fundamental political change had not taken place in Moscow." See Hannes Adomeit, *Imperial Overstretch: Germany in Soviet Policy from Stalin to Gorbachev* (Baden-Baden: Nomos Verlagsgesellshaft, 1998), 261.

39. Andrei Grachev, *Gorbachev's Gamble: Soviet Foreign Policy and the End of the Cold War* (Cambridge, U.K.: Polity Press, 2008), 136.

40. Kohl's speech is available on YouTube, "Rede von Helmut Kohl am 10. November 1989," available at www.youtube.com/watch?v=hkwcU32Oo3U, accessed February 19, 2013.

41. Sarotte, *1989,* 52–53.

42. "Memorandum of Conversation: Telephone Conversation with Helmut Kohl, Chancellor, Federal Republic of Germany," November 10, 1989, available at http://bushlibrary.tamu.edu/research/pdfs/telcon11-10-89.pdf, accessed February 19, 2013.

43. Helmut Kohl, "Ten-Point Plan for German Unity," November 28, 1989, available at http://germanhistorydocs.ghi-dc.org/sub_document.cfm?document_id =223, accessed November 25, 2012.

44. Chernyaev, quoted in Grachev, *Gorbachev's Gamble,* 150.

45. "Memorandum of Conversation: Meeting with Helmut Kohl Chancellor of the Federal Republic of Germany," Brussels, December 3, 1989, Document CK3100487420, Declassified Documents Reference System (Farmington Hills, MI: Gale, 2010).

46. Wiegrefe, "Germany's Unlikely Diplomatic Triumph."

47. Hans Dietrich Genscher, *Rebuilding a House Divided: A Memoir by the Architect of Germany's Reunification* (New York: Broadway Books, 1998), 336.

48. Klaus Wiegrefe, "Germany's Unlikely Diplomatic Triumph," Der Spiegel Online, September 29, 2010, available at www.spiegel.de/international/germany/0,1518,druck-719848,00.html, accessed February 19, 2013.

49. Zoellick to Baker, "Planning for 1990: First Quarter Outlook," James A. Baker III Papers, box 108, Public Policy Papers, Department of Rare Books and Special Collections, Princeton University Library, Princeton, New Jersey.

50. "Proposed Agenda for Meeting with the President January 24, 1990"; n.d.; James A. Baker Papers, box 115, Public Policy Papers, Department of Rare Books and Special Collections, Princeton University Library, Princeton, New Jersey.

51. Philip Zelikow and Condoleezza Rice, *Germany Unified and Europe Transformed: A Study in Statecraft* (Cambridge, MA: Harvard University Press, 1995), 159–60.

52. Minutes of Politburo meeting, in Aleksandr Galkin and Anatolii Chernyaev, eds., *Mikhail Gorbachev i Germanskii Vopros: Sbornik Dokumentov, 1986–1991* (Moscow: Ves' mir, 2006), 307–11; Mark Kramer has seen the original, full transcript of this meeting, of which a portion appears in *Mikhail Gorbachev i Germanskii Vopros.* See Mark Kramer, "The Myth of a No-NATO-Enlargement Pledge to Russia,"*Washington Quarterly* 32, no. 2 (April 2009), 39–61, available at https://csis.org/files/publication/twq09aprilkramer.pdf, accessed February 19, 2013.

53. Galkin and Chernyaev, eds., *Mikhail Gorbachev i Germanskii Vopros,* 323.

54. Ibid., 324.

55. Ibid.

56. Zelikow and Rice, *Germany Unified and Europe Transformed,* 164.

57. Ibid., 149–54.

58. Ibid., 181.

59. Iz byesyedi M.S. Gorbachyeva s J. Byeykyerom, in Galkin and Chernyaev, eds., *Mikhail Gorbachev i Germanskii Vopros,* 333.

60. Ibid., 334.

61. Ibid.

62. On this last point, Baker expressed agreement yet made no binding commitment.

63. Baker with DeFrank, *Politics of Diplomacy,* 206.

64. "Iz byesyedu M.S. Gorbacheva s G. Kolyem odyen na odyen, 10 Feyevralya 1990 goda," in Galkin and Chernayev, eds., *Mikhail Gorbachev i Germanskii Vopros,* 352–53.

65. Quoted in Melvyn P. Leffler, *For the Soul of Mankind: The United States, the Soviet Union, and the Cold War,* 1st ed. (New York: Hill and Wang, 2007), 443.

66. "Memorandum of Telephone Conversation: Telephone Call from Chancellor Helmut Kohl," available at www.margaretthatcher.org/document/B8FD4E01D24541C2B3C01845B02FEA3B.pdf, accessed November 25, 2012.

67. Quoted in Sarotte, *1989,* 189.

68. Ibid., 159.

69. "Iz byesedy M.S. Gorbacheva s X. Tel'chikom, 14 May 1990," in Galkin and Chernyaev, eds., *Mikhail Gorbachev i Germanskii Vopros,* 434, 429.

70. Brent Scowcroft, "Address to Republican National Committee Winter Meeting," January 19, 1990, available at www.c-spanvideo.org/program/SecurityAd, accessed February 19, 2013.

71. Although final passage of NAFTA did not occur until the Clinton administration, much of the agreement had already been negotiated by the Bush administration's Trade Representative, Carla Hills. For an analysis of the NAFTA negotiations, see Maxwell A. Cameron and Brian W. Tomlin, *The Making of NAFTA: How the Deal Was Done* (Ithaca, NY: Cornell University Press, 2000); Steve Dryden, *Trade Warriors: USTR and the American Crusade for Free Trade* (New York: Oxford University Press, 1995).

72. Jeffry A. Frieden, *Global Capitalism: Its Fall and Rise in the Twentieth Century* (New York: W.W. Norton, 2006).

73. George H. W. Bush, "Remarks Announcing the Enterprise for the Americas Initiative," June 27, 1990, available at http://bushlibrary.tamu.edu/research/public_papers.php?id=2041&year=1990&month=6, accessed November 25, 2012.

74. For an overview of GATT, see Sylvia Ostry, *The Post–Cold War Trading System: Who's on First?* (Chicago: University of Chicago Press, 1997).

75. Frieden, *Global Capitalism,* 476.

76. Baker with DeFrank, *Politics of Diplomacy,* 248.

77. Ibid., 249–50.

78. Bush and Scowcroft, *World Transformed,* 206.

79. Ibid., 223.

80. Baker with DeFrank, *Politics of Diplomacy,* 238.

81. George J. Church, Laurence I. Barrett, and Nancy Traver, "Clinging to The Cold War," *Time,* June 18, 1990, available at www.time.com/time/printout/0,8816,970387,00.html, accessed November 25, 2012.

82. Baker to Gorbachev, March 28, 1990, James A. Baker III Papers, box 108, Seeley G. Mudd Manuscript Library, Seeley Mudd Library, Princeton University, Princeton, New Jersey.

83. Bush and Scowcroft, *World Transformed,* 222.

84. Ibid., 216.

85. Quoted in Sarotte, *1989,* 158.

86. "Memorandum from James A. Thomson," May 24, 1990, folder "File 436, Six Power Conference," OA/ID CF01354-006, Philip Zelikow, Office of National Security Affairs, Bush Presidential Records, George H. W. Bush Presidential Library. The distribution list included Robert Blackwill, Paul Wolfowitz, Robert Zoellick; handwritten notes indicate it was sent to Brent Scowcroft.

87. "Memorandum of Telephone Conversation between George Bush and Helmut Kohl," May 30, 1990, National Security Archive, available at www.gwu.edu/~nsarchiv/NSAEBB/NSAEBB320/09.pdf, accessed November 25, 2012.

88. Bush and Scowcroft, *World Transformed,* 282.

89. Sarotte, *1989,* 184.

90. "Memorandum of Conversation between Mikhail Gorbachev and James Baker," February 9, 1990, Gorbachev Foundation Archive, Fond 1, Opis 1. This section appears neither in the portions of the meeting published Galkin and Chernyaev, eds., *Mikhail Gorbachev i Germanskii Vopros* nor that in *Otvechaia na Vyzov Vremeni.*

91. Ibid.

92. "Memorandum of Conversation between Baker and Pavlov"; March 14, 1990; James A. Baker Papers, box 108, Public Policy Papers, Department of Rare Books and Special Collections, Princeton University Library, Princeton, New Jersey.

93. Baker, "From Revolution to Democracy: Central and Eastern Europe in the New Europe," *US Department of State Dispatch,* September 3, 1990, 10–14.

94. Zoellick to Baker; September 5, 1989; James A. Baker Papers, box 108, Public Policy Papers, Department of Rare Books and Special Collections, Princeton University Library, Princeton, New Jersey.

95. "Briefing Cards: Economic Reform in the Soviet Union," undated, folder "Washington Summit, June 1990" OA/ID CF0717, Condoleezza Rice, Office of National Security Affairs, Bush Presidential Records, George H. W. Bush Presidential Library.

96. Ibid.

97. Grachev, *Gorbachev's Gamble,* 202.

98. Bush, *All the Best,* 468.

99. Robert Solomon, *Money on the Move: The Revolution in International Finance since 1980* (Princeton, NJ: Princeton University Press, 1999), 113–14.

100. Richard Darman, *Who's in Control? Polar Politics and the Sensible Center* (New York: Simon and Schuster, 1996), 243.

101. "Houston Economic Summit Political Declaration: Securing Democracy," July 10, 1990, available at http://bushlibrary.tamu.edu/research/public_papers.php?id=2063&year=1990&month=7, accessed February 19, 2013.

102. Bartholomew H. Sparrow, "Realism's Practitioner: Brent Scowcroft and the Making of the New World Order, 1989–1993," *Diplomatic History* 34 (January 2010): 161.

103. Baker with DeFrank, *Politics of Diplomacy,* 2.

104. Ibid., 1.

105. Ibid.

106. Ibid., 2.

107. Meeting of the National Security Council, August 5, 1990, available at www.margaretthatcher.org/document/8FB156AB24994C20B249A3B7855A975D.pdf, accessed February 19, 2013.

108. Ibid.

109. NSD-45, available at http://bushlibrary.tamu.edu/research/pdfs/nsd/nsd45.pdf, accessed February 19, 2013.

110. Aleksander Bessmertnykh, quoted in William Wohlforth, ed., *Cold War Endgame: Oral History, Analysis, Debates* (University Park: Pennsylvania State University Press, 2003), 91.

111. Telephone Conversation of Baker and Shevardnadze; August 6, 1990; James A. Baker Papers, box 109, Public Policy Papers, Department of Rare Books and Special Collections, Princeton University Library, Princeton, New Jersey.

112. Telephone Conversation of Baker and Shevardnadze, August 22, 1990, James A. Baker III Papers, Seeley G. Mudd Manuscript Library, Princeton University, Princeton, New Jersey.

113. James Baker's copy of Shevardnadze's speech to the UN on Iraq; September 25, 1990; James A. Baker Papers, box 109, Public Policy Papers, Department of Rare Books and Special Collections, Princeton University Library, Princeton, New Jersey.

114. "The President's News Conference on the Persian Gulf Crisis," August 30, 1990, available at http://bushlibrary.tamu.edu/research/public_papers.php?id=2189&year=1990&month=8, accessed February 19, 2013.

115. Gorbachev, *Otvechaia na vyzov vremeni*.

116. Ibid.

117. Ibid.

118. Ibid.

119. Baker with DeFrank, *Politics of Diplomacy*, 292.

120. Grachev, *Gorbachev's Gamble*, 192.

121. Memorandum of Conversation between Mikhail Gorbachev and Tariq Aziz, in *Otvechaia na Vyzov Vremeni*, 733.

122. According to Bessmertnykh, Primakov inserted himself into the equation, claiming to have influence with Saddam. See discussion in Wohlforth, ed., *Cold War Endgame*, 92.

123. Quoted in ibid., 85.

124. George H. W. Bush, "Address Before a Joint Session of the Congress on the Persian Gulf Crisis and the Federal Budget Deficit," September 11, 1990, available at http://bushlibrary.tamu.edu/research/public_papers.php?id=2217&year=1990&month=9, accessed February 19, 2013.

125. This meeting is not included in the published volumes; the original resides in Fond 1, Opis, 1, Gorbachev Foundation Archive.

126. Robert A. Mosbacher, *Going to Windward: A Mosbacher Family Memoir* (College Station: Texas A&M Press, 2010), 238.

127. These exchanges come from the original document in Fond 1, Opis 1, Archive of the Gorbachev Foundation. An abridged version of this meeting is included in *Otvechaia na Vyzov Vremeni*.

128. Baker notes; September 13, 1990; James A. Baker Papers, box 109, Public Policy Papers, Department of Rare Books and Special Collections, Princeton University Library, Princeton, New Jersey.

129. Bush, *All the Best*, 480–81.

130. George Bush, "Address before the 45th Session of the United Nations General Assembly in New York, New York," October 1, 1990, available at http://bushlibrary.tamu.edu/research/public_papers.php?id=2280&year=1990&month=10, accessed February 19, 2013.

131. Remarks to the Federal Assembly in Prague, Czechoslovakia, November 17, 1990, available at http://bushlibrary.tamu.edu/research/public_papers.php?id=2461&year=1990&month=11, accessed February 19, 2013.

132. Hitchcock, *Struggle for Europe*, 374–75.

133. Robert Hutchings, "The United States, German Unification and European Integration," in *Europe and the End of the Cold War: A Reappraisal,* ed. Frédéric Bozo, Marie-Pierre Rey, N. Piers Ludlow, and Leopoldo Nuti (New York: Routledge, 2008), 128; see also Robert L. Hutchings, *American Diplomacy and the End of the Cold War: An Insider's Account of U.S. Policy in Europe 1989–1992* (Washington, DC: Woodrow Wilson Center Press, 1997).

134. Baker with DeFrank, *Politics of Diplomacy,* 295.

135. For a description of "Western benevolence without benefaction," see Alex Pravda, "The Collapse of the Soviet Union, 1990–1991," in *Cambridge History of the Cold War,* ed. Leffler and Westad, 3:374–77.

136. Telephone conversation between George Bush and Mikhail Gorbachev, January 11, 1991, in Chernyaev et al., eds., *V Politbiuro Ts KPSS* (Moscow: Alpine Business Books, 2006), 640.

137. Ibid., 641.

138. Telephone conversation between George Bush and Mikhail Gorbachev, January 18, 1991, in ibid., 645.

139. Ibid., 646.

140. Ibid., 648.

## Conclusion

1. Jeffry A. Frieden, *Global Capitalism: Its Fall and Rise in the Twentieth Century* (New York: W.W. Norton, 2006), 363–92.

2. For accounts that ascribe U.S. Cold War victory to a grand strategy on the part of the Reagan administration, see Paul Kengor, *The Crusader: Ronald Reagan and the Fall of Communism* (New York: HarperCollins, 2006); Paul Lettow, *Ronald Reagan and His Quest to Abolish Nuclear Weapons* (New York: Random House, 2005); Peter Schweizer, *Reagan's War: The Epic Story of His Forty-Year Struggle and Final Triumph over Communism* (New York: Doubleday, 2002). See also annotated collections of primary documents: Jason Saltoun-Ebin, *The Reagan Files: The Untold Story of Reagan's Top-Secret Efforts to Win the Cold War* (Charleston, SC: CreateSpace, 2010); Martin Anderson and Annelise Anderson, *Reagan's Secret War: The Untold Story of His Fight to Save the World from Nuclear Disaster* (New York: Crown, 2009); Kiron K. Skinner, Annelise Anderson, and Martin Anderson, eds., *Reagan, In His Own Hand* (New York: Free Press, 2001). Among the more lucid interpretations written by former aides who have also detected a consistent grand strategy are: Martin Anderson, *Revolution: The Reagan Legacy* (Stanford, CA: Hoover Institution Press, 1990); Robert C. McFarlane and Zofia Smardz, *Special Trust* (New York: Cadell and Davies, 1994); Richard Pipes, *Vixi: Memoirs of a Non-Belonger* (New Haven, CT: Yale University Press, 2003); see also Richard Pipes, "Misinterpreting the Cold War: The Hardliners Had It Right," *Foreign Affairs* 74 (January–February 1995); Paul Wolfowitz, "Shaping the Future: Planning at the Pentagon, 1989–93," in *In Uncertain Times: American Foreign Policy after the Berlin Wall and 9/11,* ed. Melvyn P. Leffler and Jeffrey Legro (Ithaca, NY: Cornell University Press, 2011), 44–62. "What caused the Cold War to end will be debated for some time, but it is important to recognize that Reagan did indeed have a strategy," Wolfowitz writes on page 44, "one that recognized the important difference between what can be controlled and what is the product of uncontrollable forces."

3. See Romesh Ratnesar, *Tear Down This Wall: A City, a President, and the Speech That Ended the Cold War* (New York: Simon and Schuster, 2009); for accounts depicting the fall of the Berlin Wall as accidental, see Mary Elise Sarotte, *1989: The Struggle to Create Post–Cold War Europe* (Princeton, NJ: Princeton University Press, 2009), 28–45; William Taubman and Svetlana Savranskaya, "If a Wall Fell in Berlin and Moscow Hardly Noticed, Would It Still Make a Noise?" in *The Fall of the Berlin Wall: The Revolutionary Legacy of 1989,* ed. Jeffrey A. Engel (New York: Oxford University Press, 2009), 69–95; Vladislav Martin Zubok, *A Failed Empire: The Soviet Union in the Cold War: From Stalin to Gorbachev* (Chapel Hill: University of North Carolina Press, 2007), 326–27.

4. For a succinct interpretation of the role of strategy, see Norman A. Bailey, *The Strategic Plan That Won the Cold War: National Security Decision Directive 75* (McLean, VA: Potomac Foundation, 1998); on the role of Reagan's rhetoric, see Ratnesar, *Tear Down This Wall.* For both, see Kengor, *Crusader;* Lettow, *Ronald Reagan and His Quest;* Schweizer, *Reagan's War;* and Pipes, *Vixi.*

5. NSDD-32, available at www.fas.org/irp/offdocs/nsdd/nsdd-032.htm, accessed February 19, 2013.

6. NSDD-75, available at www.fas.org/irp/offdocs/nsdd/nsdd-075.htm, accessed February 19, 2013.

7. Melvyn P. Leffler, "The Emergence of an American Grand Strategy, 1945–1952," in *The Cambridge History of the Cold War,* ed. Melvyn P. Leffler and Odd Arne Westad (New York: Cambridge University Press, 2010), 1:88.

8. For an overview of U.S. strategy in the early Cold War, see Ernest R. May, ed. *American Cold War Strategy: Interpreting NSC-68* (New York: Bedford Books, 1993); see also Melvyn P. Leffler, *A Preponderance of Power: National Security, the Truman Administration, and the Cold War* (Stanford, CA: Stanford University Press, 1992).

9. Robert R. Bowie and Richard H. Immerman, *Waging Peace: How Eisenhower Shaped an Enduring Cold War Strategy* (New York: Oxford University Press, 1998), 5.

10. This book fits between those who say that America's pursuit of strength won the Cold War and those who contend that its role was marginal at best. In the former category, John Lewis Gaddis came to this conclusion shortly after Reagan departed. See Gaddis, "Hanging Tough Paid Off," *Bulletin of Atomic Scientists* 45 (January 1989): 11–14; Gaddis, "Ronald Reagan's Cold War Victory," in *Major Problems in American History since 1945,* ed. Robert Griffith (Lexington, MA: D.C. Heath, 1992), 705–10; for an alternative perspective, see Thomas Risse-Kappen, "Did Peace Through Strength End the Cold War? Lessons from INF," *International Security* 16 (Summer 1991), 162–88.

11. See Beth Fisher, *The Reagan Reversal: Foreign Policy and the End of the Cold War* (Columbia: University of Missouri Press, 1997); Don Oberdorfer, *From the Cold War to a New Era: The United States and the Soviet Union, 1983–1991* (Baltimore: Johns Hopkins University Press, 1998).

12. John Lewis Gaddis, *The Cold War: A New History* (New York: Penguin Press, 2005), 217.

13. Melvyn P. Leffler, *For the Soul of Mankind: The United States, the Soviet Union, and the Cold War,* 1st ed. (New York: Hill and Wang, 2007), 462. "Reagan's greatness was not his buildup of force but his inspiring of trust," writes Leffler. On the role of trust between Reagan and Gorbachev within a theoretical framework of international

behavior, see Ken Booth and Nicholas J. Wheeler, *The Security Dilemma: Fear, Cooperation, and Trust in World Politics* (London: Palgrave, 2008), 145–58. On the broader issue of trust during the Cold War, see Deborah Welch Larson, *Anatomy of Mistrust: U.S.-Soviet Relations during the Cold War* (Ithaca, NY: Cornell University Press, 1997).

14. Richard Reeves, *President Reagan: The Triumph of Imagination* (New York: Simon and Schuster, 2005).

15. Sean Wilentz, *The Age of Reagan: A History, 1974–2008* (New York: HarperCollins, 2008).

16. See, for instance, Ronald Reagan, "Address before a Joint Session of the Congress on the State of the Union," January 25, 1984, available at www.reagan. utexas.edu/archives/speeches/1984/12584e.htm, accessed February 19, 2013.

17. There are numerous accounts of how particular understandings of Reagan and end of the Cold War influenced the foreign policies of George W. Bush. See especially Peter Beinart, *The Icarus Syndrome: A History of American Hubris* (New York: Harper, 2010); Jack F. Matlock, *Superpower Illusions* (New Haven, CT: Yale University Press, 2010); Lou Cannon and Carl M. Cannon, *Reagan's Disciple: George W. Bush's Troubled Quest for a Presidential Legacy* (New York: PublicAffairs, 2008). A more balanced account is John Arquilla, *The Reagan Imprint: Ideas in American Foreign Policy from the Collapse of Communism to the War on Terror* (Chicago: Ivan R. Dee, 2006). On the influence of memories of the Cold War as a whole, see Leffler and Legro, eds., *In Uncertain Times;* Melvyn P. Leffler, "Dreams of Freedom, Temptations of Power," in *Fall of the Berlin Wall,* ed. Engel, 132–69; Michael Cox, "Another Transatlantic Split? American and European Narratives and the End of the Cold War," *Cold War History* 7 (February 2007): 121–46; Melvyn P. Leffler, "9/11 and American Foreign Policy," *Diplomatic History* 29 (June 2005); John Lewis Gaddis, *Surprise, Security, and the American Experience* (Cambridge, MA: Harvard University Press, 2004); Robert Kagan, *Of Paradise and Power: America and Europe in the New World Order* (New York: Alfred A. Knopf, 2003); see also William Kristol and Robert Kagan, "Toward a Neo-Reaganite Foreign Policy," *Foreign Affairs* 75 (July/August, 1996).

18. A vivid description of the rift between Reagan and American "realists" can be found in James Mann, *The Rebellion of Ronald Reagan: A History of the End of the Cold War* (New York: Viking, 2009).

19. Underplaying the role of Shultz—as with the notion of George H. W. Bush as an afterthought in ending the Cold War—is a theme that groups together accounts of differing perspectives. See, for instance, Mann, *Rebellion of Ronald Reagan;* Fisher, *Reagan Reversal;* Schweizer, *Reagan's War.*

20. For an account that regards his role highly, see Oberdorfer, *From the Cold War to a New Era.*

21. For Haig's worldview, see chapter 1. See also Alexander M. Haig Jr., *Caveat: Realism, Reagan, and Foreign Policy* (London: Weidenfeld and Nicolson, 1984); Alexander M. Haig Jr., *Inner Circles: How America Changed the World: A Memoir* (New York: Warner Books, 1992).

22. For an account of the role of Jack Matlock, Arthur Hartman, and other moderates toward the Soviet Union, see David S. Foglesong, *The American Mission and the "Evil Empire": The Crusade for a Free Russia since 1881* (Cambridge, U.K.: Cambridge University Press, 2007), 174–95. On the exaggerated importance of Pipes, see books listed in note 2, esp. Kengor, *Crusader.*

23. For very good accounts of the Reagan and Bush national security teams, see Peter W. Rodman, *Presidential Command: Power, Leadership, and the Making of Foreign Policy from Richard Nixon to George W. Bush* (New York: Knopf, 2009); David Rothkopf, *Running the World: The Inside Story of the National Security Council and the Architects of American Power* (New York: PublicAffairs, 2004); Ivo H. Daalder and I.M. Destler, *In the Shadow of the Oval Office: Profiles of the National Security Advisers and the Presidents They Served—From JFK to George W. Bush* (New York: Simon and Schuster, 2009).

24. Hal Brands, *From Berlin to Baghdad: America's Search for Purpose in the Post–Cold War World* (Lexington: University of Kentucky Press, 2008); Derek Chollet and James Goldgeier, *America Between the Wars: From 11/9 to 9/11* (New York: Penguin, 2008); Bartholomew H. Sparrow, "Realism's Practitioner: Brent Scowcroft and the Making of the New World Order, 1989–1993," *Diplomatic History* 34 (January 2010): 141–75. The reputation of George H. W. Bush has increased since 2003—if only for the simple reason that he was not George W. Bush. Works published on and around the twentieth anniversary of the fall of the Berlin Wall reconsider George H. W. Bush as more hands-on than recognized during his day and bestow praise independent of the foreign policies of his son. These include Sarotte, *1989;* Jeffrey A. Engel, ed., "The End of the Cold War: New Evidence and Interpretations from the First Bush Administration," Special Edition of *Diplomatic History* 34 (January 2009); Leffler, "Dreams of Freedom, Temptations of Power," in *Fall of the Berlin Wall,* ed. Engel. My contribution in chapters 6 and 7 is to go even beyond these recent interpretations.

25. George Herring, *From Colony to Superpower: U.S. Foreign Relations since 1776* (New York: Oxford University Press, 2008), 922.

26. See Philip Zelikow and Condoleezza Rice, *Germany Unified and Europe Transformed: A Study in Statecraft* (Cambridge, MA: Harvard University Press, 1995). While it is true that Zelikow and Rice employed an evidentiary source base that few other historians have the ability to investigate, I do not believe that newly available sources from Moscow, Berlin, London, and Paris and elsewhere call into question their fundamental assertions.

27. Robert B. Zoellick, "An Architecture Of U.S. Strategy after the Cold War," 26–43; Wolfowitz, "Shaping the Future," 44–62; and Eric S. Edelman, "The Strange Career of the 1992 Defense Planning Guidance," 63–77, all in *In Uncertain Times,* ed. Leffler and Legro. For an account that employs "openness" as an interpretative framework for U.S. foreign relations and regards the first Bush administration as operating firmly within it, see Andrew J. Bacevich, *American Empire: The Realities and Consequences of U.S. Diplomacy* (Cambridge, MA: Harvard University Press, 2002); for insights into the "open door" and American foreign relation, see especially Henry W. Berger, *A William Appleman Williams Reader: Selections from his Major Historical Writings* (Chicago: Ivan R. Dee, 1992). For accounts of the triumph of liberal capitalist order, see Frieden, *Global Capitalism;* see also Sarotte, *1989,* 195–214.

28. William Wohlforth and Stephen Brooks, "Economic Constraints and the Turn Towards Superpower Cooperation in the 1980s," in *From Conflict Escalation to Conflict Transformation: The Cold War in the 1980's,* ed. Olav Njølstad (London: Frank Cass, 2004); William C. Wohlforth and Stephen G. Brooks, "Economic Constraints and the End of the Cold War," in *Cold War Endgame: Oral History, Analysis, Debates,* ed. William C. Wohlforth (University Park: Penn State University Press, 2003);

William C. Wohlforth and Stephen G. Brooks, "Power, Globalization, and the End of the Cold War: Reevaluating a Landmark Case for Ideas," *International Security* 53 (Winter 2000–01): 5–53; William Wohlforth, *The Elusive Balance: Power and Perceptions during the Cold War* (Ithaca, NY: Cornell University Press, 1993).

29. David Hoffman, *The Dead Hand: The Untold Story of the Cold War Arms Race and Its Dangerous Legacy* (New York: Random House, 2009); Richard Rhodes, *Arsenals of Folly: The Making of the Nuclear Arms Race* (New York: Knopf, 2007); Lettow, *Ronald Reagan and His Quest;* David Reynolds, *Summits: Six Meetings That Shaped the Twentieth Century* (New York: Basic Books, 2007), 343–400.

30. For accounts of Gorbachev told from the perspective of the political science concept of "learning," see Akan Malic, *When Leaders Learn and When They Don't: Mikhail Gorbachev and Kim Il Sung at the End of the Cold War* (Albany: SUNY University Press, 2008); Janice Gross Stein, "Political Learning by Doing: Gorbachev as Uncommitted Thinker and Motived Learner," *International Organization* 48 (Spring 1994): 156–83. See also Archie Brown, *The Gorbachev Factor* (New York: Oxford University Press, 1996), 114–15. For accounts of the evolution of Gorbachev's thinking with respect to Afghanistan, see especially Artemy M. Kalinovsky, *A Long Goodbye: The Soviet Withdrawal from Afghanistan* (Cambridge, MA: Harvard University Press, 2011); Sarah Mendelson, *Changing Course: Ideas, Politics, and the Soviet Withdrawal from Afghanistan* (Princeton, NJ: Princeton University Press, 1998). In my opinion, the two best memoirs with respect to Gorbachev's thought process are Anatoly Chernyaev, *My Six Years with Gorbachev,* trans. and ed. Robert English and Elizabeth Tucker (University Park: Pennsylvania State University Press, 2000); and Pavel Palazchenko, *My Years with Gorbachev and Shevardnadze: The Memoir of a Soviet Interpreter* (University Park: Pennsylvania State University Press, 1997). An excellent hybrid of primary and secondary source is Andrei Grachev, *Gorbachev's Gamble: Soviet Foreign Policy and the End of the Cold War* (Cambridge, U.K.: Polity Press, 2008).

31. For an account that captures the interconnectedness of Gorbachev's foreign and domestic policies, see Chernyaev, *My Six Years with Gorbachev.*

32. Zubok, *Failed Empire,* 294.

33. Ibid., 335.

34. See Padraic Kenney, *A Carnival of Revolution: Central Europe 1989* (Princeton, NJ: Princeton University Press, 2003); Charles Maier, *Dissolution: The Crisis of Communism and the End of East Germany* (Princeton, NJ: Princeton University Press, 1997); Timothy Garton Ash, *The Magic Lantern: The Revolution of '89 Witnessed in Warsaw, Budapest, Berlin, and Prague* (New York: Random House, 1990). On the role of Pope John Paul, see John O'Sullivan, *The President, the Pope, and the Prime Minister: Three Who Changed the World* (Washington, DC: Regnery, 2006); George Weigel, *Witness to Hope: The Biography of Pope John Paul II, 1920–2005* (New York: Harper, 2005); see also Gaddis, *Cold War,* 195–204. For accounts of that describe how Gorbachev enabled the revolutions of 1989, see Marie-Pierre Rey, "The End of the Cold War: Soviet-American Relations and the Radical Changes in Europe," in *From Fulton to Malta: How the Cold War Began and Ended,* ed. Pavel Palazhchenko and Olga Zdravomyslova (Moscow: Gorbachev Foundation, 2008); see also Marie-Pierre Rey, "'Europe Is Our Common Home': A Study of Gorbachev's Diplomatic Concept," *Cold War History* 4 (January 2004): 33–65.

# Index